Routledge Guides to

The Routledge Guidebook to Mill's *On Liberty*

John Stuart Mill's *On Liberty* is widely regarded as one of the most influential and stirring pieces of political philosophy ever written. Ever relevant in our increasingly surveillance-dominated culture, the essay argues strongly in favour of the moral rights of individuality, including rights of privacy and of freedom of expression. *The Routledge Guidebook to Mill's On Liberty* introduces the major themes in Mill's great book and aids the reader in understanding this key work, covering:

- the context of Mill's work and the background to his writing
- each separate part of the text in relation to its goals, meanings and impact
- the reception the book received when first published
- the relevance of Mill's work to modern philosophy.

With further reading included at the end of each chapter, this is an essential guidebook for all students of philosophy and political theory, and all those wishing to get to grips with this classic work.

Jonathan Riley is Professor of Philosophy at the Murphy Institute, Tulane University, USA.

THE ROUTLEDGE GUIDES TO THE GREAT BOOKS

Series Editor: Anthony Gottlieb

The *Routledge Guides to the Great Books* provide ideal introductions to the work of the most brilliant thinkers of all time, from Aristotle to Marx and Newton to Wollstonecraft. At the core of each Guidebook is a detailed examination of the central ideas and arguments expounded in the great book. This is bookended by an opening discussion of the context within which the work was written and a closing look at the lasting significance of the text. The *Routledge Guides to the Great Books* therefore provide students everywhere with complete introductions to the most important, influential and innovative books of all time.

Available:

Gramsci's Prison Notebooks John Schwarzmantel
Thoreau's Civil Disobedience Bob Pepperman Taylor
Descartes' Meditations Gary Hatfield
Hobbes' Leviathan Glen Newey
Galileo's Dialogue Maurice A. Finocchiaro
Wittgenstein's Philosophical Investigations Marie McGinn
Aristotle's Nicomachean Ethics Gerard J. Hughes
Heidegger's Being and Time Stephen Mulhall
Hegel's Phenomenology of Spirit Robert Stern
Locke's Essay Concerning Human Understanding E. J. Lowe
Plato's Republic Nickolas Pappas
Wollstonecraft's A Vindication of the Rights of Woman Sandrine Bergès

Forthcoming:

De Beauvoir's The Second Sex Nancy Bauer
Paine's Rights of Man Frances Chiu
Aquinas' Summa Theologiae Jason Eberl

Kierkegaard's Fear and Trembling John A. Lippett
Machiavelli's The Prince John Scott
Gibbon's History of the Decline and Fall of the Roman Empire David Womersley
Foucault's History of Sexuality Chloe Taylor
Fanon's Wretched of the Earth Jean Khalfa
Jacobs' Death and Life of Great American Cities Peter Laurence
Weber's Protestant Ethic and the Spirit of Capitalism David Chalcraft
Augustine's Confessions Catherine Conybeare

Routledge Guides to the Great Books

The Routledge Guidebook to Mill's *On Liberty*

Jonathan Riley

Routledge
Taylor & Francis Group
LONDON AND NEW YORK

First published as *Routledge Philosophy Guidebook to Mill on Liberty*, 1998
This edition published as *The Routledge Guidebook to Mill's On Liberty*, 2015
by Routledge
2 Park Square, Milton Park, Abingdon, Oxon OX14 4RN

Simultaneously published in the USA and Canada
by Routledge
711 Third Avenue, New York, NY 10017

Routledge is an imprint of the Taylor & Francis Group, an informa business

© 1998, 2015 Jonathan Riley

The right of Jonathan Riley to be identified as the author of this work has been asserted by him in accordance with sections 77 and 78 of the Copyright, Designs and Patents Act 1988.

All rights reserved. No part of this book may be reprinted or reproduced or utilised in any form or by any electronic, mechanical, or other means, now known or hereafter invented, including photocopying and recording, or in any information storage or retrieval system, without permission in writing from the publishers.

Trademark notice: Product or corporate names may be trademarks or registered trademarks, and are used only for identification and explanation without intent to infringe.

British Library Cataloguing in Publication Data
A catalogue record for this book is available from the British Library

Library of Congress Cataloging in Publication Data
Riley, Jonathan, 1955-
The Routledge guidebook to Mill's On liberty / Jonathan Riley.
pages cm. -- (The Routledge guides to the great books)
Includes bibliographical references and index.
1. Mill, John Stuart, 1806-1873. On liberty. 2. Liberty. I. Title.
JC585.M63R55 2015
323.44--dc23
2015001817

ISBN: 978-0-415-66539-1 (hbk)
ISBN: 978-0-415-66540-7 (pbk)
ISBN: 978-1-315-72858-2 (ebk)

Typeset in Times New Roman
by Taylor & Francis Books

Printed and bound by CPI Group (UK) Ltd, Croydon, CR0 4YY

*In memory of Patrick Sutherland Fallis
(1948–1981)*

'le feu follet'

CONTENTS

Series editor's Preface	xiv
Preface to the first edition	xv
Preface to this edition	xviii

PART I
GENERAL INTRODUCTION — 1

1 Mill and the *Liberty* — 3
Mill's life and work — 3
'Text-book of a single truth' — 34
Early reaction — 36
Current status — 41
Suggestions for further reading — 45
Notes — 47

PART II
THE ARGUMENT OF *ON LIBERTY* — 51

2 Introductory (Chapter I, paras 1–16) — 53
Stages of liberty (I.1–5) — 53
Absence of a general principle (I.6–8) — 57

The exceptional case of religious belief (I.7)	58
'One very simple principle' (I.9–10)	60
Utilitarian form of argument (I.11–12)	62
Self-regarding conduct (I.12)	64
From one very simple principle to the maxim of self-regarding liberty (I.9–12)	65
The self-regarding sphere (I.12)	66
Absolute priority of self-regarding liberty (I.7, 10, 13)	68
The growing danger of social repression (I.14–15)	70
Suggestions for further reading	72
Notes	73
3 Of the liberty of thought and discussion (Chapter II, paras 1–44)	**74**
The grounds of some familiar liberties (II.1)	74
The harm of silencing an opinion which may be true (II.3–20)	76
The harm of silencing even a false opinion (II.21–33)	80
The harm of silencing an opinion which may be only partly true (II.34–36, 39)	85
The crucial case of Christian moral beliefs (II.37–38)	88
Must free expression be fair and temperate? (II.44)	90
Suggestions for further reading	91
Notes	93
4 Of individuality, as one of the elements of well-being (Chapter III, paras 1–19)	**96**
The grounds of liberty of action (III.1)	96
The worth of spontaneous action (III.2–6)	99
The worth of obedience to social rules (III.3–6, 9, 17)	101
An ideal type of individual character (III.5–9)	105
Utilitarian case for the equal right to liberty (III.10–19)	107
Holes in the case?	112
Suggestions for further reading	113
Notes	116

5 Of the limits to the authority of society over the individual (Chapter IV, paras 1–21) — 117
The nature of utilitarian coercion (IV.1–3) — 117
The nature of self-regarding acts (IV.4–7) — 120
The self–other distinction: some objections answered (IV.8–12) — 127
'Gross usurpations upon the liberty of private life' (IV.13–21) — 132
Suggestions for further reading — 137
Notes — 140

6 Applications (Chapter V, paras 1–23) — 142
Mill's doctrine and its application (V.1–2) — 142
Harm to others not sufficient for coercion (V.3) — 144
The liberty principle distinguished from laissez-faire (V.4) — 148
The proper limits of society's police authority (V.5–6) — 153
Society's authority to enforce 'good manners' (V.7) — 157
Liberty of public solicitation and its limits (V.8) — 158
Legitimate authority to tax sales and limit the number of sellers (V.9–10) — 163
Voluntary association and the enforcement of contracts (V.11) — 165
Voluntary release and the permission to break contracts (V.11) — 170
'Misapplied notions of liberty' (V.12–15) — 172
Liberty to refuse to co-operate (V.16–23) — 175
Suggestions for further reading — 183
Notes — 185

PART III
MILL'S DOCTRINE IN OUTLINE — 187

7 The structure of Mill's doctrine of liberty — 189
Key concepts — 189
The 'one very simple principle' — 201

Prevention of harm to others is necessary but not sufficient for coercive interference	203
The maxim of self-regarding liberty	203
The maxim of social authority	205
Determining which non-consensual harms to others are wrongful	207
Wrongful harm	210
The right of self-regarding liberty is inalienable	214
Prevention of wrongful harm to others is necessary but not sufficient for coercive interference	214
Necessary and sufficient conditions for coercive interference	215
Multiple harm principles	216
Multiple liberty principles	217
Beyond Mill's principles?	219
Suggestions for further reading	223
Notes	224

PART IV
GENERAL ISSUES 227

8 Liberal utilitarianism 229
Isn't liberalism incompatible with utilitarianism?	229
How can utilitarianism prescribe *absolute* liberty of self-regarding conduct?	240
Don't 'natural penalties' defeat Mill's self–other distinction?	243
Isn't there a danger of isolated and disturbed individuals?	248
Suggestions for further reading	251
Notes	253

9 Liberty, individuality and custom 254
Doesn't Mill's idea of individuality presuppose a radically unsituated individual?	254
How can doing as one pleases lead the individual to develop a noble Periclean character?	261

	Isn't the need for liberty inversely related to social progress?	269
	Why doesn't the individual have a right to parade his bad manners and indecent behaviour in public?	272
	Suggestions for further reading	284
	Notes	286
10	**The doctrine of *Liberty* in practice**	**288**
	How can anyone seriously think that Mill's doctrine is workable?	288
	Isn't it unreasonable to demand a complete ban on paternalism?	300
	Doesn't the maxim of self-regarding liberty give crude answers to some hard problems?	313
	Would implementation of the doctrine result in a social revolution?	325
	Suggestions for further reading	328
	Notes	329
	Bibliography	332
	Index	345

SERIES EDITOR'S PREFACE

'The past is a foreign country,' wrote a British novelist, L. P. Hartley: 'they do things differently there.'

The greatest books in the canon of the humanities and sciences can be foreign territory, too. This series of guidebooks is a set of excursions written by expert guides who know how to make such places become more familiar.

All the books covered in this series, however long ago they were written, have much to say to us now, or help to explain the ways in which we have come to think about the world. Each volume is designed not only to describe a set of ideas, and how they developed, but also to evaluate them. This requires what one might call a bifocal approach. To engage fully with an author, one has to pretend that he or she is speaking to us; but to understand a text's meaning, it is often necessary to remember its original audience, too. It is all too easy to mistake the intentions of an old argument by treating it as a contemporary one.

The *Routledge Guides to the Great Books* are aimed at students in the broadest sense, not only those engaged in formal study. The intended audience of the series is all those who want to understand the books that have had the largest effects.

AJG
October 2012

PREFACE TO THE FIRST EDITION

Mill's classic essay on individual liberty is the focus of a large literature. Surely there is nothing new to say about it, some (perhaps most) will think. Anyway, aside from his grand rhetoric, what is the interest for students of philosophy? Isn't his argument pretty straightforward, at least to the extent that we can make sense of it? Importance of moral rights, respect for rule of law and all that. Who needs a Guidebook to such ho-hum liberalism?

But a new guide to *On Liberty* is very much needed, I shall insist. Mill's radical argument has largely been obscured by commentators, where it has not been dismissed as incoherent. His doctrine is not now, and has never been, what most people understand by that ambiguous term 'liberalism'. In its place, much more conventional liberalisms continue to predominate in the philosophical literature. Today, students are likely to be misdirected toward one of these tamer alternatives, or worse, in the name of Millian liberalism.

It is my hope that this book might begin to remedy the misunderstandings surrounding Mill's radical argument. I depart very little from his own arrangement of the argument. But I have subdivided it into more sections, and have otherwise attempted to provide clarification where that seemed possible. At the same time, certain ambiguities are highlighted as they arise in the text, and reference is made to how they are ultimately resolved, to facilitate the reader's understanding without unduly interrupting the flow of Mill's discussion. This exegesis comprises Part II, the bulk of the Guidebook.

Part I of the guide generally introduces Mill's life and work, and relates the *Liberty* to his *Autobiography*. Since his defence of absolute liberty of thought and what he calls 'purely self-regarding' action is predicated in part on the great value of self-development or 'individuality', the story of his own process of development is of unusual interest. An indication of the *Liberty*'s early reception and current status in philosophy is also provided.

Part III [this edition's Part IV] presents, and briefly discusses, some familiar criticisms which are often levelled against Mill's form of argument. The criticisms are framed as a series of eleven pointed questions. It is very much a matter of continuing debate whether compelling replies can be given. Given the current state of the literature, I see no reason to take a negative view, and I sketch my corresponding series of preferred answers accordingly.

My sketch of a defence in this Guidebook is intended to encourage students to make up their own minds about Mill's doctrine, by means of further thought and discussion of the relevant issues. But, as for myself, I am not neutral between his argument and alternatives: I think his doctrine has great appeal for anyone who values individual liberty and social improvement. A more complete defence of Millian liberalism is offered in my monograph, *Mill's Radical Liberalism: An Essay in Retrieval*, which is also to be published by Routledge. It presupposes some familiarity with this Guidebook, and, as a somewhat more advanced companion, concentrates on the logical structure of Mill's utilitarian liberalism, with a view to clarifying the ways in which it diverges sharply from more familiar liberalisms, such as those of John Rawls and Isaiah Berlin. Also, the practical implications of the doctrine are worked out in more detail for a couple of issues, namely, prostitution and pornography.

I wish to take this opportunity to express my gratitude to Jonathan Wolff, for inviting me to do the Guidebook, suggesting improvements to earlier drafts and encouraging me to elaborate my views in the forthcoming monograph. I am also grateful for the advice and support offered by referees, one of whom remains anonymous, two of whom kindly identified themselves as Chin Liew Ten and Wayne Sumner. Amartya Sen and John Gray also deserve my thanks for many stimulating discussions of related themes during the past fifteen years or so, ever since my days as a graduate student at Oxford. Obviously, none of these people can be held responsible for my stated opinions. Indeed, Gray has made clear in various publications that he takes a far less sympathetic view of Mill's doctrine. But one can always hope to repay at least some of the gifts of one's teachers and colleagues.

I am indebted to Tulane's Murphy Institute of Political Economy for research support provided during the time in which this Guidebook was completed.

The book is dedicated to the memory of my dear friend, who died so young at thirty-three. Pat was the embodiment of a generous spontaneity, which it is the goal of the liberty principle to unleash and foster. He was a great joy to be around, as the many who knew and loved him will confirm. I will always miss him very much.

Last, but certainly not least, I thank Molly Rothenberg for her unfailing love and encouragement.

PREFACE TO THIS EDITION

Mill's main aim in *On Liberty,* I argue, is to defend the moral right of adults to complete liberty of self-regarding conduct, understood as conduct that does not directly affect – harm or benefit – the interests of other people, or, if it does, only with their genuine consent and participation. Whereas coercive interference with self-regarding conduct should not even be considered, society does have jurisdiction to *consider* interference with social (or other-regarding) conduct, that is, conduct that directly affects other people without their consent and participation. For Mill, then, the self–other distinction is a distinction between a self-regarding realm in which the individual should be free from coercion *to do as he pleases*, and a social realm in which society duly has authority to consider coercion but *does not necessarily decide to employ it.*

Readers must not assume that Mill is trying in *On Liberty* to provide a universal solution to the complex general problem of drawing a precise line between the field of conduct in which the individual should be free from coercion and the field in which society ought actually to employ coercion. Being free from coercion doesn't imply that one should do whatever one likes, and having jurisdiction to consider coercion doesn't imply that society is always justified in employing it within that jurisdiction. Mill doesn't believe that this complex general problem has a solution which all civil societies must endorse. Moreover, any particular solution which he may recommend for a given particular civil society depends upon his extraordinary version of utilitarianism, which is unlike any familiar version of utilitarianism. True, the moral right of self-regarding liberty, which he argues should be recognized by every civil society, is, for him, also grounded in his utilitarianism. But the right and its importance can be understood and endorsed by those of any stripe who love freedom, including theorists of natural rights. There is no need to understand and endorse his extraordinary utilitarian doctrine to appreciate the central argument of the *Liberty*. This seems to be why he says so little about his utilitarianism in the essay, beyond telling us that it is an enlarged utilitarianism that seeks to promote 'utility in the largest sense, grounded on the permanent interests of man as a progressive being'.

Mill does provide clues in his essay to the operation of his utilitarianism. He indicates, for example, that the individual ought to be free from coercive interference not only with respect to self-regarding conduct but also with respect to some classes of social conduct, including fair competitive actions and even wrongful actions in special situations. The individual should not do as he pleases within the social realm, however, even when he is properly left free from coercive interference there. By contrast with the self-regarding realm, the social realm is a realm within which the individual ought to obey social rules, including extremely important rules of justice and right as well as rules for achieving competitive success within the bounds of justice. Crucially, he ought to obey these rules *even if they cannot be expediently enforced by society.* In *On Liberty*, though, Mill does not spell out in any detail the nature of these social rules or the situations in which external sanctions are justified to prevent or punish other-regarding conduct. His focus is on the moral right of self-regarding liberty, and on the correlative moral duty not to coercively interfere with the individual's self-regarding choices.

Mill's utilitarian doctrine of individual freedom and social control, including the principle of self-regarding liberty which is the central concern of *On Liberty*, is highly sophisticated and much misunderstood by commentators. I've attempted, in a new Part III, added to this edition of my book, to outline the doctrine as I understand it on the basis of his various writings, especially *Utilitarianism*. As far as I can tell, my outline in Part III is fully compatible with, and confirmed by, the text of the *Liberty*. At the same time, my interpretation of his utilitarian doctrine has evolved somewhat since this book was originally published in 1998. Mill is a very concise writer who does not always spell out the details. He apparently expects readers to figure out many things for themselves in accordance with the remarks he makes. I think it fair to say that he expects too much since even those who are prepared to carefully study his writings, including *Liberty*, have so much difficulty grasping his utilitarian liberal doctrine.

I hope that my interpretation as it now stands is sufficient to persuade readers that Mill's utilitarian liberalism is a powerful moral and political theory. In particular, the maxim of self-regarding liberty is worthy of sustained attention by citizens as well as scholars. I do not mean to assert that my interpretation is immune to criticism. But I do insist that it captures the gist of Mill's view. Moreover, his maxim of self-regarding liberty as interpreted remains highly relevant, and will never cease to be highly relevant, for those who wish to achieve a genuine liberal democratic society.

Besides adding the new third part, I've made substantial additions and changes to the three parts which together comprised my original study, and which are now, respectively, Parts I, II and IV of this book. Some of these alterations update the book to take account of selected insights and arguments in the recent secondary literature. Others attempt to clarify the nature of Mill's unusual utilitarianism as I interpret it. Still others aim to clarify the application of Mill's maxim of self-regarding liberty, by responding to recent objections and removing some ambiguities in my original discussions. A detailed list of all of the alterations seems pointless and I leave it to readers interested in such matters to compile the alterations, which do not in any case alter the gist of my original argument.

But there are a couple of more or less minor changes which I would like to point out. In Part IV, I now frame various objections to Mill's form of argument in terms of a dozen pointed questions and not just the original eleven. My responses to many of the questions are also amplified. The second change is a semantic one. I now define harm in the descriptive sense as any type of perceptible damage excluding mere dislike or disgust, independently of whether the damage is consensual or not. Originally, I thought that, for Mill, the damage had to be non-consensual to count as harm. I was misled by his tendency to refer to self-regarding actions as if they are always harmless to others, when in fact he defines these actions such that they may 'affect' – harm or benefit – others with their genuine consent and participation. The change in the meaning of harm may seem slight but it is important as a descriptive matter. More specifically, the descriptive idea of harm is no longer tied to the normative *volenti* maxim that damage suffered voluntarily should be discounted altogether. Thus, I now emphasize that self-regarding conduct is correctly *described* as conduct that may directly cause consensual harm to others. The identification of such conduct does not necessarily involve any moral assumptions.

I continue to think that Mill views genuinely consensual harm as a kind of harm that should not be prevented. When it comes to his moral principle that the individual should have a right of self-regarding liberty, in other words, he may be taken to accept the *volenti* maxim, with the important caveat that the consent must be genuine and not the product of force or fraud. This rearrangement of the role of the *volenti* maxim in Mill's theory allows me to remove what I now consider some ambiguities and gaps in my original presentation, which I think are also present in the text of *On Liberty*. The rearrangement is reflected in my interpretation as now outlined in Part III of this book.

I should mention that *Mill's Radical Liberalism*, the companion volume which I've delayed publishing for far too long as I've struggled to understand some of the nuances of his extraordinary utilitarianism, will finally appear soon after this book is published. The companion aims to clarify in some detail the way in which his utilitarianism, his doctrine of individual liberty and social coercion, and his theory of political democracy are consistently brought together to form the core of his so-called Art of Life. I also plan to publish separate monographs on, respectively, his liberal feminism and his utilitarian theory of justice.

I have discussed Mill's thought with so many scholars and students on so many occasions (both formal and informal) over the years that I will not try to thank everyone individually. I am grateful to all for various insights and criticisms, some of which do not receive enough attention in these pages. As usual, responsibility for the views expressed remains mine alone.

I am also grateful to Tulane University's Murphy Institute of Political Economy and to the University of Hamburg's Department of Philosophy for research support provided during the period in which this new edition was completed. I held the Visiting Mill Chair in Social Philosophy at Hamburg during the first half of 2013.

On a more personal note, I take a lot of pleasure in lingering over the text of *On Liberty* because Mill's sparkling defence of the rights of liberty and individuality reminds me of my great friend from youth, Pat Fallis, whose spontaneity is impossible to forget. With the advance of age, one becomes ever more conscious of how rare and valuable is genuine friendship.

And I thank my dear wife Molly Rothenberg not only for reading and suggesting improvements to this new edition but also for being my wonderful partner in life.

Part I

GENERAL INTRODUCTION

1

MILL AND THE *LIBERTY*

MILL'S LIFE AND WORK

Mill lived for much of the nineteenth century, a period of remarkable social change in which, among much else, traditional religious beliefs continued to erode, without new faiths (whether religious or secular) taking their place as a general source of ideas and maxims of morality and politics. In his *Autobiography*, he describes the period as a 'critical' one, in the sense of the Saint-Simonians and Comte, meaning a 'period … of criticism and negation, in which mankind lose their old convictions without acquiring any new ones, of a general or authoritative character, except the conviction that the old are false'. Such transitional periods alternate throughout history with more settled 'organic' ones, in which, for the most part, 'mankind accept with firm conviction some positive creed, claiming jurisdiction over all their actions' (1873, 171).[1] The critical period in which he lived 'began with the Reformation', he thought, 'has lasted ever since, still lasts, and cannot altogether cease until a new organic period has been inaugurated by the triumph of a yet more advanced creed' (ibid.).

The more advanced creed, which he hoped might eventually replace fading Christian dogma, was what he called the 'Religion of Humanity' (1874), a comprehensive liberal utilitarian system of belief, in which the collective good or happiness is maximized by conjoining extensive liberty of the individual with a limited social code of morality, including general rules of justice that distribute and sanction equal rights and duties, designed to prevent or punish actions that are reasonably judged to cause wrongful harms to other persons. As he recalls, by the time he was about twenty-four, he 'looked forward, through the present age of loud disputes but generally weak convictions [surely reminiscent of our own age], to a future which shall unite the best qualities of the critical with the best qualities of the organic periods':

> unchecked liberty of thought, unbounded freedom of individual action in all modes not hurtful to others; but also, convictions as to what is right and wrong, useful and pernicious, deeply engraven on the feelings by early education and general unanimity of sentiment, and so firmly grounded in reason and in the true exigencies of life, that they shall not, like all former and present creeds, religious, ethical, and political, require to be periodically thrown off and replaced by others.
>
> (1873, 173)

His great essay, *On Liberty* (1859), dedicated to his beloved wife, is an impassioned defence of that 'unchecked liberty of thought' and 'unbounded freedom of individual action in all modes not hurtful to others', which are the 'best qualities' of critical periods.

Although he had grand hopes for mankind amidst the 'loud disputes' and social upheaval of the age, his own life was 'uneventful' (1873, 5). Born in London on 20 May 1806, he was the eldest of nine children of James and Harriet Mill. His father, after moving to London from Scotland to pursue a career in journalism, developed a strong friendship with Jeremy Bentham and became a leader of the reform-minded (or 'radical') intellectuals who banded together under Bentham's standard of utility. The elder Mill was a charismatic man, whose wit, upstanding character and love of discussion attracted such notable figures as David Ricardo, John Austin and George Grote to the Benthamite utilitarian school. James put his son through an extraordinary early education in history, logic and political economy, and these notable men as well as Bentham himself took an interest and contributed to that education. Although James was apparently a cold taskmaster who displayed virtually no affection for his son, the younger Mill expressed gratitude for his education, proclaimed it a success, and estimated that by age fifteen it gave him an advantage of some twenty-five years over his contemporaries in the development of his intellectual capacities to think for himself. In 1823, James, who had found employment at the East India Company shortly after the publication of his *The History of British India* (1817), arranged for his son's employment at the company. John worked there for thirty-five years (in the same office as his father until the latter's death in 1836) and retired only when the Company itself was terminated in 1858. As of 1856, he had risen to the same senior position that his father had achieved, namely, Examiner of India Correspondence, and thus was second in the chain of command, next to the Secretary.

Although raised as a Benthamite radical, he reacted against the Benthamite school of thought, as a young man of only twenty, when he suffered a severe depression for some six months upon recognizing that he would not personally feel happy even if the social and political reforms advocated by the Benthamites were fully implemented so that the general happiness could be maximized. In short, he feared that egoistic hedonism clashed irreconcilably with utilitarianism: he did not expect to *feel* much personal pleasure even though he *knew* that he ought to feel it if the institutions and actions recommended by the Benthamites were in operation. Indeed, he feared that he lacked any capacity for strong feelings at all because his Benthamite upbringing had focused exclusively on the cultivation of his intellect to the neglect of his imagination and sentiments.

He gradually emerged from his mental crisis during the spring of 1827, once he learned that he still had natural feelings that were awakened, and could be strengthened, by poetry and the fine arts. He seems to have studied the great German poets Goethe, Schiller and their Romantic followers, including Novalis and the Schlegel brothers, as well as their British counterparts such as

Coleridge, Wordsworth, Carlyle and Sterling, all of whom were vehement critics of Benthamite utilitarianism. He absorbed their ideas about willpower and the creative imagination, the need to strive endlessly for an aesthetic ideal of perfection that could never actually be realized, beauty as a symbol of moral good, the peculiar kind of aesthetic pleasure associated with the ideal of a duly balanced human character whose intellectual powers were in harmony with its feelings of motivation and habits of action, and so forth. No doubt he also became aware that these artists were deeply influenced by idealist philosophers such as Kant, Fichte and Hegel, which is not to say that he ever endorsed idealism. Nevertheless, many of these ideas, suitably modified, eventually found their way into the extraordinary version of hedonistic utilitarianism that he had grasped in outline by about 1830 and began to elaborate in detail after his father's death.

In 1830, he met his future wife Harriet Taylor (*née* Hardy), who was married at the time to her first husband, John Taylor. Harriet was best friends with Eliza Flower, who along with her sister Sarah was a ward of the Reverend William J. Fox, a Unitarian preacher and journalist about twenty years older than Mill. Fox, his wards and Harriet were devoted to poetry, literature and music and had unconventional ideas with respect to marriage and divorce. Indeed, as Mineka (1944) discusses, Fox was almost forced to resign as a leader of his church in 1834 when his wife revealed to members of his congregation his love for Eliza. But the congregation generally supported him after he denied any sexual relationship. He and Mill grew friendly as Mill's relationship with Harriet blossomed into a passionate attachment. In 1832, he first reached out to Mill and invited him to write for the *Monthly Repository*, the Unitarian magazine which Fox purchased in 1831 (after editing it as of 1828) and transformed into a secular journal of liberal opinion until he sold it in 1836. This gave Mill an opportunity to publish some views on poetry and aesthetic feeling, no doubt with the encouragement of Harriet and Eliza, and allowed him to interact with a wider circle of artists such as Robert Browning whose sympathies lay with the Romantics as opposed to the Benthamites. Mill and Fox became close confidants in the fall of 1833. As his letters to Fox make clear, Mill and Harriet became convinced that they were made for one another when they spent a fortnight together in Paris during October–November of that year. Nevertheless, despite their passion for one another, they decided not to live together because of the opposition of her first husband, for whom she retained much affection as opposed to passionate love. Instead, they chose to see each other frequently in London and take trips together while she otherwise lived with her husband, an unusual arrangement that pained all three parties and provoked considerable gossip as well as slights from family, friends and acquaintances, including some of the Benthamites. Moreover, just as Fox denied any sexual intimacy with Eliza while he was married to another, Mill denied any sexual relationship with Harriet before the death of her first husband in 1849. After waiting another two years, they finally married, with Mill expressing his contempt for the prevailing laws of patriarchy by making a public declaration that he rejected any suggestion that he should be entitled as a husband to take ownership of all property that Harriet brought to the marriage.

Harriet died just over seven years later, in 1858, only a few months after his retirement from the East India Company, while they were travelling to Montpellier. She was the love of his life and his enduring passion for her seems to have helped him to develop a due balance between reason and sentiment in his character and saved him from suffering any further severe depressions. Moreover, he insisted that she was joint author of the key moral and political works first drafted (but not published) during their marriage, including *On Liberty*, *Utilitarianism* (1861), *The Subjection of Women* (1869) and *Three Essays on Religion* (1874). After she died, he bought a cottage near her grave site in Avignon, and spent a good part of each of his remaining years there, usually accompanied by his stepdaughter, Helen Taylor.

During those fifteen remaining years, his writings were his main occupation. He continued to prepare new editions of his major treatises *A System of Logic* (1843) and *Principles of Political Economy* (1848), for instance, and he revised and published most of the works initially drafted with Harriet during their marriage, although *On Liberty* was never revised and the *Three Essays on Religion* together with his *Autobiography* and fragmentary *Chapters on Socialism* (1879) were published posthumously by Helen. He also wrote and published major new works in political theory and philosophy, including *Considerations on Representative Government* (1861), *Auguste Comte and Positivism* (1865), and *An Examination of Sir William Hamilton's Philosophy* (1865)—this last being his unduly neglected demolition of a leading version of rationalist intuitionism whose author was much influenced by the great metaphysical current of German idealism. Moreover, he clarified several aspects of his sophisticated version of hedonistic psychology in the notes he contributed to the new edition of his father's *Analysis of the Phenomena of the Human Mind* (1869), which he edited with additional notes contributed by Alexander Bain, Andrew Findlater and George Grote. And, as a leading public intellectual, he published numerous articles in newspapers and journals on the issues of the day.

During 1865–68, he also served as a Liberal Member of Parliament for Westminster. His political career gives an indication of his character. He was elected despite giving public notice to the voters of his district that he would not run a campaign, or bear any of the costs of his election or be instructed by them. As an MP, he also refused to curry popular favour. Rather, he made parliamentary speeches proposing radical liberal reforms, which he knew lacked support yet believed might get a hearing, leading to a more enlightened public opinion. His proposals included extension of the franchise to women, as well as the introduction of Thomas Hare's system of proportional representation, neither measure finding its way into the Reform Act of 1867. He also spoke out against various manifest injustices which most voters and their parliamentary representatives continued to neglect, including the extensive pattern of violence against women by their husbands, the ongoing oppression of Irish peasants by absentee British landlords who kept their tenants at bare subsistence by increasing land rents as high as the market would bear instead of fixing the rents at a reasonable customary level, and the suppression of unpopular speech as exemplified by the Crown's prosecution of Charles Bradlaugh for blasphemy and sedition in his weekly paper the *National Reformer*.

It is an interesting question why Mill was not re-elected. Many believed that it was the result of his strong public support for Bradlaugh just before the election. Bradlaugh was an avowed atheist (strictly speaking, an agnostic), fierce opponent of monarchy and hereditary privilege, and advocate of self-reliance and birth control who was eventually elected to Parliament himself in 1880, although a majority of the House of Commons refused to allow him to take his seat for six years (despite his repeated re-elections) by denying him the right to affirm or swear the oath of allegiance, because of his atheism. However, Mill was embroiled in other public controversies that may also have been important factors. Perhaps his most controversial activity was his chairmanship of the extra-parliamentary Jamaica Committee, which for two years sought in vain to persuade the government to prosecute Governor Eyre and his principal subordinates for unjustified military violence against Jamaican blacks in the fall of 1865. Mill believed that Eyre deserved capital punishment for authorizing the execution of more than 400 Jamaicans in response to minor disturbances that lasted a week, but conservatives, including such notable artists as Dickens, Ruskin and Carlyle as well as many Westminster voters, were disturbed by his relentless campaign to enforce the basic rights of blacks against this figure of British authority. In any case, Mill lost his seat to W. H. Smith, a Conservative, the son of the founder of the newsagents.

Mill died, apparently of erysipelas, at Avignon on 7 May 1873, and is buried there with Harriet.

Evidently, his story is unlikely to be confused with the tales of Pericles or Napoleon. Even so, he expects that anyone capable of rational persuasion will be interested to learn more about his 'unusual and remarkable' education (1873, 5). Although many have been interested, he might well have been surprised by the frequency with which the reaction is one of alarm and hostility. Typical is Carlyle's well-known jibe that the *Autobiography* reads like the story of a deeply troubled 'logical steam engine'. When he goes on to depict Mill's record of self-development as 'a mournful psychical curiosity', however, the latter-day Diogenes would be more persuasive if he were talking about himself.

By all accounts, Mill was a man of prodigious intellect and learning, whose moral and political opinions were not only far too progressive for the reactionary Carlyle but also far in advance of much contemporary liberal opinion. His various articles and treatises, emerging over a period of more than fifty years, span an incredibly broad range of topics in philosophy, politics and economics. Long regarded as a muddle-headed synthesizer of other people's ideas, he is seen in recent scholarship as a cogent and imaginative philosopher of liberal democracy, whose writings are of permanent importance.

To provide insight into the process of his education, he divides his life into three major periods. The first includes the period of his early education, lasting until he was about fourteen. During this time, his father was his 'schoolmaster' and directed his studies with a view to making him a fellow Benthamite reasoner. Then, after a year in France, he very gradually took control of his own education, by cultivating his intellectual and emotional capacities as *he* desired and thought best.

Initially, he merely carried on with the programme of his early education. During this first phase of his self-development or individuality, he threw himself into the path of intellectual enlightenment which his schoolmaster had laid out for him and accustomed him to pursue. After about five years, however, when he was still not yet twenty-one, he lost interest in that path and, by the spring of 1827, found that he wanted to take a more varied journey, one that embraced the cultivation of his sympathetic capacities *as well as* his reasoning powers. He thereby moved into a second period (also his second phase of self-culture), in which he reacted strongly against the narrow way in which he had been brought up by his father.

His more diversified experience led quickly to a fundamental transformation in his opinions and character. By about 1830, he could envisage an enlarged utilitarian radicalism, one that went beyond narrow Benthamism without abandoning its insights. He apparently did not scotch all that was excessive in his reaction against Benthamism, however, until about 1840.

Thereafter, he entered into his 'third period' of 'mental progress', as he calls it, 'which now went hand in hand with [Harriet's]' (ibid., 237). During this period, as lengthy as the other two combined, he, with assistance from her for nearly twenty years, tried to clarify his novel liberal utilitarian creed, through the writings that make up the bulk of his published work. The *Liberty*, composed over

1854–58 and published in 1859 (shortly after Harriet's death), was a product of this final phase of his individuality.

Given that his doctrine of liberty aims to encourage individuality as an element of general utility, his own process of education and self-development is of special interest for present purposes. His odyssey is a truly remarkable one, and further discussion of it provides an opportunity to dispel some common misconceptions and prejudices, which are afloat in the literature.

EARLY EDUCATION

The main lesson of his early education, Mill suggests, is that young people are capable of far more development than is commonly thought possible. His own case illustrates 'how much more than is commonly supposed may be taught, and well taught, in those early years which, in the common modes of what is called instruction, are little better than wasted' (1873, 5; see also 33). His father began teaching him Greek at about age three and Latin at eight. By twelve, he had read an astonishing selection of texts in those languages, though he never composed at all in Greek and rarely in Latin. He particularly liked ancient history, he says, and was 'much addicted' to writing about it throughout his boyhood, in imitation of his father, whose *History of British India* was published in 1817 (ibid., 17).

When he was about twelve, he began studying logic, and was required by his father to practise and master the Socratic dialectical method of dissecting the truth of an argument, as illustrated in Plato's dialogues (ibid., 25). He was also encouraged to pay special heed to the orations of Demosthenes, as being valuable for understanding the genius of Athenian political institutions and the art of the orator. During 1819–20, he completed an intensive course in political economy, reading and discussing with his father the well-known works of Adam Smith and David Ricardo. Indeed, he occasionally benefited from discussions with Ricardo himself, who was his father's 'loved and intimate friend' (ibid., 31).

Ricardo was not the only friend of his father's who took an interest in the son's education. Bentham himself, a lifelong bachelor who spent far more time writing than conversing with others about ideas, seems to have taken something of a paternal interest in John. He made clear that he could be counted on to provide for the son's upbringing in the event of something happening to James. The Mill family actually lived with him from time to time during 1810–17, renting accommodation for the first four or five years and then visiting in summers. But these arrangements ceased once James won permanent employment at the East India Company, shortly after the publication of his *History*.

John also met several rising liberal intellectuals who were attracted by his father's sharp mind and high moral character. Worthy of special note is George Grote, whom he apparently met about 1819. Grote and his wife Harriet saw a great deal of John, their junior by a dozen years or so, during the 1820s and 1830s. Despite some rifts, the friendship between the two men proved to be of enduring value for Mill's continuing intellectual growth. They apparently shared a great admiration for ancient Athenian culture and institutions, especially during the Periclean 'golden age'.[2] Indeed, Grote's magisterial *History of Greece*, on which he had been working for more than twenty-five years before it began to appear in 1846, seems to have supplied vital material for the argument of the *Liberty*, which gives prominence to a Greek ideal of self-development or education.

In May 1820, James Mill's role as schoolmaster came to an end. John was sent to France for more than a year, where he lived most of the time with the family of Samuel Bentham, Jeremy's brother. Among the advantages which he thereby gained were 'a familiar knowledge of the French language', continuing studies in higher mathematics and the sciences, and, perhaps most important, exposure to 'the free and genial atmosphere of Continental life', so different from the hidebound and aloof atmosphere of its English counterpart (Mill 1873, 59, 61).

FATHER AND SON

Contrary to a common view, Mill does not appear to think that his father's training method was wrong-headed or overly demanding. Though his father was severe and, at times, impatient beyond reason, the method itself was 'in the main ... right, and it succeeded' (ibid., 31). 'Mine ... was not an education of cram', he insists (ibid., 35). Rather, the 'mode of instruction was excellently calculated to form a thinker', and, focused as it was on logic and political economy, it 'made me a thinker on both' (ibid., 31, 33). As already indicated, James was devoted to the Socratic method, so highly lauded by the son in the third chapter of the *Liberty*.[3] Thus, John's early education confirmed for him the power of Socratic dialogue to improve one's intellectual capacities.

He seems duly grateful to his father for this intellectual growth: 'the early training bestowed on me by my father [gave] ... an advantage of a quarter of a century over my contemporaries' (Mill 1873, 33). By fifteen, in other words, he has learned with his father's help what most people at forty are still struggling to learn for themselves. Moreover, he has no illusions that his head start is the result of his own peculiar 'natural gifts', which he admits are 'rather below than above par'. His development is not the unfolding of some inherent personal excellence unique to himself. Rather, any young person of 'average capacity and healthy physical constitution' could accomplish the same, he emphasizes, if placed in his 'fortunate circumstances' (ibid.).

Nor does Mill ever betray resentment of his father for depriving him of his childhood. His early education, he says, 'was not such as to prevent me from having a happy childhood' (ibid., 53). True, his father had largely isolated him from children other than his own siblings, so that he apparently had few, if any, friends of his own age and had inadequate opportunities to develop physical skills or practical expertise in the conduct of daily life. But Mill confirms that this isolation prevented him from recognizing that he was mentally superior to other children, so that he never became arrogant or self-satisfied.[4] It also allowed him to 'escap[e] not only the ordinary corrupting influence which boys exercise over boys, but the contagion of vulgar modes of thought and feeling' (1873, 39). Later in the *Autobiography*, he makes clear that he agrees with his father that escape from the latter contagion is essential if the individual is to develop and maintain 'any mental superiority' (ibid., 235). The need for such escape explains why he chooses to limit his society to a 'very small' number of friends, beginning in the 1840s (ibid., 235–37). More importantly, this implicit conflict between the cultivation of individuality and the 'despotism' of vulgar social customs is a central concern of the *Liberty*.

We must be wary, then, of any suggestion that Mill bore a grudge against his father, or that his love of individual liberty is rooted in his resentment of the training regimen which his father compelled him to follow. He was justifiably proud of James and 'was always loyally devoted to him', even if he 'cannot say' that he 'loved him tenderly' (ibid., 53). Moreover, there is no doubt that he agrees with his father that 'rigid discipline, and known liability to punishment, are indispensable as means' for the education of children (ibid.). The principle of liberty, he is careful to say, does not apply to children (1859c, 224 (I.10); henceforth all references to *On Liberty* (and to *Utilitarianism*) will include the shortened form of chapter and paragraph (e.g. I.10), following the standard-edition page reference). Rather, young people are properly subject to coercion for their own good. Paternalism is a legitimate policy in their case, as when they are forced to undergo a demanding training programme designed to cultivate their capacities to think for themselves.[5]

Yet Mill does complain about his father's severity: 'I hesitate to pronounce whether I was more a loser or a gainer by his severity' (1873, 53). The problem was that James relied on fear of punishment *to the virtual exclusion of* love and praise. He was too quick to scorn and punish any failure to meet his (sometimes unreasonably) high standards, and he refused to praise his son's motivation and efforts to succeed (ibid., 51). By working his otherwise admirable teaching method in such a harsh spirit, he made it impossible for John to regard him with affection and trust, and perhaps even discouraged his son from 'frank and spontaneous' communication with others (ibid., 55). Thus, although fear is an 'indispensable' element in education, a wise paternalism will not use it indiscriminately, but will instead rely predominantly on more positive incentives to cultivate a desire to study and learn.

Mill's considered remarks convey sadness rather than anger at the absence of love between himself and his father. Whatever he may have felt as a child or young man, he seems to have recognized the obvious later in life, when drafting and redrafting the *Autobiography*, namely, that his father must have loved him very much to spend so much time and effort on his early education. Perhaps with Harriet Taylor's help, he came to appreciate the cultural constraints on his father's personality, and the extent to which prevailing English customs smothered any man's natural capacities of feeling:

> I believe [my father] to have had much more feeling than he habitually shewed [sic], and much greater capacities of feeling than were ever developed. He resembled most Englishmen in being ashamed of the signs of feeling, and, by the absence of demonstration, starving the feelings themselves.
>
> (Ibid., 53)

Under the circumstances, 'true pity' rather than resentment must be felt 'for a father who did, and strove to do, so much for his children, who would have so valued their affection, yet who must have been constantly feeling that fear of him was drying it up at its source' (ibid.).

The tension between existing social customs and the cultivation of spontaneity, already alluded to as a central theme of the *Liberty*, makes its appearance, then, within the very character of James Mill.[6] His son describes him as a 'leader' whose 'energetic' personality, impressive analytical skills and 'moral rectitude' combined to make a lasting impression on those he met (Mill 1873, 39, 105, 205). He evidently had strong feelings about education, for example, and, more generally, was an earnest advocate of social and political reforms which he thought were recommended by general utility. Yet, under the sway of prevailing custom, he depreciated spontaneity and the display of passionate emotion: 'For passionate emotions of all sorts, and for everything which has been said or written in exaltation of them, he professed the greatest contempt' (ibid., 51). For that reason, and because he seems to have mistakenly supposed that his son would acquire strong feelings like his 'without difficulty or special training', he neglected cultivation of the feelings in his conception of education (ibid., 39). Strong desires and sentiments per se were apparently of little value, until harnessed by reason and directed toward the public good. The serious business of social and political reform demanded abstract principles of logic, political economy and morality. To identify them, education must fiercely concentrate on cultivation of the powers of analysis and reasoning.

James' conventional contempt for passion had at least two important consequences for his son. First, John's early education was too narrow in scope. Since he was generally told what to do and given little encouragement to develop his own feelings, he seems to have been moulded into a 'mere reasoning machine', with no strong desires of his own (ibid., 111). This imbalance in his character, which erupted into a 'mental crisis' by the time he was twenty, was exacerbated by his isolation. He never learned to fend for himself when his wants came into conflict with those of other children, for example. Thus: 'The education which my father gave me, was in itself much more fitted for training me to *know* than to *do*' (ibid., 39, emphasis added).

Second, and related, his father's (and, apparently, mother's) failure to express love and affection left him at sixteen without much self-confidence, so that he became overly passive and withdrawn. His 'mental crisis' would soon force him to recognize that such self-abnegation and absence of desire can lead to severe depression. Evidently, a broader education than his, including development of the feelings, was needed to foster passionate emotion and aplomb. Ideally, the compulsory education of children ought to achieve this, by duly mixing affection and praise with discipline and fear. But it was too late for that in his own case. Rather, it would largely be up to *him* to remedy any imbalance in his development. Yet, remedying the problem would not be easy for a young man like himself, so socially awkward and starved of affection. Perhaps this may help to account for the immeasurable value which he was to place on the love and support he found in Harriet. But they did not meet until he was twenty-five, nearly ten years down the road, and his path of self-development was rocky in the interval.

YOUNG BENTHAMITE RADICAL

After returning from France in July 1821, Mill joined the circle of utilitarian radicals revolving loosely around his father and Bentham. During the first year or two, he read Roman law with John Austin, became friendly with Austin's younger brother

Charles and his Cambridge associates, and began studying Bentham's ideas as interpreted by Dumont in the *Traité de législation*, the reading of which was 'an epoch in my life' (ibid., 67). He also read Condillac, Locke, Helvetius, Hartley, Hume and others, but says that Grote's attack on the utility of Deism in *Natural Religion* (privately circulated in 1822, under the pseudonym of Philip Beauchamp) 'produced the greatest effect upon me' next to the *Traité* (ibid., 73).

He began publishing in newspapers and journals as of 1822, and became the most frequent contributor to the radical *Westminster Review* (founded by Bentham in 1823) until he ceased writing for it in 1828 (after a dispute with Bowring, the editor). He also wrote frequently for the radical *Parliamentary History and Review* (edited by Bingham and Charles Austin) during its three years of existence, 1825–28.

He also formed the Utilitarian Society, a small study group which met fortnightly during 1822–26. The term 'utilitarian' thereby entered into public discourse, he says, although he did not invent the word (ibid., 81). As that group waned, another (the Society of Students of Mental Philosophy) was formed, which met twice weekly in Grote's house until about 1830. In addition to studying German, its members critically discussed various sciences, including political economy (Mill's *Essays on Some Unsettled Questions of Political Economy*, though not published until 1844, dates from this period), logic and analytic psychology (James Mill's *Analysis of the Phenomena of the Human Mind*, published in 1829, was the final work discussed).

During 1825–30, he also took part in numerous public debates which pitted utilitarian radicals against competing sects, including Owenite socialists and (in the context of the London Debating Society, which he helped form) Tory lawyers and liberal disciples of Coleridge (notably Maurice and Sterling, the latter subsequently becoming a close friend of Mill and, through him, of Carlyle).

On top of these various activities, he had his duties at the East India Company as of May 1823, when he began as a clerk in his father's office. But even that was not all. Remarkably, he also agreed to devote much of his spare time during 1825–26 to condensing and constructing, from Bentham's 'three masses' of draft papers on evidence, a 'single treatise', eventually published in 1827 as the five-volume *Rationale of Judicial Evidence* (ibid., 117). Although he emphasizes that it was an invaluable spur to his powers of composition, that difficult task may have been the straw that broke the camel's back, so to speak. Perhaps because of overwork, he became disenchanted with Benthamite radicalism during the autumn of 1826. His disenchantment translated into a loss of a sense of purpose in his life, and grew into a severe depression for the next six months. Even so, his mental crisis did not interrupt his busy schedule as a utilitarian radical, and must have been quite invisible to observers.

The general direction of his life appears fairly predictable throughout the 1820s, even if appearances were deceptive after his depression, because his formidable intellectual skills continued to be displayed in the service of the 'official' utilitarian goals associated with his father and Bentham. That Benthamite type of radicalism glorified reason as an instrument of reform, to the neglect of cultivation of higher motives and noble character. Like the eighteenth-century Enlightenment *philosophes* (including Voltaire, Diderot, Helvetius and Condorcet), the Benthamites tended to attack prevailing customs and institutions, including legal rules, as irrational emanations of aristocratic class prejudice and religious superstition. At the same time, they took for granted that most people are predominantly motivated by notions of self-interest. As a result, their reform efforts were focused on improving the intellectual capacities of the masses and establishing institutions compatible with competitive pursuit of enlightened self-interest. Little if any attention was paid to visionary institutions, such as market socialism or voluntary communal lifestyles beyond the traditional family, the feasibility of which depends on cultivation of higher moral and aesthetic sentiments (including the desire for equal justice): 'While fully recognising the superior excellence of unselfish benevolence and love of justice', Mill says of the Benthamites, among whose number he counted himself at this time, 'we did not expect the regeneration of mankind from any direct action on those sentiments, but from the effect of educated intellect, enlightening the selfish feelings' (ibid., 113).

Benthamite radicalism combined at least five leading elements (ibid., 107–11). First, Bentham's version of utilitarianism provided the general philosophical underpinnings. According to Bentham, social institutions should be designed such that selfish persons, strongly motivated to acquire wealth and power, have adequate 'external' incentives (rewards and punishments) to act so as to maximize collective utility, understood as the sum of the personal utilities (enlightened self-interests), each to count for one and only one. Remarkably, he seems to have rejected the view, subsequently taken for granted by modern utilitarians ever since Henry Sidgwick and early neoclassical economists such as Stanley Jevons, Francis Edgeworth and Alfred Marshall, that personal utilities are cardinal and interpersonally comparable. Instead, he apparently relies on purely ordinalist utility information, in other words, non-comparable personal preference orderings defined over the feasible sources of utility, for instance, proposed laws, policies, actions. True, he advises individuals to take account of the intensity, duration, fecundity and so forth of the utilities which may reasonably be expected from the possible sources. But his advice is intended to facilitate the formation of enlightened preference orderings, that is, preferences that reflect reasonable estimates of the amounts of utility to be expected from the sources so that any person's ranking of the sources is also a reasonable ranking of the expected utilities, given that the person prefers more utility to less. The individuals remain fallible selfish humans who are likely to form diverse preferences, however, rather than ideal moral agents possessed of cardinal comparable utility information. Thus, instead of a familiar utilitarian aggregation calculus that claims to find an outcome at which total happiness is maximized with certainty, Bentham has in mind a purely ordinalist utilitarian procedure such as a democratic political process that yields laws and policies which enlightened popular majorities or their elected representatives agree are likely to bring the greatest happiness to most if not all individuals in light of those individuals' prudent estimates of the amounts of utility to be expected from the sources.[7]

Bentham also seems to have supposed that, with suitable education, enlightened individuals would tend to associate their self-interests with certain permanent goods or interests (including security of expectations, subsistence, abundance and equality) which are the chief ingredients of collective happiness. The joint attainment of these permanent interests should guide the design of social institutions. Indeed, he goes so far as to suggest that enlightened selfish individuals might eventually converge on an identical preference ordering that gives due weight to these ingredients of the collective welfare. As Sidgwick (1988) points out: 'in [Bentham's] *Deontology* ... , it is distinctly assumed that, in actual human life as empirically known, the conduct most conducive to general happiness *always* coincides with that which conduces most to the happiness of the agent; and that "vice may be defined as a miscalculation of chances" from a purely mundane point of view' (244, emphasis original). If enlightenment can produce such unanimity, then, of course, there is no fundamental conflict in principle between a prudent egoist's own greatest happiness and the greatest total happiness of the community. Evidently, the radicals committed to the establishment of Benthamite utilitarian institutions must be enlightened egoists whose notions of their self-interests are far in advance of the narrowly selfish feelings of ignorant majorities. And yet Bentham apparently believes that majorities can also become similarly enlightened if the radical vanguard establishes suitable institutions of national education.[8]

A second element of the 'official' radical creed was a hedonistic psychology which, as developed by James Mill from a basis provided by Hartley's *Observations on Man* (1749), viewed any person's sole ultimate motivation as his own utility or happiness—in the sense of pleasure (including absence of pain)—and treated wealth and power as sources of pleasure inseparably associated with most persons' ideas of their welfare in observed civil societies. Again, radicals themselves must be motivated by suitably enlightened ideas of their own welfare, ideas that effectively merge what they take personal pleasure in with attainment of collective happiness. In short, they are motivated by their enlightened ideas of self-interest to establish social institutions which they have reason to believe will promote the self-interests of virtually everyone in society by fostering security, subsistence, abundance and equality.[9]

The remaining elements highlight major institutional implications of this hedonistic utilitarianism. 'In politics', the radicals displayed 'an almost unbounded confidence in the efficacy of two things: representative government, and complete freedom of discussion'

(Mill 1873, 109). If aristocratic rule could be replaced by 'a democratic suffrage', it was thought, then, when most voters had been sufficiently enlightened through basic education and the free flow of opinions to make 'good choice of persons to represent them', an elected legislature would impartially 'aim at the general interest' (ibid.).

In religion, the radicals were sceptics who rejected any established church as incompatible with liberty of thought and discussion. Like James Mill, they attacked 'the vulgar prejudice, that what is called, very improperly, unbelief, is connected with any bad qualities either of mind or heart' (ibid., 47). The belief systems commonly accepted as Christian struck them not only as corruptions of Christ's own teachings, but also as incoherent in that 'an Omnipotent Author of Hell' is 'nevertheless identified' with 'perfect goodness' (ibid., 43).

In economics, they favoured private ownership of productive resources, freely competitive markets and, as a means of raising the wages of the working classes in the long run, birth control (enforced by social stigma rather than legal penalties). They relied on Ricardo's theory as elaborated in his great treatise *On the Principles of Political Economy and Taxation* (1817), a simplified account of which was published by James Mill (with substantial drafting assistance from John) as *Elements of Political Economy* (1821).

It was against utilitarian radicalism of this 'official' sort, the radicalism to which he had been bred by his father, that he rebelled as a twenty-year-old, even as he continued to pursue radical projects and to mingle with his radical associates.

MENTAL CRISIS AND REACTION

Mill's 'mental crisis' lasted for some six months, extending into the spring of 1827, when he feared that critics might be correct to denounce utilitarianism as 'cold calculation; political economy as hard-hearted; [and] anti-population doctrines as repulsive to the natural feelings of mankind' (1873, 113). He grew gloomy and suicidal as he became aware that he would not feel 'great joy and happiness' even if the reforms prescribed by the radicals were 'completely effected at this very instant' (ibid., 139). It was not that he ceased to understand that his 'greatest and surest sources of happiness' lay in working to bring about a liberal conception of the public good. He *knew* he ought to feel pleasure in promoting the good of mankind. But he did not actually *feel* that pleasure, or *expect to feel it*: 'to know that a feeling would make me happy if I had it, did not give me the feeling' (ibid., 143). The 'continual pursuit' of a Benthamite conception of the general happiness 'had ceased to charm' (139). An 'egotistical' dejection choked his 'love of mankind', so that his life seemed to have no purpose and his 'fabric of happiness' was ruined (149).

His mental crisis was tied up, he suggests, with an imbalance produced in his character by his early education, to wit, strong analytical powers combined with weak feelings and desires. His father's programme of study had left him 'irretrievably analytic', without encouraging him to develop passions and loves of his own. Moreover, he feared that there was no remedy for the imbalance. The 'habit of analysis' necessarily erodes such a complex passion as the desire for public good, he thought, by identifying it as a mere prejudice, whose force depends on 'artificial' associations – created by means of 'praise and blame, reward and punishment' – between feelings of pleasure and ideas of general welfare (ibid., 141). Only simple natural feelings could survive the 'analysing spirit' unscathed, namely, 'the purely physical and organic' desires and pleasures. But these were surely insufficient 'to make life desirable' (143). Thus, because he had never really experienced strong complex passions and emotions of his own, he seems to have been unaware at this time that he still *could* cultivate such feelings, by immersing himself in the fine arts and giving free rein to his powers of imagination. The latter powers, he was shortly to discover, are 'natural complements and correctives' (141) to the powers of analysis, so that there is no necessary incompatibility between complex moral and aesthetic feelings and analytic acumen.

The depression gradually lifted, Mill tells us, after he was 'moved to tears' by Marmontel's memoir of when, as 'a mere boy', he had acted to alleviate the distress of his beloved family at the time of his father's death (ibid., 145). By vividly imagining the scene and sympathizing with the feelings of the boy and his family, John realized that he too was capable of such feelings, and 'could again find enjoyment, not intense, but sufficient for cheerfulness', in life.

Similarly, he found that Wordsworth's poetry evoked his love of beautiful natural scenery, especially mountains, as a kind of perfect ideal, a 'perennial' source of happiness in which all humans might share, suggestive of what might be possible 'when all the greater evils of life shall have been removed' (ibid., 151). 'And the delight which these poems gave me, proved that with culture of this sort, there was nothing to dread from the most confirmed habit of analysis' (ibid., 153). Thus, 'there was, once more, excitement, though of a moderate kind, in exerting myself for my opinions, and for the public good' (145). He now recognized that he could largely remedy any character defect produced by his early education by pursuing a suitable course of self-improvement. He would never again be so bothered by depression, despite 'several' recurrences of 'the same mental malady' (143–45).

The point to emphasize is that the mental crisis did pass. It did not reveal some irremediable flaw in Mill's personality, for which his father could endlessly and justifiably be blamed. Nor did it signal that the critics of utilitarian radicalism were right on the main points. Even so, the crisis is a turning point because it did have 'two very marked effects' on his philosophy and character. First, it led him to take an indirect approach to the goal of happiness. Direct pursuit of his own happiness and pleasure had involved him in counterproductive analysis of the extent to which any idea of public good could serve as a means to the end. But now he would aim at public good as 'itself an ideal end', finding personal happiness 'by the way' (ibid., 147). That indirect strategy would produce the most personal happiness for the vast majority, he claims, who (like himself) 'have but a moderate degree of sensibility and of capacity for enjoyment' (ibid.). Perhaps some highly sensitive artists and philanthropists might do better for themselves with a direct strategy. But most people will find more happiness for themselves by adopting and following a code of general rules designed to promote a conception of the general good. Remarkably, it is not clear that his father or Bentham would have any serious quarrel with this indirect strategy.

Second, his crisis led him to cultivate 'a due balance among the faculties', rather than focusing exclusively on his powers of analysis and reasoning. As he explains:

> I, for the first time, gave its proper place, among the prime necessities of human well-being, to the internal culture of the individual. I ceased to attach almost exclusive importance to the ordering of outward circumstances, and the training of the human being for speculation and action. I had now learned by experience that the passive susceptibilities needed to be cultivated as well as the active capacities, and required to be nourished and enriched as well as guided. I did not, for an instant, lose sight of, or undervalue, that part of the truth which I had seen before; I never turned recreant to intellectual culture, or ceased to consider the power and practice of analysis as an essential condition both of individual and social improvement. But I thought that it had consequences which required to be corrected, by joining other kinds of cultivation with it. The maintenance of a *due balance among the faculties*, now seemed to me of primary importance. The cultivation of the feelings became one of the cardinal points in my ethical and philosophical creed.
>
> (Ibid., 147, emphasis added)

In short, he now saw that no fundamental incompatibility exists between intellectual enlightenment, the only form of culture pursued by the Benthamite school, and the cultivation of higher moral and aesthetic sentiments, generally ignored by that school as ineffectual for purposes of social reform. Henceforth, he would be more open to ideals of noble character and visions of social harmony, which were rejected by the 'official' utilitarians as useless if not antagonistic to their programme.

The real import of his crisis, on this interpretation, is that it stirred him to formulate a better version of liberal utilitarianism, a 'new' radicalism that retains what was valuable in the 'old' Benthamite doctrine but also makes more adequate provision for the cultivation of the higher feelings and for ideal social arrangements founded upon them. The crisis was 'the origin' of an 'important transformation in my opinions and character', he says, which preoccupied him 'for some years' (ibid., 137). He could imagine his new radicalism in outline by 1830, it seems, and was able to fill in most of the details before the summer of 1834, when he began to edit the *London Review* (as of 1836, the *London and Westminster Review*) started by Molesworth. Even so, he was unable to 'give full scope to my own opinions and modes of thought', before his father died (ibid., 215). After that, a principal goal of his conduct of the *Review*, he emphasizes, was 'to shew [*sic*] that there was a radical philosophy, better and more complete than Bentham's, while recognising and incorporating all of Bentham's which is permanently valuable' (221). Indeed, to achieve this goal of driving a wedge between philosophical radicalism and 'sectarian Benthamism', he went so far as to purchase the journal in 1837, operating it at a loss until 1840, when he sold it to Hickson.[10]

Mill insists that, despite his reaction against Benthamism, he never ceased to consider himself a kind of utilitarian radical, however peculiar his brand of radicalism might appear in relation to the 'official' brand. 'I never, indeed, wavered in the conviction that happiness is the test of all rules of conduct, and the end of life', he says (1873, 145). 'Like me', he says of John Austin, who had also undergone a transformation in his Benthamite opinions and character after living and studying for some time in Germany, 'he never ceased to be an utilitarian' (ibid., 185). Similarly, despite his Romantic turn toward the cultivation of feelings, Mill 'never turned recreant to intellectual culture' and 'never joined in the reaction against [the Enlightenment]' of the 'great' eighteenth century (147, 169).

Rather than abandon utilitarian radicalism, he proposes to modify and enlarge it into an even 'more heretical' doctrine, in which alien materials are grafted onto a Benthamite stock to breathe new life into the whole. The foreign supplements, as he tells us, included insights into will, imagination and aesthetic feeling offered by German idealists and the artists influenced by them, including, among others, Goethe, Wilhelm von Humboldt, Schiller and the Romantics such as Novalis, Coleridge and Wordsworth. He also made room for egalitarian social Utopias of the sort proposed by Owen and the French 'socialists' and 'communists', including Saint-Simon, Fourier, Cabet and Louis Blanc. Moreover, his interest in birth control and equal rights for women was heightened by his exposure to the feminist views of his future wife. She and her circle of Unitarian friends did not hold sacrosanct the prevailing social conventions relating to marriage and personal lifestyle.[11]

HARRIET

Harriet enters Mill's story just when his new radicalism seems to have assumed a definite shape in his mind. He soon came under her spell: 'I very soon felt her to be the most admirable person I had known', he says, although about ten years went by 'before her mental progress and mine went forward in the complete companionship they at last attained' (1873, 193, 197). He was ripe from the first for the passionate love she inspired in him, the deep emotion that he had missed until she came along, and that he was never to find with another after she died. She was the light of his life and, if his own testimony is believed, a brilliant and original thinker in her own right (ibid., 195–97, 251–61).

He praises her to a remarkable degree, making her into a paragon of moral and intellectual development. He apparently learned from her 'the constituent elements of the highest realizable ideal of human life' (ibid., 197), that is, an ideal conception of happiness, which he refers to in the *Liberty* as 'utility in the largest sense' (1859c, 224 (I.11)). She also seems to have taught him 'a wise scepticism' about his practical conclusions in moral and political science, saving him from a kind of dogmatism toward which his Benthamite training may have inclined him (1873, 197–99). In short, she was the 'fiery' artist and wise practitioner all rolled into one, the originator of their 'most valuable ideas', whereas he was predominantly a methodical 'interpreter', a synthesizer and systematizer of other people's important thoughts, which the original thinkers themselves did not know how, or could not be bothered, to integrate and reconcile (ibid., 251–53).

His high praise for her patently annoys some commentators, who do not take it seriously. But, even allowing for his tendencies to downplay his own originality and to exaggerate the brilliance of those whom he loved (he also lauds Helen, for example, as virtually another Harriet), it is not clear that third parties are in any position to second-guess his assessment of her abilities. Nor is it clear why anyone should *wish* to denigrate her contributions in any case. If he thinks enough of her critical advice and discussion to want to include her as the 'joint author' of some of his important texts, despite the absence of evidence that she wrote much of anything, why should that trouble anyone? He is certainly not disclaiming responsibility for the textual arguments, of which the clarity and power do not depend on such particulars of authorship.

What *is* clear is that Harriet's close friendship with Mill during her first marriage raised eyebrows. Her rather hasty remarriage may also have struck many of those who knew them (including members of his own family) as a breach of moral convention. Given his depiction of her proud personality, she would hardly have been intimidated by stigma of this sort.[12] Such a woman, deliberately forming unconventional relationships with other consenting adults as she likes, in defiance of prevailing norms of church and family, might well acquire a bad reputation, whatever her capacities of intellect and feeling. Defenders of traditional ideas and attitudes would surely deny all possibility that she might be a brilliant thinker, of impeccable moral character. Moreover, once acquired, her reputation as a thoughtless and irresponsible eccentric would tend to take on a life of its own. Perhaps Mill's emphatic praise of her good qualities ought to be considered in this context, as a calculated response to the predictable string of invective against her from the usual quarters.

In this one respect at least, the lives of Mill and Pericles do show some overlap, in the sense that Harriet is to Mill as Aspasia of Miletus is to the great Athenian.[13] According to the ancient sources, Pericles may have offended against traditional religious values and marriage customs, because he openly treated Aspasia – a freethinking resident alien – as not merely his lover but his wife and confidante (a status customarily reserved for dutiful Athenian women). She was vilified at the time, no doubt at the urging of his political opponents, and has continued to be vilified through history, as a manipulator, a whore, a seducer of an otherwise brilliant man who somehow lost all common sense in her presence and attributed his brilliance to her (Henry 1995). The doctrine of the *Liberty* signals that we should be cautious before accepting such assessments, since they may be nothing more than manifestations of more or less subtle forms of social coercion directed against extraordinary individuals for pursuing their personal affairs in their own ways, without wrongful hurt to others.

In any case, there seems little reason to deny Mill's claim that Harriet contributed valuable ideas to his new liberal utilitarian philosophy. He tells us that she encouraged him to take more seriously the possibility of a decentralized form of socialism, for example, in which co-operative associations of highly educated producers would compete on product and factor markets, men and women enjoying equal rights of participation within the enterprises (1873, 237–45, 255–57). She may also have helped him to grasp that women, as they gained equality with men, would be more likely to demand more prudent family practices (including birth control measures) than had hitherto been observed or could otherwise be expected under the prevailing system of male domination. Even more importantly for our purposes, she may have impressed on him the truth of the 'one very simple principle' of the *Liberty*. Nothing like that principle is recognized in his earlier writings, where, indeed, he seems more dubious about freedom of expression than one would expect from the author of the essay.[14]

If she did contribute such insights, Harriet had a large hand in the central project of Mill's life, to wit, his clarification of a new utilitarian radicalism, more adequate and complete than Bentham's related doctrine.

NEW UTILITARIAN RADICALISM

The essays and treatises published after 1840 are properly seen to elaborate that 'better and more complete' liberal utilitarianism. The *Liberty* is perhaps the crowning jewel of the new radical creed. But the jewel is surrounded by an unusually broad array of contributions on virtually every important aspect of a liberal democratic philosophy. Although his major texts on logic and political economy were both in print by 1848, most of his work on moral and political themes was published during 1859–69. In addition to the *Liberty*, it includes a statement of his utilitarianism, his thoughts on representative government, associationist psychology and the subjection of women, and his critiques of Hamilton's transcendental idealism and rational intuitionism and of Comte's positivism. His unfinished essays on religion and socialism, as well as the *Autobiography*, were published posthumously, by Helen, by 1879.

This is not the place to attempt to detail all of the ways in which the new radicalism modifies and enlarges upon its Benthamite ancestor. The differences between them are rooted in the fact that Mill is more cognizant than the old radicals of human capacities of imagination (including sympathy for others) and mutual co-operation, more open to the possibility that individuals might form noble characters that reflect repeated acts of imagination and co-operation, and consequently less committed to social institutions that presuppose the predominantly selfish type of characters observed hitherto. Unlike the Benthamites, he distinguishes among different kinds of pleasant feelings, some of which are intrinsically or qualitatively superior to others irrespective of quantity, and suggests that the kind of pleasant feeling which is inseparably associated with the moral sentiments (the sentiment of justice being the principal one), and which he calls a feeling of security, is higher in quality than any competing kinds of pleasant feelings. The upshot is that an optimal social code of justice, which distributes and sanctions equal rights and duties for all, is of the utmost importance for maximizing collective happiness. Moreover, Mill suggests that most people can develop noble and virtuous characters such that they will voluntarily participate in the more or less gradual construction of such a code and also voluntarily comply with the rules which they have had a voice in creating. Nevertheless, Bentham, despite his preoccupation with enlightening the selfish feelings to effect reform, also focused in the main on utilitarian moral and legal rules. Thus, the Benthamite and Millian approaches appear to coincide on giving priority to considerations of justice, even though they adopt very different versions of hedonistic psychology with distinctive implications for the design of utilitarian political and economic institutions.

At the same time, elements of the old radicalism are retained in Mill's new outlook. Like Bentham, for example, he does not rely on a standard utilitarian calculus that presupposes rich cardinal and interpersonally comparable utility information so as to add up individual pleasures into an incontestable sum total of happiness. Rather, he apparently works with a purely ordinalist utilitarian aggregation procedure, that is, a democratic process in which individual preferences over the sources of pleasure are impartially considered, or roughly 'added up', to yield a democratic collective preference or choice that is no more than a reasonable (i.e. maximum likelihood) estimate of actual total happiness. Indeed, as I understand him, Mill restricts the democratic process to the higher pleasure of security associated with the moral sentiment of justice. In other words, his ordinalist utilitarian procedure only considers individual preferences defined over possible codes (or fragments of codes) of equal rights and duties, with the aim of generating an optimal social code of justice to publicly define and regulate fair interactions among the members of society. Such a democratic process is in fact internal to any moral agent's sentiment of justice since the agent cannot complete the formation of her sentiment until the process has done its work, thereby informing her of the rules, rights and duties which (of the many possibilities) are recognized as best in her society. As an optimal social code is established, the individual has capacious freedom to pursue the other kinds of pleasures besides security in accord with her rights, so long as she fulfils her obligations to others under the code. She has considerable freedom to organize her own life in her own way since no political procedure operates to yield binding social rules to govern her actions with respect to those other kinds of utilities.

Like Bentham again, Mill works with a conception of the collective happiness in which security, subsistence, abundance and equality figure as 'constituent elements', and holds that most will attain personal happiness indirectly, by complying with a social code of rules designed to promote that conception of public good. (The code must also contain rules for utilitarian reformers to live by in situations where widespread compliance cannot be expected, though it should always be encouraged.) But Mill's conception of collective happiness is 'more heretical' than that of any Benthamite.

As conceived by Benthamites, the public good apparently involves sustained economic growth under capitalist institutions, peaceful majoritarian government under democratic institutions, sufficient redistribution to assure the subsistence of those who need help, and more or less material equality depending on the progress of intellectual education and birth control among the masses. A Benthamite utilitarian code of justice promotes abundance and reduces inequality, for example, by distributing private property rights and fostering free markets, such that the individual is guaranteed the fruits of his own labour and saving (net of fair taxation); primogeniture and entails are abolished; and aristocratic privileges regarding the natural fruits of the earth are curtailed. The code also minimizes the danger of political misrule, by distributing rights to vote that secure to each citizen an opportunity to make his voice heard by elected legislators. The individual must also be assigned rights to subsistence, personal safety, reputation and the like. The resulting system of equal rights and correlative duties supposedly promotes collective happiness in ways that any enlightened egoist can accept, by allowing each individual to enjoy security of expectations with respect to certain vital elements or 'primary goods' in his plan of life.

This Benthamite approach retained appeal for Mill as far as it went. But he also looked beyond it, by imagining that certain 'higher' aesthetic and moral feelings might eventually come to trump self-interest (enlightened or otherwise). His account of these complex higher feelings did not entail for him a departure from hedonism. Rather, their status as higher pleasures, inherently more valuable as pleasures than the pleasures of selfish behaviour, could be explained, he thought, by a more sophisticated version of the psychology championed by his father. That more sophisticated hedonism was largely developed by Bain and himself, as outlined in their notes to the new edition of the *Analysis of the Phenomena of the Human Mind* (1869). This modified and enlarged account of human nature opened his eyes to possibilities of personal nobility and social organization not entertained (or insufficiently considered) by Benthamite radicals. It also made him less sanguine than they were about the advantages of majoritarian democracy and market capitalism, in the absence of moral and aesthetic progress by the majority.

In politics, for example, Mill suggested that, unless the people have developed to a point of virtual moral unanimity, good government cannot be ensured by making the government as responsive as possible to popular majorities, as Bentham proposes in his *Constitutional Code* (1830). Good government requires marshalling the special competence of an educated minority if any exists in society. A fortiori, good government cannot be produced merely through democratic elections:

> Identity of interest between the governing body and the community at large, is not, in any practical sense which can be attached to it, the only thing on which good government depends; neither can this identity of interest be secured by the mere conditions of election.
>
> (1873, 165)

His father and Bentham were wrong to dismiss counter-majoritarian checks and balances as useless devices. Macaulay was right that good government depended on different groups having power to oppose one another. In addition to democratic elections, a prudent system of auxiliary checks and balances was essential, to forestall majority oppression of minority interests. Unlike Tocqueville, however, John did not favour the US system, with its bicameral legislature elected from, respectively, districts and states by majority or plurality vote, its independent chief executive and its fixed dates of election. Rather, as he makes clear in *Considerations on Representative Government*, he favoured a unicameral parliamentary system, with Hare's method of elections to ensure proportional representation. In addition to providing minorities with voices in the legislature in proportion to their numbers, auxiliary safeguards against majority incompetence and/or tyranny included an independent commission of experts (appointed by the executive) with exclusive authority to draft or amend legislation as requested by the legislature (which retained the authority to enact or veto whole bills), and perhaps even plural voting based on education as opposed to one person, one vote – although he clearly had some practical qualms about the latter innovation (1873, 261–62).

In economics, given the possibility that a high degree of moral solidarity (as well as intelligence) might emerge among workers and investors, he speculated that competitive capitalism might eventually be transformed, by a series of voluntary exchanges among market participants, into an ideal sort of decentralized socialism, in which competition among small-scale self-managed worker co-operatives is constrained by some higher morality of distributive justice. Also in his *Principles of Political Economy*, he hopes that highly developed producers might opt for a so-called 'stationary state' (i.e. stationary population and capital stock), rather than continued economic growth beyond a reasonable threshold of national wealth and population. By implication, economic rights associated with the interest in abundance – whether private property rights or rights to participate in socialist enterprises – come into conflict, in his view, with superior types of rights beyond that threshold. Those superior rights might include rights to breathe clean air and drink clean water, for example, as well as rights to contemplate unspoiled natural beauty in solitude, rights to engage freely and exclusively with other consensual adults in intimate activities of no legitimate concern to anyone else and so on. At some point, if growth of wealth and population continues unchecked and natural beauty is increasingly sacrificed to mankind's economic purposes, such rights will be endangered for many of us. His liberal utilitarianism at that point prescribes a halt to further economic growth (for further discussion of these points, see Riley 1996, 1998b).

In purely self-regarding matters, including opinions on all subjects as well as actions in all modes not hurtful to other people unless they like, Mill defends absolute liberty, so that the individual might develop his intellectual, imaginative and moral capacities. He generalizes the argument, accepted by Benthamites and others, for absolute liberty of religious opinion. But the old radicals do not seem to have anticipated his generalization, despite Kelly's suggestions to the contrary (1990, 150–54). In short, Mill's conception of collective happiness includes a distinctive 'permanent interest' in 'individuality', which is not found among the 'constituent elements' of the Benthamite conception.

Mill's new utilitarian radicalism modifies and enlarges Benthamism, then, by adding to Bentham's list of 'constituent elements' of the good life, by imagining the possibility of a distinctive ideal mix of those permanent ingredients, and by identifying novel codes of rules, rights and duties associated with that ideal blend of security, subsistence, abundance, equality and individuality. But the reader must go elsewhere for further discussion of the apparent structure of this distinctive Millian creed (see Riley 2009, 2010a, 2010b, 2010c, 2012, 2013b, 2014, 2015a, 2015b, forthcoming-a).

'TEXT-BOOK OF A SINGLE TRUTH'

Mill says that the *Liberty* is 'a kind of philosophic text-book of a single truth ... the importance, to man and society, of a large variety in types of character, and of giving full freedom to human nature to expand itself in innumerable and conflicting directions' (1873, 259). Most people do not really appreciate that truth, he insists. Rather, the majority tends 'to fetter the development, and, if possible, prevent the formation, of any individuality not in harmony with its own ways' (1859c, 220 (I.5)). Obedience to prevailing customs and norms is typically regarded as important, not the freedom to explore diverse paths of self-development and to form one's opinions and character as one thinks best (so crucial in his own case).

The truth affirmed by the 'text-book' is not entirely original, he admits. Its 'leading thought ... is one which, though in many ages confined to insulated thinkers, mankind have probably at no time since the beginning of civilisation been entirely without. To speak only of the last few generations', he goes on, its 'doctrine of the rights of individuality, and the claim of the moral nature to develope [*sic*] itself in its own way', has been asserted in one form or another by Pestalozzi, Wilhelm von Humboldt, Goethe and the German Romantics, William Maccall and Josiah Warren (1873, 260). Recall also his observation that broad liberty of thought and freedom of action in all modes not harmful to others, are among the 'best qualities' of critical periods in general (ibid., 173, 259–60).

Nevertheless, he also hints that his conception of this long-standing doctrine of liberty is more novel than he has been letting on: 'It is hardly necessary here to remark that there are abundant differences in detail, between the conception of the doctrine by any of the predecessors I have mentioned, and that set forth in the book' (ibid., 261). Moreover, we should not be fooled into thinking that the best qualities of transitional periods will automatically persist into subsequent organic periods, he insists, in the absence of any principled defence of those qualities. If we expect unbridled freedom of thought and of action in all modes harmless to others to be included as constituent elements of whatever new creed eventually 'rallies the majority around it', a *principle of liberty*, 'grounded in reason and in the true exigencies of life' and thus capable of persuading reasoning persons in all periods, is essential (ibid., 260, 173). It is within later *organic* periods, which he assumes will inevitably replace the critical age in which he lived, that 'the teachings of the *Liberty* will have their greatest value' (260). And he issues a warning, made to sound ominous in hindsight by the rise of fascist and totalitarian creeds—far removed from liberal reason—during the twentieth century: 'it is to be feared that [its teachings] will retain that value a long time' (ibid.).

The aim of the *Liberty* is to set forth 'one very simple principle' of liberty, of enduring value across critical and organic periods. That 'simple principle' is distinctive, I shall argue, in that it prescribes the individual's moral right to choose as he pleases among certain 'purely self-regarding' acts said not to harm or even 'affect' other people against their wishes: 'In the part [of his conduct] which merely concerns himself, his independence is, of right, *absolute*' (1859c, 224 (I.9), emphasis added). Whatever Harriet's influence in the matter, this prescription of a licence to think and do as one likes is not some offhand remark or a casual slip of the pen. As documented in Part II of this Guidebook, similar statements can be found throughout the 'text-book'.

Mill emphasizes that the *Liberty* is a carefully constructed piece of work: 'None of my writings have either been so carefully composed, or so sedulously corrected as this' (1873, 249). He first prepared an abbreviated version of it in 1854, he says, and then decided, while travelling in Italy in early 1855, to convert it into a volume. Despite other pressing business relating to the East India Company, he and Harriet revised the entire manuscript numerous times in the interval before her death, 'reading, weighing and criticising every sentence' (ibid.). The volume 'was more directly and literally our joint production than anything else which bears my name' (ibid., 257). It never received its 'final revision'. But it remains a highly polished production: '[T]here was not a sentence of it that was not several times gone through by us together, turned over in many ways, and carefully weeded of any faults, either in thought or in expression, that we detected in it' (ibid., 257–59).

He is also clearly proud of the arguments of the volume. In his view, 'the *Liberty* is likely to survive longer than anything else that I have written (with the possible exception of the *Logic*)' (ibid., 259). Indeed, he sees it as a fitting tribute to the love of his life: 'After my irreparable loss one of my earliest cares was to print and publish the treatise, so much of which was the work of her whom I had lost, and consecrate it to her memory' (ibid., 261). Its present form is apparently the best he can offer: 'Though it wants the last touch of her hand, no substitute for that touch shall ever be attempted by me' (ibid.). The first edition was published by Parker in February of 1859, only three months after Harriet's death. Aside from some minor typos, no revisions were ever made.

Under these circumstances, it seems incumbent on the reader to treat the arguments of the essay with due care and respect. Contrary to the suggestions of many critics, the doctrine of liberty is not some ill-considered musing or slapdash effort. It deserves, and repays, careful study.

EARLY REACTION

The *Liberty* seems to have been something of an instant sensation among English readers. Rees (1956, 1–2) cites some contemporary statements to that effect. Mill himself speaks of 'the great impression' made by the essay 'at a time [i.e. a critical period] which, to superficial observation, did not seem to stand much in need of such a lesson' (1873, 259). The first edition quickly sold out, and a second edition of 2,000 copies appeared in August 1859, followed by a third in 1864. Only one more Library Edition was published during Mill's lifetime, in 1869, largely because an inexpensive and oft-reprinted People's Edition appeared in 1865. Since his death, the essay has been reprinted numerous times, in various languages. It is still generally regarded as a classic statement of the case for individual liberty.

That is not to say that his argument has ever been widely accepted, or that it is now adequately reflected in the legal and moral systems of advanced societies such as Britain or the United States. But the text remains influential to some extent and continues to be admired by many who are prepared to be critical of existing law and morality. H.L.A. Hart noted in 1963, for example, that 'Mill's principles [*sic*] are still very much alive in the criticism of law' (1963, 15). Joel Feinberg (1984–88) turns to 'Mill's principles' as he reconstructs them in his critical assessment of legal rules in an American context. C.L. Ten has argued that Mill's doctrine contains important lessons for modern multicultural societies, and that '[i]t will be a long time before the message of *On Liberty* becomes redundant' (1995, 204). And, more recently, John Skorupski (2006) has offered a stirring plea for the continuing relevance of Mill's liberalism, including his doctrine of individual liberty.[15]

At the same time, the fame of the essay should not be taken to imply that its argument has been fully comprehended by most of its readers. From the start, most critical notices of the book have been infected by remarkable confusions and misunderstandings. As J.T. Mackenzie complained in 1880, in a cogent reply to the smug conservatism expressed by Max Muller during the previous year, 'scarcely anybody' seems to have understood the 'plain language' of the text (as reprinted in Pyle 1994, 397). It is difficult to know whether such incomprehension generated the qualms and outright hostility among philosophers which rather quickly surrounded the book, or whether a pre-existing climate of hostility to hedonistic utilitarianism predisposed most critics to make little effort to understand its form of reasoning in the first place, let alone to clarify that reasoning for a wider public. But it is clear that a mix of incomprehension and hostility to utilitarianism continues to linger, and still casts a shadow even over recent liberal interpretations that revise Mill's text so that its doctrine of liberty becomes merely a restatement of the liberal shibboleth that justice demands equal rights for all.

As Mackenzie continues, however, Mill's 'words contain the germ of a social revolution; there is not a corner of life into which they do not pierce' (ibid., 397–98). It is tempting to suggest that certain elements of society had a vested interest in blunting the revolutionary implications of the liberty doctrine. And, like Oscar Wilde, I can resist everything but temptation. In particular, I shall ask the reader to keep in mind the possibility that influential defenders of established social institutions may have deliberately misrepresented Mill's position, so as to obscure the radical liberal reforms that flow from his 'very simple principle'.[16] Influential defenders of the established order included many ministers and professors imbued with a faith in traditional religious and moral ideals.[17]

For instance, T.H. Green, Bernard Bosanquet and other British idealists, profoundly influenced by Rousseau and the German metaphysicians such as Kant, Fichte and Hegel firmly rejected Mill's doctrine of the rights of liberty and individuality. They misrepresented it as resting on a glaring mistake, to wit, the assumption that the individual has a sphere of self-regarding action where he has no moral responsibilities to others. In their expressed view, no such self-regarding sphere exists and so Mill is wrong to insist that society (notably, the democratic majority) must respect some right of the individual to choose as he desires among self-regarding actions. They replaced Mill's doctrine with a contrary one, according to which liberty consists in choosing to do what is worthy of a 'higher' rational and moral self that works in co-operation with others. Liberty thus understood boils down to freely obeying social rules which democratic majorities decide are worthy of the higher self and promote its realization. Such liberty is positive insofar as its exercise promotes the common good given that the ideal self to be realized is the same for everyone. Individuality is understood in terms of the higher self's realization, and is displayed by spontaneously performing one's social roles in accord with one's recognized rights and duties under the established rules. But Millian rights of self-regarding liberty and individuality are not among these recognized rights. Instead, the anti-Millian, idealist doctrine places no restrictions on the scope of society's legitimate use of coercion: no sphere of action is exempt in principle from coercive interference by state officials or concerned citizens. That doctrine replaces Mill's distinction between self-regarding and other actions with a distinction between coercion and free will: coercion, although it can be employed to prevent or compel any action as society decides, can never be a substitute for morality since a moral will must be a free will.

Nevertheless, the idealists may not have intentionally misrepresented Mill's doctrine as resting on a mistake which they knew not to be a mistake at all. They may have genuinely believed that a self-regarding action as he understands it is a fiction of his imagination. That belief has persisted among many philosophers besides the idealists even though it is clearly false, or so I maintain. Indeed, the idealist critique of Mill's doctrine received early support from thinkers who can hardly be suspected of being defenders of the established social order. For instance, Nietzsche, an open enemy of Christianity and the existing social morality, also at least implicitly dismissed the distinction between self-regarding and other conduct as mistaken. In contrast to Green and other idealists who conceived of the higher self as a moral self committed to equal rights for all, he conceived of the higher self, or 'overman', as a selfish and talented artist who is entitled if he can to trample over all those who obstruct his expression of his authentic nature. In effect, he replaced Mill's idea of a limited self-regarding sphere with an unlimited sphere of selfishness, and denied that a talented egoist ought to bend his will to respect the equal rights of all. Nietzsche preached a far-reaching revolution in which Christianity and bourgeois morality are completely overthrown, with violence if necessary, only to be replaced by a continuing struggle among the strong and talented to impose their will on the rest.

Nietzsche's thought, which is similar in important respects to Carlyle's, is arguably an offshoot of what Isaiah Berlin (2013) calls an 'unbridled' strain of romanticism that celebrated the untrammelled will as the expression of an individual's or nation's authentic and unique nature or essence, a view sometimes wrongly attributed to Mill himself, who repeatedly rejected it. Just as idealism has continued to have a strong influence, so this stream of 'unbridled romanticism' has continued to have an influence on later thought. The upshot is that various schools still converge on the claim that Mill's doctrine of liberty must be rejected as untenable, at least in the form in which he presents it. Even Berlin (1969) himself, though evidently inspired by *On Liberty*, rejected its idea of self-regarding conduct and its utilitarian form of reasoning.

The widespread misrepresentation of Mill's liberty doctrine as resting on a glaring mistake has largely succeeded in repressing its distinctive revolutionary message. The work begun by the early critics has hardened into a dogma among many scholars that, despite his uplifting rhetoric, his argument is a failure. There is no doubt that the reviews published during his lifetime and shortly thereafter, are, for the most part, hostile.[18] There are occasional exceptions. I have already mentioned Mackenzie's review. Morley's (1873) reply to Fitzjames Stephen's crude utilitarian attack on Mill (1967; originally published 1873) is also cogent and devastating.[19] Walt Whitman (1871), despite his affinity for idealism, refers to Mill in support of an argument that the rights of individuality must be protected to elevate the character of American democracy. But these are relatively rare. Many more, after expressing grudging admiration for the author, go on to charge him with fatal inconsistency, hopeless ambiguity, immoral subversion of family values and/or something akin to blasphemy. Indeed, as Rees (1956, 1–38) and Pyle (1994, vii–xx) document, the panoply of criticisms now largely taken for granted by philosophers can be found in these early reviews, including: liberalism is incompatible with utilitarianism; liberty is defined improperly by Mill, in purely negative terms; harm is not defined at all; self-regarding acts cannot be distinguished from others; the liberty principle is inapplicable—and on and on.

In this regard, many of the early reviewers are evidently offended by Mill's claims in the essay that Christianity has decayed into a 'dead dogma' for most members of advanced societies, such that what is now called Christian morality, and habitually practised as such, is something very different from the 'maxims and precepts contained in the New Testament', which no longer guide conduct and indeed are scarcely understood. Modern Christianity, he suggests, boils down for most to a doctrine of 'passive obedience' to prevailing social customs and conventions, and would be largely unrecognizable to Christ or even to Saint Paul. To put it mildly, this was unwelcome news to those who considered themselves Christians, and it may have led many to discount the value of his argument in support of the liberty principle. Even Bain was bothered. 'Such a line of observation is felt at once as challenging the pretensions of Christianity to be a divine revelation', he intoned, 'and this ought not to be done in a passing remark ... The whole subject is extraneous to his treatise, and impedes rather than assists the effect that he desires to produce' (1882a, 105–6).

The problem was exacerbated over time by the periodic outbursts of traditional religious sentiment which (in defiance of the long-term erosion) continued to sweep across America, Britain,

France and elsewhere, revivals that tended to help identify freedom with the abolition of slavery, polygamy, intemperance and any other practices which the majority had learned to condemn. Indeed, the notion that Mill's 'text-book' is anti-Christian, or hostile to religious faith as such, still resonates today among some critics.

But Bain is quite incorrect to assert that 'the whole subject' of Christian morality is 'extraneous' to the argument of the *Liberty*. Moreover, Mill (1874) evidently admires the figure of Christ, apart from the question of divinity, and would certainly include the 'golden rule', maxims of good Samaritanship and other reasonable Christian precepts, within a liberal utilitarian Religion of Humanity. Rather than anti-Christian, he is against hypocrisy and blind conformity to customary standards of conduct whose Christian pedigree is open to doubt.

CURRENT STATUS

As already suggested, the early hostility surrounding the *Liberty* hardened over time, leaving us today with an essay whose rhetoric is apparently much admired, at least by liberals, even while its identification of a purely self-regarding sphere and its hedonistic utilitarian form of reasoning are not taken seriously. Those few who might be considered early disciples of Mill's utilitarian liberalism, including Morley, Helen Taylor, perhaps Bain, Cairnes and Fawcett, and, through Morley, perhaps even Pater, were quickly swamped by a rejuvenated pan-Christian idealism among academics, which, though it was arguably more egalitarian and democratic than its ancestors, largely reflected the evolution of majoritarian customs and practices.[20] The majority's understanding of traditional religious and moral values continued – and continues yet – to be revised as a result of sustained economic growth and the extension of democratic institutions. But the 'one very simple principle' of liberty has never gained wide acceptance. Indeed, if, as seems doubtful, a new organic period has ever arrived in Western societies to supplant the critical period in which Mill lived, its creed has not been his liberal utilitarianism. At best, we now have some pallid imitation, a somewhat more liberal democratic version of Judaeo-Christian ethics or American constitutionalism, which most accept more or less intuitively as providing justification for the general shape of social institutions as they have evolved.

And yet, the eloquence of the 'text-book' still inspires those who recognize the immense value of individual freedom. In our times, many thinkers have turned to Mill for insights into the construction of a credible doctrine of liberty, including, among others, Berlin (1969), Rawls (1999, 2005, 2007), Ten (1980, 1995), Hart (1982), Gray (1989, 1996, 2000), Berger (1984), Feinberg (1984–88), Rees (1985), Raz (1986), Skorupski (1989, 2006), Donner (1991, 2009), Brink (1992, 2013), Jacobson (2000, 2003, 2008), Kateb (2003), Devigne (2006), Miller (2010), and Rosen (2013). Even these thinkers typically alter or abandon his own explicit arguments, however, and propose alternative doctrines that attempt to better capture his liberal spirit. They charge him with incoherence and ignore what he says, in the course of elaborating whatever form of liberalism strikes them as an adequate substitute for his allegedly flawed hedonistic utilitarian form.[21]

These friendly critics downplay or ignore his key distinction between self-regarding and other conduct as well as his hedonistic utilitarianism. In my view, they are mistaken to do so. His doctrine, properly understood, restricts the individual's moral right to do as she pleases to the self-regarding sphere, and recognizes that society has legitimate authority to frame and enforce rules of other-regarding, or what he calls 'social', conduct. There is no clash between absolute self-regarding liberty and obligations to obey moral and legal rules whose scope is limited to the other-regarding domain. Rather, this mix of self-assertion and obedience to social rules is grounded on his extraordinary version of hedonistic utilitarianism.

Unlike the friendly critics, other critics are not inspired to construct revised doctrines that attempt to preserve Mill's liberal spirit while remedying his supposed inconsistencies. These unfriendly critics apparently believe that his self–other distinction and his hedonistic utilitarian form of reasoning are so flawed that he cannot be considered a serious theorist of any stripe, liberal or otherwise. Such thinkers generally attribute to Mill severe confusions of their own making. For example, Justman (1990) and Posner (2003) leave the impression, as Matthew Arnold (1993) did soon after the *Liberty* was published, that Mill is asserting the individual's right to pursue her self-interest not only in her self-regarding conduct but also in her social conduct that affects others' interests against their wishes. Such a blanket right to personal liberty evidently conflicts with obligations to other people and leads to anarchy. The critics are not deterred even if they notice that Mill restricts the scope of the individual right and gives society the right to decide whether to interfere with social conduct to prevent harm to others. He never clearly defines what he means by 'harm', so the familiar story goes, and, besides, his theory puts incredible psychological strains on the individual: she cannot be expected to square her right to pursue her self-interest with her duty to sacrifice it so as to help others to meet their needs, for example, nor with her duty to participate in democratic politics showing an impartial concern for the collective good. There is no doubt that Mill is committed to those moral duties.

Some of the unfriendly critics do not confine themselves to objections that Mill contradicts himself or relies on untenable psychological assumptions. They go much further and launch an assault on his moral character. They accuse him of being shallow and lacking in moral fibre, of hostility to Christian virtues, of contempt for the working classes, of lying about his real goal to oppress the majority, and so on. Thus, Himmelfarb (1974, 1994) derides him as a weak and incoherent figure, pushed and pulled in contradictory directions by others. She seems to think that he was manipulated by Harriet into a deviant brand of radical liberalism, sharply at odds with the classical liberalism to which he otherwise seemed attracted. The radical Mill, spouting nonsense about individual licence, abrasive feminism and socialism, is seen mainly in *On Liberty* and perhaps *The Subjection of Women*. The classical Mill, voicing more or less reasonable support for conventional pieties, family values, private property and free markets, predominates in his other writings. But it is the radical Mill, let loose upon the world by the evil Harriet, who now 'sets the terms of debate' in advanced liberal cultures, with his perverse model of individual licence in matters that are properly of moral concern, and government interference in markets and family activities that are properly left alone by classical liberals.

Hamburger (1991a, 1991b, 1995, 1999) accuses him of deliberately misrepresenting his true convictions in the *Liberty*, apparently out of wild political ambition. To preserve the Radicals' electoral appeal during the 1830s, and, when that failed, to foster acceptance of a new utilitarian religion that, despite what he said, really involved subtle forms of coercion against the lower and middle classes, he was prepared to disguise his truly illiberal belief that some utilitarian vanguard of journalists, professors and public intellectuals ought to *impose* its notion of a morally superior type of character on the ignorant and passive majority. The majority, he supposedly thought, displayed a 'miserable individuality' that included, inter alia, a commitment to Christianity. But these miserable creatures could be fooled into accepting new forms of coercion, foisted upon them by their betters in the name of liberty. Once the new religion was accepted and utilitarian radicals like himself could gain electoral majorities, suitable laws could be enacted, if necessary, to compel any dissenters to refashion themselves in the preferred mould. Cowling (1990) takes this line to its logical extreme. He charges bluntly that Mill is a moral totalitarian, bent on destroying Christian civilization and replacing it with his barbaric all-encompassing 'Religion of Humanity'. A similarly extreme line is taken by Raeder (2002).

Contemptuous critiques of this sort are rather jolting, if taken seriously. They surely test any liberal's sense of humour. But they also reveal something about the critic. The critic is either deeply confused about what Mill is saying, or, assuming otherwise, intensely dislikes his liberal doctrine and is prepared to distort and caricature it for partisan purposes. The confusions, at least, can be remedied, by properly attending to the conceptual distinction between purely self-regarding and other conduct, or so I shall suggest. Absolute liberty of self-regarding conduct *is* compatible with the enforcement of reasonable rules of other-regarding conduct, designed to prevent harm to others against their wishes. Given a reasonable idea of 'harm', these two aspects of Mill's liberalism are harmonious in principle and, indeed, combine to form a powerful doctrine, worthy of careful study. By implication, we ought to abandon any thesis of 'two Mills', or of a strategic Mill seeking to fool people and win political power by hiding the true Mill, or of an aristocratic and elitist Mill motivated, like Nietzsche, by a hatred of Christianity and equal justice for all, or of a totalitarian Mill lurking behind the facade of a champion of liberty.[22]

SUGGESTIONS FOR FURTHER READING

For details of the life of Mill, see Richard Reeves, *John Stuart Mill: Victorian Firebrand* (London: Atlantic, 2007); Nicholas Capaldi, *John Stuart Mill: A Biography* (Cambridge: Cambridge University Press, 2004), although Capaldi makes the common mistake of transforming Mill into some sort of idealist; and Michael St John Packe, *The Life of John Stuart Mill* (London: Secker & Warburg, 1954). A variorum edition of the *Autobiography* is included in John M. Robson and Jack Stillinger (eds), *Autobiography, and Literary Essays*, vol. 1 of J.M. Robson (gen. ed.), *Collected Works of John Stuart Mill*, 33 vols (London and Toronto: Routledge and University of Toronto Press, 1981), 1: 1–290. His early years are reconsidered by Bruce L. Kinzer, *J.S. Mill Revisited: Biographical and Political Explorations* (New York: Palgrave Macmillan, 2007). A focus on his years in Parliament is provided by Bruce L. Kinzer, Ann P. Robson and John M. Robson, *A Moralist In and Out of Parliament: J.S. Mill at Westminster 1865–68* (Toronto: University of Toronto Press, 1992) (the Governor Eyre affair is treated in chapter 6).

For further discussion of his father's view of education, see James Mill, 'Education' (1818?), in F.A. Cavenagh (ed.), *James and John Stuart Mill on Education* (Westport, CT: Greenwood Press, 1979), 1–73. On John's relationship with his father, some insights may be gleaned from Alexander Bain, *John Stuart Mill: A Criticism* (London: Longmans, Green, 1882), and *James Mill: A Biography* (London: Longmans, Green, 1882).

On his relationship with Harriet, see F.A. Hayek, *John Stuart Mill and Harriet Taylor* (London: Routledge & Kegan Paul, 1951); John M. Robson, 'Harriet Taylor and John Stuart Mill: Artist and Scientist', *Queen's Quarterly* 73 (Summer 1966): 167–86; and Kinzer, *J.S. Mill Revisited*, chapter 3.

For perspectives on the social circles in which he moved, see M.L. Clarke, *George Grote: A Biography* (London: Athlone

Press, 1962); Francis E. Mineka, *The Dissidence of Dissent: The Monthly Repository 1806–38* (Chapel Hill: University of North Carolina Press, 1944), esp. chs 4–7, relating to W.J. Fox, Eliza Flower, Robert Browning and others with whom Harriet and John Taylor were associated; Emery Neff, *Carlyle and Mill*, 2nd edn, rev. (New York: Octagon Books, 1964); Fred Kaplan, *Thomas Carlyle: A Biography* (Ithaca: Cornell University Press, 1983); E. Alexander, *Matthew Arnold and John Stuart Mill* (New York: Columbia University Press, 1965); Lotte Hamburger and Joseph Hamburger, *Troubled Lives: John and Sarah Austin* (Toronto: University of Toronto Press, 1985); Graham Wallas, *The Life of Francis Place, 1771–1854*, 4th edn (London: George Allen & Unwin, 1951); W. Robbins, *The Newman Brothers: An Essay in Comparative Intellectual Biography* (Cambridge, MA: Harvard University Press, 1966); and Bryan Nisbett, *Dare to Stand Alone: The Story of Charles Bradlaugh, Atheist and Republican* (Oxford: Kramedart Press, 2011).

The argument of the *Liberty* is self-contained. But it is usefully read in conjunction with Mill's essay on *Utilitarianism* (1861), esp. ch. 5 ('On the Connexion between Utility and Justice'). See also his *Three Essays on Religion* (1874), esp. 'The Utility of Religion' and 'Theism'. These companions to the 'text-book' are all reprinted in J.M. Robson (gen. ed.), *Collected Works of John Stuart Mill*, 33 vols (London and Toronto: Routledge and University of Toronto Press, 1969), 10: 203–59, 369–489.

Also useful is to compare and contrast Mill's argument with some of those which he cites as similar in nature. Perhaps the most interesting are K. Wilhelm von Humboldt, *The Limits of State Action* (in German, 1851), ed. J.W. Burrow (London: Cambridge University Press, 1969); and Josiah Warren, *Equitable Commerce: A New Development of Principles, as Substitutes for Laws and Governments, for the Harmonious Adjustment and Regulation of the Pecuniary, Intellectual, and Moral Intercourse of Mankind: Proposed as Elements of a New Society* (1846), ed. S.P. Andrews (New York: Fowlers and Wells, 1852). Humboldt's book was first translated by J. Coulthard, as *The Sphere and Duties of Government*, in 1854, about the time Mill began to compose his essay. A quote from the translation serves as the frontispiece to the *Liberty*. Mill says he took the term 'sovereignty of the individual' from 'the Warrenites' (1873, 261).

It is worth mentioning at this point that Goethe and Schiller were close associates of von Humboldt. Like him, they envisioned an ideal human character in which reason and sentiment are duly balanced or harmonized such that the individual willingly obeys moral rules that he asserts are reasonable for himself and others. They all seem to have had a deep faith that the creative imagination, if allowed free play, necessarily seeks beauty in accordance with an internal natural law of operation. In conjunction with reason, they suggested, the imagination can guide the will to develop and express a noble character that is both moral and beautiful. Mill apparently found much to agree with in their picture of the noble target of self-development, although he rejected Kant's view that reason can deduce moral maxims prior to experience as well as the view that the imagination necessarily seeks beauty independently of experience. He accepts that humans can freely learn to improve their characters on the basis of experience, rising from a 'miserable individuality' to a 'noble' one that he apparently sees as inseparable from maximum happiness. See Chapter 4 below.

A good selection of the early reviews of the *Liberty* is contained in A. Pyle (ed.), *Liberty: Contemporary Responses to John Stuart Mill* (Bristol: Thoemmes Press, 1994). Early books whose arguments continue to find favour with critics of Mill's doctrine include Matthew Arnold, *Culture and Anarchy* (1869), esp. chapter 2, 'Doing as One Likes', repr. in *Culture and Anarchy and Other Writings*, ed. S. Collini (Cambridge: Cambridge University Press, 1993), 53–210; and James Fitzjames Stephen, *Liberty, Equality, Fraternity* (1873), ed. R.J. White (Cambridge: Cambridge University Press, 1967).

NOTES

1 All references to Mill's texts are to the *Collected Works of John Stuart Mill*, as listed in the Bibliography at the end of this book.
2 Bain says that '[John] was, quite as much as Grote, a Greece-intoxicated man' (1882a, 94). The same was true of James Mill. See also Clarke 1962, 105, 115, 134–49, 168–86.
3 Indeed, Grote writes in 1866 that

> of all persons we have known, Mr. James Mill was the one who stood least remote from the lofty Platonic ideal of Dialectic ... (the giving and receiving of reasons), competent alike to examine others, or to be examined by them on philosophy.
>
> (Quoted in Clarke 1962, 21)

4 At the same time, Mill admits that 'various persons who saw me in my childhood ... thought me greatly and disagreeably self-conceited; probably because I was disputatious'. He apparently acquired a 'bad habit' of contradicting adults, 'having been encouraged in an unusual degree to talk on matters beyond my age, and with grown persons, while I never had inculcated in me the usual respect for them'. 'Yet with all this I had no notion of any superiority in myself; and well was it for me that I had not' (1873, 37).

5 Also unpersuasive is any suggestion that Mill was so influenced by his father that he conflated liberty with voluntary conformity to social rules of reasonable conduct, such as the rules imposed on him in the context of his early training programme. In *On Liberty*, 'liberty' does not mean self-government or self-discipline in accord with certain impartial dictates of reason. It means acting spontaneously, as one pleases or desires, independently of social rules of reasonable behaviour. Liberty in that sense must be kept distinct from familiar ideas of rational or moral 'autonomy'. The latter term is not found in Mill's essay.

6 Mill makes a similar point in connection with Roebuck's character (1873, 153–57).

7 For further relevant discussion, see Riley 1990.

8 Like Sidgwick, Mill rejects Bentham's claim that enlightened egoists will always find their own greatest happiness in harmony with the greatest collective happiness. In Mill's view, the radical vanguard must be impelled by noble and virtuous principles rather than by enlightened selfishness. For illuminating discussions of Bentham's philosophy, see Hart 1982; R. Harrison 1985; Rosen 1983, 1992, 1996; Kelly 1990; Postema 2006; and Schofield 2006.

9 Postema (2006) suggests that Bentham works with two conceptions of pleasure, to wit: a *quale* conception that sees pleasure as a private feeling of enjoyment, where the focus is on the immediate tone of the feeling; and a distinct attitudinal conception that sees pleasure as the object of public likes or other attitudes, where the focus is on the more or less shared preferences of people regarding the observable sources of pleasure rather than on the feeling. But there is no need to assume two distinct conceptions once we recognize that Bentham rejects cardinal interpersonal comparability of utility and works with preferences defined over the feasible sources of pleasure.

10 Mill claims that his use of the *Review* as a vehicle for this purpose 'to a certain extent, succeeded' (1873, 221). But his attempt to use the journal for a second purpose, 'to stir up the educated Radicals ... and induce them to make themselves' into 'a powerful party capable of taking the government of the country', 'was from the first chimerical' (ibid., 221–23).

11 As mentioned earlier in the text, the minister of the Unitarian congregation (South Place Chapel) was W.J. Fox, in whose journal the *Monthly Repository* Mill

published most of his essays during 1831–35. After the majority of his congregation refused to accept his offer of resignation during the public scandal which ensued in 1834 when his wife revealed his love for Harriet's dear friend Eliza Flower, Fox began to live openly with Eliza and continued to serve as a minister until 1852, subsequently going into Parliament. She was apparently a distinguished composer but died young in 1846. Browning adored her (she seems to have been the inspiration for *Pauline*) and Mill describes her as 'a person of genius' (1873, 195). For related discussion, see Mineka 1944, 188–96.

12 Mill himself was annoyed by rumours of impropriety in their relationship, and he did not hesitate to distance himself even from old friends such as the Austins or Grotes if he associated them with such gossip. Thus, he became estranged from the Grotes about 1837, for example, after Harriet Grote apparently made some catty remarks. (Although intelligent and gregarious, Harriet Grote could also be meddlesome and overbearing, it seems, since she alienated Molesworth and Roebuck for similar reasons.) Mill was also disappointed at the time (as he later admitted, unreasonably so) by George's performance as a leader of the embryo Radical party in Parliament, and George disapproved of Mill's modified radicalism as exhibited in his conduct of the *Review*. But the two men seem to have resumed their friendship by 1845, and Mill reconciled with Harriet Grote shortly after the death of his own Harriet. Indeed, Mill became sufficiently close to her that he tried to comfort her when George had a protracted affair with Susan Durant during 1862–68. See Clarke 1962, 55–102.

13 For different reasons, Clarke speculates that Harriet Grote is to Grote as Aspasia is to Pericles (1962, 124).

14 On this point, see Himmelfarb 1974, 36–56.

15 It should be noted that Hart, Feinberg, Ten and Skorupski depart in important ways from what they consider the simplistic liberalism of Mill.

16 Some interpretations of Mill's argument are so preposterous that the charge of deliberate misrepresentation is difficult to avoid. Nevertheless, as he says himself, it is often impossible to distinguish such unfair discussion from honest mistakes (1859c, 258–59 (II.44)).

17 It must be remembered that most professors in Britain, if not the US, were also ministers when Mill was writing, and that the liberal struggle to separate higher education from undue religious influence was regarded by conservatives as yet more evidence of the erosion of traditional moral values and the decline of civilization. Mill called Oxford and Cambridge 'impostor-universities' in 1834, and the inroads into the curriculum subsequently made by his *Logic*, *Political Economy* and other writings were bitterly resisted by many. For Grote's fights to make lay appointments even to the faculty at University College (founded in London about 1828, as perhaps the first institution of higher education which aimed to keep free of church control), see Clarke 1962, ch. 7.

18 Rees (1956) provides a synopsis of much of the commentary appearing during Mill's lifetime, which he depicts as largely hostile. Pyle (1994) collects selected reviews which were published in journals during 1859–83. Most are fairly described as hostile.

19 The exchange between Morley and Stephen is reminiscent of the well-known debate between Hart (1963) and Devlin (1965), which raised similar issues.
20 Eisenach (1995) suggests other disciples. But if people such as Fitzjames Stephen are to be included as 'disciples', it is pointless to speak of enemies. Even friends like Bain and Grote, devotees of James Mill, could not wholeheartedly accept John's novel radical creed but restricted their admiration to many smaller points.

This is not to deny that Mill's essay on liberty exerted an influence on religious intellectuals such as Mark Pattison, by encouraging free discussion of received church doctrines and stimulating interest in ecclesiastical history. But, of course, Newman, Pusey and other leaders of the Oxford Movement (in which Pattison was involved) had long been arguing to similar effect (see e.g. Mill 1842). More generally, while the new religious and moral idealism defended by Green, Bradley, Bosanquet and many others may have been somewhat more liberal than would have been the case without Mill's influence, it is a serious mistake to see such idealism as similar to, or continuous with, his novel utilitarian liberalism.
21 For an excellent discussion of what's wrong with standard utilitarianism, see Kymlicka 2002, ch. 2. It must be emphasized, however, that Mill's utilitarianism is a non-standard version of the doctrine which is not vulnerable to the objections that are so telling against the standard versions.
22 Some of the flaws in the arguments of Himmelfarb and Cowling have been discussed by Rees (1985, 106–15, 125–36) and Ten (1980, 144–73), among others. Ten (2002) also identifies some of the mistakes made by Hamburger (1999). Miller (2010, 199–201) offers some pointed criticisms of Justman's view. I say something in Part IV about Hamburger's arguments and about Posner's. See Chapters 8 and 10, respectively.

Part II

THE ARGUMENT OF *ON LIBERTY*

2

INTRODUCTORY (CHAPTER I, PARAS 1–16)

STAGES OF LIBERTY (I.1–5)

Mill introduces his subject as 'the nature and limits of the power which can be legitimately exercised by society over the individual' (1859c, 217 (I.1)). That subject, though rarely treated in philosophical terms, 'is so far from being new', he says, 'that, in a certain sense, it has divided mankind, almost from the remotest ages' (ibid.). Even so, in the more advanced societies of his day (as well as our own), 'it presents itself under new conditions, and requires a different and more fundamental treatment' (ibid.). To clarify why the problem needs a novel philosophical treatment under 'new conditions' of large-scale industrial democracy, he identifies four stages of social development.

During the earliest stage, the struggle between liberty and authority was between subjects and rulers 'conceived (except in some of the popular governments of Greece) as in a necessarily antagonistic position to the people whom they ruled' (ibid., 217

(I.2)). '[L]iberty ... meant protection against the tyranny of the political rulers', in other words, limitations on the legitimate power of government (ibid.). Political liberty in this sense was secured, at first, 'by obtaining a recognition of certain ... political liberties or rights' which, if infringed by the rulers, justified individual 'resistance, or general rebellion'; and, later, by adding 'constitutional checks' which, by dividing government power and setting one group of rulers against another, helped the community to avoid injustice at the hands of its political leaders (ibid., 218 (I.2)).

It is important to see that this doctrine of balanced and limited government (exemplified by Machiavelli's *Discourses* (1531), Contarini's *Commonwealth and Government of Venice* (1543) and Locke's *Second Treatise* (1690)) does not necessarily involve a due regard for individual spontaneity. The doctrine is rather intended to secure the community from political oppression.

At a second stage of social progress, the struggle between liberty and authority was reinterpreted as a battle between a democratic party and other parties – defenders of aristocracy, for example, or supporters of monarchy – for the reins of political power: 'By degrees, this new demand for elective and temporary rulers became the prominent object of the exertions of the popular party, whenever any such party existed; and superseded, to a considerable extent, the previous efforts to limit the power of rulers' (1859c, 218 (I.3)). Liberty came to mean not limitation of government power but popular self-rule, if not by the people directly, then by means of temporary representatives revocable at the majority's pleasure:

> What was now wanted was, that the rulers should be identified with the people; that their interest and will should be the interest and will of the nation. The nation did not need to be protected against its own will. There was no fear of its tyrannizing over itself.
>
> (Ibid.)

Again, this doctrine of popular self-government (exemplified by Rousseau's *Of the Social Contract* (1762), James Mill's *Essay on Government* (1821) and Bentham's *Constitutional Code* (1830)) does not necessarily involve any due respect for individual spontaneity. The doctrine is intended to make government reflect the will of the majority, on the assumption that 'the people have no need to limit their power over themselves' (1859c, 219 (I.4)).

At a third stage, entered first by the United States, it was recognized that the need to limit government power loses none of its importance when the government is controlled by the popular majority:

> [Popular] 'self-government' ... is not the government of each by himself, but of each by all the rest. The will of the people, moreover, practically means the will of the most numerous or the most active *part* of the people; the majority, or those who succeed in making themselves accepted as the majority; the people, consequently, *may* desire to oppress a part of their number ... The limitation, therefore, of the power of government over individuals loses none of its importance when the holders of power are regularly accountable to the community, that is, to the strongest party therein.
>
> (Ibid., emphasis original)

The struggle for liberty became a struggle for limited democratic government, in which the rulers are accountable to the majority yet at the same time legitimate government power is limited by constitutional checks and a bill of fundamental political rights. Liberty now meant popular self-rule within certain fundamental legal limits designed to secure minorities against injustice by the popular majority and its elected representatives.[1]

But this doctrine still does not recognize the rightful liberty of the individual, in Mill's view. It is merely a combination of the two earlier doctrines of political liberty, neither of which manifests a due regard for individual spontaneity. The laudable purpose of the third doctrine is to make government accountable to the deliberate sense of the community, on the understanding that this 'deliberate sense' entails limitations on legitimate political power. In short, this kind of freedom demands that the *government* should limit its *legal* authority so as not to infringe on certain rights or liberties due equally to all citizens. But no limitations are placed in principle on the authority of popular *opinion* to enforce its standards of conduct. Although the government must not enact laws which violate the individual's rights to free speech and religious liberty, for example, the majority can interfere with those rights in other ways, by stigmatizing certain forms of speech and religious expression as unacceptable.[2]

Mill is concerned about a fourth stage of social development in which, as a result of technological improvements in mass transportation and communications, the popular majority has vastly expanded power to ensure, by means other than legal punishment, that all conform to its opinions and customs. As he emphasizes in his review of Tocqueville's *Democracy in America*, he fears the growing power of the 'middle class' to stamp its commercial type of character upon the rest of society because he associates any unduly homogeneous community with moral and cultural (and thus, eventually, material) stagnation and decline: 'the most serious danger to the future prospects of mankind is in the unbalanced influence of the commercial spirit' (1840b, 198; see also 1859c, 272–75 (III.16–19)). Indeed, he argues that Tocqueville's study properly documents the cultural and moral influences not of social equality but of a preponderant commercial class, influences which for the most part are also 'in full operation in aristocratic England' (1840b, 196).[3]

In any case, the struggle for liberty takes on a new dimension at this fourth stage. The individual requires protection not merely from government authority but also from increasingly oppressive popular opinion (mainly commercial in spirit) that achieves its meddlesome aims without relying on legislation or other government commands at all:

> Protection, therefore, against the tyranny of the magistrate is not enough: there needs protection also against the tyranny of the prevailing opinion and feeling; against the tendency of society to impose, by means other than civil penalties, its own ideas and practices as rules of conduct on those who dissent from them; to fetter the development, and, if possible, prevent the formation, of any individuality not in harmony with its ways, and compel all characters to fashion themselves upon the model of its own. There is a limit to the legitimate interference of collective opinion with individual independence: and to find that limit, and maintain it against encroachment, is as

indispensable to a good condition of human affairs, as protection against political despotism.

(1859c, 220 (I.5))

He concedes that most people by now would accept the general proposition that there is some limit to legitimate coercion – whether in the form of legal penalties or social stigma. Yet 'the practical question, where to place the limit – how to make the fitting adjustment between individual independence and social control – is a subject on which nearly everything remains to be done' (ibid., 220 (I.6)).

ABSENCE OF A GENERAL PRINCIPLE (I.6–8)

In his view, there is no recognized general rule or principle by which the legitimacy or illegitimacy of coercion can be consistently tested across different social contexts – ignoring 'backward states of society in which the race itself may be considered as in its nonage' (ibid., 224 (I.10)). Rather, men have usually decided the question by 'a mere appeal to a similar preference felt by other people' (221 (I.6)). Little concern has been shown for an impartial principle, based on a rational assessment of the observed consequences of human behaviour. Rather, a remarkable variety of answers has been more or less arbitrarily dictated by social custom, and the limit placed on coercion by one society 'is a wonder to another':

> All that makes existence valuable to any one, depends on the enforcement of restraints upon the actions of other people. Some rules of conduct, therefore, must be imposed, by law in the first place, and by opinion on many things which are not fit subjects for the operation of law. What these rules should be, is the principal question in human affairs; but if we except a few of the most obvious cases, it is one of those which least progress has been made in resolving. No two ages, and scarcely any two countries, have decided it alike; and the decision of one age or country is a wonder to another. Yet the people of any given age and country no more suspect any difficulty in it, than if it were a subject on which mankind had always been agreed. The rules which obtain among themselves appear to them to be self-evident and self-justifying. This all but universal illusion is one of the examples of the magical influence of custom.
>
> (Ibid., 220 (I.6))

The magical influence of custom is 'all the more complete' in the present instance because most people are in the habit of thinking that existing rules of conduct do not need to be impartially justified by reason: most 'are accustomed to believe, and have been encouraged in the belief by some who aspire to the character of philosophers, that their feelings, on subjects of this nature, are better than reasons, and render reasons unnecessary' (ibid.).

Custom itself, in other words, has generally implanted 'the feeling in each person's mind that everybody should be required to act as he, and those with whom he sympathizes, would like them to act', without any further need for reasons (ibid., 221 (I.6)). Shared likings and dislikings, emanating from various sources (class interest, for example, or religious conviction) have thus been the usual standard of judgment, often glorified as common sense or moral sense. 'The likings and dislikings of society, or of some powerful portion of it, are thus the main thing which has practically determined the rules laid down for general observance, under the penalties of law or opinion' (ibid., 222 (I.7)).

Even intellectual leaders and social reformers have generally failed to recognize a general principle by which the propriety or impropriety of freedom from coercion can be tested: 'They have occupied themselves rather in inquiring what things society ought to like or dislike, than in questioning whether its likings or dislikings should be a law to individuals' (ibid.). These elites have not sought to place a limit in principle on society's authority to enforce, by means of social stigma or civil penalties, compliance with its rules of conduct. Rather, they have tried merely to rechannel that authority in directions of which they approved, by 'endeavouring to alter the feelings of mankind on the particular points on which they themselves were heretical' (ibid.)

THE EXCEPTIONAL CASE OF RELIGIOUS BELIEF (I.7)

The only exceptional case, where 'the higher ground has been taken on principle and maintained with consistency', is that of religious belief: 'The great writers to whom the world owes what religious liberty it possesses, have mostly asserted freedom of conscience as an *indefeasible* right, and denied *absolutely* that a human being is accountable to others for his religious belief' (ibid., emphasis added). Among these great writers, he might have added, are Jefferson and Madison, who went well beyond Locke's doctrine of toleration to defend the full and free exercise of religion, first in the context of Virginia and later in the context of the United States.[4]

Madison claims, for example, that complete liberty of conscience is an 'unalienable' right because it is 'a duty towards the Creator': 'It is the duty of every man to render to the Creator such homage and such only as he believes to be acceptable to him' (1973, 299). Moreover, this unalienable right should never be subject to interference by law and opinion:

> This duty is precedent, both in order of time and in degree of obligation, to the claims of Civil Society ... We maintain therefore that in matters of Religion, no man's right is abridged by the institution of Civil Society and that Religion is *wholly* exempt from its cognizance.
> (Ibid., emphasis added)

Thus, 'freedom of conscience' is 'a *natural and absolute right*' (Madison, in Adair 1945, 199, emphasis original). In effect, the Creator, not man, draws the line that separates the individual's life into a private sphere of absolute religious liberty, and a public sphere to which social authority is properly confined.

Such a principle of religious liberty initially took root, Mill makes clear, when each church or sect was unable to win 'a complete victory' over its multiple competitors: 'minorities, seeing that they had no chance of becoming majorities, were under the necessity of pleading to those whom they could not convert, for permission to differ' (1859c, 222 (I.7)). Even so, the principle emerged victorious 'hardly anywhere' until 'religious indifference ... added its weight to the scale' (ibid.). By implication, any victory of this sort might prove to be short-lived. The right of the individual to religious liberty remains precarious, and might well crumble if a revival of religious enthusiasm sweeps over the majority: 'Wherever the sentiment of the majority is still genuine and intense, it is found to have abated little of its claim to be obeyed' (ibid.). There are ample signs in the essay that he takes seriously the possibility of such revivals of religious intolerance, and even fears the advent of despotic secular religions of the sort we now usually classify as 'totalitarianism'.

'ONE VERY SIMPLE PRINCIPLE' (I.9–10)

Excepting the case of religious belief, the lack of any general principle of liberty has resulted in frequent serious mistakes on both sides of the question. People's naked preferences are as often wrong about the impropriety of coercion, he suggests, as they are about its propriety (ibid., 222–23 (I.8); see also 304–5 (V.15)). The purpose of his essay is to deal with the problem, by supplying the missing principle of liberty:

> The object of this essay is to assert one very simple principle, as entitled to govern *absolutely* the dealings of society with the individual in the way of compulsion and control, whether the means used be physical force in the form of legal penalties, or the moral coercion of public opinion. That principle is, that ... the only purpose for which power can be rightfully exercised over any member of a civilized community, against his will, is to prevent harm to others. His own good, either physical or moral, is not a sufficient warrant.
>
> (Ibid., 223 (I.9), emphasis added)

Thus, the principle states a necessary condition for legitimate use of coercion against any individual: his liberty of action should be restrained by law or opinion only if his action is reasonably expected to harm other persons. Put in other words, the principle states a sufficient condition for legitimate protection of individual liberty: the individual ought to be free from all forms of coercion if his action does not harm others. 'In the part [of his conduct] which merely concerns himself, his independence is, of right, *absolute*' (ibid., 224 (I.9), emphasis added).

It is worth emphasizing a couple of points relating to Mill's statement of this simple harm principle or liberty principle. First, he does not make clear what he means by 'harm', and this ambiguity has led to all sorts of confusions and disagreements among commentators about what the principle amounts to. Still, he has just finished complaining how unreasonable it is for mere likes and dislikes to determine where the individual should be free from coercion, and so a reasonable reading of 'harm' as he understands it would exclude mere dislike. His simple principle grounded on reason can hardly be saying that, for example, the majority's mere dislike is a reason for coercive interference with an individual's actions.[5] Moreover, while it may seem puzzling that he does not provide a clear definition of harm, we should keep in mind the possibility that he takes for granted a common-sense notion of harm as some form of 'perceptible damage'. In that case, harm to others means perceptible damage in some object of concern to them, either as individuals or as the public at large, that is, collectively. Such objects can include one's body, finances, reputation, contractual agreements, and so on but also various public goods such as public health and a clean natural environment.

I will argue in due course that this straightforward descriptive idea of harm fits best with Mill's doctrine of liberty. For him, harm means perceptible damage and excludes mere dislike or disgust, that is, mere displeasure without any associated perceptible injury to account for the displeasure. I will just assume this for now, however, and shift attention to the status of his simple principle within his doctrine. Considered as a harm principle, the simple principle states a necessary but not sufficient condition for legitimate coercive interference with an individual's action. Considered as a liberty principle, the same simple principle states a sufficient but not necessary condition for the individual's action to be free from interference. These are two ways of saying the same thing.

The second point worth emphasizing is that Mill states that the individual's 'own good' is not a 'sufficient' reason for coercive interference with his actions. That is not to say that the individual's own good is never a reason to consider. If harm to others is involved, then, given that the simple harm principle states a necessary but not sufficient condition for interference, the agent's own good can have some weight in society's considerations as to whether coercion is justified. If harm to others is not involved, however, then the individual has a moral right to do as he pleases, whatever others may think or feel about his conduct.

Mill expresses the caveat that his simple principle is meant to apply only to human beings capable of 'spontaneous progress', that is, self-development guided by their own judgment and inclinations: 'Liberty, as a principle, has no application to any state of things anterior to the time when mankind have become capable of being improved by free and equal discussion' (1859c, 224 (I.10)). Anyone who has not attained some minimal capacity for self-improvement should not be granted liberty, even if his conduct is harmless to others. Others must substitute their judgment and inclinations for his, to help him develop his capacities, or at least protect him from self-harm as well as injury at the hands of others. Thus, the liberty principle does not apply to 'children', 'young persons below the age which the law may fix as that of manhood or womanhood', 'those [including the mentally retarded and the insane] who are still in a state to require being taken care of by others' or 'barbarians' in 'backward states of society' (ibid.). But for most adults of civilized states of society (including our own), 'compulsion, either in the direct form or in that of pains and penalties for non-compliance, is no longer admissible as a means to their own good, and justifiable only for the security of others' (ibid.).

UTILITARIAN FORM OF ARGUMENT (I.11–12)

In addition to its apparent novelty, putative simplicity and restriction to adults capable of self-improvement, Mill points to several other distinctive features of the simple liberty or harm principle. It is a utilitarian principle, for example, rather than a principle of 'abstract right' (ibid., 224 (I.11)). Its general limit on legitimate coercion is ultimately justified by general utility, he insists, 'but it must be utility in the largest sense, grounded on the permanent interests of man as a progressive being' (ibid.).

General utility thus understood authorizes society to consider coercive interference with actions or inactions that are harmful to others, although society may properly decide after due consideration not to interfere because the harms are outweighed by benefits. In the case of economic trade or exchange, for instance, society legitimately considers intervention in markets and yet, according to Mill, a general policy of laissez-faire is the proper policy because the collective benefits of free markets, including efficient allocation and economic growth, outweigh the harms suffered by competitive losers. But there are expedient exceptions to the laissez-faire policy. The exceptional situations involve a grievous kind of harm which is distinct from the harm suffered by losers in a fair competition conducted without force, fraud or treachery. Producers may cause grievous harm to workers by adopting unsafe production methods, for instance, or they may cause grievous harm to the public by severely polluting the environment. Society properly decides that such harms are unjust and that no individual ought to be forced to suffer them. Coercive intervention in the market to prevent them is justified.[6]

Man's permanent interest in 'self-protection' or 'security' authorizes society to establish moral and legal rules that distribute and sanction equal duties not to inflict these grievous harms on others. Yet there are sometimes good reasons for society not to employ external sanctions to enforce the duties:

> either because it is a kind of case in which [the individual] is on the whole likely to act better, when left to his own discretion, than when controlled ... or because the attempt to exercise control would produce other evils, greater than those which it would prevent.
>
> (1859c, 225 (l.11))

In these cases, where 'special expediencies' give society good reasons not to coerce the individual by law or opinion, 'the conscience of the agent himself should step into the vacant judgment seat, and protect those interests of others which have no external protection' (ibid.). The agent should enforce internally, as his own dictates of conscience, impartial rules which he thinks are generally expedient for all to follow in circumstances like his.[7]

Apart from this, general utility in the largest sense also rules out social control altogether over actions or inactions that are harmless to other people, even if the others in question intensely dislike the relevant conduct. More specifically, man's permanent interest in 'self-development' or 'individuality' authorizes the absolute protection, by right, of individual liberty with respect to such actions. This leads us to a related feature of the liberty principle, what might be termed its practical bite.

SELF-REGARDING CONDUCT (I.12)

Mill insists that the principle has bite because there really does exist conduct which is reasonably viewed as harmless to other persons:

> [T]here is a sphere of action ... comprehending all that portion of a person's life and conduct which affects only himself, or if it also affects others, only with their free, voluntary, and undeceived consent and participation. When I say only himself, I mean directly, and in the first instance: for whatever affects himself may affect others through himself.
> (1859c, 225 (I.12))

Such conduct, which he refers to as 'private' or 'self-regarding' (ibid., 226 (I.14)), either does not directly affect others at all or, if it does, only with their genuine consent and participation. If it does not affect their interests, then it does not cause any perceptible damage or perceptible improvement in objects of concern to them. It does not harm or benefit them, although they may still dislike or like the conduct. If it does affect their interests, however, then it does cause perceptible damage or improvement in (some of) the various objects making up their social position, but only with their genuine consent and participation. It does not harm or benefit them against their wishes. Thus, self-regarding conduct may be harmful to others with their consent and yet Mill rejects any thought of interference with it. Society may legitimately take non-coercive steps to make sure that the others' consent to harm is genuine rather than the product of deception or force but, once assured, coercive interference must be dismissed. And so society has jurisdiction to investigate and assure itself that self-regarding conduct really is self-regarding but it has no legitimate power to employ coercion against genuine self-regarding conduct.

Notice that Mill's treatment of consensual harm is consistent with his one very simple principle. The simple principle says that prevention of harm to others is a necessary but not sufficient condition for coercive interference. Now he tells us that coercion is properly off the table if the harm is consensual. According to utility in the largest sense, apparently, society should not employ coercion to prevent consensual harm because the freedom to experience it is essential to the self-development of competent adults as opposed to children, the insane and so forth—a claim to which we will return in due course. Thus, the self-regarding sphere is the proper sphere of individual liberty under Mill's unusual version of utilitarianism: 'This, then, is the appropriate region of human liberty' (ibid., 225 (I.12)). In short, freedom from coercion ought to be guaranteed, by right, for self-regarding conduct.

FROM ONE VERY SIMPLE PRINCIPLE TO THE MAXIM OF SELF-REGARDING LIBERTY (I.9–12)

Before proceeding, it should be remarked that, strictly speaking, the principle of self-regarding liberty is distinct from, though compatible with, the 'one very simple principle'. The self-regarding liberty maxim incorporates a judgment that *consensual* harm ought to be ignored altogether by society in its deliberations about when to employ coercion to prevent harm to others. This normative judgment may reflect Mill's implicit endorsement of the *volenti* maxim, as I suggested in my earlier work: 'volenti non fit injuria' (Mill 1861b, 253 (V.28), quoting Ulpian). Even if 'harm cannot be made willingly', however, we must be careful to interpret the *volenti* maxim such that it applies only to genuinely consensual harm and not to any harm which the individual seemingly accepts under duress, when he has no real choice in the matter, or under conditions of extreme ignorance, where it would also be a blatant injustice to hold him to his agreement. In that suitably tailored form, the *volenti* maxim is consistent with society taking non-coercive steps to ensure that seemingly consensual harm is truly consensual. It is also compatible with society's utilitarian moral authority to declare that no reasonable individual can really consent to certain grievous harms to himself or to the public at large. Some contracts may be refused enforcement, for example, because the perceptible injury to at least one of the parties is of a kind that cannot reasonably be accepted by any person who seeks to promote utility in the largest sense. Any person who willingly negotiates an unconscionable contract such as voluntary slavery must be considered a child or delirious or insane, or, if he is found competent, a person whose wishes have adapted to existing features of society, including poverty, biased promotional advertising, and so forth, which Mill's utilitarianism refuses to endorse.

If Mill endorses the *volenti* maxim thus understood, as limited to genuine consensual harm, then that would explain his rather confusing practice of treating purely self-regarding actions as if they are always literally harmless to others when in fact they may directly cause consensual harm to others. It would also explain why he does not clearly distinguish between his one very simple principle and his maxim of self-regarding liberty, even though, strictly speaking, they are distinct. At any rate, his practice has led to some confusion. In what follows, I will typically emphasize that self-regarding conduct may harm others with their genuine consent. By contrast, actions that harm others against their wishes are not self-regarding but instead are 'social' or 'other-regarding' actions. Such actions affect the interests of others without their genuine consent and participation. Even if a 'social' action directly causes perceptible improvement in objects of concern to others, society has jurisdiction to consider interference if the improvement is non-consensual. A competent individual is not likely to oppose a perceptible improvement such as an improvement in his health promised by a medical procedure or drug, but, if he does, it must be treated as a non-consensual harm to him from his fallible self-regarding perspective.

THE SELF-REGARDING SPHERE (I.12)

The self-regarding region, Mill says, may be described as follows:

> It comprises, first, the inward domain of consciousness; demanding liberty of conscience, in the most comprehensive sense; liberty of thought and feeling; *absolute* freedom of opinion and sentiment on all subjects, practical or speculative, scientific, moral, or theological. The liberty of expressing and publishing opinions may seem to fall under a different principle, since it belongs to that part of the conduct of an individual which concerns other people; but, being almost of as much importance as the liberty of thought itself, and resting in great part on the same reasons, is practically inseparable from it. Secondly, the

principle requires liberty of tastes and pursuits; of framing the plan of our life to suit our own character; of *doing as we like*, subject to such consequences as may follow: without impediment from our fellow-creatures, so long as what we do does not harm them, even though they should think our conduct foolish, perverse, or wrong. Thirdly, from this liberty of each individual, follows the liberty, within the same limits, of combination among individuals; freedom to unite, for any purpose not involving harm to others: the persons combining being supposed to be of full age, and not forced or deceived.

(1859c, 225–26 (I.12), emphasis added)

Noteworthy even at this preliminary stage is his caveat that freedom of expression, though it really involves conduct which 'concerns others' (since publication of an opinion can harm another's reputation without his consent, for example, or harm competing speakers by depriving them of an audience against their wishes), is 'practically inseparable' from liberty of thought itself, and 'almost' as important. This may seem puzzling or worse. But he has already given us some hint of how it should be read.

Strictly speaking, coercive interference with expression can be legitimately considered, he seems to be saying, since expression is not self-regarding conduct but rather social conduct that harms others against their wishes or poses a credible risk of doing so. Even so, society should 'almost' never bother to exercise its control because laissez-faire is virtually always generally expedient here. In particular, the benefits of self-development associated with freedom 'almost' always outweigh the non-consensual harms to others which can be prevented by regulation of expression. That utilitarian argument is similar in form to the one used to justify absolute freedom of thought itself. There is some difference because thought, unlike expression, *never* harms others, and thus is truly self-regarding. Social regulation of thought should never even be considered, whereas regulation of expression may be justified in some situations. Nevertheless, the reasons for granting liberty are 'in great part ... the same' in the two sorts of cases, and allow us to treat expression in 'almost' all instances *as if* it were self-regarding. Moreover, as we will see, Mill has strategic reasons for assimilating expression to thought in this way. He wants to exploit the fact that liberties of conscience, of speech and of the press are already recognized to a large extent in advanced societies, so as to facilitate acceptance of his more general liberty principle.

ABSOLUTE PRIORITY OF SELF-REGARDING LIBERTY (I.7, 10, 13)

Yet another key feature of the liberty principle, which Mill points to in introducing it, is the *absolute* priority it gives to individual liberty over other moral or social considerations within self-regarding limits. As I have already tried to emphasize, he says repeatedly that the individual's liberty – in the sense of thinking and doing as he pleases, without fear of any coercive form of interference, legal or moral – is, by right, *absolute* with respect to self-regarding matters that are properly of no concern to others (because others do not experience any non-consensual harm). The individual's right to liberty can never be defeated by other considerations, if he is choosing among self-regarding actions. Nor can a voluntary group's right to liberty be defeated, provided the members of the group are choosing among actions that are jointly self-regarding for them, that is, all members consent to any harms they may suffer and the actions do not harm third parties. This feature of the liberty principle, whereby its prescription of liberty is indefeasible within the self-regarding region, gives it a foundational quality, a fundamental ethical status akin to that of the principle of utility from which, Mill insists, it directly flows.

This foundational quality of the liberty principle harkens back to a similar quality in the extraordinary principle of religious freedom, whose defenders, he claims, 'asserted freedom of conscience as an *indefeasible* right, and denied *absolutely* that a human being is accountable to others for his religious belief' (ibid., 222 (I.7), emphasis added). Their common foundational character suggests that he sees his principle as a generalization of the religious liberty maxim already recognized by the US Constitution when he wrote. Without arguing the point here, there is evidence for such a view. In his *Notes on the State of Virginia*, for example, Jefferson does argue that absolute freedom should be extended to religion insofar as one person's convictions and practices do not harm other people:

> The legitimate powers of government extend to such acts only as are injurious to others. But it does me no injury for my neighbour to say there are twenty gods, or no god. It neither picks my pocket nor breaks my leg.
> (1982, 159)

Consistently with this, Madison says that the individual is entitled to the full and free exercise of his religion unless, under the guise of religion, he acts so as to disturb the peace or safety of society.

The fundamental status of Mill's liberty principle also implies that it should be accepted as a basic maxim by *every* civil society, whatever that society's cultural and moral circumstances: 'No society in which these liberties [in self-regarding matters] are not, on the whole, respected, is free, whatever may be its form of government; and none is completely free in which they do not exist absolute and unqualified' (1859c, 226 (I.13)). Thus, even if society advances toward intellectual and moral perfection, the liberty principle remains applicable. But its universal application to civil societies is possible only if the self-regarding sphere can be defined in a way that remains reasonable from the perspective of any civil society's cultural and moral norms. Otherwise, those norms may refuse to admit the existence of any actions that directly cause no non-consensual harm to others. More specifically, non-consensual harm to others, in the sense that others suffer against their wishes some form of perceptible damage in objects of concern to them, must be recognizable by any human being who is capable of self-improvement, whatever his particular moral and cultural outlook. This does not mean that the members of different societies must agree on the particular objects that comprise an individual's position in society. But they all must be able to see when perceptible damage occurs in external objects without the consent of the relevant individual. At the same time, all must recognize that some conduct does not give rise to non-consensual harm in that sense.

WHAT THE SELF-REGARDING LIBERTY PRINCIPLE IS NOT

The foregoing survey of its distinctive features allows us to emphasize what Mill's liberty principle is *not*, namely, a familiar liberal principle of equal basic rights or liberties, of the sort defended by Rawls (1999,

2005, 2007), R. Dworkin (1977, 2000, 2011) or Harsanyi (1982, 1992). Certainly, all liberals (including Mill) will defend some such familiar principle, even if the nature of the rights defended varies with the defence under consideration. Classical liberals may give prominence to private property rights and rights of contract, for example, as well as the rights enumerated in the US Bill of Rights. New liberals may downgrade private ownership of capital and natural resources and assign more importance to welfare rights, rights to a suitably participatory democratic political system, rights to clean air and a safe working environment, rights to non-discrimination on the basis of race, sex, ethnic background, age and so on. Myriad lists of rights and relative priorities are conceivable.

Mill is not arguing in his essay for rights to vote, own property, sell goods, receive subsistence from the state, be free from undue discrimination and the like. He surely defends such rights in some of his other writings. But his 'text-book' is a defence of a special sort of equal rights, to wit, rights to self-regarding liberty – in the sense of choosing as one pleases among one's self-regarding actions, with suitable caveats about expression. Of course, since there are many distinct sorts of self-regarding actions, self-regarding liberty can be broken up into many distinct self-regarding liberties such as religious liberty, liberty of thought on all subjects, liberty of taste, liberty of personal lifestyle and choice of career, liberty to buy and consume all products with self-regarding uses, liberty to combine with others for jointly self-regarding purposes, and so on. The fundamental right to self-regarding liberty covers all of these basic liberties, always on the understanding that self-regarding conduct does not directly cause any non-consensual harm to others. Mill is defending, in short, the individual's right to have absolute control of what goes on within his self-regarding sphere. Such a defence is uncommon even within liberalism. Indeed, it is so rare that it makes his utilitarian liberalism distinct within the liberal family.

THE GROWING DANGER OF SOCIAL REPRESSION (I.14–15)

After outlining his doctrine, Mill proposes to focus attention on the one division of his subject where the liberty principle is, 'to a certain point, recognized by the current opinions', namely, 'liberty of thought [including, of course, religious thought]: from which it is impossible to separate the cognate liberty of speaking and writing' (1859c, 227 (I.16)). The 'grounds' on which these liberties rest, 'when rightly understood, are of much wider application' (ibid.).

Before going on to clarify those grounds, however, he warns us that 'the general tendency of existing opinion and practice' is to meddle far more deeply into self-regarding matters (ibid., 226 (I.14)). The use of the law for this unduly meddlesome purpose has perhaps diminished relative to earlier ages, he admits, largely because of 'the greater size of political communities, and above all, the separation between spiritual and temporal authority' (ibid.). But the use of social stigma has not diminished: '[T]he engines of moral repression have been wielded more strenuously against divergence from the reigning opinion in self-regarding, than even in social matters' (ibid.). The main culprit seems to be traditional organized religion:

> [R]eligion [is] the most powerful of the elements which have entered into the formation of moral feeling, having almost always been governed either by the ambition of a hierarchy, seeking control over every department of human conduct, or by the spirit of Puritanism.
> (Ibid., 226–27 (I.14))

Indeed, the liberties of thought and expression themselves might even be overwhelmed from this quarter in the future, a salient theme of the next chapter.

Although he evidently fears that religion will continue to spur tyrannical majority opinion and feeling, he also seems concerned about the rise of totalitarian social systems (such as that proposed by Auguste Comte) which, while strongly opposed to Christianity and other 'religions of the past', seek to establish 'a despotism of society over the individual, surpassing anything contemplated in the political ideal of the most rigid disciplinarian among the ancient philosophers' (ibid., 227 (I.14); see also 1873, 219–21). The general danger is that a new organic period will arrive, of a remarkably illiberal nature, to replace the critical period that was ongoing for the moment. He concludes his introduction with a dire prediction that all too soon proved prophetic in the twentieth century:

> The disposition of mankind, whether as rulers or as fellow-citizens, to impose their own opinions and inclinations as a rule of conduct on others, is ... hardly ever kept under restraint by anything but want of power; and as the power is not declining, but growing, unless a strong barrier of moral conviction can be raised against the mischief, we must expect, in the present circumstances of the world, to see it increase.
>
> (1859c, 227 (I.15))

SUGGESTIONS FOR FURTHER READING

It makes good sense at this stage to study some literature relating to the history of the principle of religious liberty, given that Mill's principle appears to be a generalization of the religious principle. On the American argument for the sovereignty of the individual with respect to religious opinions and practices in all modes not harmful to others, see James Madison, 'Memorial and Remonstrance against Religious Assessments' (1785), in Robert A. Rutland and William M. E. Rachal (eds), *The Papers of James Madison* (Chicago and London: University of Chicago Press, 1973), 8: 295–306; and Thomas Jefferson, *Notes on the State of Virginia* (1785), ed. W. Peden (New York: Norton, 1982), Query 17, on 'Religion', pp. 157–61.

For further discussion of the historical context and consequences of the Virginia Statute for Religious Freedom, see T.E. Buckley, *Church and State in Revolutionary Virginia, 1776–87* (Charlottesville: University Press of Virginia, 1977); and Merrill D. Peterson and Robert C. Vaughan (eds), *The Virginia Statute for Religious Freedom: Its Evolution and Consequences in American History* (Cambridge: Cambridge University Press, 1988).

Among other great defenders of the principle of religious liberty may be mentioned Baruch Spinoza. See the *Theological-Political Treatise* (1670), ed. J. Israel, trans. M. Silverthorne and J. Israel (Cambridge: Cambridge University Press, 2007), esp. ch. 20; and S. Nadler, 'Baruch Spinoza', in E. N. Zalta (ed.), *The Stanford*

Encyclopedia of Philosophy (Fall 2013 edn), <http://plato.stanford.edu/archives/fall2013/entries/spinoza/>.

NOTES

1 This view of liberty is emphasized in the Federalist papers written during 1787–88 by James Madison, Alexander Hamilton and John Jay to encourage the people of the State of New York to ratify the US Constitution.
2 Under the amendment formula of the US Constitution, moreover, the people can legally alter the list of basic rights with which government must not interfere. Supermajorities have supreme authority to amend or even abrogate such constitutional rights as free speech or free exercise of religion. Those popular decisions, should they occur, would in principle be binding on the courts. Thus, there are no legal (as opposed to moral) limits on popular consensus, even though limits are placed on simple majorities and their elected representatives.
3 On this point, see also Hamburger 1965, 103 n. 62; and 262 n. 47. More generally, the failure of Mill and other 'philosophical radicals' during the 1830s to form a new political party in England was due at least in part to popular apathy, which they tended to blame on middle-class preoccupation with business and commerce. Hamburger depicts the radical political movement as 'doctrinaire', a vain grasp for power by uncompromising intellectuals with preconceived notions of the general good which were far removed from what was actually wanted by the majority at the time. A more sympathetic observer might say that the majority was not yet sufficiently educated to appreciate radical liberal reforms far in advance of their time.
4 I have in mind such documents as the Virginia Statute for Religious Freedom (drafted by Jefferson in 1777, enacted 1786), Madison's 'Memorial and Remonstrance against Religious Assessments' (written in 1785 to help enact Jefferson's Statute for Religious Freedom), and the First Amendment to the US Constitution. For relevant discussion, see Buckley 1977 and Peterson and Vaughan 1988.
5 Strictly speaking, a person's actions include his inactions or deliberate omissions. For Mill, an action is an intention or plan combined with whatever physical movements are needed to carry out the plan. An inaction is an intention that requires a lack of movements.
6 For further clarification of Mill's economic policy of laissez-faire, see Mill 1871a, 936–71.
7 Even here, social coercion has an indirect role to play in the moral education of the individual since, for Mill, education is legitimately made compulsory for young people and discipline is an essential tool of effective teaching. But teachers cannot force their students to endorse moral maxims once the students become adults. Rather, the teachers can only hope that their students will have learned to think for themselves and so will arrive at right conclusions.

3

OF THE LIBERTY OF THOUGHT AND DISCUSSION (CHAPTER II, PARAS 1–44)

THE GROUNDS OF SOME FAMILIAR LIBERTIES (II.1)

Mill thinks it convenient to begin with 'a thorough consideration' of the liberties of thought and discussion, partly because most people in advanced countries already take for granted that these freedoms are rightful: 'these liberties, to some considerable amount, form part of the political morality of all countries which profess religious toleration and free institutions' (1859c, 227 (I.16)). In England, for example, 'there is not … any intolerance of differences of opinion' on most of 'the great practical concerns of life', including politics and culture (254 (II.36)).

Not so common is a proper understanding of the moral justification for these familiar liberties. Moreover, there *is* deep and growing intolerance of diversity of opinion on at least one great practical concern, he suggests, namely, principles of morality. An underlying theme is the grave danger to liberty of thought and discussion lurking in the increasingly popular claim that 'Christian morality ... is the whole truth on that subject' (ibid., 254 (II.37)). Thus, he complains that the 'narrow' and 'one-sided' 'theological morality' which now passes for Christianity 'is becoming a grave practical evil' (256 (II.38)). A 'revival of religion [of the sort under way in both Europe and America as he wrote] is always, in narrow and uncultivated minds, at least as much the revival of bigotry' (240 (II.19)).

The central point of the chapter is that the considerable protection already extended to freedom of thought and discussion ought to be extended further, until it is, by right, *absolute* for all thought and 'almost' all expression. All thought is self-regarding, he makes clear, and virtually all expression is reasonably treated as if it were self-regarding as well, even though it is really social conduct that concerns others. In special circumstances, however, the expression of an opinion cannot be treated as self-regarding because it has 'at least a probable connexion' to an act that seriously harms others without their consent. In those special cases, where we can no longer reasonably pretend that expression is self-regarding conduct, coercive interference is legitimate, although it might not always be expedient for society to actually employ it. Thus, while insisting that 'there ought to exist the fullest liberty of professing and discussing, as a matter of ethical conviction, any doctrine, however immoral it may be considered' (ibid., 228 n. (II.1)), Mill also points to exceptional situations in which expression ought to be prevented or punished because it is 'a positive instigation to some mischievous act' that is grievously harmful to others against their wishes (260 (III.1)). The upshot is that utility in the largest sense recommends a broad social policy of laissez-faire for expression instead of a moral right to absolute liberty of expression. The individual should enjoy a great deal of freedom to express her views but she has no moral right to express any opinion she likes at any time and place.[1]

It is important to keep in mind that Mill excludes some expression from the self-regarding sanctuary, so that his liberty principle does not pretend to grant absolute protection to *all* expression. With that caveat, his prescription of absolute liberty for what may be termed 'self-regarding expression' *is* compatible with his claim that society has legitimate authority to control expression in the special cases. Moreover, if 'almost' all expression is reasonably treated as if it does not cause non-consensual harm to others, despite the fact that successful speakers do take listeners away from other speakers without their consent, his emphasis on liberty to the neglect of authority in this context is understandable, even though it may mislead the careless reader into a belief that an absolute right to liberty with respect to *all* expression of opinion is being defended. His liberty doctrine is radical enough, without going to that extreme.

Suppressing the caveat for ease of exposition, Mill denies 'the right of the people' to exert any power of coercion, by law or stigma, against the expression of opinion: 'The power itself is illegitimate' (1859c, 229 (II.1)). He 'altogether condemn[s]' even a reference to 'the immorality and impiety of an opinion' as such (234 (II.11)). In support of his contention that the individual ought to enjoy absolute freedom from coercion, he argues that 'silencing the expression of an opinion is … a peculiar evil', namely, 'robbing the human race' of truth or, of 'what is almost as great a benefit, the clearer perception and livelier impression of truth' (ibid., 229 (II.1)). His argument provides, among much else, insights into the nature of his utilitarianism.

THE HARM OF SILENCING AN OPINION WHICH MAY BE TRUE (II.3–20)

The first step is to consider the peculiar evil of silencing an opinion which 'may possibly be true' (ibid., 229 (II.3)).

THE ASSUMPTION OF INFALLIBILITY (II.3–11)

Part of the problem is that the silencers make an unwarranted assumption of their own infallibility: 'All silencing of discussion is an assumption of infallibility' (ibid., 229 (II.3)). They not only deny the truth of the opinion for themselves; they also presume to know for certain that the opinion is false, thereby deciding the question for everyone else. But nobody can really have such absolute certainty in complex moral issues. By acting as if he had it, a silencer merely reveals his desire to impose his judgment on others, without letting them make up their own minds. That sort of undue moral coercion is what is *meant* by the assumption of infallibility:

> [I]t is not the feeling sure of a doctrine (be it what it may) which I call an assumption of infallibility. It is the undertaking to decide that question *for others*, without allowing them to hear what can be said on the contrary side.
>
> (Ibid., 234 (II.11), emphasis original)

It might be objected that 'there is no greater assumption of infallibility in forbidding the propagation of error, than in any other thing which is done by public authority on its own judgment and responsibility' (ibid., 230 (II.5)). Granted that all men are fallible, says the objector, the majority ought still to have the power to impose their 'conscientious convictions' on others when 'quite sure of being right' (ibid.). The power might sometimes be mistakenly exercised, resulting in the suppression of truth. Yet 'governments and nations have made mistakes in other things, which are not denied to be fit subjects for the exercise of authority' (231 (II.5)). Bad taxes and unjust wars do not justify the denial of authority to lay taxes or make war. Similarly, occasional suppression of truth does not justify the denial of authority to 'forbid bad men to pervert society by the propagation of opinions which we regard as false and pernicious' (ibid.).

That objection, often made even by utilitarians such as Fitzjames Stephen, is treated seriously by Mill, as the very argument of his chapter suggests is appropriate. It leads him to reconsider the evil of silencing an opinion which might be true, when the silencer admits he lacks absolute certainty of the truth. His rejoinder is that silencing an opinion is inconsistent with that admission of fallibility: '[I]t is *not the feeling sure* of a doctrine (be it what it may) which I call an assumption of infallibility. It is *the undertaking to decide* that question *for others*, without allowing them to hear what can be said on the contrary side' (ibid., 234 (II.11), emphasis added). Given fallibility, absolute liberty of thought and discussion is the only way in which warranted belief (as opposed to absolute certainty) can be acquired:

> Complete liberty of contradicting and disproving our opinion, is the very condition which justifies us in assuming its truth for purposes of action; and on no other terms can a being with human faculties have any rational assurance of being right.
>
> (Ibid., 231 (II.6))

Complete liberty is the *very test* of such truth as humans are capable of acquiring:

> The beliefs which we have most warrant for, have no safeguard to rest on, but a standing invitation to the whole world to prove them unfounded ... This is the amount of certainty attainable by a fallible being, and this is the sole way of attaining it.
>
> (Ibid., 232 (II.8))

Free and open discussion is essential so that fallible beings can rectify their mistakes: 'There must be discussion, to show how experience is to be interpreted' (231 (II.7)).

TRUTH VERSUS UTILITY (II.10)

Mill also rejects any sharp distinction between truth and utility: 'In the opinion, not of bad men, but of the best men, no belief which is contrary to truth can be really useful' (ibid., 233–34 (II.10)). Another way to put this is to say that utilitarianism in its best form will respect warranted belief and the liberty essential to it. Indeed, complete liberty of thought and discussion of alternative conceptions of utility is the test of a warranted conception of utility itself. As he makes clear toward the end of the chapter, he is urging us to recognize 'the necessity to the mental well-being of mankind (on which all their other well-being depends) of freedom of opinion, and freedom of the expression of opinion' (ibid., 257–58 (II.40)).

THE MISCHIEF ILLUSTRATED AND EMPHASIZED (II.11–17)

To illustrate the 'mischief' of silencing an opinion which might be true, Mill also identifies some 'instances memorable in history' when legal coercion has been used to suppress noble opinions widely regarded at the time as impious and immoral attacks on received doctrines of religion and morality. He points in particular to the condemnation of Socrates, the crucifixion of Christ, and the persecution of Christianity by the otherwise enlightened and impartial (even proto-Christian) Emperor Marcus Aurelius (ibid., 235–37 (II.12–14)).[2]

Evidently, 'ages are no more infallible than individuals' (1859c, 230 (II.4)). Moreover, once-persecuted opinions have survived in one form or another to become the received doctrines of a later age, in which they are, 'as if in mockery', invoked to justify another round of persecution of dissenting opinions (235 (II.11)). Under the circumstances, the people of any age (including our own) should not 'flatter' themselves that they can know when silencing an opinion is warranted or useful.

Nor should they indulge themselves in the 'pleasant falsehood' (associated with Samuel Johnson) that 'truth always triumphs over persecution', with the implication that coercion is justified because it only works against error anyway (ibid., 238 (II.17)). Coercion is as effective at silencing warranted opinions as unwarranted ones: 'Men are not more zealous for truth than they often are for error, and a sufficient application of legal or even of social penalties will generally succeed in stopping the propagation of either [at least for a time]' (238–39 (II.17)).

LINGERING RELIGIOUS PERSECUTION (II.18–20)

Before going on to the second step of his argument in this chapter, Mill returns to his underlying theme of the serious and rising intolerance of diversity of religious and moral opinion in advanced societies. In contemporary England, he says, the silencing of opinions as impious and immoral is highly effective, even though coercion is usually in the form of stigma rather than legal punishment: 'It is the stigma which is really effective' (ibid., 241 (II.19)). That stigma results in 'a general atmosphere of mental slavery', an oppressive state of intellectual peace in which 'there is a tacit convention that [religious and moral] principles are not to be disputed' (243 (II.20)). Many of even the best minds are too intimidated to engage in a 'fair and thorough discussion of heretical opinions', resulting in a false uniformity, an ill-considered conformity to conventional ideas (242 (II.20)).

He mentions that there have been only three quite brief moments within the ongoing critical period stemming from the Reformation, when liberty of thought and discussion were encouraged and burst forth. The impulses given to self-development at these moments account for the relatively advanced state of contemporary European societies, he suggests. But it seems pretty clear that 'all three impulses are well nigh spent' (ibid., 243 (II.20)). No further social progress can be expected 'until we again assert our mental freedom' (ibid.).

THE HARM OF SILENCING EVEN A FALSE OPINION (II.21–33)

The second step of Mill's argument is to consider the 'peculiar evil' of silencing an opinion which, for the sake of argument, may be supposed entirely false.

DEAD DOGMA VERSUS LIVING TRUTH (II.21–23)

The problem now is that the silencers rob even themselves of the only warrant a fallible being can have of the truth: 'however true [the received opinion] may be, if it is not fully, frequently, and fearlessly discussed, it will be held as a dead dogma, not a living truth' (ibid., 243 (II.21)). Unless he can hear and answer objections to it, a person does not have any knowledge of the grounds of the true belief. Authority, as opposed to evidence, determines his judgment. He accepts the true opinion blindly, 'as a prejudice, a belief independent of, and proof against, argument' (244 (II.22)). But 'this is not the way in which truth ought to be held by a rational being ... Truth, thus held, is but one superstition the more, accidentally clinging to the words which enunciate a truth' (ibid.).

Someone might object that a person can be '*taught* the grounds' of a true opinion, without ever hearing what can be said on the other side (ibid., 244 (II.23)). The objection is decisive in the case of mathematical truths, Mill admits, where proof of a theorem negates the possibility of a reasonable difference of opinion. But on more complex subjects, including morals and religion, 'the truth depends on a balance to be struck between [at least] two sets of conflicting reasons', where the act of balancing consists in large measure of 'dispelling the appearances which favour some opinion' other than a warranted one (244–45 (II.23)). To carry out the balancing, it is imperative to hear and, where possible, refute what can be said by persons 'in earnest' on the different sides of the argument, so that one can identify a warranted opinion. Fully carried out, he implies, this process will distil the truth, that is, a belief warranted by the available evidence.

Mill is not content with the rational 'suspension of judgment' required when one is 'equally unable to refute the reasons' on different sides of a conflict (ibid., 245 (II.23)). Rather, he insists that 'those who have attended equally and impartially' to the different sides, will be able to gather together and reconcile the various parts of the truth that remain unrefuted. Thus, he speaks of the capacity of 'a completely informed mind' to acquire 'that part of the truth which turns the scale, and decides the judgment' (ibid.). But one can become completely informed about the available evidence only by throwing oneself 'equally and impartially' into the different mental positions of the combatants to hear and, where possible, refute their reasons.

> So essential is this discipline to a real understanding of moral and human subjects, that if opponents of all important truths do not exist, it is indispensable to imagine them, and supply them with the strongest arguments which the most skilful devil's advocate can conjure up.
>
> (Ibid.)

This is the dialectical method of Socrates as depicted by Plato. Its negative aspect involves posing questions with a view to casting doubt on received concepts and maxims and refuting their claim to be true opinions. Those who defend these allegedly true opinions are expected to explain why any competing opinions are false. The positive aspect of the dialectical method involves recovering warranted ideas and maxims on the basis of complete liberty of discussion and debate. Warranted opinions are those that remain unrefuted to date.

A UTILITARIAN ELITE? (II.24–26)

Even if this process of free thought and discussion is accepted as the sole way in which truth can be acquired by a rational being, however, someone might go on to object that it is only necessary for some instructed elite, rather than 'mankind in general', to go through the process (1859c, 246 (II.24)). Conceding for the sake of argument that there is nothing to be said against such a division of society into a rational elite and non-rational mass, that objection still does not touch the claim that complete liberty of thought and expression is essential for the elite:

> If not the public, at least the philosophers and theologians who are to resolve the difficulties, must make themselves familiar with those difficulties in their most puzzling form; and this cannot be accomplished until they are freely stated, and placed in the most advantageous light which they admit of.
>
> (Ibid., 246 (II.25))

But there is much to be said against the relevant social hierarchy. If forced to adopt warranted opinions merely on the authority of the elite, the public will be left ignorant not only of the grounds of the truth but also, eventually, of its very meaning: 'not only the grounds of the opinion are forgotten in the absence of discussion, but too often the meaning of the opinion itself' (ibid., 247 (II.26)). Free discussion is in effect mental *exercise*, the absence of which causes the powers of the mind to atrophy, until at last the person cannot really grasp the truth behind the words:

> The words which convey it, cease to suggest ideas, or suggest only a small portion of those they were originally employed to communicate. Instead of a vivid conception and a living belief, there remain only a few phrases retained by rote; or, if any part, the shell and husk only of the meaning is retained, the finer essence being lost.
>
> (Ibid.)

Lurking in the background is Mill's concern that, unless mental exercise of this sort is widespread, neither competent government nor tolerant public opinion can be expected as the balance of power shifts toward the working-class majority. Without widespread free discussion, democracy is likely to be incompetent and oppressive, as words and ideas lose their significance. At the same time, an ignorant majority is easily manipulated and misled by false prophets and leaders, whose ability to flatter and pander to the crowds negates any attempt by instructed minorities to offer criticism.

HIERARCHY AND DOGMA (II.27, 30)

Absence of free discussion facilitates the emergence of 'dead dogma', perhaps actively propagated by some influential minority, charged with the care and study of its ideas and maxims. Such a creed is received 'passively' by most people: it 'remains as it were outside the mind, incrusting and petrifying it against all other influences addressed to the higher parts of our nature' (ibid., 248 (II.27)). Thus, organic periods, it seems, have typically involved a settled social hierarchy and dogma.

Mill insists that the tendency of living beliefs to degenerate into dead dogma through absence of free discussion is 'illustrated in the experience of almost all ethical doctrines and religious creeds' (ibid., 247 (II.27)). They are 'full of meaning and vitality' to their originators and expounders who struggle to defend them against their critics, yet they lose their animating force as controversy dies, until, eventually, they take their place as dead dogma, 'if not as a received opinion, as one of the admitted sects or divisions of opinion' which excite little interest and are no longer really understood (247–48 (II.27)).

THE EXAMPLE OF CHRISTIANITY AGAIN (II.28–30)

Such is the experience of Christianity itself, he remarks. The New Testament was 'assuredly' full of meaning and vitality to 'the early Christians', whose conduct and character largely reflected its principles during their struggle to establish their doctrine as the received 'religion of the Roman empire' (ibid., 249 (II.29)). But what passes for Christianity in modern Europe or America is something much different. Those who are called Christians now, he points out, do not really believe the doctrine of the New Testament 'in the sense of that living belief which regulates conduct' (ibid., 249 (II.28)). It is rare to see anybody give away their wealth to become one of the 'blessed', for example, or to observe people loving their neighbours as themselves (a suspiciously communistic outlook). Rather, most so-called Christians believe and act upon the rules of the true Christian doctrine just up to the point at which it is *customary* at the moment to do so. 'They have an habitual respect for the sound' of the words (ibid.). But 'whenever conduct is concerned, they look round for Mr. A and B to direct them how far to go in obeying Christ' (ibid.). In a predominantly commercial culture, he might have added, the conventional directions given and accepted by most will tend to be imbued with a commercial spirit, yielding a so-called 'Christian' dogma whose rules are bent to fit capitalistic expectations rather than anything Christ and his early followers had in mind.[3]

Evidently, with that example, Mill has sounded the alarm among those of his readers who consider themselves Christians. But the point he wants to illustrate is that even the Christian religion has not been immune from the evil caused by suppression of allegedly false opinions. Christianity has lost its meaning for most of those who still profess to believe in it, for want of free discussion of the ideas held out as 'Christian' by church authorities. Original Christian maxims of morality, even if entirely warranted, no longer motivate most so-called Christians, who now mistakenly apply the term 'Christianity' to quite different ideas: 'The fatal tendency of mankind to leave off thinking about a thing when it is no longer doubtful, is the cause of half their errors' (1859c, 250 (II.30)). He is trying to provoke modern Christians to examine whether they might be in error to call themselves Christians. Such self-examination requires them to think and discuss their 'living beliefs' with their critics. Before anyone can really be said to believe in the New Testament, he must have learned the meaning and grounds of its doctrine, defended that doctrine from its critics and shaped his conduct in accord with its maxims. Until they are committed to all that, he implies, people should desist from calling themselves Christians and see themselves in a truer light.[4]

UNANIMITY VERSUS TRUTH? (II.31–33)

Yet even a non-Christian might object that the argument at this stage carries an unwelcome implication, namely, that unanimous agreement among people on a warranted belief causes the meaning of the opinion to 'perish within them' (1859c, 250 (II.31)). Without critics who 'persist in error', the essential process of free thought and discussion apparently comes to a halt, causing the truth to waste away.

But the objection is too quick, Mill replies. Even if unanimity were achieved, the essential process would remain necessary for fallible beings to retain the meaning of their warranted opinions. Complete liberty of thought and discussion can be carried on by a 'contrivance' such as 'the Socratic dialectics', in which skilled devil's advocates take the place of committed critics (ibid., 251–52 (II.32–33)).

THE HARM OF SILENCING AN OPINION WHICH MAY BE ONLY PARTLY TRUE (II.34–36, 39)

Mill now turns to the last step of his argument, where he considers a third case, 'commoner ... than either' of the other two (ibid., 252 (III.34)). In this case, the opinion to be silenced is neither entirely warranted nor completely refutable. Rather, it shares the truth with received opinion. The 'peculiar evil' of silencing such an opinion is thus a conjunction of the evils already considered, to wit, the failure to acquire all sides of the truth, united with the lack of a lively appreciation of the grounds and meaning of even that portion of truth found in received opinion.

His discussion of this case allows him to clarify some aspects of his argument before returning to the particular problem that concerns him most in practice, that is, intolerance of diversity of opinion on religious and moral principles.

POPULAR OPINION IS GENERALLY BIASED (II.34)

Received opinions 'on subjects not palpable to sense' are generally one-sided, containing only part of the truth, Mill suggests, because heretical opinions which contain complementary parts of the truth are silenced at any given time. History is viewed by him not as a victorious march of inevitable improvement but rather as a largely cyclical process in which different parts of the truth repeatedly supersede one another, one part setting as another rises:

> Even progress, which ought to superadd, for the most part only substitutes, one partial and incomplete truth for another; improvement consisting chiefly in this, that the new fragment of truth is more wanted, more adapted to the needs of the time, than that which it displaces.
>
> (Ibid., 252–53 (II.34))

TRUTH AND TOLERATION (II.34–36)

Given the 'partial character' of any received ideas on complex subjects (including religion and morality), heretical opinions that perhaps embody some neglected side of the truth 'ought to be considered precious' by fallible beings, 'with whatever amount of error and confusion that truth may be blended' (ibid., 253 (II.34)). Those who seek to learn the many sides of a warranted opinion on morality or politics, that is, ought to be grateful even to one-sided critics and committed ideologues who attempt to 'explode' the 'compact mass' of received opinion, 'forcing its elements [of truth] to recombine in a better form and with additional ingredients' (253 (II.35)).

A case in point, he remarks, is Rousseau's Romantic attack on the received opinion among eighteenth-century Europeans that the civility and enlightenment of their culture made it wholly superior to simpler states of society (ibid.). Another illustration is provided by a freely competitive party system, which has the generally beneficial effect of keeping received political opinion 'within the limits of reason and sanity' (ibid., 253–54 (II.36)).

COMPLETE LIBERTY OF DISCUSSION IS UTILITARIAN (II.36, 39)

More generally, Mill re-emphasizes his argument that complete liberty of thought and discussion is the *only* way fallible beings can hope to develop the capacities required to infer, and retain a lively understanding of, warranted beliefs (see ibid., 22–23, 31–33 (II.6–10)). Complete liberty is essential because we cannot expect impartial observers with warranted beliefs to appear like magic in its absence:

> Truth, in the great practical concerns of life, is so much a question of the reconciling and combining of opposites, that very few have minds sufficiently capacious and impartial to make the adjustment with the approach to correctness, and it has to be made by the rough process of a struggle between combatants fighting under hostile banners.
>
> (Ibid., 254 (II.36))

He is under no illusions that complete freedom of discussion somehow automatically leads the combatants themselves to grasp many-sided truths: 'I acknowledge that the tendency of all opinions to become sectarian is not cured by the freest discussion', he says, 'but is often heightened and exacerbated thereby; the truth which ought to have been, but was not, seen, being rejected all the more violently because proclaimed by persons regarded as opponents' (ibid., 257 (II.39)). Despite its costs, however, the 'rough process' is utilitarian because there is no other way for impartial persons (including the combatants themselves upon reflection) to acquire the truth and sustain a lively appreciation for it:

> [I]t is not on the impassioned partisan, it is on the calmer and more disinterested bystander, that this collision of opinions works its salutary effect. Not the violent conflict between parts of the truth, but the quiet suppression of half of it, is the formidable evil ... And since there are few mental attributes more rare than that judicial faculty which can sit in intelligent judgment between two sides of a question, of which only one is represented by an advocate before it, truth has no chance but in proportion as every side of it, every opinion which embodies any fraction of the truth, not only finds advocates, but is so advocated as to be listened to.
>
> (Ibid.)

Minority opinions, unpopular with the majority, ought nevertheless to be encouraged by the majority, and their free expression protected by right, because otherwise there is no hope of finding warranted opinions.

THE CRUCIAL CASE OF CHRISTIAN MORAL BELIEFS (II.37–38)

But someone may still object that some received beliefs, for example, Christian principles, are special in the sense that they comprise 'the whole truth' on the vital subject of morality. That objection returns Mill to what he considers the crucial test case for his principle of absolute liberty of thought and discussion: 'As this is of all cases the most important in practice, none can be fitter to test the general maxim' (ibid., 254 (II.37)). His strategy is to show that Christian principles contain only a part of the truth about morality, so that a fully adequate morality (utilitarian or otherwise) requires them to be modified and supplemented by non-Christian elements.

In the first place, there is doubt about the meaning of 'Christian morality'. If it means the maxims of the New Testament, he argues, then it was clearly intended to be only a part of moral truth: 'The Gospel always refers to a pre-existing morality, and confines its precepts to the particulars in which that morality was to be corrected, or superseded by a wider and higher [one]' (ibid.). It can only be completed by specifying the relevant 'pre-existing' rules. But the usual suggestions, including codes drawn from the Old Testament, for example, or from the Greeks and Romans, are 'in many respects barbarous', even going so far (in Saint Paul's case) as to give 'an apparent sanction to slavery' (ibid., 254–55 (II.37)). Granted, better suggestions can be made. Indeed, the 'sayings of Christ' can be reconciled with everything which 'a comprehensive morality requires' (256 (II.38)). But this does not alter the point that Christian principles in this sense 'contain, and were meant to contain, only a part of the truth' (ibid.).[5]

If 'Christian morality' means the 'theological morality' gradually devised by the early Catholic Church and subsequently modified by 'moderns and Protestants', then, apart from the fact that this is distinct from the maxims of the New Testament, 'it is ... incomplete and one-sided' (1859c, 255 (II.37)). Mill affirms that 'mankind owe a great debt to this [so-called Christian] morality' (ibid.). But 'it is, in great part, a protest against Paganism', and must be modified and completed by that part of the truth which Paganism contains:

> Its ideal is negative rather than positive; passive rather than active; Innocence rather than Nobleness; Abstinence from Evil, rather than energetic Pursuit of Good ... It is essentially a doctrine of passive obedience; it inculcates submission to all authorities found established; who indeed are not to be actively obeyed when they command what religion forbids, but who are not to be resisted, far less rebelled against, for any amount of wrong to ourselves.
>
> (Ibid.)

A complete morality must make room for so-called Pagan ideals, for example, 'duty to the state' and the associated virtues of public service and honour (ibid., 255–56 (II.37)).

The incomplete theological morality hardly notices the idea of constitutional obligation, looking instead beyond this life for the motives to virtue. In so doing, it tends to

> give to human morality an essentially selfish character, by disconnecting each man's feelings of duty from the interests of his fellow-creatures, except so far as a self-interested inducement [hope of heaven or threat of hell] is offered to him for consulting them.
>
> (Ibid., 255 (II.37))[6]

Even the New Testament largely ignores the idea of constitutional obligation on the parts of political leaders and citizens alike, he insists.[7]

However we define it, Mill argues, Christian morality must be supplemented by non-Christian principles if we hope to get a complete picture of the many different sides of warranted moral opinion: 'the Christian system is no exception to the rule, that in an imperfect state of the human mind, the interests of truth require a diversity of opinions' (1859c, 257 (II.38)). The insistence by so-called Christians, contrary to Christ's own intentions, that their religious doctrine provides 'a complete rule for our guidance' is 'a great error' and is 'becoming a grave practical evil' (256 (II.38)). Unless the requisite Pagan elements are given freedom to breathe, he fears, 'there will result, and is even now resulting, a low, abject, servile type of character' in the majority (ibid.). Complete liberty of religious thought and expression is essential to avoid this result, for otherwise the Pagan elements of truth will be silenced:

> If Christians would teach infidels to be just to Christianity, they should themselves be just to infidelity. It can do truth no service to blink the fact ... that a large portion of the noblest and most valuable moral teaching has been the work, not only of men who did not know, but of men who knew and rejected, the Christian faith.
>
> (Ibid., 257 (II.38))[8]

MUST FREE EXPRESSION BE FAIR AND TEMPERATE? (II.44)

Before moving on to examine more generally the extent to which men ought to be free from coercion when acting upon their opinions, Mill considers briefly the objection that complete freedom of expression is permissible only if 'the manner be temperate, and do not pass the bounds of fair discussion' (1859c, 258 (II.44)). Such a requirement of fair and temperate discussion has lately enjoyed a revival in our own age, as a requisite of political liberalism. He rejects the requirement for several reasons. People commonly take offence whenever their opinions are subjected to a 'telling and powerful' attack, for example, and are liable to brand a skilled opponent an intemperate one.

Even more importantly, legal penalties or stigma can never be employed effectively against the 'gravest' sorts of unfairness, namely, 'to argue sophistically, to suppress facts or arguments, to misstate the elements of the case, or misrepresent the opposite opinion' (ibid.). The problem is that people do this sort of thing all the time 'in perfect good faith', mistakenly rather than with the intention to harm others. As for the use of 'invective, sarcasm, personality, and the like', these are weapons which are generally advantageous only to the defenders of received opinion, as minorities have little incentive to give unnecessary offence to majorities (ibid., 259 (II.44)). In any case, law and stigma 'have no business' in restraining vituperative expressions of opinion (ibid.).

'[T]he real morality of public discussion', he emphasizes, involves a disposition to distinguish between what a person says and how he says it. Complete liberty ought to be granted to both the content and the manner of expression, with the usual caveat about expression which is not reasonably treated as if it is self-regarding. But observers must develop the capacity to see the truth in what a person says, and separate that truth from how he says it. At the same time, observers ought to make up their own minds as to whether a person's manner of discussion reveals an unjust intent to defraud others of the truth, by deliberately misrepresenting opposing arguments and so on. If a person reveals himself a liar and a cheat by repeatedly engaging in unfair ways of conducting a discussion, observers have the moral right to freely stop listening to him and to warn others of his unfairness. Legal penalties or public stigma designed to silence him or to force him to be a fair discussant are inexpedient and unnecessary.

SUGGESTIONS FOR FURTHER READING

There is no finer argument than Mill's for freedom of thought and discussion. His views continue to inspire many liberal writers today, although his utilitarian underpinnings are usually rejected and there is disagreement about what his views really are. For various readings of Mill's approach, see e.g. C.L. Ten, *Mill on Liberty* (Oxford: Clarendon Press, 1980), ch. 8; John Skorupski, *John Stuart Mill* (London: Routledge, 1989), ch. 10; and Kevin C. O'Rourke, *John Stuart Mill and Freedom of Expression: The Genesis of a Theory* (London: Routledge, 2001). My own interpretation is discussed further in Jonathan Riley, 'J.S. Mill's Doctrine of Freedom of Expression', *Utilitas* 17 (2005): 147–79, and 'Racism, Blasphemy and Free Speech', in C.L. Ten (ed.), *Mill's On Liberty: A Critical Guide* (Cambridge: Cambridge University Press, 2008), 62–82.

C. Edwin Baker, in *Human Liberty and Freedom of Speech* (Oxford: Oxford University Press, 1989), is critical of what he calls Mill's 'market model' of free speech, according to which an unregulated market in expression allows true opinions to emerge in triumph over false ones. But Mill evidently does not hold such a market model, despite the common practice of attributing it to him. He does not subscribe to a policy of unrestrained laissez-faire for expression, economic trade, or any other sorts of social actions. Rather, he defends a policy of limited laissez-faire and joins those who argue that government intervention is legitimate in situations where free markets are reasonably expected to fail. Indeed, Mill's approach to freedom of expression, properly interpreted, is far closer to Baker's own 'liberty' approach than to the 'market model'. See also C. Edwin Baker, *Media, Markets and Democracy* (Cambridge: Cambridge University Press, 2002), and *Media Concentration and Democracy: Why Ownership Matters* (Cambridge: Cambridge University Press, 2006).

Frederick Schauer, in *Free Speech: A Philosophical Enquiry* (Cambridge: Cambridge University Press, 1982), offers a provocative and skilled critique of the liberal consensus that favours broad freedom of expression. Mill would greatly appreciate Schauer's challenge as being essential for preventing liberal views from deteriorating into 'dead dogma'.

At the same time, it is important to remember that Mill admits that acts of 'expressing and publishing opinions' are not truly self-regarding acts, since they always pose some risk of non-consensual harm to other people (if only because successful speakers deprive others of an audience for their competing opinions). Such acts do not really fall within the ambit of the self-regarding liberty principle, which prescribes complete liberty of thought and self-regarding action. But he treats them as 'practically inseparable' from the liberty of thought itself, and suggests that they should be given 'almost' as much protection as the absolute protection afforded to thought. For him, it seems, coercive interference with the content and manner of expression is rarely expedient, even though society has legitimate authority to consider intervention and actually should intervene to prevent speakers from causing grievous injuries to other people against their wishes. So, for example, utility in the largest sense may prescribe time and place restrictions on expression to prevent people from being unduly disturbed, leaving speakers ample opportunities to express their opinions. And it would presumably authorize government to prevent or punish criminal activities such as blackmail and fraudulent advertising that are mistakenly depicted as forms of discussion or expression of an opinion.

An interesting general issue is whether social conditions in countries like Britain and the US are now so different from Mill's times that he might reasonably change his mind about how often interference with the content of public expression is expedient. Given the rise of global motion picture, television and computer networks with which he was not familiar, for example, perhaps he would admit more opportunities for censorship of such visual forms of expression as violent movies, pornographic films and racist websites. For insights into the issue of free speech in advanced modern societies, see e.g. Cass R. Sunstein, *Democracy and the Problem of Free Speech* (New York: Free Press, 1993), and *Republic.com 2.0* (Princeton: Princeton University Press, 2009); L. Wayne Sumner, *The Hateful and the Obscene: Studies in the Limits of Free Expression* (Toronto: University of Toronto Press, 2004); and Danielle K. Citron, *Hate Crimes in Cyberspace* (Cambridge, MA: Harvard University Press, 2014).

The issue of when it is expedient to censor public expression evidently overlaps with the more general issue of when it is expedient to employ coercion against indecent or unruly behaviour in public. Yet, unfortunately, Mill doesn't say much to clarify his views in the *Liberty* (see 1859c, 295–96 (V.7)). We return to these questions below in Chapters 6, 9 and 10.

NOTES

1 The limits of a Millian utilitarian policy of laissez-faire for expression are a matter for further debate. Mill's admission that coercive interference is legitimate against expression that instigates 'mischievous acts' evidently covers incitement to violence. But it might be seen as covering more than incitement. Consider malicious libel, for example. It might legitimately be prohibited on the grounds that deliberately and recklessly lying about a person instigates others to wrongfully cease doing business with him. In any case, Mill may have intended expression that instigates mischievous acts as only one example among others. Like his father, he apparently takes for granted that 'freedom of expression' cannot be

used to justify or excuse expression that is properly deemed criminal, such as blackmail or fraudulent advertising or theft of copyright. In general, all of these exceptional forms of expression should be distinguished from 'discussion', that is, the expression of an opinion in the context of a debate that seeks to find warranted opinions. See Riley 2005a, 2008b.

2 Mill's picture of Aurelius seems to have had an impact on Matthew Arnold and Walter Pater, among others. See the suggestions for further reading in Chapter 4.

3 Mill says later in the text that Christ himself preached an admirable, if incomplete, morality (1859c, 254–57 (II.37–38)). But Christian doctrine has evolved into something quite different, its content apparently for the most part a reflection of prevailing social customs. In a predominantly commercial culture, Christian doctrine so-called becomes tied up with norms of work, saving and wealth in ways discussed by Marx and Weber, among others.

4 Various writers in the Victorian era claimed that early Christian teachings had been corrupted by the subsequent development of the Roman Catholic Church and/or Protestant sects. A version of the claim is associated with Newman, Pusey and the so-called 'Oxford Movement', for example. See Mill 1842 and Nockles 1994. Analogous themes are sounded during the Renaissance. Thus, for example, Machiavelli, Guicciardini, Paruta and Sarpi emphasize that the emergence of a highly centralized Roman church, controlled by a papacy with imperialist pretensions, represented a corruption of the true spiritual church, as well as a constant threat to the republics of Florence and Venice. For relevant discussion, see Bouwsma 1968.

5 Mill says that Christ was 'probably the greatest moral reformer, and martyr to that mission, who ever existed upon earth', a man of 'preeminent genius' who

> supposed himself to be – not God, for he never made the smallest pretension to that character and would probably have thought such a pretension as blasphemous as it seemed to the men who condemned him – but a man charged with a special, express and unique commission from God to lead mankind to truth and virtue.
>
> (1874, 488)

Moreover,

> religion cannot be said to have made a bad choice in pitching on this man as the ideal representative and guide of humanity; nor, even now, would it be easy, even for an unbeliever, to find a better translation of the rule of virtue from the abstract into the concrete, than to endeavour so to live that Christ would approve our life.
>
> (Ibid.; see also 421–22)

A utilitarian 'Religion of Humanity' would, therefore, certainly make room for Christ's maxims of conduct. More generally, see Mill 1874, for his discussion of the Religion of Humanity and his rational 'scepticism' or agnosticism about the existence and attributes of a divine Creator.

LIBERTY OF THOUGHT AND DISCUSSION 95

6 This sort of isolation among self-interested individuals is usually attributed to political liberalism itself, rather than to Christian morality.
7 Mill's assertions about Christian passivity may require some modification now, if not then. Consider, for example, the modern doctrine of 'passive resistance' which Christian leaders such as Martin Luther King found in Gandhi's work and elaborated during the struggle against racial segregation in the United States. Or consider the insistence of many Christians that all have a constitutional duty to protect the lives of the unborn and the terminally ill, where the duty is often understood as correlative with rights that cannot be alienated or waived.
8 Mill's insistence that a complete morality must find room for both Christian and Pagan elements is echoed by various Victorian and Renaissance writers who admire Periclean Athens and/or the Roman Republic as well as Christ's teachings. He returns to this theme in the next chapter.

4

OF INDIVIDUALITY, AS ONE OF THE ELEMENTS OF WELL-BEING (CHAPTER III, PARAS 1–19)

THE GROUNDS OF LIBERTY OF ACTION (III.1)

With his case made for absolute liberty of thought and expression of thought, Mill next considers 'whether the same reasons do not require that men should be free to *act* upon their opinions' (1859c, 260 (III.1), emphasis added). He says immediately that 'no one pretends that actions should be as free as opinions', and then reminds us that even expression is subject to legitimate social control in special circumstances which render unreasonable its classification as a self-regarding act (ibid.). Specifically, in rare situations where it is 'a positive instigation' to violence, molestation or other serious damage, expression can no longer be reasonably treated as if it causes no non-consensual harm to others. Yet, just as thought and 'almost' all expression are reasonably seen as self-regarding, so a significant field of action is also reasonably seen as self-regarding, he claims, and for the same reasons:

INDIVIDUALITY AND WELL-BEING

> [I]f [the individual] refrains from molesting others in what concerns them, and merely acts according to his own inclination and judgment in things which concern himself, the same reasons which show that opinion should be free, prove also that he should be allowed, without molestation, to carry his opinions into practice at his own cost ... As it is useful that while mankind are imperfect there should be different opinions, so is it that there should be different experiments of living; that free scope should be given to varieties of character, short of injury to others.
>
> (Ibid., 260–61 (III.1))

By implication, absolute liberty ought to be guaranteed, by right, with respect to certain 'self-regarding' acts, which do not cause non-consensual harm to others.

INDIVIDUALITY AND HAPPINESS

By analogy with the case of thought and discussion, such liberty of action is essential for the individual to acquire, and sustain a lively appreciation of, a many-sided truth, namely, that of *his own nature or character*. The only way to gather this sort of warranted opinion about oneself, it seems, is to think, express, and act as one likes, 'short of injury to others'. Choosing spontaneously, in accord with one's own judgment and inclinations, is a constituent element, apparently, of what Mill means by 'individuality' and (what is 'the same thing') self-development (ibid., 267 (III.10)). As such, '[i]t is desirable', he says,

> that in things which do not primarily concern others, individuality should assert itself. Where, not the person's own character, but the traditions and customs of other people are the rule of conduct, there is wanting one of the principal ingredients of human happiness, and quite the chief ingredient of individual and social progress.
>
> (Ibid., 261 (III.1))

The main purpose of his discussion in this chapter is to underline the high value of individuality, and thereby make clear why the complete liberty of self-regarding acts essential to its realization is justified.

AN AMBIGUITY

Before proceeding with his discussion, it is worth noting a large ambiguity which has cropped up at this stage. Although he clears it up by the final chapter, and, indeed, has already given some hint of the way he will do so, the ambiguity is one which continues to baffle many readers. The problem is this. Mill has assimilated freedom of acting upon one's opinion to freedom of expressing it. Yet we know that expression is something of an exceptional case from the perspective of his liberty doctrine, to wit, expression is really 'social' or *other-regarding* conduct which, though it concerns others and can be legitimately prevented through coercion, is 'almost' always reasonably treated *as if* it were self-regarding conduct, harmless to others unless they consent to the harm. The question then arises: is the sphere of self-regarding action that comes within the purview of his 'very simple principle' *really* self-regarding (in the sense that no non-consensual harm to others is involved), or is it really other-regarding, yet treated as if it were not (in the sense that, although non-consensual harm to others is involved, regulation is generally inexpedient for one reason or another, so that laissez-faire should prevail)? How we answer that question is extremely important.

If there are no truly self-regarding actions, for example, then the simple liberty principle is arguably a sham since we must await (possibly complex) utilitarian calculations before we can determine which other-regarding acts ought to be treated 'as if' they are self-regarding. If there truly are actions which are harmless to other people or only harm them with their consent, on the other hand, actions with respect to which the agent ought to be perfectly free to do as he likes, independently of any further social calculation relating to their consequences, then which actions are these? That last question of identification raises the vexed issue of the definition of 'harm', about which Mill appears rather cavalier. Even if we confine our attention to the first couple of pages of this chapter, he seems to use interchangeably with 'harm' such terms as 'mischief', 'nuisance', 'molestation', and the like (ibid., 260–61 (III.1)). I have already indicated my view that he takes for granted a straightforward descriptive idea of harm as perceptible damage, and I will say more about this in due course, but it must be admitted that he is not as clear about this as he might have been.

The ambiguity as to whether there are any truly self-regarding actions, and the associated ambiguity as to whether the simple liberty maxim relating to self-regarding actions is really a complicated utilitarian policy of laissez-faire with exceptions relating to other-regarding actions, will linger with us until the final chapter. In the meantime, it is worth recalling Mill's remark that liberty of expression 'rest[s] in great part on the same reasons' as liberty of thought itself, where, he makes clear, thought truly *is* self-regarding whereas expression is not. So, the distinction between the two forms of reasoning might not be that crucial at this stage of his argument. His present focus is on the great importance of individuality as a component of well-being. Perhaps for ease of exposition, if for no other reason, he decided to postpone clarifying some key distinctions which were not needed for the moment.

THE WORTH OF SPONTANEOUS ACTION (III.2–6)

Mill begins by insisting on the 'intrinsic worth' of 'individual spontaneity' because it 'is hardly recognised', he feels, by either defenders or critics of received opinions and practices:

> The majority, being satisfied with the ways of mankind as they now are (for it is they who make them what they are), cannot comprehend why those ways should not be good enough for everybody; and what is more, spontaneity forms no part of the ideal of the majority of moral and social reformers.
>
> (Ibid., 261 (III.2))

He points to Wilhelm von Humboldt as a notable exception, and applauds his doctrine that '"the end of man"' ought to be seen as the cultivation of individuality, in other words, '"the highest and most harmonious development of his powers to a complete and consistent whole"' (ibid., quoting from von Humboldt 1969, 16). As the quotation makes clear, a fully cultivated individuality – the most complete idea of individuality, individuality in all its glory – is in effect an ideal type of noble and moral character, a character in which the many different sides of the individual's true nature have a chance to flourish as much as possible in mutually compatible ways.[1]

Mill's subsequent remarks are directed at clarifying what he thinks are warranted inferences about the different sides of the relevant character ideal, and how they are combined into a 'consistent whole'. This brings him back to his earlier claim that the part of the truth contained in the Christian (also Platonic) ideal of 'passive obedience' must be integrated with the distinct part that is contained in a non-Christian (or Pagan) ideal of 'energetic' self-assertion (1859c, 255–57 (II.37–38); see also 265–66 (III.8–9)). At the same time, in the course of providing this clarification, he says more about the high utility of self-assertion, or, in other words, of liberty itself, in the sense of doing as one likes. Liberty is essential not only to sustain the ideal many-sided character once it has been developed. Liberty is also necessary to self-development, the process of cultivating and acquiring that ideal.

He devotes quite a lot of time to his point that complete liberty of choosing as we like, 'short of injury to others', is essential to individuality and its cultivation. Rather than blindly follow the customs of the majority, without any inclination to consider and experiment with alternatives, the individual should desire to make up his own mind and choose for himself, at least when non-consensual harm to others is not involved:

> The human faculties of perception, judgment, discriminative feeling, mental activity, and even moral preference, are exercised only in making a choice. He who does anything *because* it is the custom [rather than because he chooses to do it, in accord with his own judgment and inclinations], makes no choice.
>
> (Ibid., 262 (III.3), emphasis added)

Just as a licence to think and discuss is needed to develop one's capacities to identify, and retain an understanding of, warranted opinions, a licence to choose (at least among self-regarding acts) is needed to develop one's capacities to acquire, maintain and *act upon* warranted opinions about one's own enjoyments, desires, loves and plans of life.

> The mental and moral, like the muscular powers, are improved only by being used. The faculties are called into no exercise by doing a thing merely because others do it, no more than by believing a thing only because others believe it.
>
> (Ibid.)

THE WORTH OF OBEDIENCE TO SOCIAL RULES (III.3–6, 9, 17)

But his emphasis on the worth of liberty and spontaneity should not make us lose sight of other valuable ingredients in the ideal type of noble and moral character, which he insists is the true 'end of man', and, thus, for him, the best conception of personal happiness. That character ideal, he makes clear, involves a 'complete and consistent' blend of human powers or capacities, implying some sort of harmony between the general ability to obey social rules (designed to prevent non-consensual harm, or certain kinds of non-consensual harm, to others), and the capacity to think and choose as one likes, in accord with one's own judgment and desires.[2]

He emphasizes that individuality should be cultivated 'within the limits imposed by the rights and interests of others' (1859c, 266 (III.9)). Some 'compression' of individual spontaneity 'is necessary to prevent the stronger specimens of human nature from encroaching on the rights of others' (ibid.). But social control for that purpose is justified even if we restrict attention to 'human development', he points out, because such control allows every person (including the weaker) to cultivate his individuality without fear of grievous non-consensual injury. Indeed, the requisite compression is justified even from the perspective of any individual's *self-development*:

> [E]ven to himself there is a full equivalent in the better development of the social part of his nature, rendered possible by the restraint put upon the selfish part. To be held to rigid rules of justice for the sake of others, develops the feelings and capacities which have the good of others for their object.
>
> (Ibid.)

It helps the individual (including the strongest) along the road to an ideal moral character, to be forced (if necessary) to develop the 'feelings and capacities' of goodwill toward others, at least to the extent of not doing them serious injury against their wishes. But for the individual 'to be restrained in things not affecting [the] good [of others], by their mere displeasure, developes [*sic*] nothing valuable' (ibid.).

Within an ideal type of character, then, self-restraint in accord with general rules that regulate other-regarding matters is consistently mixed with self-assertion in self-regarding matters.

SELF-ASSERTION NOT THE SOLE SOURCE OF IMPROVEMENT (III.5, 17)

The propriety of a balance between spontaneity and rule-abidingness is made clear by him at other points as well. For example, he argues for different self-regarding experiments of living so that people may learn from their own and others' experiences which of the many different desires and impulses possible to human nature are best for *them*. People are capable of self-improvement, in the sense that they can choose to acquire or strengthen some desires and weaken or discard others, if they judge such a change to be desirable for them. But liberty of self-regarding experiments, while it may be 'the only unfailing and permanent source of improvement' in morality and personal plans of life, is *not* the only source of it: 'the spirit of improvement is not always a spirit of liberty, for it may aim at forcing improvements on [the] unwilling' (ibid., 272 (III.17)). Rather, improvement may require coercion in some contexts, to force the recalcitrant to obey rules designed to secure others from experiencing serious harm against their wishes.

Consistently with this, Mill does not advocate free scope for *other-regarding* experiments of living incompatible with a due regard for the rights and interests of other people. Rather, he calls for development of an ideal moral character involving a 'proper balance' of strong desires and impulses, including a desire to do right:

> [S]trong impulses are only perilous when not properly balanced; when one set of aims and inclinations is developed into strength, while

others, which ought to co-exist with them, remain weak and inactive. It is not because men's desires are strong that they act ill; it is because their consciences are weak. There is no natural connexion between strong impulses and a weak conscience. The natural connexion is the other way.

(Ibid., 263 (III.5))

Such a character is depicted as 'energetic', embodying an array of strong desires and impulses under the self-government of a powerful rational will (264 (III.5)). A strong conscience, or desire to do right, is an essential ingredient.

COERCION MAY BE NEEDED TO HELP CULTIVATE CONSCIENCE

To foster self-development in that direction, society must encourage the individual to cultivate a 'proper balance' of strong desires and impulses. In part, this is done by giving free scope to self-regarding experiments of living: there is no other way to gain warranted opinions about the 'proper balance'.

But society can also legitimately use coercion where need be, to enforce general rules of other-regarding conduct. Threats of legal penalties and social stigma may be useful to encourage the unwilling to acquire or strengthen a desire to do right. This remains so even if coercion alone can never lead the individual to develop his conscience.

OBEDIENCE AND INDIVIDUALITY

It emerges that there is no necessary conflict between the cultivation of individuality and obedience to expedient social rules. A person ought to think freely for himself and choose his own lifestyle rather than *blindly* imitate other people in self-regarding matters. But that does not preclude him from choosing, after reflection, to imitate others to the extent implied by common obedience to reasonable rules governing conduct that harms others without their consent. Indeed, he *ought* to choose to obey laws and customs which most people think are reasonable means of governing other-regarding conduct (even if he thinks better rules might be devised). He *ought* to suppress, by means of his own moral willpower (which must be developed), those of his desires and impulses which, if he acted upon them, would harm other people in unreasonable ways. He *ought* to develop his capacity to recognize when he is likely to cause serious injury to others against their wishes, and he *ought* to develop a sufficiently strong conscience, or desire to do right, that he chooses to respect their rights, pay his fair share of taxes and otherwise suitably 'compress' his behaviour. Until he develops the requisite willpower and character (habits of acting), however, the individual may legitimately be coerced to do as he ought.

Society has legitimate authority to coerce the individual (if need be) to follow whichever rules of other-regarding conduct are in the majority's estimation generally expedient. No person is infallible – nobody is absolutely sure what an ideal code looks like in this respect. But, provided complete liberty of discussion of the alternatives is guaranteed, the majority is warranted in establishing such laws and customs as it (at least tacitly) considers reasonable. That does not mean that the individual must *agree* with the existing rules governing other-regarding conduct (let alone any which meddle with self-regarding acts), or that he must sit quietly rather than work at social reform.

But it does mean that society has legitimate authority to punish him for deviations from those of its existing moral and legal rules which are designed to prevent other-regarding conduct that is harmful to others against their wishes. Society has no legitimate authority, however, to enforce rules of self-regarding conduct.

Even with respect to self-regarding conduct, the individual should consult 'traditions and customs', which he is properly taught in youth, 'to find out what part of recorded experience is properly applicable to his own circumstances and character' (ibid., 262 (III.3)). Those customs include, of course, the prevailing conventions of warranted inference per se. As Mill remarks, 'it would be absurd to pretend that people ought to live as if nothing whatever had been known in the world before they came into it' (ibid.). Consistently with this, however, any person capable of self-improvement should be granted complete liberty of thought and action, short of injury to others.

AN IDEAL TYPE OF INDIVIDUAL CHARACTER (III.5–9)

Mill's emphasis on liberty and individuality, as opposed to compression and rule-abidingness, reflects his view that the 'proper balance' has been tipped dangerously against individuality in the present age, and is likely to get even worse: 'In our times, from the highest class of society down to the lowest, every one lives as under the eye of a hostile and dreaded censorship' (ibid., 264 (III.6)). In 'some early states of society' the balance was tipped too much the other way: 'But society has now fairly got the better of individuality' (ibid.). Even 'in what concerns only themselves', people blindly follow custom rather than consider what they would most like to try: 'I do not mean that they *choose* what is customary, in preference to what suits their own inclination. It does not occur to them to have any inclination, except for what is customary' (ibid., 264–65 (III.6), emphasis added). Moreover, just as lack of free thought and discussion can result in loss of any acquired understanding of the grounds and even meaning of warranted opinions, so lack of self-regarding choices and experiments can cause people to lose all desire to depart from custom, since they no longer have any idea of what might be suitable to their own nature: 'their human capacities are withered and starved' (265 (III.6)).

Self-denial of that sort exhausts the so-called Christian interpretation (now referred to as 'the Calvinistic theory') of an ideal moral character, Mill argues: 'All the good of which humanity is capable, is comprised in obedience', whether to the will of God or some other authority sanctioned by the divine (ibid., 265 (III.7)). He ties this in with his earlier theme of the rising danger of religious intolerance of competing moral ideals: 'In some such insidious form there is at present a strong tendency to this narrow theory of life, and to the pinched and hidebound type of human character which it patronizes' (265 (III.8)). That Christian theory contains a part of the truth. But it must be modified and supplemented by other warranted opinions concerning what besides obedience comprises an ideal noble and moral character.

In particular, account must be taken of the value of self-assertion, not merely the importance of obedience to rules: '"Pagan self-assertion" is one of the elements of human worth, as well as

"Christian self-denial'" (ibid., 266 (III.8); quoting from Sterling 1848, 1: 190). He points to a 'Greek ideal' which apparently combines these different sides of the truth into a 'complete and consistent whole'. Since he explicitly mentions Pericles, that warranted character ideal might be referred to as *Periclean*. It apparently involves liberty and spontaneity, duly balanced with self-government in the sense of freely choosing to obey rules. Moreover, the cultivation of this Periclean ideal presupposes individual rights to liberty within the self-regarding sphere, consistently mixed with legitimate social enforcement of reasonable rules of conduct outside that sphere.

Evidently, this 'Greek ideal' of character is not purely 'Platonic' since Mill equates the latter with the 'Christian ideal of self-government' (1859c, 266 (III.8)). Rather than Periclean, it is sometimes labelled as Aristotelian, even though the golden age of Pericles in Athens ended with the coming of the Peloponnesian War about 431 BC. Aristotle was born in 384 BC, almost half a century after the death of Pericles is recorded. The ideal might be referred to as Socratic, since Socrates was a contemporary of Pericles. Yet Mill chooses to speak of Pericles. A major reason for this may be that, in his view, Pericles anticipates the liberty doctrine during the course of his great funeral oration (see Mill 1853, 333–34; for further discussion, see Riley 2006c).

Another reason may be to call attention to the fact that Pericles, in addition to his attainments as a great political leader and orator, seems to have done as he pleased in his self-regarding matters. As already mentioned in Part I, he seems to have sustained a passionate love affair with Aspasia, a foreigner, outside the marriage conventions of Athens. She was also apparently his trusted political and philosophical adviser, as well as a teacher and confidante of Socrates. Indeed, she seems to have advocated true love between equals as a model for all intimate relationships (heterosexual and homosexual). Her unusual position, as a woman not bound by social conventions and treated as an equal by men such as Pericles and Socrates, apparently made her the object of severe criticism as a whore, a manipulator of men, another Helen who instigated wars and so on. Like Socrates, she was even formally charged with impiety, though her trial ended in acquittal (after Pericles wept in open court for her release, so Plutarch tells us). Perhaps Mill was even reminded by all this of his own beloved Harriet, and of the hostility and stigma they faced as a result of their own unconventional relationship.

UTILITARIAN CASE FOR THE EQUAL RIGHT TO LIBERTY (III.10–19)

Mill goes on to clarify his utilitarian form of argument for giving the individual absolute liberty, by right, to choose among opinions and self-regarding acts in accord with his own judgment and inclinations.

SELF-DEVELOPMENT AND TRUE HAPPINESS (III.10)

For those who seek warranted opinions about their own feelings, who want knowledge of which of their desires and impulses to strengthen and which to weaken, the utility of liberty within the self-regarding sphere is clear: it is essential to their self-development. They expect to learn which actions have pleasant consequences and which have painful ones for them. Such persons recognize that choosing as they like is essential to their progress toward an ideal noble and moral character, which reflects a *warranted belief about their own happiness.*

Complete liberty of self-regarding action is the very test of a true conception of their personal utility, just as complete liberty of discussion is the test of warranted opinions in general. Moreover equal rights to liberty in self-regarding matters would maximize social development without causing non-consensual harm to others, if each member of society sought his self-development and desired liberty.

But, as Mill recognizes, not all people do value self-development and the liberty essential to it. Thus,

> it is necessary [for a utilitarian] further to show that these developed [and truly happy] human beings are of some use to the undeveloped – to point out to those who do not desire liberty, and would not avail themselves of it, that they may be in some intelligible manner rewarded for allowing other people to make use of it without hindrance.
>
> (1859c, 267 (III.10))

He offers at least four related reasons to persuade 'the undeveloped', that is, the majority whose culture and religion is infused with the predominantly selfish spirit of commercial society rather than any perfectionist spirit of self-development toward an ideal Periclean character.

BETTER SOCIAL CUSTOMS AND PRACTICES (III.11–12)

First, 'they might possibly learn something' (ibid., 267 (III.11)). Even if they do not develop habits of free inquiry and free experimentation themselves, they might benefit as new warranted opinions (including opinions about lifestyles) are put into practice and converted into customs through imitation of the developed persons who originated them:

> There is always need of persons not only to discover new truths, and point out when what were once truths are true no longer, but also to commence new practices, and set the example of more enlightened conduct, and better taste and sense in human life.
>
> (Ibid.)

In short, there is always need of individuals with a passion for liberty to point out to the majority over time which 'uncustomary things … are fit to be converted into customs' (ibid., 269 (III.14)). This applies not only to self-regarding matters, where respect for liberty ought to be made the custom. It applies as well to other-regarding matters where, for example, new warranted beliefs about other people's interests and rights, or about what harms them in grievous ways, should be put into general practice.

Admittedly, only a relatively few persons will actually discover new truths worthy of adoption by the majority. But, since we cannot know beforehand who these 'salt of the earth' will be, the general '*atmosphere* of freedom' which they need to breathe and flourish ought to be secured (ibid., 267 (III.11), emphasis original). Equal rights to liberty of self-regarding choices must be distributed, therefore, so that individuals who desire liberty, and will 'avail themselves of it', can choose in accord with their own judgment and inclinations. Otherwise, even that portion of the truth embodied in existing practices will tend to lose its significance, and may eventually lose its very meaning for virtually everyone, who have nothing to contrast it with or to defend it from: 'There is only too great a tendency in the best beliefs and practices to degenerate into the mechanical' (ibid.).

MORE EFFECTIVE GOVERNMENT (III.13)

Second, the undeveloped cannot expect fair and reasonable government in the absence of a body of developed individuals. 'Mediocrity' is 'the ascendant power among mankind', Mill insists: ill-considered popular opinions, spewed at the majority by 'men much like themselves' through the mass media, are everywhere gaining political influence as democracy takes hold in advanced commercial societies (ibid., 268–69 (III.13); see also 274–75 (III.18–19)). To counteract this and promote competent government, it is essential to have competent individuals, with complete liberty to advise and cajole the majority:

> No government by a democracy or a numerous aristocracy ... ever did or could rise above mediocrity, except in so far as the sovereign Many have let themselves be guided (which in their best times they always have done) by the counsels and influence of a more highly gifted and instructed One or Few.
>
> (Ibid., 269 (III.13))

He emphasizes that he does not countenance Carlyle's (1841) brand of 'hero-worship', whereby the 'strong man of genius' seizes power and uses it to coerce the masses to behave in accord with some ideal code (Mill 1859c, 269 (III.13)). Rather than such a power of coercion, the developed should merely have 'freedom to point out the way' (ibid.). He seems to have in mind something like Coleridge's (1818, 1839) notion of a 'clerisy', a national corps of intellectuals, ministers and professors, suitably independent of the government, accessible to the people and serving them (as well as political leaders) as a source of learning and friendly advice.[3]

More generally, to help 'break through' the tyranny of majority opinion, he thinks it expedient for society to encourage 'exceptional individuals' to deviate as they like from majoritarian ideas and practices, short of causing injury to others against their wishes. The point, it seems, is that such deviations help remind people that popular opinion often reflects mediocrity rather than excellence, and unfairness to minorities rather than justice. Effective government is thus facilitated by the mere example of non-conformity: 'In this age, the mere example of nonconformity, the mere refusal to bend the knee to custom, is itself a service ... That so few now dare to be eccentric, marks the chief danger of the time' (Mill 1859c, 269 (III.13)).

DIVERSITY MORE CONGENIAL THAN FORCED UNIFORMITY (III.14–16)

A third reason for the undeveloped to welcome a free scope for individuality within the self-regarding sphere is that they too (not the developed alone) will generally be happier than they would be if society tried to make everyone conform to a code of self-regarding conduct: 'If a person possesses any tolerable amount of common sense and experience, his own mode of laying out his existence is the best, not because it is the best in itself, but because it is his own mode' (ibid., 270 (III.14)). People have different tastes and 'also require different conditions for their spiritual development' (ibid.). General rules laying out how everyone ought to act in their self-regarding concerns could never effectively take account of such diversity:

> Such are the differences among human beings in their sources of pleasure, their susceptibilities of pain, and the operation on them of different physical and moral agencies, that unless there is a corresponding diversity in their modes of life, they neither obtain their fair share of happiness, nor grow up to the mental, moral, and aesthetic stature of which their nature is capable.
>
> (Ibid.)

Moreover, rules in this context have no justification in terms of preventing non-consensual harm to others.

Mill returns yet again at this point to his theme of rising religious intolerance, arguing that the public is currently 'more disposed than at most former periods' to try to make everyone behave as if his desires and impulses are moderate or weak: the 'standard, express or tacit, is to desire nothing strongly' (ibid., 271 (III.15)). He is evidently referring to the 'movement' by Christians (so-called) to make their standard of self-denial into a complete guide of conduct:

> Its ideal of character is to be without any marked character; to maim by compression, like a Chinese lady's foot, every part of human nature which stands out prominently, and tends to make the person markedly dissimilar in outline to commonplace humanity.
>
> (Ibid., 271–72 (III.15))

Pagan self-assertion and diversity of lifestyles are to be stamped out. Everyone is to obey whichever rules the majority decides are needed for all alike to mould for themselves the same maimed character. That character's defining feature is 'obedience', that is, 'Platonic and Christian … self-government' in accord with the social rules (ibid., 265–66 (III.7–8)).

He thinks that the religious movement has already gone too far in England, though its unintended effect has been to produce an 'outward conformity' to religion and morality with little genuine interest in either (ibid., 272 (III.16)). Strong desires and impulses, or what is left of them, have largely been redirected elsewhere: 'There is scarcely any outlet for energy in this country except business' (ibid.). This emerging pattern, of 'outward conformity' to an incomplete and overextended moral ideal conjoined with a passion for commerce, leads him to his fourth reason for the undeveloped to respect liberty and individuality within the self-regarding sphere: the spectre of social stagnation and even decline.

PREVENTION OF SOCIAL STAGNATION AND DECLINE (III.17–19)

Liberty and individuality are necessary not merely for social improvement, he insists, but to prevent a kind of social paralysis associated with the complete 'despotism of custom' (ibid., 272

(III.17)). He speaks of China, 'stationary' in its customs 'for thousands of years' and no longer capable of progress without foreign intervention, as 'a warning example' (273 (III.17)). But he thinks the despotism of custom which threatens Europe (and, in all likelihood, America) will take a somewhat different form, more consonant with advanced industrial society and its consumption possibilities. The threat is 'not precisely stationariness' but rather endless changes of fashion, 'change ... for change's sake' in self-regarding matters like dress and opinions on all subjects, 'provided all change together' (ibid.). A constant flux of mass desires and impulses, a continual grabbing and tossing away of commercial products and ideas, an habitual restlessness with little consideration or discussion of alternative ways of life, awaits the majority unless steps are taken immediately to protect self-regarding liberty and individuality by right.

HOLES IN THE CASE?

Mill evidently does make a rather elaborate utilitarian case for the rights of liberty and individuality, then, despite the familiar chorus of protests that he fails even to address the question. Warranted opinions about personal happiness are possible, he insists, only if complete liberty is granted to self-regarding experimentation. Consistently with that, developed individuals are warranted up to now in believing that their happiness is associated with the Periclean character ideal, which integrates liberty and spontaneity in self-regarding matters with rule-abidingness and self-government in other-regarding ones. The individual who has developed such an ideal character will, of course, voluntarily govern himself in accord with an ideal code restricted to other-regarding concerns. But before he attains that character, during the development process when he lacks the strong conscience that governs him to do right, he may be legitimately coerced by society to obey its existing rules of other-regarding conduct.

Apart from those who desire liberty and seek self-perfection, individuals who do not desire to develop themselves beyond some modicum of common sense separating the barbarian from the person capable of rational persuasion are also given utilitarian reasons for respecting rights of self-regarding liberty and individuality.

But are there holes in the case? For example, why does Mill believe that complete liberty of self-regarding conduct will tend to lead the individual in the direction of developing an ideal noble and moral character? Put in other words, what justification does he have for thinking that the individuals who are passionate about doing as they please in their self-regarding affairs will develop themselves into moral agents who wish to respect the rights of others and may even view such respect as beautiful and sublime? Such moral agents are essential to society's improvement, of course, since it is they who must point out the way to the predominantly selfish majority and persuade these relatively undeveloped people to recognize and comply with reasonable social rules that distribute and sanction equal rights not to suffer certain grievous harms.

Before we can make an attempt to answer such questions, several related issues of interpretation cry out to be cleared up, namely: are there *truly* self-regarding acts, or is the self-regarding category merely an artificial utilitarian construction in the seamless web of other-regarding conduct? If there really are acts that are harmless to others or that only harm them if they like, what is meant by harm? If all acts really cause one or another form of non-consensual harm to others, on the other hand, why all the fuss about self-regarding acts? Is his talk of these merely a subterfuge, a way to hide from the reader of liberal sympathies the utilitarian form of reasoning at the heart of the argument? These sorts of questions begin to receive more attention in his next chapter.

SUGGESTIONS FOR FURTHER READING

Mill's admiration for the ancient Athenian way of life, as envisioned by Pericles in his great funeral oration near the beginning of the long Peloponnesian War, is discussed further in Jonathan Riley, 'Mill, *On Liberty*', in John Shand (ed.), *Central Works of Philosophy*, 5 vols (London: Acumen, 2006), vol. 3, ch. 5, and 'Mill's Neo-Athenian Model of Liberal Democracy', in Nadia Urbinati and Alex Zakaras (eds), *J.S. Mill's Political Thought: A Bicentennial Reassessment* (New York: Cambridge University Press, 2007),

221–49. On Pericles, see George Grote, *A History of Greece*, 12 vols (London: John Murray, 1846–56), vol. 6; Philip Stadter, *A Commentary on Plutarch's Pericles* (Chapel Hill: University of North Carolina Press, 1989); Donald Kagan, *Pericles of Athens and the Birth of Democracy* (New York: Free Press, 1991); and Vincent Azoulay, *Pericles of Athens*, trans. Janet Lloyd (Princeton: Princeton University Press, 2014), although Azoulay, unlike Mill, apparently believes that Pericles' character is not suitable to serve as a universal ideal. A rich discussion of Aspasia and her biographical tradition is provided by Madeleine Henry, *Prisoner of History: Aspasia of Miletus and Her Biographical Tradition* (Oxford: Oxford University Press, 1995).

Mill's Periclean ideal of self-development or individuality is a many-sided noble and virtuous character in which man's intellectual, imaginative and moral capacities have been developed into a complete and consistent whole. This ideal character, in which reason and sentiment work in harmony such that the individual is motivated to freely assert himself in self-regarding matters and to willingly obey reasonable moral and legal rules that govern social or other-regarding conduct, is the ultimate goal prescribed for the individual by Mill's extraordinary utilitarian Art of Life. Collective happiness is truly maximized if, and only if, all members of society develop this ideal character, or at least all who are capable of self-improvement (by assumption, the vast majority) attain it.

Von Humboldt, Goethe, Schiller and early Romantics also draw on ancient Greece and Rome to propose ideals of a beautiful human character. But they all rejected utilitarianism and endorsed moral psychologies of a broadly Kantian sort rather than any hedonistic 'associationist psychology' of the sort endorsed by Mill. For further discussion, see e.g. Elizabeth M. Wilkinson and L.A. Willoughby, *Models of Wholeness: Some Attitudes to Language, Art and Life in the Age of Goethe*, ed. J. Adler, M. Swales and A. Weaver (Oxford: Peter Lang, 2002); Ernst Cassirer, 'Goethe and the Kantian Philosophy', in his *Rousseau-Kant-Goethe: Two Essays*, trans. J. Gutmann, P.O. Kristeller and J.H. Randall Jr (Princeton: Princeton University Press, 1945), 61–98; J.C. Friedrich von Schiller, *On the Aesthetic Education of Man in a Series of Letters*, ed. E.M. Wilkinson and L.A. Willoughby (Oxford:

Oxford University Press, 1983); Frederick C. Beiser, *The Romantic Imperative: The Concept of Early German Romanticism* (Cambridge, MA: Harvard University Press, 2006), and *Schiller as Philosopher: A Re-examination* (New York: Oxford University Press, 2008); and Jonathan Riley, 'Mill's Greek Ideal of Individuality', in K.N. Demetriou and A. Loizides (eds), *John Stuart Mill: A British Socrates* (London: Palgrave Macmillan, 2013), 97–125.

Candace A. Vogler argues, in *John Stuart Mill's Deliberative Landscape* (New York: Garland, 2001), that the hedonistic associationist psychology adopted by Mill cannot do the work required for his defence of the importance of individuality as an ingredient of human well-being. Her argument is deeply flawed, in my opinion, largely because she attributes views to him that he does not hold, to wit: an instrumentalist model of practical reason according to which reason has nothing to say about basic ends – reason guides only the choice of means to given ends—and a crude form of associationist psychology in which reason is divorced from sentiment, beliefs are unrelated to desires, and an ontological gulf is maintained between cognitive ideas and contentless feelings such as pleasure and pain. I say a bit more about her argument later, in Chapter 9 below.

Mill's Periclean ideal attempts consistently to combine Christian virtues with Pagan self-assertion. Many other Victorians defended what they saw as appealing mixtures of Christianity and Paganism. They included Matthew Arnold and Walter Pater. See e.g. Arnold, 'Marcus Aurelius' (1863), in his *Essays in Criticism: First Series* (1865), ed. Sister T.M. Hoctor (Chicago and London: University of Chicago Press, 1968), 204–24; and Pater, *Marius the Epicurean* (1885), ed. M. Levey (Harmondsworth: Penguin, 1985).

Arnold glorifies Christianity as a supreme moral ideal, and extols the Stoicism of Marcus Aurelius as an approximation to that Christian idealism. Unlike Mill, he seems to see a suitably revitalized Christianity as a complete morality, requiring nothing else to supplement it. He rejects any right to choose as one pleases in self-regarding matters, as well as hedonistic utilitarianism more generally.

Pater also elaborates on Mill's discussion of Aurelius (1859c, 236–37 (II.14)), in a way that emphasizes a potential harmony between Millian utilitarianism and Christian idealism. His 'Marius' follows a course of self-development through which his simple youthful Epicureanism or Cyrenaicism is transformed into a 'noble' version of that doctrine. That noble Cyrenaicism is (like Mill's utilitarianism) a hedonistic philosophy which affirms the development of a beautiful character, involving a complete harmony of human virtues. At the same time, the ideal character is identified (as in Arnold's idealism) with true Christian virtue. Pater seems more open than Arnold to something like a right to pursue aesthetic personal ideals as one pleases.

On the mixture of Greek and Christian cultural influences in Britain and America more generally, see D.J. DeLaura, *Hebrew and Hellene in Victorian England: Newman, Arnold, Pater* (Austin: University of Texas Press, 1969); Peter Hinchcliff, *Benjamin Jowett and the Christian Religion* (Oxford: Clarendon Press, 1987); Frank M. Turner, *The Greek Heritage in Victorian Britain* (New Haven: Yale University Press, 1981), and 'The Triumph of Idealism in Victorian Classical Studies', in his *Contesting Cultural Authority: Essays in Victorian Intellectual Life* (Cambridge: Cambridge University Press, 1993), 322–61; and Simon Goldhill, *Victorian Culture and Classical Antiquity: Art, Opera, Fiction, and the Proclamation of Modernity* (Princeton: Princeton University Press, 2011).

NOTES

1 Although he singles out von Humboldt, Mill might also have mentioned various other German philosophers who were just as committed to a 'many sided' character ideal, in which some sort of harmonious fusion of different human capacities and powers is attained. Goethe says, for example: 'Man ... can only accomplish the unique, the wholly unexpected, if all his qualities unite within him and work together as one. This was the happy lot of the ancients, especially the Greeks in their golden age' (1994b, 100–1).

2 The social rules may include rules that a competent person ought to act on to prevent a child or incompetent adult from unintentionally harming himself. In short, certain inactions (intentional omissions to act) may be ruled out, even though the agent himself has not caused any non-consensual harm to others through his physical movements.

3 The idea of a 'clerisy' can be construed to mean something like a system of universities, perhaps subsidized by the taxpayer, whose faculties control appointments and enjoy job tenure during good behaviour.

5
OF THE LIMITS TO THE AUTHORITY OF SOCIETY OVER THE INDIVIDUAL (CHAPTER IV, PARAS 1–21)

THE NATURE OF UTILITARIAN COERCION (IV.1–3)

Mill now starts to lend more precision to his general doctrine of 'the nature and limits' of legitimate coercion. He has made his utilitarian case for the right to absolute liberty in self-regarding matters, so that those who desire self-development may make use of the freedom of thought and action essential to its achievement. More needs to be said, however, not only about the general boundary of the self-regarding realm within which coercion should not even be considered, but also about how coercion should be exercised by society in the other-regarding realm where its use is legitimate. His attempt to clarify these things preoccupies him for the remaining two chapters.

In return for the valuable general security which society provides, he says, all individuals have a duty to obey its rules of other-regarding conduct: 'every one who receives the protection of society owes a return for the benefit, and the fact of living in society renders it indispensable that each should be bound to observe a certain line of conduct towards the rest' (1859c, 276 (IV.3)).

First, the individual ought not to injure 'certain interests' of other people, 'which, either by express legal provision or by tacit understanding, ought to be considered as rights' (ibid.). Second, he ought to 'bear his share (to be fixed on some equitable principle) of the labours and sacrifices incurred for defending the society or its members from injury and molestation' (ibid.). 'These conditions society is justified in enforcing *at all costs to those who endeavour to withhold fulfilment*' (ibid., emphasis added).

But third, the individual ought also to refrain from hurting others in ways that do not 'go the length of violating any of their constituted rights' (ibid.). In that type of case, '[t]he offender may ... be justly punished by opinion, though not by law' (ibid.).

Utilitarian coercion thus has the following nature and limits, as Chapter V of Mill's *Utilitarianism* confirms. Legal coercion, the form symbolic of society's deepest contempt and the most costly to implement, is expediently used to prevent *only* certain egregious kinds of harms to others to which no reasonable person who seeks to promote the collective welfare can consent. These egregious harms include harms to the public at large such as refusing to pay one's fair share of the taxes required to defend the society. Suitable legal penalties (including death, incarceration, fines and the like) ought to be enforced by government officials only to prevent a person from violating others' moral rights and justified legal rights, including the rights of officials to perform their legitimate public duties. Officials must have a right to collect a fair share of taxes, for example, and a right to draft citizens into military service when necessary for the defence of the country.

Social stigma, but not legal punishment, ought to be used to prevent less serious kinds of harms which do not rise to the level of rights violations. Public contempt (including organized *displays* of condemnation, publicized messages intended to humiliate their targets, and so on) ought to be showered on the individual who repeatedly disappoints others' customary expectations for help when he can easily afford to help, for example, or who otherwise exhibits unusually bad will toward others, without due cause.

Of course, the conduct which is legitimately subject to these forms of coercion is other-regarding. It 'affects prejudicially the interests of others' (1859c, 276 (IV.3)); it 'affects others' *without* 'their free, voluntary, and undeceived consent' (225 (I.12)); and it is 'the part [of life] which chiefly interests society' (276 (IV.2)). Moreover, it is not merely harmful to others without their consent. It is so remarkably harmful that it is properly viewed as *immoral* conduct according to utility in the largest sense. Coercion to prevent it ought to be employed, except in special situations where external sanctions are inexpedient and society must rely (perhaps in vain) solely on the agent's internal sanctions of conscience for deterrence. Special situations of this sort include secret promises between intimate friends, where one person can grievously harm the other by breaking the promise and yet society cannot expediently use legal penalties or public stigma to prevent or punish the harm. Aside from such special cases, coercion should not merely be *considered* to prevent these wrongful kinds of harms. It ought to be *employed*.

In contrast, 'there should be perfect freedom' from all forms of coercion, Mill says, 'when a person's conduct affects the interests of no persons besides himself, or needs not affect them unless they like (all the persons concerned being of full age, and the ordinary amount of understanding)' (ibid., 276 (IV.3)). Coercion should not even be 'open to discussion' in such cases.

It is worth remarking, however, that a third possibility is still being ignored at this stage of his argument, namely, other-regarding actions which, though, legitimately open to coercive interference because they cause non-consensual harm to others, are not so harmful as to render coercion *expedient*. This raises yet again the ambiguity noted earlier in the context of freedom of expression (see pp. 98–9). Is the third possibility, where social control of conduct admittedly harmful to others without their consent is not generally expedient, really distinct from the self-regarding sphere of liberty? Or is the self-regarding sphere just another name for that part of the seamless web of other-regarding conduct where coercive interference is not expedient? He does not give a complete answer

THE NATURE OF SELF-REGARDING ACTS (IV.4–7)

'Selfish indifference' to others in their self-regarding concerns, Mill insists, is no part of his doctrine (1859c, 276–77 (IV.4)). Absence of coercion does not imply absence of all forms of interaction. People should try to persuade each other to cultivate 'self-regarding virtues' such as prudence, moderation and self-respect. They should advise and warn each other to think more carefully and to act more wisely. But, ultimately, the individual must choose in accord with his own judgment and desires in his self-regarding concerns because '[h]e is the person most interested in his own well-being' (ibid., 277 (IV.4)). 'Considerations to aid his judgment, exhortations to strengthen his will, may be offered to him, even obtruded on him, by others; but he himself is the final judge' (ibid.).

Self-regarding acts, he admits, can and should affect the *feelings* of other people. It is 'neither possible nor desirable' for others to remain unaffected altogether by the individual's conduct, even though that conduct is harmless to them unless they consent to be harmed (ibid., 278 (IV.5)). By implication, *harm* to others cannot mean merely affecting their feelings, or causing them to feel aversion, without any injury or damage beyond that. Others are reasonably expected to like or dislike self-regarding actions, as the case may be. Self-degrading conduct, for example, can and should occasion intense dislike in other people: 'Though doing no wrong to any one, a person may so act as to compel us to judge him, and feel to him, as a fool, or as a being of an inferior order' (ibid.).

Moreover, others are properly free to act upon their contempt for the individual's self-regarding conduct. They have 'a right to avoid' him, for example, as well as a right (and perhaps a duty) to warn others to avoid him (ibid.). But nobody has a right to 'parade the avoidance', in other words, make a coercive public display of their contempt as would be justified if he were guilty of an other-regarding fault such as lack of charity (ibid.).

NATURAL PENALTIES (IV.5–7)

It emerges that the agent may suffer *harm* 'at the hands of others' as a result of his self-regarding conduct:

> In these various modes a person may suffer very severe penalties at the hands of others, for faults which directly concern only himself; but he suffers these penalties only in so far as they are the natural, and, as it were, the spontaneous consequences of the faults themselves, not because they are purposely inflicted on him for the sake of punishment.
> (Ibid.)

These natural penalties are apparently 'strictly inseparable from the unfavourable judgment of others', in the sense that no further deliberation is required to bring them about (ibid.). They flow immediately from others' dislike: 'the natural penalties ... cannot be prevented from falling on those who incur the distaste or the contempt of those who know them' (ibid., 282 (IV.11)). Thus, a self-regarding action, although harmless to others, can trigger their aversion and thereby result in harm to the agent himself.

Mill contends that the natural penalties 'are the only ones to which a person should ever be subjected' for his self-regarding conduct (ibid., 278–79 (IV.6)). Nevertheless, the fact that such penalties are inseparable from mere dislike may seem to contradict his earlier suggestion that harm must mean something other than mere dislike, and even to contradict his claim that there is a self-regarding sphere comprised of actions that do not cause any non-consensual harms to others. Self-regarding actions cannot be said to cause only consensual harms if any harms at all, someone might object, because such actions inspire dislike and the non-consensual harms that are inseparable from it. In particular, says the objector, others' dislike may directly cause non-consensual harm not only to the agent of the self-regarding conduct but also to themselves. And yet, while it sounds ominous, this is not an insurmountable objection. Self-regarding actions do not cause any non-consensual harms, either to others or to the agent. There are really two aspects to consider.

On the one hand, self-regarding actions admittedly can result in harm to the agent through the reactions of others. But that self-harm is not harm to others. Others' mere dislike is not harm to them, and their actions based on their dislike are chosen, however reluctantly, by them. True, the others may suffer from the natural penalties which they choose to inflict as a result of their dislike of the self-regarding conduct. They may regret losing the affection and friendship of a person whom they choose to avoid because of what they see as intolerable self-regarding faults, for example, and yet they consent to suffer these harms. The natural penalties inflicted by them cannot be said to be non-consensual harms to them.

On the other hand, what about the harm implied for the agent by the natural penalties inflicted on him as a result of others' dislike of his self-regarding actions? That harm too is consensual harm. Given that others have tried to persuade him to change his ways, that they have warned him that they will cease to associate with him if he fails to heed their advice, and that they have intimated that they will warn mutual acquaintances of what they consider his self-regarding vices, he must reasonably expect to experience these harmful consequences if he persists in his disliked self-regarding conduct. By acting on their dislike in these ways, Mill insists, the others are exercising their own self-regarding liberty: they are not causing non-consensual harm to the agent. It is not quite right, however, to say that these natural penalties are largely self-inflicted. Others do inflict the penalties but the agent accepts them if he chooses to persist in his self-regarding actions. The others should be perfectly free to avoid anyone who does not accept their advice. Their freedom does not imply any deliberate intention to punish the person. Rather, the natural penalties are incidental by-products of their equal rights to avoid what they dislike in their self-regarding concerns. Thus, 'it is not our part to inflict any suffering on him except what may incidentally follow from our using the same liberty in the regulation of our own affairs, which we allow to him in his' (ibid., 280 (IV.7)). Equal rights to complete liberty of self-regarding acts are thus compatible with natural penalties because such harms are consensual harms. Liberty is choosing in accord with one's own judgment and likes; natural penalties are inseparable from dislike of another's self-regarding act; natural penalties are suffered willingly, if reluctantly, by those who inflict them and by the agent who continues to do as he likes in the face of them; and so natural penalties are inseparable from self-regarding liberty itself. Other-regarding actions are simply not involved.

NATURAL PENALTIES VERSUS ARTIFICIAL PUNISHMENT (IV.7)

Mill insists on a distinction between natural penalties and artificial penalties. Whereas the former are suffered consensually by individuals who persist with their unpopular self-regarding conduct, the latter are deliberately inflicted on the individual without his consent because society decides to retaliate against his *immoral* conduct, that is, conduct which the majority judges causes wrongful harm to other people by damaging their rights and other essential interests.[1] This distinction between natural and artificial penalties calls to mind Hume, whose influence on Mill's philosophy is not sufficiently appreciated in the literature.[2]

This 'is not a merely nominal distinction', Mill says (1859c, 279 (IV.7)). Two distinct psychological phenomena are involved. If we become aware of another person's self-regarding faults, for example, then we recognize that the harmful consequences of his self-regarding actions fall on himself. Thus:

> [W]e may express our distaste, and we may stand aloof ... but we shall not therefore feel called on to make his life uncomfortable. We shall reflect that he already bears, or will bear, the whole penalty of his error; if he spoils his life by mismanagement, we shall not, for that reason, desire to spoil it further: instead of wishing to punish him, we shall rather endeavour to alleviate his [self-inflicted] punishment, by showing him how he may avoid or cure the evils [including natural penalties] his [self-regarding] conduct tends to bring upon him. He may be to us an object of pity, perhaps of dislike, but not of anger or resentment.
> (Ibid., 279–80 (IV.7))

But 'it is far otherwise' if we become aware of another person's moral vices (ibid., 280 (IV.7)). For 'the evil consequences of his acts do not then fall on himself, but on others' (ibid.). We feel anger and resentment toward anyone whose conduct has caused, or is likely to cause, harm to another's essential interests. Moreover, his wrongful other-regarding conduct ought to be deliberately punished, although external sanctions are inexpedient in special situations. In those special situations, his conscience ought to deliver the punishment, preferably by a force of habit so firm that it overrides any momentary desires and whims to the contrary. Aside from those special situations, society rightfully imposes suitable artificial penalties on any person 'of mature years' who infringes its moral rules of other-regarding conduct:

> [I]f he has infringed the rules [of justice and of charity] necessary for the protection of his fellow-creatures, individually or collectively ... [then] society, as the protector of all its members, must retaliate on him [by law or by opinion]; must inflict pain on him for the express purpose of punishment, and must take care that it be sufficiently severe.
>
> (Ibid.)

Those artificial penalties are strictly separable from anybody's mere dislike of the other-regarding conduct per se. Their rationale is the prevention of grievous harm to others without their consent, which is something other than mere dislike and the natural penalties which flow from it.

BEYOND MORALITY (IV.6)

Mill is careful to highlight his view that 'self-regarding faults ... are not properly immoralities, and to whatever pitch they may be carried, do not constitute wickedness' (ibid., 279 (IV.6)).[3] Such faults by themselves do not cause non-consensual harm to other people. We may have self-regarding duties to correct such faults but the duties are

> not socially obligatory, unless circumstances render them at the same time duties to others. The term duty to oneself, when it means anything more than prudence, means self-respect or self-development; and for none of these is any one accountable to his fellow creatures.
>
> (1859c, 279 (IV.6))

But certain *other-regarding* faults *are* properly immoralities *because* they grievously harm other persons against their wishes. Immoral acts include

> encroachment on [the] rights [of other persons]; infliction on them of any loss or damage not justified by [the agent's] own rights; falsehood or duplicity in dealing with them; unfair or ungenerous use of advantages over them; even selfish abstinence from defending them against injury.
>
> (Ibid.)

'And not only these acts, but the dispositions which lead to them, are properly immoral' (ibid.). Immoral dispositions include cruelty, malice, envy, dishonesty, love of domineering, habitual egotism, vain enjoyment of others' misfortunes and so on: 'these are moral vices, and constitute a bad and odious moral character' (ibid.). Society legitimately has jurisdiction over morality thus understood, and should impartially interfere with immoral conduct as a means of promoting each person's permanent interests. But society has no legitimate authority over self-regarding matters.

THE MEANING OF HARM

It seems quite clear that Mill believes there are truly self-regarding actions, 'properly' beyond morality, which do not affect other people in the sense of harming their interests, or do so only with their genuine consent and participation. Such actions, he admits, can and should affect others' feelings. Others may feel intense dislike, for example, and thus seek to avoid the agent. But mere dislike does not amount to harm, and the natural penalties which flow from dislike do not amount to non-consensual harm for anybody.

Since self-regarding actions may be disliked by others whose interests are not harmed, Mill apparently excludes mere dislike from his notion of harm. As I have already indicated, harm is something other than mere dislike, namely, 'perceptible damage'. It may appear in myriad forms, including physical injury (not excepting death), forcible confinement, financial loss, damage to reputation, broken promises (contractual or otherwise) and so on.

A self-regarding action does not directly cause any form of perceptible damage to others, or, if it does, only with their genuine consent and participation. By contrast, other-regarding conduct directly causes damage to the interests of others *without their genuine consent and participation*, or carries a reasonable probability of doing so.

An important caveat is that society must not artificially distort this simple notion of harm, by recognizing (in law or custom) rights not to suffer the mere disgust or dislike or subjective pain which anyone may feel at another's purely self-regarding conduct. Violation of such recognized rights would, after all, constitute a type of perceptible damage suffered against the right-holder's wishes (ignoring cases of forfeiture or voluntary waiver). Unfortunately, societies generally have recognized such rights and correlative duties, and have thereby hidden truly self-regarding actions, by transforming them into fake other-regarding actions that cause no non-consensual harm other than to violate the rights in question. Mill's claim is that a civilized society ought never to interfere with purely self-regarding conduct, by recognizing such illiberal rights and duties. Rather, equal rights to absolute liberty of self-regarding conduct ought to be recognized.

The idea of harm, around which the argument of the *Liberty* seems to cohere, is this simple idea of perceptible damage, with the caveat that the perceptible damage must exist independently of any rights and correlative duties recognized by the majority or its representatives. It is worth noticing that Mill actually uses the term 'perceptible hurt' when speaking of self-regarding conduct 'which neither violates any specific duty to the public, nor occasions perceptible hurt to any assignable individual except himself' (ibid., 282 (IV.11)). It may well be wondered why he adds the rider that self-regarding conduct does not violate any duties to the public. As it turns out, there are actions that look as if they are self-regarding because they do not cause any perceptible injury to the interests of others considered as separate individuals, and yet the actions are really wrongful other-regarding actions that cause grievous perceptible damage to the interests of the public at large without the consent of the public or its political representatives. So Mill is being careful to signal that self-regarding actions must not be confused with wrongful other-regarding actions that violate duties to the public. I will return to this important point in the next section and again in Part III.

At the same time, Mill, although he has still not been very clear about this up to now, believes that some other-regarding actions are also 'properly' considered morally permissible according to utility in the largest sense, even though the actions, unlike self-regarding actions, do harm others' interests against their wishes. These other-regarding actions are successful competitive actions, and they are morally permissible because the total non-consensual harms suffered by the losers in a fair competition are outweighed by the total benefits that accrue to society as a result of the competition, at least in the estimation of a fallible majority. Such other-regarding actions do more than affect the feelings of the disappointed competitors; the losers suffer perceptible damage to their interests against their wishes, for example, they lose sales or are even driven into bankruptcy. And yet their competitive losses, although non-consensual, are a kind of harm that should not be seen as wrongful, as long as force or fraud has not been employed to make the competition into an unfair one.

THE SELF-OTHER DISTINCTION: SOME OBJECTIONS ANSWERED (IV.8–12)

Mill certainly recognizes that 'many persons will refuse to admit' the distinction he wants to draw between self-regarding and other-regarding conduct (ibid., 280 (IV.8)). He identifies three general objections. First, critics will object that 'no person is an entirely isolated being' (ibid.). By harming himself, he may harm his dependents and creditors. Moreover, he may become incapable of rendering the customary level of help to others, and eventually depend entirely on their charity for his subsistence.

Second, the individual's self-injurious conduct will be said to set a bad example to others. Thus, he 'ought to be compelled to control himself, for the sake of those whom the sight or knowledge of his conduct might corrupt or mislead' (ibid.).

Third, even supposing for the sake of argument that 'the consequences of misconduct could be confined to the vicious or thoughtless individual', critics will still object that society should interfere for the same reasons, admittedly dispositive, in the case of children or mental defectives:

> There is no question here (it may be said) about restricting individuality, or impeding the trial of new and original experiments in living. The only things it is sought to prevent are things which [are known] ... not to be useful or suitable to any person's individuality. There must be some length of time and amount of experience, after which a moral or prudential truth may be regarded as established; and it is merely desired to prevent generation after generation from falling over the same precipice which has been fatal to their predecessors.
>
> (Ibid., 281 (IV.9))

He takes these three objections seriously but insists that they are not fatal to his doctrine.

NO PERSON IS ENTIRELY ISOLATED (IV.10–11)

Concerning the first objection, he begins by saying that if a person's self-injurious conduct causes him at the same time 'to violate a distinct and assignable obligation to any other person or persons, the case is taken out of the self-regarding class, and becomes amenable to moral disapprobation in the proper sense of the term' (ibid., 281 (IV.10)). Thus, if self-harm is inseparable from violation of some other person's rights, or from violation of the agent's own duty to pay his taxes or serve as a public official, then the misconduct is properly identified as *other-regarding* misconduct – indeed, unjust action – properly subject to legal and moral interference. Mill gives some illustrations, including the man whose extravagant personal consumption leads him to violate his creditors' rights; and the soldier or policeman whose drunkenness prevents him from performing the duties which society has a right to expect from him (ibid., 281–82 (IV.10)).

Moreover, he says, self-injurious conduct is also properly seen as other-regarding misconduct – more specifically, uncharitable action – if the self-injury is inseparable from a failure to observe the customary level of beneficence towards others: 'Whoever fails in the consideration generally due to the interests and feelings of others, not being compelled by some more imperative duty, or justified by allowable self-preference, is a subject of moral [but not legal] disapprobation for that failure' (ibid., 281 (IV.10)). If a cocaine addict harms others through his extraordinary unkindness in situations where his assistance is reasonably expected under existing customs, for example, then 'he deserves reproach' for his failure to give due consideration, 'but not for the cause of it, nor for the errors, merely personal to himself, which may have remotely led to it' (ibid.).

Thus, where circumstances conjoin self-regarding faults to unjust or uncharitable other-regarding conduct that wrongfully damages the interests of others (so that the conduct is not properly seen as self-regarding), the person is legitimately punished by law or by opinion for his breach of duty:

> Whenever, in short, there is a definite damage, or a definite risk of damage, either to an individual or to the public, the case is taken out of the province of liberty, and placed in that of morality or law.
> (Ibid., 282 (IV.10))

But the province of liberty is not thereby rendered empty because, in many situations, self-regarding faults remain separable from other-regarding misconduct. The point is that the extravagant man who nevertheless is able to pay his debts and taxes, the public servant who is drunk only while off duty and the cocaine addict who is as kind and helpful to others as they may reasonably expect under prevailing social conventions, should remain perfectly free from legal or social penalties.

The question still arises, however, whether those putatively self-regarding actions are, like expression, really other-regarding ones which, when violations of others' rights and other important interests are absent, may be treated as if they were self-regarding because coercion is generally inexpedient. The answer, it seems, is that these actions are not like the case of expression. Expression of an opinion always carries a risk of non-consensual harm to others, by depriving them of listeners for their competing opinions, or damaging their reputations, or misleading them, and so on. It remains other-regarding even outside the special situations where its suppression is held to be expedient. But drinking on duty, or drinking with a known tendency to become violent toward others when drunk, is other-regarding whereas drinking with other consenting adults, of the usual tendencies, on a free evening seems genuinely self-regarding. Unlike expression, consuming alcohol does not pose any risk of non-consensual harm to others beyond their mere dislike. To be removed from the self-regarding class, drinking, it seems, must be conjoined with some additional factor from which the drinking itself is logically separable. The drinker must have some pre-existing tendency to harm others without their consent, for example, or a tendency to ignore his recognized duties of employment, marriage, loan repayment and so on. But such tendencies are not necessarily associated with drinking.

What about the damage to society occasioned when self-indulgent behaviour eventually leads to a complete dependence on the taxpayer? In Mill's view, that 'merely contingent, or, as it may be called, constructive injury which a person causes to society ... is one which society can afford to bear, for the sake of the greater good of human freedom' (ibid., 282 (IV.11)). He argues that society has better means than coercion to influence its members to be prudent and temperate workers:

> Armed not only with all the powers of education, but with the ascendency which the authority of a received opinion always exercises over the minds who are least fitted to judge for themselves; and aided by the natural penalties which cannot be prevented from falling on those who incur the distaste or the contempt of those who know them; let not society pretend that it needs, besides all this, the power to issue commands and enforce obedience in the personal concerns of individuals.
> (Ibid.)

He apparently assumes that, in general, an ordinary person, capable of 'being acted on by rational consideration of distant motives', will not voluntarily become dependent on others for his subsistence (ibid.). If society fails to educate 'any considerable number of its members' up to this threshold level of rationality, or if it creates foolish social programs that give able-bodied and able-minded people strong incentives to become dependent on the state or on charity for their subsistence, then it has only 'itself to blame for the consequences' (ibid.).

That assumption is also implicit in his responses to the other two objections.

BAD EXAMPLES (IV.11)

Mill admits that 'a bad example may have a pernicious effect, especially the example of doing wrong to others with impunity to the wrong-doer' (ibid., 283 (IV.11)). But he emphasizes that 'we are now speaking of conduct which, while it does no wrong to others, is supposed to do great harm to the agent himself' (ibid.). Such self-regarding misconduct must generally set 'a more salutary than hurtful' example to other people capable of self-improvement (ibid.). For 'if [the example] displays the misconduct, it displays also the painful or degrading consequences which, if the conduct is justly censured, must be supposed to be in all or most cases attendant on it' (ibid.).

PATERNALISM (IV.12)

As for the third objection, Mill argues in effect that the majority is far more likely than the individual to be wrong about what is useful or suitable to him in his self-regarding concerns. The lessons drawn from experience by the majority are more likely to be right when it comes to other-regarding concerns:

> On questions of social morality, of duty to others, the opinion of the public, that is, of an overruling majority, though often wrong, is likely to be still oftener right; because on such questions they are only required to judge of their own interests; of the manner in which some mode of conduct, if allowed to be practised, would affect themselves.
> (Ibid., 283 (IV.12))

In short, majoritarian laws and customs of other-regarding conduct are more likely than not to be generally expedient because most adults can be expected to make reasonable judgments about whether this or that sort of non-consensual damage to their own interests ought to be permitted. But majoritarian rules of self-regarding conduct are 'quite as likely' to be generally inexpedient because 'in these cases public opinion means, at the best, some people's opinion of what is good or bad for *other* people' (ibid., emphasis added).

Interference with self-regarding conduct *denies* the assumption that most adults capable of self-improvement can be expected to make reasonable judgments about which harms to accept to their own interests. Since he wants to maintain that key assumption, he argues that society should never interfere with liberty and individuality in purely self-regarding matters.

'GROSS USURPATIONS UPON THE LIBERTY OF PRIVATE LIFE' (IV.13–21)

Mill concludes the chapter with several examples of the majority's tendency to encroach on individual spontaneity in self-regarding concerns. He says he is 'not writing an essay on the aberrations of existing moral feeling' (ibid., 284 (IV.13)). But he wants to show that his principle of self-regarding liberty 'is of serious and practical moment', as opposed to 'a barrier against imaginary evils' (ibid.).

The public's tendency to translate its mere likes and dislikes into rules of self-regarding conduct, rules which are improperly called moral rules at all because they are not designed to prevent non-consensual harm to others, is easy to illustrate: 'one of the most universal of all human propensities ... [is] to extend the bounds of what may be called moral police' (ibid.). After considering some cases of religious intolerance which, though not actually found in English-speaking societies at the time, would be unobjectionable if the majority has authority to regulate self-regarding conduct, he discusses three cases drawn from those societies, presumably to drive home the point that no 'superior excellence' (ibid., 274 (III.18)) inheres in English-speaking majorities, which keeps them from committing 'gross usurpations upon the liberty of private life' (287 (IV.18)).

His three examples are: legal prohibition (except for medical purposes) of 'fermented drinks' in New Brunswick and 'nearly half the United States' (the so-called Maine laws, after the state which first enacted prohibition in 1851), which the United Kingdom Alliance was pressing to have similarly enacted in the United Kingdom (despite the beginnings of repeal throughout North America) when he was writing (ibid., 287–88 (IV.19)); Sabbatarian legislation, re-enacted in Britain in 1850 to forbid the greater part of work and public amusements on Sundays (288–89 (IV.20)); and the relentless persecution of Mormonism, chiefly on account of 'its sanction of polygamy', despite the attempt of the Mormons to voluntarily remove themselves from the larger American society by relocating during the 1840s to the remote Utah Territory (ibid., 290–91 (IV.21)).

As these cases make clear, he has returned to his earlier theme of rising religious intolerance. All of them illustrate a revivified religious bigotry put into practice by (so-called) Christian majorities in the English-speaking societies. Needless to add, similar examples can still be drawn from the practices of English-speaking countries in our own time. Laws prohibiting the sale and possession of drugs, Sabbatarian legislation, and legal bans on polygamy are all found in the United States today, for example, among many other rules meddling with self-regarding conduct.

During the course of his discussion, he makes some remarks relating to the application of his doctrine. Although he presents a more sustained treatment of problems of application in his final chapter, it seems useful to highlight those remarks now, to facilitate study of the three cases.

CONSUMPTION VERSUS TRADING (IV.19)

When discussing temperance laws, Mill suggests that 'the act of drinking fermented liquors' is self-regarding, whereas 'selling fermented liquors ... is trading, and trading is a social act' (ibid., 288 (IV.19)). This distinction between consumption and 'trading' or marketing is of great importance in understanding his doctrine. The individual ought to be given complete liberty, by right, to consume alcohol, or any other product that can be used without causing non-consensual perceptible damage to the interests of others, in accord with his own judgment and desires. Other people may intensely dislike his consumption activities, but mere dislike is not harm. Marketing those same products, however, is *not* self-regarding conduct, and thus is *not* covered by his maxim of self-regarding liberty. Market competitors can cause each other unwanted financial loss through their selling activities. Society thus has legitimate authority to regulate the market, in his view, even if general expediency usually recommends a policy of laissez-faire rather than legal or social coercive interference. But society's regulation of the sellers can never legitimately amount to outright prohibition of the sale of products with self-regarding uses. For prohibition would interfere with the right of consumers to freely buy and use such products.

PERSONAL LIFESTYLE VERSUS MARKETING OF LABOUR (IV.20)

A similar distinction is at work in his discussion of Sabbatarian legislation. '[S]elf-chosen occupations' are self-regarding activities, he suggests, whereas contractual employer–employee relationships are other-regarding because they involve the selling of labour on the market. The individual ought to have absolute liberty to employ himself in whatever productive activities he pleases short of injury to others, assuming he has a legal right or permission to use any natural resources he proposes to use. Others may dislike what he does. But they can avoid him and his products, without directly causing non-consensual harm to anybody.

In contrast, self-interested behaviour by some workers in the labour market can directly affect other workers against their wishes. By breaking a customary agreement not to work on one day of the week, for example, some workers can increase their own wages while tending to depress the weekly wage rate for others: 'The operatives are perfectly right in thinking that if all worked on Sunday, seven days' work would have to be given for six days' wages' (ibid., 289 (IV.20)).[4] Society thus has legitimate authority to regulate the labour market by enforcing a day of leisure. But Mill goes on to provide strong arguments for concluding that Sabbatarian legislation, or, more generally, legislation forcing *all* workers to take the *same* day off, is not generally expedient. 'The only ground, therefore, on which restrictions on Sunday amusements can be defended, must be that they are religiously wrong; a motive of legislation which can never be too earnestly protested against' (1859c, 289 (IV.20)).

CONTRACTS-IN-PERPETUITY (IV.21)

When discussing the Mormons, he says, despite his general conclusion that they should be left alone under the circumstances, that the institution of polygamy 'is a direct infraction' of his self-regarding liberty principle (ibid., 290 (IV.21)). The problem, it seems, is that any contract-in-perpetuity, including a marriage contract, polygamous or otherwise, is incompatible with the moral right of the individual to do as she pleases in her self-regarding affairs. This can be inferred from his discussion of slavery contracts in the next chapter (ibid., 299–300 (V.11)). He also makes a general case against contracts-in-perpetuity elsewhere (Mill 1870; 1871a, 953–54).

Given that they can never be revoked by one of the parties without the consent of the other(s), such contracts (including international treaties) bind the parties together in a permanent relationship, despite the possibility of unforeseen changes of circumstances leading to subsequent changes of mind not shared by all. Agreements of this sort are generally an unreasonable restriction on individual liberty (or, by analogy, a country's liberty), he argues, and thus on self-development (or national development):

> if [the law] ever does sanction them, it should take every possible security for their being contracted with foresight and deliberation; and in compensation for not permitting the parties themselves to revoke their engagement, should grant them a release from it, on a sufficient case being made out before an impartial authority.
>
> (1871a, 954)

'These considerations are eminently applicable to marriage', he goes on to emphasize as of 1852 (just after his own marriage had taken place), 'the most important of all cases of engagement for life' (ibid.). A marriage in which there is no possibility of divorce without unanimous consent of the parties is not compatible with the rights of the individual to self-regarding liberty and individuality.

Even so, he recognizes that Mormon contracts of polygamous marriage, like other marriage contracts-in-perpetuity, are made by willing participants in the given culture. Thus, there is no ground, aside from religious intolerance, for coercively interfering with the Mormon community on this score, given that the community is not aggressive toward others, grants complete freedom of exit to its dissatisfied members and is not otherwise roiled by internal dissensions in which appeals for external intervention are made by those whose liberty is being repressed:

> So long as the sufferers by the bad law do not invoke assistance from other communities, I cannot admit that persons entirely unconnected with them ought to step in and require that a condition of things with which all who are directly interested appear to be satisfied, should be put an end to because it is a scandal to persons some thousands of miles distant, who have no part or concern in it.
>
> (1859c, 291 (IV.21))

FOREIGN INTERVENTION (IV.21)

Elsewhere, in *Representative Government* (1861a, 546–77) and 'A Few Words on Non-intervention' (1859a, 118–24), Mill clarifies the conditions under which he thinks intervention by one community in the domestic affairs of another is justified. Among other things, he says that one country can rightfully intervene in the affairs of another, to counter the previous intervention of a third party determined to support the side of despotism against that of free institutions (including political democracy and market capitalism): 'Intervention to enforce non-intervention is always right, always moral, if not always prudent' (1859a, 123). If, in the context of a civil war, a foreign despot offers financial or military support to an oppressive government, for example, the friends of liberty have a moral right to interfere similarly on the side of domestic rebels fighting for their freedom, with some prospect for success were it not for the initial foreign interference. This includes a civil war between different ethnic groups in the same state, of course, one of which is fighting the other for national liberation and its own free institutions.

By analogy, one individual, including a government official, is permitted to intervene in the self-regarding affairs of a second individual to prevent third parties from coercively interfering with the second individual's self-regarding choices.

SUGGESTIONS FOR FURTHER READING

Piers Norris Turner, in '"Harm" and Mill's Harm Principle', *Ethics* 124 (2014): 299–326, has challenged my argument that, for Mill, harm means some form of 'perceptible damage' and excludes mere dislike. In Turner's view, mere dislike is a form of non-consensual harm and, so, actions that cause others to feel dislike are other-regarding actions rather than self-regarding ones. As I have argued in response, however, that turns Mill into an illiberal utilitarian and cannot be squared with the text of the *Liberty*. See Jonathan Riley, 'Is Mill an Illiberal Utilitarian?', *Ethics*, forthcoming.

It remains an interesting question whether Mill might have seen mere dislike as a form of *consensual* harm that the individual inflicts on himself. It may seem odd to say that people consent to their own dislikes. Nevertheless, we do hold people responsible for their desires and aversions on the assumption that the individual can alter his likes and dislikes if he wishes. Mill stresses in the *Logic* and the *Examination of Sir William Hamilton's Philosophy* that we are born with a power of will that can be used and developed into a strong force for picking out the desires and aversions we wish to maintain and to be held responsible for. So, to the extent that an individual does not extinguish given likes and dislikes, he might be said to tacitly consent to them. If mere dislike is seen as consensual harm, then my reading of Mill's doctrine of liberty goes through without any need to distinguish between harm and mere dislike. For, in that case, harm would include mere dislike but, since it is consensual harm, self-regarding actions could give rise to it in other people in accordance with the definition of self-regarding conduct. Mill gives no sign of treating mere dislike as consensual harm but, if he did, that might help to explain why he appears so cavalier about the meaning of harm. Harm could be seen as any negative consequence including pain or dislike, and the crucial distinction would be between consensual and non-consensual harm. Still, I think it is a stretch to classify mere dislike as consensual harm that the individual chooses to inflict on himself. The individual's desires and aversions are shaped in part by cultural factors beyond his control, at least until he has developed a powerful will that is strong enough to override those external factors. So I prefer to distinguish mere dislike from harm as perceptible damage.

As a prelude to identifying and analysing current examples of 'gross usurpations upon the liberty of private life', it is useful to read more about the three examples discussed by Mill. There is a large literature on nineteenth-century temperance crusades in general, and the Maine laws in particular. See e.g. Neal Dow, *The Reminiscences of Neal Dow: Recollections of Eighty Years* (Portland, ME: Evening Express Publishing Co., 1898); J.K. Chapman, 'The Mid-Nineteenth-Century Temperance Movement in New Brunswick and Maine', *Canadian Historical Review* 35 (1954): 43–60; J.S. Blocker, *American Temperance Movements: Cycles of Reform* (Boston: Twayne, 1989); J. Noel, *Canada Dry: Temperance Crusades before Confederation* (Toronto: University of Toronto Press, 1995); L.L. Shiman, *Crusade against Drink in Victorian England* (New York: St Martin's Press, 1988); and I.R. Tyrrell, *Sobering Up: From Temperance to Prohibition in Ante-bellum America, 1800–1860* (Westport, CT: Greenwood Press, 1979), 252–89.

For the career of the United Kingdom Alliance, see Brian Harrison, *Drink and the Victorians: The Temperance Question in England 1815–72* (Pittsburgh: University of Pittsburgh Press, 1971); and A.E. Dingle, *The Campaign for Prohibition in Victorian England: The United Kingdom Alliance, 1872–95* (New Brunswick, NJ: Rutgers University Press, 1980).

The history of Sabbatarian legislation is analysed by D.N. Laband and D.H. Heinbuch, *Blue Laws: The History, Economics, and Politics of Sunday Closing Laws* (Amherst: Lexington Books, 1987).

The Mormons are of special interest, as a Christian sect founded as recently as 1830, by Joseph Smith, who led his followers from New York to settle initially around Nauvoo, Illinois. Quickly driven into Missouri, they faced more harassment and violence there, and eventually relocated to Utah.

Their trials were far from over when Mill wrote. During the 'Mormon Wars' of 1857–58, President James Buchanan sent federal troops to occupy the Utah Territory. By 1862, in the midst of the larger Civil War, the Republican majority in Congress had enacted anti-bigamy legislation. Although the law was largely ignored until the 1879 *Reynolds* decision of the Supreme Court sanctioned federal enforcement, the US government conducted an intense campaign of persecution against the Mormons thereafter, with popular majority support. Mormons were repeatedly prosecuted for bigamy (a felony) and 'cohabitation' (an ambiguous misdemeanour), they were effectively stripped of the franchise (under the power of Congress to regulate the territories) and, finally, their church was driven into bankruptcy, with the Court upholding federal seizure of its assets in an infamous 1890 decision, *Church of Jesus Christ of Latter-Day Saints v. US*. Shortly after the decision, church leaders issued a manifesto which abandoned polygamy as an article of the official Mormon faith, although polygamy continues to be practised even today by scattered 'fundamentalists'. By 1893, Mormon polygamists were given a general amnesty by presidential proclamation. In 1896, Congress granted Utah admission into the union as a state. Further discussion can be found in Leonard J. Arrington and Davis Bitton, *The Mormon Experience: A History of the Latter-Day Saints*, 2nd edn (Champaign: University of Illinois Press, 1992); D. Michael Quinn, *Early Mormonism and the Magic World View*, 2nd edn (Salt Lake City: Signature Books, 1998); Sarah B. Gordon, *The Mormon Question: Polygamy and Constitutional Conflict in Nineteenth-Century America* (Chapel Hill: University of North Carolina Press, 2002); Ronald W. Walker, Richard E. Turley Jr and Glen M. Leonard, *Massacre at Mountain Meadows* (New York: Oxford University Press, 2008); E.L. Lyman, *Political Deliverance: The Mormon Quest for Utah Statehood* (Champaign: University of Illinois Press, 1986); Richard L. Jensen and Malcolm R. Thorp (eds), *Mormons in Early Victorian Britain* (Salt Lake City: University of Utah Press, 1990); Richard S. Van Wagoner, *Mormon Polygamy: A History*, 2nd edn (Salt Lake City: Signature Books, 1989); and Sanjiv Bhattacharya, *Secrets and Wives: The Hidden World of Mormon Polygamy* (Berkeley: Soft Skull Press, 2011).

For some horrific stories of criminal abuse relating to the forced marriage of teenage girls to much-older 'fundamentalist' polygamists who see themselves as genuine Mormons, see e.g. Carolyn Jessop, with Laura Palmer, *Escape* (New York: Broadway Books, 2007); and Rebecca Musser, with M. Bridget Cook, *The Witness Wore Red: The 19th Wife Who Brought Polygamous Cult Leaders to Justice* (New York: Grand Central, 2013). The criminal activities of these cult leaders have no necessary connection to the institution of genuine consensual polygamy, of course, just as similar crimes committed by any other extremists have no essential link to the institution of monogamous marriage contracts.

For a discussion of some general lessons for liberalism to be drawn from Mill's approach to the Mormons, see C.L. Ten, 'Mill's Place in Liberalism', *Political Science Reviewer* 24 (1995): 179–204, esp. 185–87. Some commentators are highly critical of Mill's approach. See e.g. Richard Posner, '*On Liberty*: A Revaluation', in David Bromwich and George Kateb (eds), *On Liberty: John Stuart Mill* (New Haven: Yale University Press, 2003), 197–207; and Wendy Donner, 'Autonomy, Individuality, and Community: The Case of Mormon Polygamy', in Wendy Donner and Richard Fumerton, *Mill* (Malden, MA: Wiley-Blackwell, 2009), 68–74. I take up the criticisms of Posner and Donner in Chapter 10 below.

For a helpful commentary on Mill's still-influential approach to foreign intervention, see Georgios E. Varouxakis, *Liberty Abroad: J.S. Mill on International Relations* (Cambridge: Cambridge University Press, 2013).

NOTES

1 Mill certainly does not advocate indifference to self-regarding vices, as Hart emphasizes (1963, 76–77). But natural penalties are not the same thing as deliberate moral blame or punishment. Social stigma, the intentional display in public of disapproval, does not legitimately extend to self-regarding conduct because such conduct is harmless to others unless they consent.

2 For Hume's distinction between natural and artificial virtues and vices, see Hume 1978, 294–98, 474–75, 477–621; and Hume 1975, 169–284, 303–11.

3 Recall his related claim that thoughts and opinions are not properly termed immoral (Mill 1859c, 234 (II.11)).
4 This situation, where the individual has an incentive to defect from an agreement under which everyone (including himself) would be better off, is a classic example of what is sometimes called the 'Prisoners' Dilemma' in the theory of games.

6

APPLICATIONS (CHAPTER V, PARAS. 1–23)

MILL'S DOCTRINE AND ITS APPLICATION (V.1–2)

It has emerged that the principle of liberty is directed at opinions and truly self-regarding actions, which do not directly cause any perceptible damage to the interests of others against their wishes. Others may intensely dislike the self-regarding conduct. But mere dislike, without any evidence of perceptible damage, does not constitute harm. Others may *choose* to avoid the agent as a result of their dislike, thereby imposing possibly severe natural penalties on him and even themselves. But any loss which others may suffer because of their decision to avoid the agent is not suffered against *their* wishes. And any perceptible damage which the agent may suffer by persisting in his displeasing self-regarding conduct is not suffered against *his* wishes.

Of course, the self-regarding liberty maxim has as its corollary what may be termed the social authority principle. The authority principle says that society has legitimate power to consider framing and enforcing moral rules of social or other-regarding conduct.

The individual has no moral right to choose as he pleases with respect to other-regarding actions, which do directly cause non-consensual perceptible damage to the interests of others, or pose a credible risk of doing so. Rather, he ought to obey the general moral customs and laws established by the majority to regulate other-regarding conduct, and may justifiably be forced to obey if necessary.

When introducing the concluding chapter, Mill emphasizes that he is defending these 'two maxims', the self-regarding liberty maxim and its logical complement. After referring to 'the two maxims which together form the entire doctrine of this Essay', he restates the maxims:

> The maxims are, first, that the individual is not accountable to society for his [self-regarding] actions ... Advice, instruction, persuasion, and avoidance by other people if thought necessary by them for their own good, are the only measures by which society can justifiably express its dislike or disapprobation of his conduct. Secondly, that for [other regarding] actions ... the individual is accountable, and may be subjected to social or to legal punishment, if society is of opinion that the one or the other is requisite for its protection.
>
> (1859c, 292 (V.2))

Strictly speaking, the two maxims are not identical to the 'one very simple' harm principle but they are both compatible with it. The liberty maxim says that society ought not to be concerned to prevent *consensual* harm to others whereas the social authority maxim says that society ought to consider coercion to prevent *non-consensual* harm to others. Even where consideration of coercion is legitimate, however, society may properly decide not to enforce moral or legal rules because utility in the largest sense recommends against their enforcement. Mill's subsequent discussion is intended to clear up remaining ambiguities surrounding his doctrine, and to illustrate how the maxims can be consistently applied.

Many situations arise in practice, he suggests, where it is not immediately clear which of the maxims applies. He offers 'specimens of application' to help us learn how to go about arriving at reasonable practical conclusions in these sorts of situations. The sample cases are chosen, he says, with a view 'to assist the judgment in holding the balance between [the two maxims], in the cases where it appears doubtful which of them is applicable to the case' (ibid., 292 (V.1)). As it turns out, he argues that a reasonable balance can invariably be struck, as we would expect in light of his comments in Chapter II about the decisiveness of 'a completely informed mind' (ibid., 245 (II.23)). Even in hard cases where he himself cannot make up his own mind between conflicting answers, both of which appear reasonable, he suggests that further debate and discussion among the members of a given society would lead to a contextual resolution of the conflict.

It is important to emphasize at the outset that there is no doubt in any of these cases about the meaning of self-regarding acts, or about the logical distinction between self-regarding and social or other-regarding spheres upon which the doctrine of the essay depends. Rather, any doubts are inherent in the practical situation, and they generally vanish once certain reasonable distinctions are made to deal with the situation. In short, further reflection usually reveals what was not immediately apparent, namely, which of the two maxims applies, or, to be more precise, whether the conditions are satisfied for application of the self-regarding liberty maxim or for the social authority principle. Even where doubts are expressed by Mill himself about what to do, the integrity of the principle of self-regarding liberty is not compromised.

HARM TO OTHERS NOT SUFFICIENT FOR COERCION (V.3)

He begins by reminding us that, according to his 'one very simple principle' (ibid., 223 (I.9)), the prevention of harm to others is necessary but not sufficient for coercive interference: 'it must by no means be supposed, because damage, or probability of damage, to the interests of others, can alone justify the interference of society, that therefore it always does justify such interference' (ibid., 292 (V.3)). The maxim of self-regarding liberty itself tells us that coercion is never justified to prevent genuine consensual harm to others. Moreover, even if the harm is non-consensual, there are many situations in which coercion should not be employed to prevent it: 'In many cases, an individual, in pursuing a legitimate object, necessarily and therefore legitimately causes pain or loss to others, or intercepts a good which they had a reasonable hope of obtaining' (ibid.).

Freedom from coercion should be granted in 'many cases' not because the actions are self-regarding actions that the individual has a moral right to perform as he pleases, but because social control of the actions, though it can be legitimately considered because the actions are other-regarding, is commonly admitted to be generally inexpedient. The examples Mill gives are of fair competitions:

> Whoever succeeds in an overcrowded profession, or in a competitive examination; whoever is preferred to another in any contest for an object which both desire, reaps benefit from the loss of others, from their wasted exertion and their disappointment. But it is, by common admission, better for the general interest of mankind, that persons should pursue their objects undeterred by this sort of consequences.
> (Ibid., 292–93 (V.3))

There is no denying that the successful agent directly causes his unsuccessful competitors to suffer non-consensual perceptible damage to their interests, to wit, 'wasted exertion' and the loss of valuable things which they had 'a reasonable hope of obtaining'. Nevertheless, coercion for the purpose of preventing such non-consensual harms would, 'by common admission', result in even more damage to the interests of the members of society than the alternative of laissez-faire. In other words, the harms suffered by losing competitors are of a less weighty kind, which does not justify enforcement of social rules:

> society admits no right to immunity from *this kind* of suffering; and feels called on to interfere, only when means of success have been employed which it is contrary to the general interest to permit – namely, fraud or treachery, and force.
>
> (Ibid., 293 (V.3), emphasis added)

At least two implications must be kept in mind if Mill's doctrine is to be consistently applied 'with any prospect of advantage' (ibid., 292 (V.1)).

THE EXPEDIENT SCOPE OF INDIVIDUAL LIBERTY

First, the self-regarding liberty principle is not intended to determine the expedient scope of negative liberty or freedom from coercion. The liberty maxim says that each individual has a moral right to choose as he pleases among those of his actions which do not directly cause any damage to others' interests, or, if they do cause such harm, only with the genuine consent and participation of those other people. The purely self-regarding sphere, to which the maxim applies, is a *minimum* domain of negative liberty protected by right, the violation of which ought to be considered an injustice in any civil society. In general, the expedient field of negative liberty will include more than that inviolable minimum.

What *additional* domain is called for, beyond the self-regarding minimum, is not the subject of the liberty principle. Rather, it falls within the legitimate jurisdiction of society, recognizing that majoritarian notions of general expediency may well vary across social contexts. In this regard, the social authority maxim, which applies only to other-regarding acts, does not imply that society ought invariably to exercise its legitimate power to coerce the individual to prevent non-consensual harm to others. Negative liberty with respect to other-regarding actions is not necessarily illegitimate. Rather, a policy of laissez-faire is commonly held to be generally expedient in many cases. Enforcement of rules of other-regarding conduct is viewed as inexpedient in such cases,

> either because it is a kind of case in which [the individual] is on the whole likely to act better, when left to his own discretion ... or because the attempt to exercise control would produce other evils, greater than those which it would prevent.
>
> (Ibid., 225 (I.11))

In short, absence of harm to others, while sufficient, is not necessary for freedom from coercion to be generally expedient. Thus, the expedient scope of negative liberty may extend beyond the ambit of the self-regarding liberty principle, which tells us where the individual has an inviolable moral right to choose as he pleases. Choosing as one wishes, or doing as one likes, is a form of positive liberty. As it turns out, when he says that the self-regarding sphere is the appropriate region of human liberty, Mill is saying that this is the region where the individual ought to choose whatever he wishes. Positive liberty in this sense is never appropriate in the other-regarding sphere.

THE EXPEDIENT REALM OF PRIVATE ACTION

A second implication is that, for analogous reasons, the expedient domain of private action will extend beyond the purely self-regarding sphere, if by private action we mean any action (including competitive market behaviour) that individuals are expediently left alone to perform, free from coercive interference by others (including government officials). Some private actions in this sense will be other-regarding. Indeed, some will be immoral actions which cannot be expediently prevented through external sanctions but which the individual ought not to perform – he ought to develop a strong conscience to prevent himself from doing wrong. Thus, the expedient realm of negative freedom should not be conflated with the self-regarding sphere, where the individual has a moral right to choose as he wishes (a form of positive freedom).

Note that what is then called 'private' action may take place 'in public', as many market transactions do. This alerts us to the vagaries of any private–public distinction, and should make us suitably cautious when using these terms.[1] But, more importantly, it tells us that, for Mill, the mere performance of an action 'in public' cannot be sufficient to justify coercive interference with that action. At the same time, it leaves open the possibility that acts which are self-regarding when performed 'in private', in the sense of behind closed doors, may become other-regarding when performed 'in public'. Sex 'in public' between consenting adults might perhaps be shown to pose some sort of perceptible damage to others against their wishes, for example, so that consensual sex in that case loses its otherwise purely self-regarding character (see 1859c, V.7). Yet society might nevertheless properly view coercion against sex in public as inexpedient in some locations such as country fields or woods, so that it would continue to be 'private' in the sense of being expediently left free from coercive interference in those situations.

Indeed, if the locations are so remote that there is no chance that anyone else is around, sex in public is brought back within the class of self-regarding actions.

THE LIBERTY PRINCIPLE DISTINGUISHED FROM LAISSEZ-FAIRE (V.4)

We can now make sense of Mill's claim that his maxim of self-regarding liberty must not be conflated with the economic doctrine of laissez-faire: 'the principle of individual liberty is not involved in the doctrine of free trade' (ibid., 293 (V.4)). Market sales are *not* self-regarding acts, and thus do *not* fall within the ambit of his liberty maxim. Rather,

> trade is a social act. Whoever undertakes to sell any description of goods to the public, does what affects the interest of other persons, and of society in general; and thus his conduct, in principle, *comes within the jurisdiction of society.*
>
> (Ibid., emphasis added)

Selling goods to others is an other-regarding act within the ambit of the social authority maxim. Society can legitimately consider imposing rules of exchange and production, yet, 'by common admission', laissez-faire is often (though not always) more expedient than social regulation:

> [I]t is now recognised, though not till after a long struggle, that both the cheapness and the good quality of commodities are most effectually provided for by leaving the producers and sellers perfectly free, under the sole check of equal freedom to the buyers for supplying themselves elsewhere. This is the so-called doctrine of free trade, which rests on grounds different from, though equally solid with, the principle of individual liberty asserted in this essay.
>
> (Ibid.)

Social control of exchange and production is not illegitimate in principle: 'the restraints in question affect only that part of conduct which society is competent to restrain' (ibid.). But it is 'now recognised' that such control is often inexpedient – it causes more non-consensual harm than it prevents. The restraints directly harm efficient producers and suppliers without their consent, by preventing them from transacting on the terms they wish; taxpayers, who must bear enforcement costs; and consumers, who face higher prices and lower quality goods as compared with laissez-faire. Thus, the restraints 'are wrong solely because they do not really produce the results which it is desired to produce by them' (ibid.).

Mill argues in his *Political Economy* that there are various 'large exceptions' to the laissez-faire doctrine (1871a, 936–71). But 'most of the questions which arise respecting the limits of that doctrine' also have nothing to do with his liberty maxim (1859c, 293 (V.4)). '[H]ow far sanitary precautions, or arrangements to protect workpeople employed in dangerous occupations, should be enforced on employers', for example, are questions of justice and general expediency relating to other-regarding conduct (ibid.).

Yet 'there are questions relating to interference with trade, which are essentially questions of liberty' (ibid.). The self-regarding liberty maxim is involved in 'all cases ... where the object of the interference is to make it impossible or difficult to obtain a particular commodity', for example, temperance laws, 'prohibition of the importation of opium' and 'restriction of the sale of poisons' (ibid.). In these cases, society violates the right of the individual to buy or use any products he likes, so long as he doesn't cause any non-consensual harm to other people: 'These interferences are objectionable, not as infringements on the liberty of the producer or seller, but on that of the buyer' (ibid.).

The clear implication is that the liberty principle can be applicable to consumer choices, whereas the laissez-faire doctrine applies to the activities of producers and sellers. It does not follow that all consumption behaviour is purely self-regarding. That claim is highly implausible. Rather, there is some field of consumption activity which can be seen as self-regarding. Mill suggests later in this chapter that the individual should have a right to spend his income as he wishes on any good which can be used in ways that pose no significant risk of non-consensual damage to the interests of other people. Even a product such as poison, which in some uses poses grave danger to others, ought not to be forbidden to consumers, because it also has innocent uses. Still, if a commodity is designed solely to cause injury to others, he allows, its use may be prohibited consistently with the liberty maxim.

Granting all this, there must be more to the story, even though he does not tell it in this place. For even if a product has innocent uses, someone may object that its purchase and consumption by one person can directly injure another against his wishes, by denying that other person the opportunity to use that particular scarce commodity. But the objection is, in general, misplaced. One way to answer it might be to draw a distinction between harm and the denial of goods or benefits which a person had a reasonable hope of obtaining. But such an avenue is closed to Mill, who, after all, admits that the losing competitors for jobs and the like do suffer non-consensual perceptible hurts at the hands of the winners.

A far more persuasive answer is available in any event: the consumption of a product by one person does not, in general, preclude its consumption by others at the same price. Given that a good can be reproduced indefinitely at a competitive cost of production, its use by one individual in no way prevents others from acquiring like goods. Moreover, in reasonably competitive markets characterized by free entry and exit (though not necessarily by large numbers of sellers or buyers at any one time), one person's consumption choices have no perceptible impact on market prices. Current market supply is determined by producers' expectations, at a previous time, of potential market demand. Any person's current consumption cannot affect past producer decisions, but can only help to call forth an adequate market supply at competitive cost in the future.

No doubt there are exceptions. Non-consensual harm to others may be caused by large-scale purchases, which temporarily disrupt competitive market prices, for example, or by the use of irreplaceable objects which are in fixed supply. But these special cases do not alter the fact that many acts of consumption do belong in the self-regarding realm.

It transpires that, according to the liberty principle, the individual ought to be given complete liberty, by right, to consume any product which, first, has self-regarding uses and, second, can be reproduced indefinitely at a competitive cost. But no person has a moral right to produce or sell anything as he wishes. Society has legitimate authority to organize production and exchange as the majority thinks expedient. Should scarce inputs of natural resources, labour and capital be employed to create this type of product or that? Should production and allocation be organized in terms of central planning or decentralized markets? Should market enterprises be organized as socialistic co-operatives or capitalistic corporations? Should these enterprises be left alone to buy their inputs and sell their products on any terms they agree to negotiate without force or fraud, or should government intervene for various reasons to regulate market prices? For Mill, these are all questions of utility in the largest sense, legitimately within the purview of social authority. At the same time, he emphasizes, general expediency is commonly held to dictate a continuing reliance on capitalistic firms and free markets, at least for the foreseeable future. Private ownership of the means of production ought to be conjoined with a general presumption in favour of laissez-faire. (For further discussion and caveats relating to these points, see Riley 1996.)

When applying Mill's doctrine, then, we must not suppose that there is a neat correspondence between the expedient scope of negative individual liberty (or private conduct) and the liberty maxim on the one hand, and between the expedient scope of public coercion and the authority maxim on the other. His support for laissez-faire implies that freedom from coercion for some other-regarding acts is utilitarian, whereas the liberty maxim says the same for all purely self-regarding acts. Indeed, the liberty maxim also says that the self-regarding realm is the rightful realm of positive liberty in the sense of choosing as one pleases.

WHY DRAW THE DISTINCTION?

The question arises whether there is really much point in distinguishing between the liberty maxim and a laissez-faire principle. In both cases, it might be said, the value of individuality or self-development outweighs competing considerations, even if non-consensual harm to others is involved in the one case and not in the other.

Nevertheless, there are crucial differences. The liberty maxim prescribes equal rights to complete liberty of self-regarding actions. Equal rights of this sort can be enjoyed in harmony, since one person's exercise of his right does not directly affect other people against their wishes. The laissez-faire doctrine says, in contrast, that individuals have no moral obligations to each other with respect to some other-regarding activities. Rather, individuals have moral permission (and perhaps legal rights founded on that permission) to compete under certain terms and conditions. But an equal permission to compete is a much weaker moral position than an equal claim to do as one likes. Indeed, it is impossible to guarantee self-interested producers and sellers an equal right to choose as they wish in a competitive scramble for scarce resources. Some competitors can succeed only at the expense of others. Thus, society needs good reasons – the efficient production and allocation of resources, for example – for permitting the individualities of some to flourish at the expense of others under laissez-faire. The exact form of reasoning that justifies the liberty maxim, namely, that it affords an equal opportunity for the cultivation of individuality without non-consensual harm to others, is not available.

THE EXTRAORDINARY CASE OF EXPRESSION

Before considering a second sort of practical insight offered by Mill, we should return briefly to the ambiguity which has been lingering around his treatment of the expression of thoughts and opinions. The ambiguity must be resolved, it seems, by saying that expression is an extraordinary case.

In general, unlike expression, self-regarding actions do not cause non-consensual harm to others. These actions can never be immoral. They are not really other-regarding actions which, because interference with them is calculated to be generally inexpedient, are treated *as if* they are self-regarding when in fact they cause non-consensual harm (or carry a significant risk of non-consensual harm) to others.

Expression is extraordinary because, although truly other-regarding because competing speakers always pose some risk of depriving one another of listeners who support their particular views, it is virtually never the object of expedient coercive interference: the non-consensual risks and perils to others are 'almost' always outweighed by the expected collective benefits of finding warranted opinions, of developing better personal lifestyles, of exposing and counteracting political corruption, and so on. But 'almost' means 'almost': there are rare situations in which expression causes such grievous non-consensual harms to others that it is properly seen as immoral conduct according to utility in the largest sense. In those rare cases, such as incitement to violence and malicious libel, coercive interference may become expedient. Nevertheless, an expedient laissez-faire doctrine for expression is very broad, with far fewer exceptions than in the case of free markets. Thus, expression can be seen as a peculiar element of the other-regarding class. Since it is 'almost' self-regarding, it may conveniently be treated in general as if it were self-regarding, and practically inseparable from thought.

THE PROPER LIMITS OF SOCIETY'S POLICE AUTHORITY (V.5–6)

Mill next turns to another practical issue, opened up, as he says, by the example of 'the sale of poisons' touched on in his treatment of the laissez-faire doctrine. The 'new question' is 'the proper limits of what may be called the functions of police; how far liberty may legitimately be invaded for the prevention of crime, or of accident' (1859c, 293–94 (V.5)). It is indisputable, he says, that social authority is legitimately employed to prevent crimes, understood as actions involving serious harms to others to which no reasonable person can consent, and accidents, including unintentional self-injury. Public officials may interfere with 'any one evidently preparing to commit a crime', for example, and may also prohibit the manufacture and sale of any product which is only ever used to commit crimes (ibid., 294 (V.5)). Moreover, they, 'or any one else', may prevent a person from 'attempting to cross a bridge which had been ascertained to be unsafe', if 'there were no time to warn him of his danger' (ibid.). Such interference does not constitute 'any real infringement of his liberty' when the bridge is *known* to be unsafe, because his attempt to cross it will result with *certainty* in an accident: '[L]iberty consists in doing what one desires, and he does not desire to fall into the river' (ibid.).

Notice that Mill does not allow for special cases where a suicidal person does wish to plunge into the river. Perhaps he thinks that such a person must be 'a child, or delirious, or in some state of excitement or absorption incompatible with the full use of the reflecting faculty' (ibid.). In any case, the desire for self-annihilation is evidently at odds with self-development or individuality, the cultivation of which is the very purpose of protecting the individual's liberty, by right, in self-regarding matters. Still, it remains an open question whether he would advocate coercive interference with a competent person's suicidal action. It seems that he cannot do so, consistently with his maxim of self-regarding liberty.

PRACTICAL UNCERTAINTIES (V.5)

These more or less clear-cut cases are not, however, the only ones in practice. It may be unclear whether a person is preparing to commit a crime, for example, because the products which he has bought have 'innocent' and 'useful purposes' as well as criminal ones. The buyer of poison might be preparing to murder his wife, or he might be intending to use it to help protect the plants in his garden from insects. Such situations seem problematic because we are uncertain about whether a person intends to perform an other-regarding action or a self-regarding action. If we could know beforehand how he will act, we could decide in a straightforward way whether the social authority maxim or the liberty maxim applies. But we do not know what he will do.

Again, it may be unclear just how unsafe a bridge is, in which case a person's attempt to cross it will result in an accident only with some probability less than unity. He might be an adventuresome soul fully aware of the danger to himself, or he might be someone who is ignorant of the risk and who would not wish to take it once suitably informed. Such situations seem problematic because we are uncertain about how much information the person has concerning the probable consequences of his behaviour. If we could know beforehand how much he knows, we could again quite easily decide which of the two maxims applies to the case. But we do not know his state of knowledge, and will never know unless we seize him at the entry of the bridge. What to do?

The problem in these situations is to find a reasonable balance between the maxims with which to resolve the uncertainty inherent in the situation itself. Precisely because we do not know enough at the moment to be able to say whether conditions justify application of one maxim or the other, we must give due weight to both until we have acquired the relevant knowledge. Otherwise, if we dismiss either maxim *ex ante*, we preclude ourselves from gaining the very information required to decide which of the two properly applies *ex post*. In order to resolve our ignorance in a way that allows for due application of whichever maxim is called for in the situation as it materializes, we must place certain restrictions on the individual's right to choose as he wishes in what may ultimately prove to be his self-regarding concerns (though we cannot be sure of this when the restrictions are imposed). The restrictions are reasonable in light of society's legitimate authority to take precautions against crimes and accidents whose burdens will fall on unwilling victims as well as the general taxpayer.

REASONABLE COMPROMISES (V.5)

Mill thinks a reasonable balance can be struck in these cases without any real encroachment on the individual's freedom to choose as he wishes in his self-regarding concerns. Society can legitimately take precautions against accidents, for example, by forcing the individual to attend to a warning of the risk he incurs when he crosses a dangerous bridge or uses toxic drugs. Once warned, however, the person should be free to choose as he likes, at least as long as self-injury is not a certainty: 'when there is not a certainty, but only a danger of mischief, no one but the person himself can judge of the sufficiency of the motive which may prompt him to incur the risk' (ibid., 294 (V.5)). Society properly has authority to assure itself that he is informed about the possibly grave consequences of his self-regarding acts. But the informed individual should not be 'forcibly prevented from exposing himself to [the danger]' which he *desires* to undertake (ibid.).

Again, Mill is leaving open the question of deliberate suicide. But it seems that he must say that society has no legitimate authority to interfere, once it has assured itself that the suicidal individual is competent. Obtaining such assurance is likely, however, to involve more than a warning or a brief detention to learn whether the person really knows what he is doing. A proper psychological assessment may take some time. Nevertheless, once assurance of his competence has been obtained, the self-regarding liberty maxim kicks in.

Similarly, society can legitimately take precautions against crimes by forcing the individual to observe 'certain formalities' as a condition of sale in the case of 'articles adapted to be instruments of crime' (ibid., 295 (V.5)). A buyer of poisons or guns should be required to provide what 'Bentham … called "preappointed evidence"' of how he intends to use these products:

> The seller, for example, might be required to enter in a register the exact time of the transaction, the name and address of the buyer, the precise quality and quantity sold; to ask the purpose for which it was wanted, and record the answer he received.
>
> (Ibid.)

The provision of such evidence is no 'material impediment' to the buyer's freedom to do as he likes short of causing non-consensual injury to others. But it may help to ward off crimes, by facilitating their detection: 'Such regulations would in general be no material impediment to obtaining the article, but a very considerable one to making an improper use of it without detection' (ibid.).

SPECIAL INSTANCES OF LEGITIMATE POLICE AUTHORITY (V.6)

Mill goes on to argue that society's legitimate power, to 'ward off crimes against itself by antecedent precautions', can even extend to coercion against what seems to be self-regarding action in special circumstances. It is 'perfectly legitimate', for example,

> that a person, who had once been convicted of any act of violence toward others under the influence of drink, should be placed under a special legal restriction, personal to himself; that if he were afterwards found drunk, he should be liable to a penalty, and that if when in that

> state he committed another offence, the punishment to which he would be liable for that other offence should be increased in severity.
>
> (Ibid., 295 (V.6))

Such a person's consumption of alcohol, although apparently self-regarding, carries a significant probability, based on his own special experience, of becoming in fact a violent act toward others. What looks like a self-regarding act is really an other-regarding one, posing a risk of evil to others: 'The making himself drunk, in a person whom drunkenness excites to do harm to others, is a crime against others' (ibid.). But most consumers are not similarly excited by alcohol, even if they drink it in excessive amounts. Thus, the extraordinary interference with his liberty, though justified in his case, is not justified in general.

For analogous reasons, Mill thinks it perfectly legitimate that an idle person, who has a special financial obligation towards others as a result of contractual arrangements or kinship, should be coerced to fulfil that obligation, 'by compulsory labour, if no other means are available' (ibid.).

SOCIETY'S AUTHORITY TO ENFORCE 'GOOD MANNERS' (V.7)

Mill completes his discussion of 'obvious limitations' of this extraordinary sort to the self-regarding liberty maxim, by claiming that many actions which are self-regarding when done in private, behind closed doors, can become other-regarding, and indeed immoral, if done in public:

> there are many acts which, being directly injurious only to the agents themselves, ought not to be legally interdicted, but which, if done publicly, are a violation of good manners, and coming thus within the category of offences against others, may rightfully be prohibited.
>
> (Ibid., 295 (V.7))

The claim is puzzling as it stands, and he provides virtually no clarification. 'Of this kind are offences against decency', he says, yet 'the objection to publicity' is 'equally strong in the case of many actions not in themselves condemnable, nor supposed to be' (ibid., 295–96 (V.7)). He seems to be saying that publicity as such can lend a special quality to what is otherwise a self-regarding action, transforming it into an other-regarding action that harms others without their consent, indeed, harms them in a way sufficiently grievous as to justify coercive interference by stigma but not by law. Examples might include self-mutilation in public, eating disgusting foods that lead one to vomit or otherwise show signs of illness in public, defecation in public, sexual intercourse between consenting adults in public, or the publication of intimate details of one's personal relationships contrary to the wishes of the others involved. The last case might be read, broadly, to include publication of gossip about one's friends and their acquaintances, as communicated in private conversations, letters and the like.

Non-consensual harm to others in these instances apparently involves the violation of certain rules of polite behaviour and kindness, which constitute 'good manners' in a particular social context. Such rules might be viewed as reasonable contrivances for protecting each individual's interest in his good reputation, for example, in which case a violation of the rules could be seen as harmful to others' reputations without their consent. Self-mutilation or deliberately vomiting in front of others might be seen as insults to their good names, for instance, just as publication of an intimate friend's confidences may damage that person's reputation. Even if Mill has something like this in mind, however, it cannot be the whole story. More needs to be said. The line between mere dislike and harm may well vanish for actions performed in public, if harm to others without their consent can include whatever others feel is too rude or impolite to be suffered in public. This admittedly hard case requires further discussion (see Chapter 9, pp. 272–84).

LIBERTY OF PUBLIC SOLICITATION AND ITS LIMITS (V.8)

Mill next considers practical cases that are prompted by the question: 'what the agent is free to do, ought other persons to be equally free to counsel or instigate?' (1859c, 296 (V.8)). Given that the individual should be completely free, by right, to engage in self-regarding conduct which is disliked by most, should others be equally free to encourage such self-regarding conduct? 'This question', he admits, 'is not free from difficulty' (ibid.). Strictly speaking, soliciting another to do an act is not a self-regarding action: 'To give advice or offer inducements to any one, is a social act, and may, therefore, like actions in general which affect others, be supposed amenable to social control' (ibid.). Yet he argues that, like expression, it can reasonably be treated as if it were self-regarding, since it is practically inseparable from deliberation over self-regarding acts:

> If people must be allowed, in whatever concerns only themselves, to act as seems best to themselves at their own peril, they must equally be free to consult with one another about what is fit to be so done; to exchange opinions, and give and receive suggestions. Whatever it is permitted to do, it must be permitted to advise to do.
>
> (Ibid.)

The benefits of self-development made possible by liberty of advice and consultation generally outweigh any non-consensual harms to others' interests.

Nevertheless, just as complete liberty of expression is not recommended, so exceptions ought to be considered to liberty of solicitation. Mill argues that treating solicitation as if it were self-regarding becomes dubious 'only when the instigator derives a personal benefit from his advice; when he makes it his occupation, for subsistence or pecuniary gain, to promote what society and the state consider to be an evil' (ibid.). The 'new element of complication' in these exceptional cases is the existence of classes of producers and sellers, 'with an interest opposed to what, is considered [by the majority] as the public weal' (ibid.). Ought society to prohibit these sellers, or adopt a policy of laissez-faire? 'Fornication, for example, must be tolerated, and so must gambling; but should a person be free to be a pimp, or to keep a gambling house?' (ibid.). This is a hard case, he admits, which 'lie[s] on the exact boundary line between two principles, and it is not at once apparent to which of the two it belongs' (ibid.).

On the one hand, it may be argued that such a case ought to be assimilated to the self-regarding liberty principle, since that principle admittedly applies already not only to the *buyer* of the product or service which the pimp or casino-owner is promoting and offering to sell but also to friends and acquaintances of the buyer who offer their advice without any thought of making money. The fact that the commercial advisers and promoters are prejudiced because they are seeking to make money should make no difference with respect to liberty of solicitation:

> On the side of toleration it may be said, that the fact of following anything as an occupation, and living or profiting by the practice of it, cannot make that criminal which would otherwise be admissible; that the act should be either consistently permitted or consistently prohibited; that if the principles which we have hitherto defended are true, society has no business, as society, to decide anything to be wrong which concerns only the individual; that it cannot go beyond dissuasion, and that one person ought to be as free to persuade, as another to dissuade.
>
> (Ibid.)

In short, a broad policy of laissez-faire ought to apply to the self-interested producers and marketers in the same way that it admittedly applies to non-commercial advisers because the consumer has complete freedom, by right, to buy and use the products or services in question. It cannot be wrong for people to make a living by persuading the individual to consume that which he has a right to consume as he wishes.

On the other hand, it may be argued that society should coercively interfere with the social actions of these profit-seeking sellers so as

> to exclude the influence of solicitations which are not disinterested, of instigators who cannot possibly be impartial – who have a direct personal interest on one side, and that side the one which the state believes to be wrong, and who confessedly promote it for personal objects only.
>
> (Ibid., 297 (V.8))

Given that all are fallible, the majority is justified in assuming that the individual ought to decide for himself, with as little influence as possible from biased sellers, whether the product or service is good or bad for his purposes:

> There can surely, it may be urged, be nothing lost, no sacrifice of good, by so ordering matters that persons shall make their election, either wisely or foolishly, on their own prompting, as free as possible from the arts of persons who stimulate their inclinations for interested purposes of their own.
>
> (Ibid.)

To minimize the influence of biased advertising, so the argument goes, public brothels and casinos should be prohibited whereas private ones, which do no promotional advertising and are confined to homes, or members-only clubs, or out-of-the-way 'red light districts', should be permitted. This would confine the self-regarding activities of the buyers and the solicitations of the sellers to private establishments, out of view of the general public: 'all persons should be free to gamble [or buy sex] in their own or each other's houses, or in any place of meeting established by their own subscriptions, and open only to the members and their visitors' (ibid.). Even 'the prohibition [against public establishments] is never effectual', he admits (ibid.). Yet it serves its purpose. Public brothels and gambling houses can only be carried on 'with a certain degree of secrecy and mystery, so that nobody knows anything about them but those who seek them' (ibid.).

Mill thinks 'there is considerable force' in the argument that public casinos and brothels should be prohibited but he never actually endorses it. Even if he is read as not opposing it, the argument just carves out an exception to the otherwise broad laissez-faire policy with respect to solicitation. More specifically, society should exercise its legitimate authority to control social conduct by prohibiting commercial solicitation in public and yet allowing it in private, beyond the eyes of everyone but those who actively seek to engage in the self-regarding activities disliked by most people. Mill cannot recommend complete prohibition because consumers have a moral right to gamble or to engage in consensual sex as they please, as long as they do not cause non-consensual perceptible damage to the interests of others. Coercive interference could only be justified to prevent public advocacy by the sellers of fornication and gambling, he suggests, and yet the sellers should be left alone, under certain terms and conditions, to offer these same activities in private. The police might legitimately shut down public brothels and casinos, and also make sure that private establishments operate according to the terms and conditions of their licences: for example, they must be open only to paying members and their guests. But complete prohibition of commercial gambling and prostitution would be inconsistent with the self-regarding liberty of the buyers, and so is rejected by utility in the largest sense.

And yet Mill does not positively recommend coercive interference with public casinos and brothels. He says that he 'will not venture to decide whether [the arguments for public prohibition] are sufficient to justify the moral anomaly of *punishing* the accessary, when the principal is (and must be) allowed to go free; of fining or imprisoning the procurer, but not the fornicator, the gambling-house keeper, but not the gambler' (ibid., emphasis added). In other words, he refuses to say that public advocacy of gambling and prostitution by the sellers is immoral and ought to be made illegal. We can infer as much because, according to his utilitarian theory as outlined in *Utilitarianism*, if the sellers do not deserve to be punished for their public advocacy, then they have no moral duty not to do it. So, in the end, he seems to leave this moral decision up to the particular society, which may decide the matter either way. What is judged immoral in one social context may be considered morally permissible in another. Still, he does seem reluctant to opt for punishment, as he speaks of it as a 'moral anomaly' when the principal must be allowed to go free (ibid.).

He clearly rejects any claim that 'the common operations of buying and selling [ought] to be interfered with on analogous grounds' (ibid.). The sellers of virtually every commodity 'have a pecuniary interest in encouraging' excess consumption of it. But 'no argument' in favour of prohibition 'can be founded on this', because the sellers are essential to consumers who have a right to buy and use articles as they wish, short of non-consensual harm to others. Temperance laws cannot be justified on that basis, for example, 'because the class of dealers in strong drinks, though interested in their abuse, are indispensably required for the sake of their legitimate use' (ibid.).

This does not preclude special regulations, akin to those imposed on pimps and casino operators, which are designed to prevent public encouragement of alcohol consumption: 'The interest, however, of these dealers in promoting intemperance is a real evil, and justifies the state in imposing restrictions and requiring guarantees which, but for that justification, would be infringements of legitimate liberty' (ibid.). The public authorities might properly require that dealers post warnings against abuse of alcohol, for example, and refuse to serve apparently intoxicated patrons. Repeated violation of these conditions would result in revocation of the licence to sell drinks to the public.

LEGITIMATE AUTHORITY TO TAX SALES AND LIMIT THE NUMBER OF SELLERS (V.9–10)

Mill now turns to yet another question, namely, 'whether the state, while it permits, should nevertheless indirectly discourage [purely self-regarding] conduct which it deems contrary to the best interests of the agent'(ibid., 297 (V.9)). He asks, for example, whether government 'should take measures to render the means of drunkenness more costly, or add to the difficulty of procuring them by limiting the number of the places of sale' (ibid., 297–98 (V.9)). To give an adequate answer, he insists, 'many distinctions require to be made' (298 (V.9)).

SPECIAL TAXATION OF STIMULANTS (V.9)

On the one hand, it is an illegitimate use of social authority to tax 'stimulants' solely for the purpose of limiting their consumption: 'Every increase of cost is a prohibition, to those whose means do not come up to the augmented price; and to those who do, it is a penalty laid on them for gratifying a particular taste' (ibid.). The individual should be free to spend his income on alcohol and drugs as he likes, provided he does not harm others against their wishes.

On the other hand, taxation for purposes of revenue is a legitimate exercise of social authority, if only because revenues are evidently required to maintain government and run the legal system which any civilized society creates as an important component of its moral code. Since 'in most countries it is necessary that a considerable part of that taxation should be indirect', society 'cannot help imposing penalties, which to some persons may be prohibitory, on the use of some articles of consumption' (ibid.). Given that such penalties are inevitable, society properly has the right to focus taxation on those commodities 'of which it deems the use, beyond a very moderate quantity, to be positively injurious [to the consumer]' (ibid.). Thus, special taxation of stimulants for revenue purposes is 'not only admissible, but to be approved of' (ibid.).

Mill's argument here distinguishes between legitimate and illegitimate purposes of special taxes on self-regarding acts of which the majority disapproves. Specifically, taxation of self-regarding conduct is legitimate for the purpose of raising revenues needed by the state to carry out certain generally expedient functions.[2] But it is illegitimate when employed merely to interfere with consumption, raising no necessary revenues. This distinction may seem very fine in the context of the modern welfare state, where government's appetite for funds appears virtually unlimited. Note, however, that in addition to taking for granted a liberal theory of government as limited to certain expedient functions, Mill does not rule out the possibility that indirect taxation for fiscal purposes will cease to be necessary. In advanced societies with massive wealth, for example, necessary revenues might be raised entirely through direct taxation of income and wealth. If so, because it is not needed to raise revenues, special taxation of stimulants is an illegitimate interference with individual liberty in that social context.

LIMITS ON SUPPLY (V.10)

As for social authority to limit the number of sellers of intoxicants, its propriety also depends on the purpose of its exercise. On the one hand, it is illegitimate to set a 'limitation in number, for instance, of beer and spirit houses, for the express purpose of rendering them more difficult of access, and diminishing the occasions of temptation' (1859c, 298 (V. 10)). Such paternalism treats as children those (notably workers) who want to drink, and violates the right of the individual to spend his income as he likes, short of non-consensual harm to others.

On the other hand, some limitation in the number of sellers may be a justified by-product of society's exercise of legitimate authority to regulate the market and take precautions against crime:

> All places of public resort require the restraint of a police, and places of this kind peculiarly, because offences against society are especially apt to originate there. It is, therefore, fit to confine the power of selling these commodities (at least for consumption on the spot) to persons of known or vouched-for respectability of conduct; to make such reguations respecting hours of opening and closing as may be requisite for public surveillance, and to withdraw the licence if breaches of the peace repeatedly take place through the connivance or incapacity of the keeper of the house, or if it becomes a rendez-vous for concocting and preparing offences against the law.
>
> (Ibid.)

Again, there is no absolute right to sell commodities, free of all forms of coercion, because marketing is not a purely self-regarding act. The doctrine of laissez-faire is distinct from the principle of self-regarding liberty. The latter is implicated only to the extent that society interferes in the market for the sole purpose of prohibiting the consumption of particular commodities. The individual does have a right to spend his income on whatever he wants, short of non-consensual harm to others.[3] Note that an indefinite number of places of drink, open at all hours, could be justified if sufficient keepers of good repute were available and round-the-clock police surveillance were not inexpedient.

VOLUNTARY ASSOCIATION AND THE ENFORCEMENT OF CONTRACTS (V.11)

Mill next turns to the question of applying his two maxims in cases where 'any number of individuals' choose 'to regulate by mutual consent such things as regard them jointly, and regard no persons but themselves' (1859c, 299 (V.11)). It is straightforward that any such group ought to have complete liberty, by right, to conduct its self-regarding affairs in accord with the unanimous wishes of its members. But, recognizing that their unanimity may not persist, the members may choose to negotiate contracts of various sorts with one another, and rely on society to enforce the contracts: 'it is often necessary, even in things in which they alone are concerned, that they should enter into engagements with one another; and when they do, it is fit, as a general rule, that those engagements should be kept' (ibid.). Failure to keep to the terms of a contract harms other parties, by disappointing legitimate expectations raised by the contract itself. Society properly has authority to coerce all parties, by law or opinion, to satisfy contractual obligations which have been voluntarily incurred.

Even though society legitimately has authority to enforce the terms of all contracts, however, it is, by common admission, not always generally expedient for society actually to exercise that enforcement authority: 'in the laws, probably, of every country, this general rule [that engagements should be kept] has some exceptions' (ibid.). Indeed, 'it is sometimes considered a sufficient reason for releasing [persons] from an engagement, that it is injurious to themselves' (ibid.). If a party's contractual obligations are properly seen as unconscionable according to utility in the largest sense, for example, then society properly refuses to enforce them for the common good. It not only refuses to use coercion to force the party to fulfil his contractual duties against his wishes. It also refuses to recognize the contract as valid *ab initio*, and so denies that such contractual duties even exist. Thus, society refuses to lend its authority to give effect to the parties' wishes in this case. It denies that the *volenti* maxim applies and so 'interferes' with the self-regarding liberty of people to make blatantly unreasonable and unjust contracts as they please 'in things in which they alone are concerned'.

VOLUNTARY SLAVERY

One example, an 'extreme case', is slavery contracts: 'an engagement by which a person should sell himself, or allow himself to be sold, as a slave, would be null and void; neither enforced by law nor by opinion' (ibid.). The reason why society ought to refuse to recognize such contracts is 'apparent', Mill says, even though third parties are not suffering any damage to their interests against their wishes. The seller ought to be prevented from alienating his liberty:

> [B]y selling himself for a slave, he abdicates his liberty; he foregoes [*sic*] any future use of it beyond that single act. He therefore defeats, in his own case, the very purpose which is the justification of allowing him to dispose of himself. He is no longer free; but is thenceforth in a position which has no longer the presumption in its favour, that would be afforded by his voluntarily remaining in it.
>
> (Ibid., 299–300 (V.11))

If slavery contracts are enforced, a person who sells himself as a slave can no longer freely choose whether to remain in that position. Because he can no longer make a voluntary choice, his subsequent conduct provides no evidence that his continuing slave status is 'desirable, or at the least endurable, to him' (ibid., 299 (V.11)). A fortiori, there can be no presumption that his remaining a slave is conducive to his self-development, the essential ingredient of his well-being which is '[t]he reason for not interfering, unless for the sake of others, with [his] voluntary acts' in the first place (ibid.). Thus, no society which purports to value liberty and individuality can properly recognize slavery contracts: 'The principle of freedom cannot require that he should be free not to be free. It is not freedom, to be allowed to alienate his freedom' (ibid., 300 (V.11)).

Mill's claim that society can legitimately 'interfere' with voluntary slavery has puzzled many commentators, since it seems to contradict his liberty doctrine. Admittedly, society has every right to regulate the sellers of any commodity in the market: 'trade is a social act' (ibid., 293 (V.4)). Society can even properly prohibit the sale of any commodity whose only possible uses involve harming others: buyers have no right to use such commodities. In the slavery case, however, the marketed commodity, namely, the seller's very person, need not be used by the buyer to harm other people against their wishes. Thus, it seems that the buyer should be free to use voluntary slaves short of non-consensual injury to others, in which case prohibition of selling oneself into slavery is not only inexpedient but illegitimate.

Nevertheless, Mill does not seem to be guilty of inconsistency in this case. There are other pertinent considerations. What is peculiar about a slavery contract is that the seller is marketing his very person, including his liberty to act in accord with his own judgment and inclinations. This poses no problem so long as the seller-slave wishes to act as his buyer-master wishes him to act. If he comes to regret his slave status, however, and wishes to recover his freedom against the master's wishes, unanimous consent no longer exists between the parties to the slavery contract. The difficulty is that society, if it has recognized the contract in the first place, is then committed to enforcing involuntary servitude as a permanent condition. For, once authority is exercised to enforce the individual's contractual promise to give up his liberty completely, society can no longer legitimately intervene on behalf of the slave.

Application of the self-regarding liberty maxim is complicated in this situation by the fact that there is uncertainty about the nature of the durable commodity which the buyer is purchasing. Is he buying a voluntary slave who will always wish to remain a slave, or a voluntary slave who will sooner or later become an unwilling slave? Given such uncertainty, we cannot simply say that the buyer should have complete liberty to use voluntary slaves, short of non-consensual harm to others. Rather, the real issue is how to balance that liberty against society's legitimate authority to prohibit involuntary slavery. But to speak of balancing in this extreme case is misleading. Society must decide either permanently to enforce slavery contracts (since, once such contracts are recognized, no distinction can be drawn in practice between voluntary and involuntary slavery), or never to enforce them. Evidently, any society which values individuality, and the moral right of the individual to choose as he likes in self-regarding matters which is essential to its cultivation, must decide not to recognize slavery contracts.

Moreover, and of utmost importance, Mill does not actually say that society ought to employ coercion to prohibit voluntary slavery. He says that society should refuse to enforce slavery contracts. Even though refusal to recognize a slavery contract does constitute 'interference' with the parties' choice to arrange their self-regarding affairs as they wish, it is not *coercive* interference. Society is not employing force to prohibit people from voluntarily selling themselves into slavery, and is not threatening to punish those whom it finds have entered into slavery contracts. In short, it is not declaring that voluntary slavery is immoral. The practice might still persist even though society refuses to endorse it. Individuals can still sell themselves as slaves in return for whatever they deem suitable compensation, despite the fact that society signals its disapproval by refusing to recognize any moral or legal *right* to do so. If this reasoning is correct, then it follows that society's refusal to recognize the *volenti* maxim in some cases does not imply that society is committed to coercive interference with self-regarding conduct in those cases.

Mill seems correct, then, to insist that a society committed to his liberty maxim must refuse to recognize any practice of selling oneself into slavery. Society cannot recognize any right to buy and control another's very person as one pleases. Slavery contracts are by their nature irrevocable. Society cannot recognize them without sacrificing all means of discriminating between voluntary and involuntary servitude on the part of the seller-slave. Unless prepared to enforce in perpetuity a state of absolute vulnerability, which the once-willing slave may have come to regret and now wish to alter, society must refuse to enforce slavery contracts.

It might be suggested that such a refusal would not achieve the goal of stamping out slavery. And to some degree this must be admitted: society's refusal to enforce slavery contracts would not eradicate voluntary slavery overnight. But non-enforcement has the practical effect of strongly discouraging voluntary slavery such that it is reasonably expected to gradually disappear. No reasonable buyer can be expected to pay a price to a seller who has permission from society to remove what has been sold (namely, himself) from the buyer's hands at will. Moreover, individuals must increasingly lose interest in becoming slaves as they learn that they have better ways to manage their self-regarding affairs. Of course, if anyone tries to coerce another into slavery, society retains legitimate authority to prevent such non-consensual harm to others.

It is true that a person may yet freely sell his services or promise his love (rather than give up his very person) to another for some time. But employment contracts, marriage contracts and the like must be distinguished from the resignation of liberty involved in slavery contracts. Subsistence, affection and other 'necessities of life ... continually require, not indeed that we should resign our freedom, but that we should consent to this and the other limitation of it' (ibid., 300 (V.11)). Moreover, as we have already seen in our earlier discussion of the Mormon case (290–91 (IV.21)), Mill is reluctant ever to recommend contracts-in-perpetuity. Employment contracts, marriage contracts, international treaties and the like ought to include automatic termination ('sunset') clauses that come into effect after a suitably expedient fixed period, he suggests, at which time they would be open to renegotiation.

VOLUNTARY RELEASE AND THE PERMISSION TO BREAK CONTRACTS (V.11)

Mill goes on to point out that his self-regarding liberty maxim implies that the parties to all contracts in self-regarding matters should have complete liberty, by right, to release each other by mutual consent: 'those who have become bound to one another, in things which concern no third party, should be able to release one another from the engagement' (ibid., 300 (V.11)). '[E]ven without such voluntary release', he continues, 'there are perhaps no contracts or engagements, except those that relate to money or money's worth, of which one can venture to say that there ought to be no liberty whatever of retraction' (ibid.).

Evidently, dissolving an engagement against the wishes of another party is not a self-regarding act. Society properly has authority to prohibit an individual from harming others by disappointing their expectations, which he himself has encouraged, 'either by express promise or by conduct' (ibid.). Even though society has legitimate authority to enforce contracts, however, general expediency might sometimes dictate letting a party disappoint the contractual expectations of others. Such a laissez-faire policy is quite distinct from the liberty maxim.

To illustrate his view that social authority generally ought to be applied to force unwilling parties to observe the terms of their contracts, Mill briefly discusses, and rejects as simplistic, Wilhelm von Humboldt's conviction that all 'engagements which involve personal relations or services' should be of limited legal duration, and that marriage in particular 'should require nothing more than the declared will of either party to dissolve it' (ibid.). Against

Humboldt, he argues that, while a wife or husband should be legally free to dissolve the marriage without the consent of the other, coercion is legitimate to prevent them from ignoring their moral obligations to one another as well as to third parties such as children peculiarly associated with the partnership:

> When a person, either by express promise or by conduct, has encouraged another to rely upon his continuing to act in a certain way – to build expectations and calculations, and stake any part of his plan of life upon that supposition – a new series of moral obligations arises on his part toward that person, which may possibly be overruled, but cannot be ignored. And again, if the relation between two contracting parties has been followed by consequences to others; if it has placed third parties in any peculiar position, or, as in the case of marriage, has even called third parties into existence, obligations arise on the part of both the contracting parties toward those third parties ... [E]ven if, as Von Humboldt maintains, [these obligations] ought to make no difference in the *legal* freedom of the parties to release themselves from the engagement (and I also hold that they ought not to make *much* difference), they necessarily make a great difference in the *moral* freedom. A person is bound to take all these circumstances into account, before resolving on a step which may affect such important interests of others; and if he does not allow proper weight to those interests, he is morally responsible for the wrong.
>
> (Ibid., 300–1 (V.11), emphasis original)

Society ought to allow a person to legally dissolve his marriage against the wishes of his partner, because enforcing the contract harms him in ways that he finds intolerable and, in particular, impedes his ability to develop his character in his own way. Even so, the individual should not have complete liberty, by right, of divorce. He has moral obligations to his partner and to third parties which he ought to fulfil, and stigma as well as legal penalties are instruments which society may legitimately employ to force him to fulfil them if need be. Of course, the same is true for any woman who wishes to dissolve her marriage. And this applies to same-sex marriages as well as to heterosexual ones, and to polygamous marriages as well as to monogamous ones.

'MISAPPLIED NOTIONS OF LIBERTY' (V.12–15)

Mill next discusses cases in which individual liberty cannot be justified by application of his self-regarding liberty maxim, even though prevailing majority sentiment 'in the modern European world' is strongly in favour of granting liberty in these cases. The most important of these 'in its direct influence on human happiness', he says, is 'family relations', where it is commonly held that a husband should be virtually free to do as he likes in acting for his wife and children, 'under the pretext that the affairs of the other are his own affairs' (ibid., 301 (V.12)). But the moral right to *liberty* in self-regarding matters must not be conflated with a right to dominate, or exercise *power* over, others.[4] No individual should have any power at all, for example, to coerce other adults in their respective self-regarding concerns. Rather, all adults should have equal rights to liberty of self-regarding action. Thus, no argument based on utility in the largest sense exists for the 'almost despotic power of husbands over wives' (1859c, 301 (V.12)). Rather, 'wives should have the same rights, and should receive the protection of the law [including enforcement of contracts] in the same manner, as all other persons' (ibid.).[5]

Moreover, although public officials and even private citizens must be legally entrusted with social authority to prevent non-consensual harm to others, Mill recommends a democratic political system with checks and balances, such that no person has unfettered power to lay down rules of other-regarding conduct as he likes: 'The state, while it respects the liberty of each in what specifically regards himself, is bound to maintain a vigilant control over his exercise of any power which it allows him to possess over others' (1859c, 301 (V.12)).[6]

Mill is even more preoccupied with 'misapplied notions of liberty' in the case of parents' control over their children (ibid.). His liberty maxim evidently does not apply to children per se: anyone not yet capable of rational persuasion and self-development needs to be taken care of by others, for his own good. Society properly has authority to make sure that those (including parents) who are entrusted to take care of children act in ways which society deems essential for the good of the children.

EDUCATION (V.12–14)

In particular, society has every right to compel parents by law to provide a suitable education:

> It still remains unrecognised, that to bring a child into existence without a fair prospect of being able, not only to provide food for its body, but instruction and training for its mind, is a moral crime, both against the unfortunate offspring and against society; and that if the parent does not fulfil this obligation, the state ought to see it fulfilled, at the charge, as far as possible, of the parent.
>
> (1859c, 302 (V.12))

This does not imply that government must monopolize the provision of education, establish the professional qualifications of teachers, or even provide any schools at all:

> It might leave to parents to obtain the education where and how they pleased, and content itself with helping to pay the school fees of the poorer classes of children, and defraying the entire school expenses of those who have no one else to pay for them.
>
> (Ibid., 302 (V.13))

Indeed, Mill rejects the idea that government should direct 'the whole or any large part of the education of the people', unless society is 'so backward' that there is no alternative (ibid., 302–3 (V.13)).

But it does imply that government must administer 'public examinations, extending to all children, and beginning at an early age', as a means of enforcing the law which makes education compulsory (ibid., 303 (V.14)). In his view, such examinations, given annually, should cover a 'gradually extending range of subjects' and require 'a certain minimum of general knowledge' to pass. To give them an incentive to fulfil their obligations, parents might be subjected to 'a moderate fine' for the failure of their children to pass an exam (ibid.).

In addition to these compulsory minimum examinations, 'there should be *voluntary* examinations on all subjects, at which all who come up to a certain standard of proficiency might claim a certificate' (ibid., emphasis added). Even these 'higher classes of examinations' are expediently 'confined to facts and positive science exclusively', to prevent government from having 'an improper influence over opinion' on 'disputed topics' such as religion and politics (ibid.).

Given his view that the state should not monopolize or control the schools, Mill sees no problem with children 'being taught religion, if their parents chose, at the same schools where they were taught other things', provided they are 'not required to profess a belief' (ibid., 303–4 (V.14)). Despite his concerns over rising religious bigotry, he apparently thinks that the state can even administer public examinations in religion, without unduly interfering with the religious liberty of the individual.

Examinations 'in the higher branches of knowledge', including knowledge of religion, should, however, be 'entirely voluntary' (ibid., 304 (V.14)). Persons who attain advanced certificates and degrees in any subject might thereby gain an advantage over competitors for professional employment of one sort or another. Yet there is no improper government influence, so long as government does not have power to 'exclude any one from professions, even from the profession of teacher, for alleged deficiency of qualifications' (ibid.; see also Mill 1842).

BIRTH CONTROL (V.15)

Mistaken notions of liberty also obscure the recognition of society's legitimate authority to regulate the act of 'causing the existence of a human being' (1859c, 304 (V.15)). Society has every right legally to prevent couples from bestowing a life of misery on another person, by bringing him into the world without 'the ordinary chances of a desirable existence' (ibid.). It can properly 'forbid marriage', for example, 'unless the parties can show that they have the means of supporting a family' (ibid.). By extension, it can also force couples to use suitable birth control devices to prevent the creation of wards of the state.

Even if couples have the requisite means to raise a child, society can properly enact such laws to prevent non-consensual harm to the working classes, resulting from excess supply of labour:

> [I]n a country either overpeopled, or threatened with being so, to produce children, beyond a very small number, with the effect of reducing the [long-run] reward of labour by their competition, is a serious offence against all who live by the remuneration of their labour.
>
> (Ibid.)

Whether expedient or not, such measures 'are not objectionable as violations of liberty' (ibid.). Nobody has a moral right to produce as many children as he likes. 'Such laws are interferences of the state to prohibit a mischievous act – an act injurious to others, which ought to be a subject of reprobation, and social stigma, even when it is not deemed expedient to superadd legal punishment' (ibid.).

Yet prevailing majority sentiment rebels against those coercive interferences, as illegitimate infringements of liberty:

> When we compare the strange respect of mankind for liberty, with their strange want of respect for it, we might imagine that a man had an indispensable right to do harm to others, and no right at all to please himself without giving pain to any one.
>
> (Ibid., 304–5 (V.15))

LIBERTY TO REFUSE TO CO-OPERATE (V.16–23)

By way of conclusion, Mill turns to cases 'which, though closely connected with the subject of this essay', he says, 'do not, in strictness, belong to it' (ibid., 305 (V.16)). In these cases, the reasons against coercive interference 'do not turn upon the principle of [self-regarding] liberty' (ibid.). The right of the individual to act as he pleases in his self-regarding concerns is not involved. Indeed, the question is not about coercive interference with the actions of individuals, Mill says. Instead, it is about whether the government should help individuals to achieve their goals, and perhaps even before they see any need for the help:

> [T]he question is not about restraining the actions of individuals, but about helping them: it is asked whether government should do, or

> cause to be done, something for their benefit, instead of leaving it to
> be done by themselves, individually, or in voluntary combination.
>
> (Ibid.)

Now, an individual who deliberately improves his own circumstances, without directly affecting – harming or benefiting – the interests of others against their wishes, is engaged in self-regarding conduct covered by the liberty maxim. Moreover, individuals who wish to co-operate to confer perceptible advantages on one another, without affecting the interests of others against their wishes, are engaged in jointly self-regarding behaviour. Self-regarding conduct includes actions that cause consensual benefits, and not only consensual harms, to the interests of other people. But it does not include actions that cause non-consensual benefits or harms: such actions are other-regarding ones, and are legitimately subject to social control. It may seem that a competent person would never object to perceptible improvements in his circumstances. But we must allow for the fact that fallible people will at times disagree over whether a given other-regarding action is likely to be beneficial or harmful to their interests. Some individuals will reject recommended medical procedures and medication as detrimental to their health, for example, and thus view as damaging what others believe is beneficial to their interests. Notice that this disagreement over whether the direct effects of an action are harmful or beneficial to others without their consent has no bearing on the definition of self-regarding conduct or on the application of the self-regarding liberty maxim. The liberty maxim is not in play if the effects are non-consensual, whether they are classified as harmful or beneficial.

A major concern of Mill's in this concluding section seems to be the provision of public goods, that is, goods such as national security, public education, the general state of the natural environment, and works of fine art displayed in museums freely open to the public, which are advantageous to the interests of the public, or at least appear so to some citizens and government officials, and yet some members of the public do not wish to help contribute to their production while profit-seeking entrepreneurs have no incentive to produce them.[7] Given that some individuals do not consent to help produce them or to help pay for their production whereas others believe that a failure to produce them damages their interests as members of the public, society must decide whether to force people to help produce public goods or to adopt a policy of laissez-faire such that public goods will be undersupplied or not produced at all until most people develop the intellectual, moral and practical capacities required to produce them through voluntary combination. Notice that society is deciding here between other-regarding actions. Should recalcitrant people be coerced, either directly or through the tax system, to contribute to the production of a public good, even though this harms them without their consent? Or should society leave everyone alone, even though this means that people who desire the public good will lose the advantages to their interests which they associate with its production? This issue has nothing to do with the self-regarding liberty maxim but instead is a question of the most expedient deployment of society's legitimate coercive authority within the realm of other-regarding actions.

I do not mean to suggest that Mill is exclusively concerned here with the problem of public goods. The government can intervene to help others by subsidizing private enterprise, for example, or by conducting the business itself instead of leaving it to private entrepreneurs. The government can also help others by providing welfare payments to support people in need instead of leaving it entirely to private philanthropy. Again, these government interventions do not implicate the self-regarding liberty maxim. Subsidies to private industry involve a redistribution of income from the general taxpayer to the industry, and taxpayers may not consent to this use of their taxes which they are forced by law to pay. Trade is not a self-regarding action in any case. Similarly, welfare payments involve a redistribution of income from the general taxpayer to those in need, whether or not individual taxpayers consent to this use of their taxes.

There is no doubt in any of this that individuals ought to be inclined to help each other, and that society ought to advise and educate people to develop the requisite motivations. Moreover, it may be fair to assume that, especially as the general level of education improves, individuals will often agree on which other-regarding actions would be helpful rather than harmful to their interests, whether the actions are performed voluntarily by themselves in concert with others or demanded by government. They may often agree on what constitutes a public good rather than a public bad, for example, or on what sort of profit-seeking enterprise produces net benefits rather than net harms for the members of the public, or on whether help for those in need is a good thing rather than a bad thing.[8] Even so, however, most individuals may not have learned to co-operate with one another to mutual advantage. As a result, the public goods, useful enterprises, and support for subsistence will not be provided through voluntary co-operation. The question is whether society ought to employ its authority to prevent such benefits to the shared interests of the public from being lost when citizens lack the requisite norms of mutual co-operation. Should government intervene, either to perform the beneficial actions itself, or to force people to perform them in accord with its laws and policies? Or should individuals be left alone to learn to co-operate among themselves, with advice and encouragement but no coercion?

These cases are 'closely connected with the subject of this essay', it seems, because, although no interference with the individual's liberty of self-regarding action is contemplated, interference with his failure to perform certain other-regarding acts is under consideration. The question is whether government should intervene to prevent certain non-consensual harms that result from the failure of individuals to help one another, namely, the forgone benefits of mutual co-operation which some people, if only a minority, do not wish to forgo. Indeed, it might well be true that all members of society, were their capacities more highly developed, would not wish to forgo these benefits. In that ideal situation, the public goods, beneficial enterprises, and help for the needy would be supplied spontaneously through joint self-regarding actions. The cases under consideration, however, fall outside that ideal situation.

Mill counsels against government intervention in these cases, except as a last resort. Admittedly, society has legitimate authority to compel its members to perform all sorts of mutually beneficial actions, either directly, or indirectly through tax contributions to support a suitably active government. But utility in the largest sense apparently dictates a presumption in favour of laissez-faire.[9]

RATIONALE FOR LAISSEZ-FAIRE (V.18–22)

He identifies three sorts of arguments in favour of letting individuals or groups learn to help each other with their projects, rather than relying on government to help them.

RELATIVE INEFFICIENCY OF GOVERNMENT (V.18)

Non-intervention is expedient 'when the thing to be done is likely to be better done by individuals than by the government' (1859c, 305 (V.18)). Since those whose material self-interest is tied to a business are generally the most fit to manage its operations or at least choose the managers, for example, government ought not to interfere with 'the ordinary processes of industry' by forcing some people to subsidize others through the tax system (ibid.). But this economic doctrine of laissez-faire is treated in detail by him elsewhere, in his *Political Economy* (1871a, 936–71), and, as he has already made sufficiently clear, 'is not particularly related to the principles of this essay' (ibid.; see also 293 (V.4)).

CULTIVATION OF INDIVIDUALITY (V.19)

Even if government officials might do the thing more competently 'on the average', non-intervention can still be expedient because it is desirable that individuals should do the thing 'as a means to their own mental education' (1859c, 305 (V.19)). This is a major reason for trial by jury rather than trial by judge alone, for example, and for voluntary philanthropic associations rather than government departments which provide support for the welfare of the individual beyond some minimum level of subsistence. It is also a strong argument for co-operative industrial enterprises of all sorts, and for voluntary associations of firefighters, street cleaners and other providers of local and municipal services, rather than government agencies set up for those purposes. Though the individual's participation in such beneficial other-regarding activities is generally not the same thing as choosing as he likes in his self-regarding concerns (because it generally affects the interests of some other people against their wishes), it does similarly promote self-development, more specifically, the development of his capacities to understand 'joint interests', manage 'joint concerns' and act habitually 'from public or semi-public motives' in pursuit of 'aims which unite' rather than isolate him from his fellows (ibid.). 'Without these habits and powers, a free constitution can neither be worked nor preserved' (ibid.).

By leaving individuals and voluntary associations alone to experiment in various ways to discover what can be accomplished through mutual co-operation, government can promote, among other things, the cultivation of that Periclean character ideal which is also the target of the basic right to liberty in self-regarding concerns.

> What the state can usefully do, is to make itself a central depository, and active circulator and diffuser, of the experience resulting from many trials. Its business is to enable each experimentalist to benefit by the experiments of others; instead of tolerating no experiments but its own.
> (Ibid., 306 (V.19))

PREVENTION OF TOTALITARIAN STATE (V.20–22)

A final, 'and most cogent', reason for non-intervention in these cases 'is the great evil of adding unnecessarily to [government] power' (ibid., 306 (V.20)). Mill dismisses the idea that a utilitarian society would involve a large-scale bureaucracy comprised of the most able persons in society. If an attempt were made to run society by means of such a 'numerous bureaucracy' of the most skilled and ambitious, he insists, there would cease to be any social support for critics of the bureaucratic elite. Rather than help each other with their various projects in their own ways, everyone would look to the bureaucracy, 'the multitude for direction and dictation in all they had to do; the able and aspiring for personal advancement' (ibid., 307 (V.20)).

A bureaucratic despotism would tend to arise, involving some uniform system of rules and regulations governing all the details of life: 'where everything is done through the bureaucracy, nothing to which the bureaucracy is really adverse can be done at all' (ibid., 308 (V.21)). 'And the evil would be greater, the more efficiently and scientifically the administrative machinery was constructed—the more skilful the arrangements for obtaining the best qualified hands and heads with which to work it' (306 (V.20)). The 'more perfect' the organization and discipline of the bureaucracy, 'the more complete is the bondage of all, the members of the bureaucracy included' (308 (V.21)). At an extreme, virtually nobody would even consider acting in opposition to the customs and standards of the bureaucracy, as in Russia, where the 'Czar himself is powerless against the bureaucratic body' (307 (V.20)), or in China, where a 'mandarin is as much the tool and creature of a despotism as the humblest cultivator' (308 (V.21)).

In contrast, where individuals and voluntary associations are accustomed to undertake various co-operative ventures without government intervention, as in America and to some extent in France, the danger of bureaucratic tyranny recedes: 'No bureaucracy can hope to make such a people as this do or undergo anything that they do not like' (ibid.). This is not to say that there will be no danger of majority despotism, in the form of illegitimate interference, by stigma if not law, with individual liberty of self-regarding action. But the majority will not suffer the government to gather power beyond certain limits, under the guise of helping the people to do what they can more expediently do by themselves through mutual co-operation.

Mill also emphasizes that a society run by a bureaucratic elite would inevitably suffer stagnation and decline: 'the absorption of all the principal ability of the country into the governing body is fatal, sooner or later, to the mental activity and progressiveness of the body itself' (ibid., 308 (V.22)). Unless subject to external 'watchful criticism of equal ability', the bureaucracy will tend to sink into 'indolent routine' or embrace 'some half-examined crudity which has struck some leading member of the corps' (ibid.). To promote a spirit of individuality and improvement within the bureaucracy and society, it is imperative to let various independent groups serve as an expedient check on the administration. Independent associations should be empowered to criticize the bureaucracy freely, for example, and to experiment with their own co-operative ventures: 'if we would not have our bureaucracy degenerate into a pedantocracy, this body must not engross all the occupations which form and cultivate the faculties required for the government of mankind' (ibid.).

A MAXIM OF LIBERAL UTILITARIAN GOVERNMENT (V.23)

According to Mill, a utilitarian form of government must balance the benefits of social order and co-ordination which an active bureaucracy can provide, against the evils of oppression and stagnation which will result if that bureaucracy discourages individuals and voluntary associations from transacting with each other to mutual advantage.[10]

Without laying down any 'absolute rule' akin to the self-regarding liberty maxim, Mill calls for 'the greatest dissemination of power consistent with efficiency; but the greatest possible centralization of information and diffusion of it from the centre' (1859c, 309 (V.23)). He seems particularly concerned that a central bureaucracy should limit itself, beyond enforcing certain general rules of justice enacted by the legislature, to the collection and dissemination of knowledge which will facilitate co-operation to mutual advantage by people outside the bureaucracy: 'A government cannot have too much of the kind of activity which does not impede, but aids and stimulates, individual exertion and development' (ibid., 310 (V.23)). But the bureaucracy should not force individuals into some pattern of co-operative activities in accord with certain administrative criteria:

> The mischief begins when, instead of calling forth the activity and powers of individuals and bodies, it substitutes its own activity for theirs; when, instead of informing, advising, and, upon occasion, denouncing, it makes them work in fetters, or bids them stand aside and does their work instead of them.
>
> (Ibid.)

It is worth recalling that this recommendation, that government should provide relevant information but otherwise leave individuals alone to pursue various other-regarding projects within the recognized bounds of justice, is, 'in strictness', distinct from the self-regarding liberty maxim. Both are directed at the cultivation of individuality or development. Whereas the liberty maxim urges complete liberty of self-regarding action, however, the present recommendation is for government to refrain from undertaking allegedly beneficial social projects, or from forcing individuals to undertake them, prior to the emergence of the relevant norms of mutual co-operation. By refusing to exercise coercion, society makes possible the development of the norms in question by its members. Until the individual acquires such dispositions, however, he will fail to act co-operatively with others.

At the same time, there is a 'close connection' between the liberty maxim and the present recommendation. For, once individuals have learned norms of mutual co-operation, spontaneous acts to mutual advantage will be included among their self-regarding acts. Prior to that time, these people simply do not choose to perform such beneficial acts, for want of the essential intellectual, moral and practical capacities. Instead, as a last resort, government must force them to perform the acts, or perform them itself.

This co-operative aspect of self-development seems to be the decisive consideration underlying Mill's recommendation for laissez-faire in this context. It might have turned out, contrary to his reasoning, that social benefits could be maximized by government intervention rather than laissez-faire with respect to mutually beneficial actions. Thus, the general expediency of laissez-faire requires further argument, to show why people are benefited more than they would be under mandated projects of mutual co-operation. His answer seems to turn on the idea that most people who are left alone to spontaneously help themselves will develop norms of mutual co-operation, which they would not otherwise develop in the presence of legal coercion.[11]

SUGGESTIONS FOR FURTHER READING

Much of the literature relating to application of the liberty doctrine is unhelpful. Some commentators are so hostile and/or confused that they claim Mill perversely abandons his 'one very simple principle' in this fifth chapter, leading them roundly to dismiss his whole approach. See e.g. Bernard Bosanquet, *The Philosophical Theory of the State* (1899), 4th edn (London: Macmillan, 1923), esp. 55–63, 117–19; and Gertrude Himmelfarb, 'Liberty: "One Very Simple Principle?"', in her *On Looking into the Abyss: Untimely Thoughts on Culture and Society* (New York: Knopf, 1994), 74–106.

A more careful discussion is provided by C.L. Ten, *Mill on Liberty* (Oxford: Clarendon Press, 1980), esp. chs 6–8. Even those as sympathetic as Ten clearly is to the spirit of Mill's liberalism, however, tend to reinterpret his 'text-book', in such a way that we lose sight of any clear connection between his stated doctrine and what he tells us are its practical implications. For the most elaborate of these influential attempts, see Joel Feinberg, *The Moral Limits to the Criminal Law*, 4 vols (Oxford: Oxford University Press, 1984–88). The respective approaches of Ten and Feinberg are taken up below in Chapters 8–10, where I try to spell out some of the main points of contrast with the approach favoured in this Guidebook.

Part III of this edition provides an outline of the structure of Mill's doctrine as I understand it. His 'specimens of application' all seem to fit consistently within this general framework, despite the charges of inconsistency or ambiguity levelled by even his sympathetic admirers. See Chapter 7, 'Suggestions for Further Reading', for references to leading scholars, in addition to Ten and Feinberg, whose interpretations differ markedly from mine.

It might be objected against Mill that the performance of a self-regarding action always implies the omission of an other-regarding action, and vice versa, so that it is pointless to draw the self–other distinction in the field of individual conduct. But the objection is misplaced. True, a self-regarding action chosen at time t implies that the individual fails to choose alternative self-regarding actions as well as other-regarding ones at t. Moreover, society has legitimate authority to consider coercive interference with other-regarding inactions, that is, failures to act that directly cause non-consensual harm or benefit to the interests of others. Yet it does not follow that society ought always to coercively interfere. A general policy of laissez-faire seems expedient, allowing for exceptions. If the agent has a recognized moral duty to others which he fails to fulfil as a result of his putatively self-regarding action at t, then, as Mill argues, the action is taken out of the self-regarding class because it is inseparable from duties to others at t. Failure to fulfil recognized duties to others is a grievous form of non-consensual harm to them, properly open to coercive interference. It should also be noted that the individual's choice of a self-regarding action at t does not necessarily preclude him from choosing a different self-regarding action or an other-regarding action at time $t+1$.

For further discussion of Mill's views on the economic doctrine of laissez-faire, on the need for birth control duly to restrict the general supply of labour in the long run, and on capitalism versus socialism, see J. Riley, 'Justice under Capitalism', in J. Chapman and J.R. Pennock (eds), *Markets and Justice: NOMOS XXXI* (New York: New York University Press, 1989), 122–62; the Introduction to J. Riley (ed.), *John Stuart Mill: Principles of Political Economy and Chapters on Socialism* (Oxford: Oxford University Press, 2008), vii–xlvii; and 'J.S. Mill's Liberal Utilitarian Assessment of Capitalism versus Socialism', *Utilitas* 8 (1996): 39–71.

For an important public disclaimer, consistent with his liberty doctrine, that Mill added to his own marriage contract, see 'Statement on Marriage' (1851), in J.M. Robson (gen. ed.), *Collected Works of John Stuart Mill*, 33 vols (London and Toronto: Routledge and University of Toronto Press, 1984), 21: 97–100.

For further discussion of his views on education, see e.g. Mill, 'Inaugural Address at St Andrews' (1867) and 'Endowments' (1869), in J.M. Robson (gen. ed.), *Collected Works of John Stuart Mill*, 33 vols (London and Toronto: Routledge and University of Toronto Press, 1967), 21: 215–57 and 5: 613–29.

NOTES

1 For an illuminating discussion of different private–public distinctions, see Kymlicka 2002, 386–98. Kymlicka does not discuss Mill's idea of the self-regarding sphere, however, and it's not entirely clear how the idea might fit in with the notions of privacy that he discusses. Mill's idea may overlap with the Romantic notion of a sphere of privacy or intimacy, for example, but self-regarding conduct goes well beyond that to include actions 'in public', outside of a 'room of one's own'.

2 For his view of the generally expedient functions of government, see Mill 1871a, 797–971.

3 Recall that if a commodity only has uses which involve harm to other people, society can legitimately prohibit its production altogether.

4 'In whatever way we define or understand the idea of a right', Mill insists in his *Representative Government*, 'no person can have a right (except in the purely legal sense) to power over others: every such power, which he is allowed to

possess, is morally, in the fullest force of the term, a trust' (1861a, 488). The power of the franchise, for example, is a moral trust, as is the power of attorney or the authority granted to parents over children. See also Mill's distinction between two 'intrinsically very different' dispositions, namely, 'the desire to exercise power over others' and the 'disinclination to have power exercised over [oneself]' (ibid., 420).

5 Mill 1869b elaborates on this argument.

6 For further discussion of Mill's preferred system of liberal democratic political institutions, which he apparently associated with utility in the largest sense, see his *Considerations on Representative Government* (1861a); Thompson 1979; Urbinati 2002; and Riley 2007. It is generally not appreciated that he was severely critical of American political institutions. Prochaska (2012) makes some suggestive remarks in this regard but he underestimates the depth of Mill's dissatisfaction with the presidential system, congressional control over the drafting of bills, the electoral system, and so on. Moreover, Mill was no fan of an aristocracy of blood or wealth. Rather, he proposed ways in which a representative democracy might be designed so as to give what Jefferson called a 'natural aristocracy' a crucial role to play in discouraging the popular majority and its representatives from enacting incompetent legislation and tyrannizing over minorities.

7 Private enterprise has no incentive to supply public goods because the benefits of such a good cannot be excluded from any members of the public at large, including 'free riders' who refuse to pay anything for them.

8 Even support for the needy can be seen as a mutually advantageous action once we recognize that anyone might occupy the positions of the needy and that the needy, once back on their feet, can reciprocate the help they have received, not necessarily to the individuals who helped them but to others in need, either directly or through the tax system. Granted, some individuals will be permanently in need. This may raise issues as to how much support from others can reasonably be expected, whether through voluntary action or government subsidy. But I cannot discuss such issues, which are well beyond the scope of Mill's doctrine of liberty.

9 This is one place (among many others) where Mill evidently rejects traditional act-utilitarian reasoning. See also his letter of 10 January 1862 to Grote, in Mill 1862.

10 Mill develops this theme much further in his *Considerations on Representative Government*, where he rejects the received wisdom that the most competent form of government is found in the aristocratic republics of ancient Rome and Venice because they were administered by powerful bureaucratic elites. See Riley 2007.

11 For further discussion pertinent to this point, see M. Taylor 1982, 1987.

Part III

MILL'S DOCTRINE IN OUTLINE

7
THE STRUCTURE OF MILL'S DOCTRINE OF LIBERTY

I propose to distil from the discussion of Part II the structure of Mill's doctrine of individual liberty and social coercion as I understand it. This seems convenient for readers, including those who may wish to challenge aspects of my interpretation. My interpretation of the doctrine also relies on my understanding of Mill's other writings, especially *Utilitarianism*.

I begin by clarifying my reading of some of Mill's key concepts, including 'harm', 'self-regarding conduct', 'social, or other-regarding, conduct', 'individual liberty', 'individual rights', 'individuality' and 'social authority'.

KEY CONCEPTS

HARM

What does Mill mean by harm? Admittedly, he is not as clear as he might have been about the meaning of harm, and this has led to confusion and controversy. But he does seem to conceive of harm as excluding mere dislike or disgust, what we might call subjective hurt without any accompanying perceptible injury. This is hardly surprising: if the individual is to have the liberty of doing as he likes in his self-regarding affairs, then he must be guaranteed by right that his likes will not be overridden by the contrary likes and dislikes of other people with respect to his self-regarding affairs. Others must have correlative duties to mind their own business. By the same token, self-regarding conduct cannot be reduced to conduct to which others are indifferent or which they like: the fact that someone dislikes a particular action does not mean that he or she is being *harmed*. If the self-regarding liberty maxim meant that the individual only has the right to make personal choices which others like or don't care about, then the maxim would be empty.[1]

Consequently, liberals would regard such an interpretation of Mill's self-regarding maxim as either useless or dangerous, because it would give the individual no protection from the tyranny of the majority in his personal affairs. Standard utilitarians may see nothing objectionable in the interpretation. But Mill is not a standard utilitarian. Rather, as a liberal, he believes that individuals have the power to shape their own likes and dislikes and so are responsible for personal actions which they choose on the basis of their likes and dislikes, except in dire circumstances where they effectively have no choice but to do what they do. Thus, if a person merely feels displeasure at another's self-regarding conduct, he can choose to avoid the source of his dislike or to tolerate it, without being obstructed in the pursuit of his own personal lifestyle. He has no reason to claim that his own self-regarding liberty has been coercively interfered with or that his interests have been damaged against his wishes.

The idea of harm that fits best with *On Liberty* is a broad descriptive idea of 'perceptible hurt', a term which Mill does use in the essay (1859c, 282 (IV.11)).[2] This term needs to be unpacked. In *A System of Logic*, he defines a 'perception' as the direct recognition of an external object and says that it amounts to an intuitive belief – a belief held to be self-evident – that the object exists as the source of 'certain sensations which I receive from it' (1843, 53–54).[3] So perceptible hurt is damage in an external object that can in principle be directly recognized by any suitably situated competent observer. And by perceptible hurt to an individual's interests, Mill apparently means damage in any external thing which the individual has a *reason* to be concerned about, including his body, mobility, residence, finances, contracts, reputation, friendships, other kinds of relationships, and so on, since noticeable changes in those objects alter his personal circumstances and thus affect his capacity to make his own choices and to cultivate his higher faculties.

To digress a bit, the individual's view of his interests is, for Mill, his idea of utility. Given that all humans are fallible, any individual's idea of utility may be mistaken. Moreover, utility means happiness in the sense of feelings of pleasure including relief from pain, so the individual's view of his interests is his possibly mistaken idea of happiness. But Mill also rejects any suggestion that pleasant or painful feelings are free-floating entities that appear out of nowhere or are purely subjective creations of our mental faculties. Instead, he maintains that they are embodied in external objects that can be treated as the sources of pleasure and pain or, strictly speaking, of *sensations* of pleasure and pain, the elementary 'bodily feelings' that are experienced by the senses and automatically conveyed by the nervous system into our consciousness. These elementary sensations are ingredients of every other kind of pleasant or painful feeling, however complex. So it may be clearer to say that, for Mill, the individual's view of his interests is his idea of the things or objects which he associates with happiness, in so far as he believes (though perhaps incorrectly) that these things are sources of the most pleasure including absence of pain for him.

It is worth emphasizing that the idea of harm as perceptible damage is descriptive rather than normative. There is no implication that the individual should dislike the perceptible damage, for instance, or that he ought to find it undesirable, all things considered. He has a reason to be concerned about it, but that reason may be outweighed by other considerations for him so that he freely consents to the damage to his interests. Moreover, even if the damage is non-consensual, his reason for concern may not be morally justified. His reason may be decisive in terms of his selfish interests so that he opposes the damage in the objects of his concern. But it does not follow that he has a moral claim on society to prevent or punish others' actions that cause the perceptible damage or that fail to intercept it. Whether he does have such a claim is a separate question to be answered by a moral theory. But at least his reasonable concern for his self-interest must be among the considerations which a moral calculus will take into account. Society or its representatives may properly decide, however, that the non-consensual damage to his interests is not of a kind that everyone needs to be protected, by equal right, from suffering.[4]

By contrast, the individual's mere dislike is not a *reason* to consider coercive interference with another's conduct, a point Mill repeatedly emphasizes throughout the essay. As he puts it: 'But to be restrained [by others] in things not affecting their good, by their mere displeasure, developes [*sic*] nothing valuable, except such force of character as may unfold itself in resisting the restraint' (1859c, 266 (III.9)). Given that coercion to prevent mere dislike develops nothing valuable, individuals who seek happiness 'grounded on the permanent interests of man as a progressive being' have no reason to be concerned about protecting each other from experiencing mere dislike.

SELF-REGARDING CONDUCT

Self-regarding conduct does not directly harm or benefit the interests of other people, or, if it does, only with their genuine consent and participation. Although it can and at times should affect the feelings of others, so that they will like or dislike it, the conduct does not cause any perceptible damage or improvement in any objects which they have a reason to be concerned about.

Remarkably, Mill appears not to take consensual harm very seriously in so far as he rejects its prevention as a reason for coercive interference. Perhaps, some might think, he assumes that competent adults can only genuinely consent to, and participate in, quite trivial forms of perceptible damage to their interests, and that readers would recognize this and accept that such trivial harms can be treated as if they are not harms at all. This would explain the rather puzzling way in which he refers to self-regarding actions as if they are always literally harmless to others, whereas in fact he defines them such that they can harm others' interests with their genuine consent. I seriously doubt that he assumes that consensual harms are invariably trivial ones, however, since it is so obviously false: competent adults can consent to and participate in serious damage to their interests, such as selling themselves into slavery. The more likely explanation for his puzzling way of referring to self-regarding conduct, I think, is ease of exposition: it is true that some self-regarding actions *are* harmless to others, and he does not wish to keep repeating that some do cause consensual harm, after he has alerted readers to this fact.

In any case, I now emphasize that self-regarding actions may directly cause consensual harm to others. This emphasis allows me to define harm as perceptible damage, whether experienced with or without consent, instead of defining it such that consensual harm is not harm at all.[5] Moreover, consensual harm may amount to grave perceptible damage to one's interests.

Before moving on, it is important to clear up why Mill at one point refers to self-regarding conduct as 'conduct which neither violates any specific duty to the public, nor occasions perceptible hurt to any assignable individual except himself' (1859c, 282 (IV.11)). Why is there a need to add that it does not violate any specific duty to the public? This reference, I think, shows his subtlety of reasoning. The point is that conduct which *appears* to be self-regarding because it does not cause any perceptible damage to the interests of any other *assignable individual* is nevertheless *not* self-regarding, because it causes non-consensual perceptible damage to the interests of the *public at large*. The people or its representatives have decided, after due deliberation, that everyone has a duty not to cause this specific form of non-consensual harm to the public interest.

For Mill, a utilitarian code of social justice distributes and sanctions 'specific duties to the public' which are not correlative with individual rights, such as the duty to help defend the country against foreign aggressors, the duty to pay one's fair share of the taxes needed to support the government, the duty to serve on juries, and the duty not to pollute the environment by, say, defecating on city streets (ibid., 276 (IV.3), 282 (IV.11)). The individual who fails to fulfil these public duties causes perceptible damage to the interests of the public at large rather than to those of assignable individuals.[6] Such perceptible damage to the public interest is deemed non-consensual and wrongful by the political representatives of the polity. These public duties help to resolve certain puzzles that arise if the term 'harm to others' is mistakenly confined to harm to other assignable individuals.

In this regard, there can be perceptible damage to the public at large which is imperceptible with respect to the interests of any assignable member of the public. Conduct that appears to be harmless to the interests of any other particular individual may yet cause perceptible hurt to the public if it is performed by many individuals simultaneously or in succession. One individual may fail to pay his fair share of taxes without any perceptible effect on another assignable individual, for instance, and yet if many or all people did the same, perceptible damage to the public treasury would be the result. Or one person might trespass across a beautiful part of a national park without harming the interests of any other determinate individual, and yet if many or all did the same, that area of the park would be ruined.

Perceptible damage to the public interest is not necessarily wrongful: it may be permissible for many people to trample over the vegetation in designated areas of a national park, for example, and it might even be praiseworthy for many people to refuse to pay taxes to support a government that engages in unjustified military strikes against innocent civilians around the world. But the prevention of perceptible damage is a necessary condition for the authorities to create an enforceable 'specific duty to the public'.

According to utility in the largest sense, some forms of perceptible damage to the public at large are unjust and thus deserving of punishment. Any action that would, if performed repeatedly by many people, cause such grievous perceptible damage ought to be prevented to promote the public interest. Political representatives have legitimate power to protect the public by creating duties not to cause such perceptible damage: the duties signal that the public's representatives regard the damage as non-consensual and wrongful. For instance, such duties may include duties not to endanger the public health by defecating in the city streets, even though any isolated act of public defecation may not seem to endanger the health of any assignable individual. The enlarged utilitarian criterion thereby generates specific public duties not to engage in conduct that might otherwise be mistaken for self-regarding conduct if we only considered its effects on the interests of other assignable individuals. But duties not to do things which others merely dislike remain illegitimate: the people and its representatives have no legitimate power to create such duties.

This discussion shows that, for Mill, the individual's view of his interests (and thus his idea of utility) is not necessarily confined exclusively to narrowly selfish interests. An enlightened moral agent conceives of his interests as a member of the public and regards wrongful damage to the interests of the public as non-consensual harm to his own interests.

SOCIAL, OR OTHER-REGARDING, CONDUCT

Social, or other-regarding conduct, is the complement of self-regarding conduct. Unlike the latter, the former does directly cause *non-consensual* harm or benefit to the interests of others. Society rightfully has authority to regulate the individual's social conduct, Mill emphasizes, so as to prevent others from suffering grievous damage to their interests without their consent.

In this regard, it should be kept in mind that any fallible person's idea of his interests, that is, his utility, may be mistaken: he may regard as a harm what others see as a benefit, and so he may refuse to accept what others view as beneficial to his interests. But it is the competent individual's view of his interests that matters, and so any attempt to force him to accept what others regard as a benefit must be seen as a non-consensual harm *to him*. This interpersonal variation in the classification of harms and benefits does not raise any problems for the definition of other-regarding conduct, which is tied to the *non-consensual* effects on others' interests. Nor does it raise any problems for the definition of self-regarding conduct, since it does not matter whether others view the conduct's effects as harmful or beneficial to them so long as they genuinely consent to them. Nor does the interpersonal variation cause any problems for the idea of social authority, provided we recognize that the majority's ideas of what is harmful may not be shared by everyone in society.

The individual's social conduct includes actions that directly cause non-consensual damage to the interests of the public. Society has legitimate power to consider coercive interference with such actions and may properly decide to interfere if it or its representatives are persuaded, after due deliberation, that coercion is needed to protect the public interest as opposed to the interests of any assignable individual. True, highly developed individuals of strong moral character will associate their own interests with those of the polity instead of viewing them in a narrowly selfish way. But not every person can be assumed to be an ideal moral agent at present, and so coercion may be required to prevent him from putting his selfish interests before the interests of the public at large. It may be convenient to dump garbage on public property, for example, but society properly has authority to declare that such other-regarding conduct is wrongful and subject to punishment.

INDIVIDUAL LIBERTY

There is no doubt that, for Mill, liberty means 'doing as we like' (1859c, 226 (I.12)), 'doing what one desires' (ibid., 294 (V.5)), 'act[ing] according to [one's] own inclination and judgment' (ibid., 260 (III.1)).

Keeping in mind his caveat that his doctrine is intended only for fallible adult members of civil societies who are capable of rational persuasion, we can say that this is a descriptive notion according to which the individual has liberty with respect to a given set of feasible actions only if two conditions are satisfied: first, while fallible, he must have some threshold level of competence that enables him to make reasonable choices among the actions, in which case he is able to grasp the likely consequences of the choices he makes; and second, he must choose as he wishes, likes, desires, and judges as best or maximal for promoting his interests as he views them, in which case there must not be any coercive interference with his choices by other people or their institutions.

It is worth remarking that, for Mill, liberty is 'positive' in Isaiah Berlin's sense.[7] It is positive in that the individual who has it does as he wishes, is the master of his own actions and is not making choices dictated by other people. It is also 'negative' in that the individual is free from coercive interference with respect to the actions he performs, even if he merely wishes to be idle for the time being.[8] Indeed, if a person does as he wishes, then it must be the case that others are not preventing him from acting in accord with his judgment and inclinations. It is not quite true, however, that, for Mill, liberty itself is negative in Berlin's sense. For Berlin, negative liberty seems to require that the individual has a field or sphere of actions with respect to which he is aware that he can make choices free from coercive interference, even if he does not currently have any wish at all. The guarantee of such a field of actions is, for Mill, provided by an individual *right* to liberty, which is correlative with duties for everyone else not to coercively interfere in that field. This guaranteed field is the self-regarding sphere. So, we may say that the *right* of self-regarding liberty captures something like Berlin's negative aspect, whereas the *liberty* itself is positive.

Moreover, Mill does not introduce any distinction between the 'empirical self' and a higher 'ideal rational and moral self' in the way German and British idealists do, and so he does not work with a metaphysical notion of positive freedom that involves doing what the higher self finds worthy of choosing, even if the actual self does not wish to make such a choice and must be coerced to do whatever is assumed to be 'worthy'.

INDIVIDUAL RIGHTS

In Mill's doctrine, liberty is not the same thing as rights. Individual liberty is a purely descriptive idea whereas individual rights are normative claims that specify, among other things, where and under what conditions the individual ought to have liberty in the sense of doing as he wishes.

Again, there is no doubt that, for Mill, a right is a claim on society to protect some vital interest of the individual: 'When we call anything a person's right, we mean that he has a valid claim on society to protect him in the possession of it, either by the force of law, or by that of education and opinion' (1861b, 250 (V.24)). A right of private property, for example, is a claim (or bundle of claims) on society to protect the individual's vital interest in the exclusive use and control of the objects which his community permits to be owned, with the caveat that the objects cannot be used in immoral ways that cause grievous harms to other individuals or to the public at large. Protection consists of duties for others which are correlative with his claim and which, if not voluntarily fulfilled, may be enforced by the state. As Mill makes clear in *Political Economy*, however, the right of private property, if it were properly designed, would protect the individual's interest only in the exclusive use and control of the things which he has produced through his own efforts, or which he has acquired through voluntary exchanges stemming from the producer. In that case, the right would protect the individual's interest in providing a living for himself and his family through his own labour and investment. So designed, however, the right would not cover ownership of natural resources, although rights to use them in ways deemed permissible by society are evidently essential.[9]

A right of private property, even designed as Mill recommends, gives the individual some liberty to use his property in ways permitted by society but not in other ways. Strictly speaking, he does not have liberty in the sense of doing whatever he likes. Rather, he can do what he wants only within the moral and legal limits established by society. Moreover, such liberty as is permitted is with respect to other-regarding actions that cause non-consensual harm to others. For instance, the production of finished goods requires social permission to use scarce natural resources, and permission for one individual or group is prohibition for another, which at some point must begin to damage the interests of the losing competitors. As well, trade is an other-regarding act: successful sellers and marketers of products cause their competitors to lose sales and perhaps be driven into insolvency against their wishes.

By contrast, the right of self-regarding liberty gives the individual complete freedom to choose among self-regarding actions as he wishes. No limits on his use of self-regarding liberty are legitimately enforced by society. This right protects the vital interest in self-assertion or individuality, which is 'the same thing' as self-improvement or 'development' (1859c, 267 (III.10)). Liberty in the sense of asserting oneself as one pleases, without any limits set by society, is 'the only unfailing and permanent source of improvement' (ibid., 272 (III.17)).

THE STRUCTURE OF MILL'S DOCTRINE OF LIBERTY 199

This right to liberty is not merely a moral or legal permission in the sense of having no duty not to choose this or that self-regarding action: such a permission is compatible with other people having no duties not to obstruct or compete with the individual's self-regarding choices. Rather, the right is a claim on society to protect the individual from others' obstruction and competition so that he can freely make self-regarding choices in accordance with his own judgment and inclinations, discover whether he enjoys or regrets the outcomes, learn from his mistakes, and develop his higher mental faculties, including his intellect and imagination as well as his desires and sentiments. Thus, Mill speaks of 'a just *claim* [of individuals] to carry on their lives in their own way' (ibid., 270 (III.14), emphasis added). By insisting that 'over his own body and mind, the individual is sovereign' (224 (I.9)), he is urging us to recognize the individual's valid claim to choose as he pleases among his self-regarding actions so that he can develop his own individuality, 'one of the principal ingredients of human happiness' (261 (III.1)).[10]

INDIVIDUALITY

It is worth emphasizing right away that Mill does *not* say that the cultivation of individuality reveals some unique essence or nature of the individual, and indeed he repudiates such talk as a fantasy of 'metaphysics, that fertile field of delusion propagated by language' (1843, 127).[11] So what is individuality? For Mill, it seems to be the individual's character, or set of dispositions or habits of will, as developed by the individual himself through his own assertions or efforts, that is, by doing as he pleases. The sphere of self-regarding liberty is a minimum sphere in which the individual is guaranteed by right to be able to think, discuss his opinions, and act in accord with his own judgment and inclinations, and thus develop his character.

Mill argues that there is a ladder or progressive series of individualities or characters, not unique to any particular individual, such that the individual can ascend through his own efforts from having a 'miserable individuality' (1861b, 216 (II.14)) to having a 'noble character' (ibid., 213 (II.9)). Whereas a miserable character features narrowly selfish dispositions, degrading tastes, and passive acceptance of existing laws and customs, a noble individuality is represented by the ideal Periclean character in which a powerful conscience, or disposition to fulfil one's moral duties to others, is integrated with a cultivated appreciation of the beautiful and sublime as well as a disposition to actively struggle to reform unjust laws and practices.

Nevertheless, it is an interesting question why Mill seems to believe that the individual can ascend this ladder by doing as he pleases in his self-regarding affairs: why does self-regarding liberty lead the individual to develop a balanced character in which strong moral dispositions to respect the rights of other people and to help them with their projects, treat them with kindness, and so on, figure prominently? Some commentators suggest that he faces severe problems here: either he cannot give a convincing answer, they charge, or he must abandon his extremely individualistic doctrine of liberty.[12] By contrast, I argue that a convincing answer lies in his claim, as indicated in *Utilitarianism*, that there are higher kinds of pleasant feelings, including relief from suffering, which are superior in quality to lower kinds, irrespective of quantity. Those individuals who exercise their self-regarding liberty to experiment with different ideas and personal lifestyles will tend to discover these qualitatively superior elements of happiness and, in particular, learn that the pleasant feeling of the moral sentiment of justice is of higher quality than any competing pleasure. I will return to this issue in Part IV, Chapter 9.

SOCIAL AUTHORITY

Social authority is the legitimate power of society, or of those who succeed in making themselves its representatives, to employ coercion to force people to obey its rules, including laws and customs, that regulate social, or other-regarding, conduct. This legitimate power over others is not unlimited: it is not a moral right or entitlement to compel others to obey any rule whatsoever subject to punishment. Rather, it is a moral trust consisting of two components: first, a limited power and privilege to enforce reasonable social rules that govern which forms of non-consensual harm to others are morally permissible and which are not; and second, a disability and duty not to enforce any social rules that govern self-regarding conduct. The individual, not the public or the majority or the government, is sovereign within the self-regarding realm.

In principle, every civil society has such authority, whatever its form of government. But Mill argues in his *Representative Government* that this legitimate power is most likely to become manifest and to be used competently in civil societies that adopt a representative form of democratic government in which, among other things, there is proportional representation under a universal franchise, a distinctive system of counter-majoritarian checks and balances which gives an unusual degree of influence to highly educated members of society in political deliberations, and a skilled professional bureaucracy to draft and enforce the laws that govern other-regarding conduct. In short, for him, a utilitarian government is a distinctive form of liberal democracy, in which unusual steps are taken to encourage competent deliberation about which social rules are most likely to promote collective happiness 'in the largest sense'.

I will next use these key concepts to clarify the structure of Mill's doctrine of liberty as I understand it. My discussion will be fairly brief, as my intention is to provide an outline rather than a more detailed analysis. Readers may find it helpful to refer to Figure 1 overleaf, which depicts the structure of Mill's doctrine.

THE 'ONE VERY SIMPLE PRINCIPLE'

The 'one very simple principle' really is simple. It says that the only reason for society or its representatives to employ coercion to interfere with the actions of a competent adult is to prevent harm to others, where harm means perceptible damage to their interests. It can be expressed either as a simple harm principle or as a simple liberty principle. As a liberty principle, it says that the individual has a moral right to choose any actions that are harmless to others, since society has no reason to coercively interfere with such actions. Everything else Mill says in *On Liberty* is compatible with, and revolves around, this simple principle.

Despite its simplicity, the principle is of great importance. It implies, for example, that society cannot legitimately appeal to

```
                                    One very simple principle: Prevention of
                                    harm to others is a necessary but not
                                    sufficient condition for coercive interference

                                              The individual's life
                                                 and conduct
```

```
                                                                    Social sphere:
                                                                     Actions cause
                                                              non-consensual harm to others
```

```
Self-regarding sphere:
Actions do not cause
harm to others or, if they do,
only consensual harm
```

```
                                                              Simple maxim of social authority:
                                                              Society has legitimate authority to consider
                                                              coercive interference to prevent the harm
Simple maxim of self-regarding liberty:
Society has no legitimate authority to even
consider coercive interference
```

```
                                                                                                Sphere of morality and law: Immoral and
                                          *Sphere of competition:                               properly illegal actions cause non-consensual
                                          Successful actions cause non-consensual              and wrongful harm to others
The individual has a                      but permissible harm to others
moral right (claim)
to do as he pleases                                                                             Principle of moral and legal freedom:
                                                                                                Individuals should willingly refrain from      Sphere of beneficence and charity: Society
                                          Principle of laissez-faire:                           wrong-doing but, if they refuse to, society ought    should not employ legal punishment to prevent
                                          Society ought not to employ                           to employ coercive interference to prevent it,       unkind actions but instead should rely solely
                                          coercive interference                                 except in special situations where coercion          on public stigma and guilt
                                                                                                is not expedient
                                          The individual has no utilitarian
                                          duties to refrain from competing                                                                      The individual has imperfect duties
                                          with others under fair conditions                                                                     that are not correlative with others' rights
```

```
                                                                                    Sphere of justice: Society legitimately
                                                                                    employs legal punishment to
                                                                                    prevent injustice


                                              The individual has perfect                        The individual has perfect
                                              duties correlative with                           absolute duties to the
                                              others' rights, including rights                  public at large, enforceable
                                              of self-regarding liberty                         by public officials
```

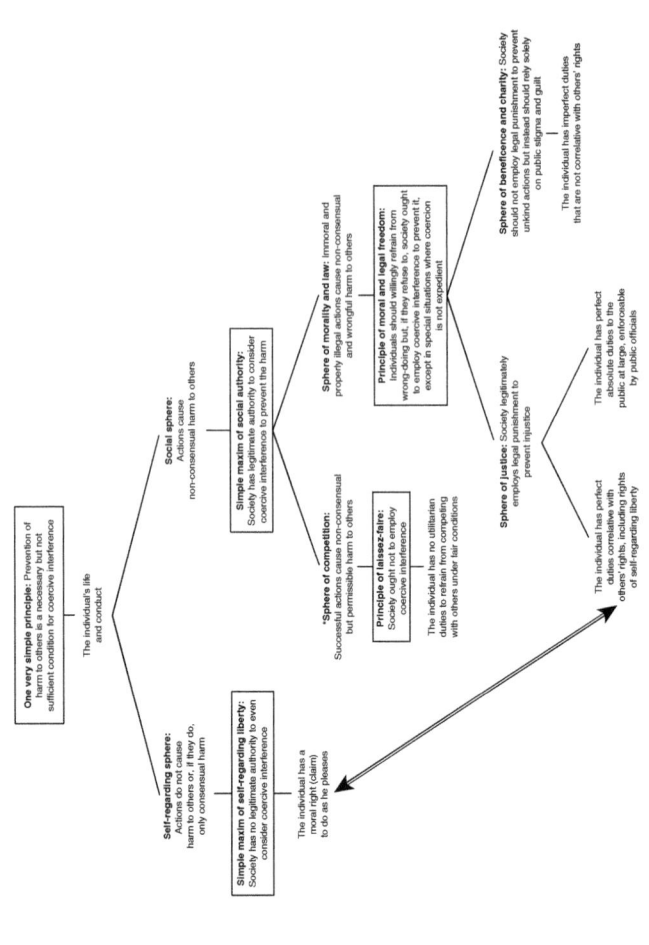

Figure 1 Mill's extraordinary utilitarian doctrine of individual liberty

*Note: The competitive sphere is nested within the sphere of morality and law, i.e. it is protected by moral and legal rules. So a utilitarian policy of laissez-faire does not countenance violations of duties to others.

other reasons for coercive interference. The people or their government cannot legitimately employ coercion to prevent mere dislike or disgust, since such mere displeasure is not perceptible damage. Nor can coercive interference be employed to prevent a competent individual from harming himself alone, if the interests of others are not damaged.[13] Society is permitted to check that self-harm is not unintentional but the steps taken to check must not amount to coercion: any 'interference' must be brief, consist only of advice or warnings, and cease once the individual is made aware of the likely consequences of his actions.

The simple principle also implies that society can only legitimately enforce duties that are duties not to directly cause harm to others. Duties not to cause damage to one's own interests alone cannot be legitimately enforced, nor can duties not to perform actions at which others feel mere dislike or contempt. Society must not make such duties into moral or legal duties and threaten to punish people for not fulfilling them. Instead, the individual ought to be perfectly free to do as he wishes if what he does is harmless to others.

PREVENTION OF HARM TO OTHERS IS NECESSARY BUT NOT SUFFICIENT FOR COERCIVE INTERFERENCE

As Mill emphasizes, the simple principle states a necessary but not sufficient condition for coercive interference with a competent individual's action. Thus, the fact that an action directly causes perceptible damage to the interests of others does not mean that coercive interference is therefore justified. For example, Mill quickly indicates that society should not even consider coercive interference to prevent *consensual* harm to others.

THE MAXIM OF SELF-REGARDING LIBERTY

The maxim of self-regarding liberty, which may be expressed more fully as the maxim of individual liberty with respect to self-regarding conduct, says that a competent member of any civil society has a moral right to do as he pleases with respect to the self-regarding portion of his life and conduct. Coercive interference with self-regarding actions should not even be considered. Society has no legitimate power to use coercion within the individual's self-regarding sphere, which, for Mill, is properly seen as beyond morality.

Strictly speaking, this principle of self-regarding liberty is distinct from the 'one very simple principle' because the former, unlike the latter, embodies the judgment that society ought to ignore consensual perceptible damage to the interests of others when deliberating over how to employ coercion. The self-regarding maxim extends the rightful liberty of the individual not only to actions that are harmless to others but also to actions that harm others with their genuine consent and participation. Evidently, the self-regarding maxim is a refinement of the 'very simple principle' and consistent with it.

The self-regarding liberty maxim refines the 'one very simple principle' by combining it with the *volenti* maxim, on the understanding that 'harm is not made by consent' is valid only if the consent is genuine, that is, given by a competent individual without force or fraud. Although it is a bit more complex than the 'one very simple principle', it seems fair to say that the self-regarding liberty maxim itself remains pretty simple.

Perhaps it is also worth stressing that the right of self-regarding liberty encompasses a variety of liberties insofar as there are various self-regarding activities. To have a right of self-regarding liberty is to have the right to choose among many self-regarding actions as one pleases, choosing to do one thing at one time and then doing another thing later if one likes, reverting to the first activity after that, and so forth. More specifically, the self-regarding liberties include 'the liberty of conscience ... ; absolute freedom of opinion and sentiment on all subjects ... ; the liberty of expressing and publishing opinions ... ; liberty of tastes and pursuits; ... of doing as we like ... without impediment from our fellow-creatures, so long as what we do does not harm them, even though they should think our conduct foolish, perverse, or wrong ... ; [and] freedom to unite, for any purpose not involving harm to others' (1859c, 225–26 (I.12)). Thus, self-regarding actions include forming opinions and feelings (including feelings of like and dislike), discussing them with other people, choosing careers, lifestyles (including sexual lifestyles) and commitments (including artistic and spiritual projects) that do not force others to experience perceptible injury even though others may dislike them, consuming any products and services (including drugs, alcohol and so forth) that can be used in self-regarding ways, and forming voluntary associations that do not inflict non-consensual harm on non-members. Competent adults should by right have complete liberty to choose any of these self-regarding actions: 'No society in which these [self-regarding] liberties are not, on the whole, respected, is free, whatever its form of government; and none is completely free in which they do not exist *absolute and unqualified*' (ibid., 226 (I.13), emphasis added).

For Mill, the self-regarding sphere is 'the appropriate region of human liberty' (ibid., 225 (I.12)). 'In this department, therefore, of human affairs, Individuality has its proper field of action ... [I]n each person's own concerns, his individual spontaneity is entitled to free exercise' (ibid., 277 (IV.4)). Notice that mere dislike of or disgust at another's conduct *is* counted in Mill's unusual utilitarianism: each individual has an equal right to avoid whatever he merely dislikes, as long as he does not cause any non-consensual harm to others. But mere dislike is never counted as a reason for coercive interference: 'We have a right ... to act upon our unfavourable opinion of any one, not to the oppression of his individuality, but in the exercise of ours' (ibid., 278 (IV.5)).

THE MAXIM OF SOCIAL AUTHORITY

The maxim of social authority, which may be expressed more fully as the maxim of society's authority with respect to social, or other-regarding, conduct, is the logical complement of the self-regarding liberty maxim. It says that the individual has no moral right to do as he pleases with respect to the social portion of his life and conduct. In other words, society does have legitimate power to consider coercive interference with respect to other-regarding conduct, for the purpose of protecting others from suffering damage to their interests without their genuine consent and participation.

This maxim is obviously consistent with both the self-regarding liberty maxim and the 'one very simple principle'. Unlike the latter, it implicitly incorporates the *volenti* maxim, and thus directs society to focus exclusively on non-consensual harm to others when deliberating over how and where to use coercion. Again, although it is a bit more complex than the 'one very simple principle', the social authority maxim remains pretty simple. The maxim says nothing specific about how and where society should actually employ coercive interference *within the social sphere*. It says only that society's jurisdiction is confined to the social sphere.

For Mill, how and where to use coercion within any person's other-regarding sphere is answered by his extraordinary version of utilitarianism. I can only give a brief, and no doubt inadequate, indication of the way I think it works, although I have explained this in more detail elsewhere and will also say a bit more about it from time to time in Part IV of this study.[14] To appreciate its method of operation, it is important to see that his utilitarianism carves up the other-regarding sphere into subspheres. Unlike both the self-regarding and other-regarding spheres themselves, which are in principle observable independently of his utilitarianism or of any other theory of morality and law, these various subspheres of social conduct are created by his utilitarianism itself in the course of prescribing how society ought to go about maximizing 'utility in the largest sense'.

More specifically, the social portion of any individual's life and conduct is broken down into a sphere of competition, where the non-consensual harms caused to others by successful competitors are permissible because they do not violate any recognized duties to others, and a sphere of morality and law, where the non-consensual harms caused to others by malicious individuals are wrongful and impermissible because they do violate recognized duties to others. Strictly speaking, the competitive sphere is a separate sphere nested inside the sphere of morality and law: individuals are permitted to compete with one another only if they comply with society's moral and legal rules that distribute duties to others.

The sphere of morality and law is itself split further into two subspheres, to wit, a sphere of beneficence and charity in which duties are 'imperfect' in the sense that they are owed to others only under certain conditions and so the individual has some discretion about when to fulfil them, and a sphere of justice in which duties are 'perfect' in the sense that they are always owed to others so that the individual is required to continuously fulfil them. And 'perfect duties' may also be divided into two classes, those owed to other 'assignable individuals' whose rights are correlative with the duties, and those owed to the public at large which are not correlative with any assignable individual's rights. The perfect duty which correlates with any assignable individual's right of self-regarding liberty is what brings Mill's utilitarian theory of justice and right into harmony with his radical liberal maxim of self-regarding liberty.

Evidently, more must be said to clarify how Mill's utilitarianism creates these various regions within the other-regarding sphere, and how it creates the various moral and legal duties, including those perfect duties that are correlative with individual rights. I will focus attention on the link between his utilitarianism and a liberal democratic political system.

DETERMINING WHICH NON-CONSENSUAL HARMS TO OTHERS ARE WRONGFUL

Roughly, Mill's utilitarianism says that collective decisions about duties to others with respect to social conduct, and thus about which non-consensual harms are wrongful and which are not, ought to be made by popular majorities or their representatives, after due discussion and deliberation, in the context of a liberal democratic political system of the distinctive sort mentioned earlier. Such a political system is essential for the promotion of utility in the largest sense. True, humans are fallible and will sometimes, perhaps often, make mistakes. Even in the present low level of general education, however, deliberative majorities have learned to accept broad laissez-faire doctrines with respect to speech and economic markets, he points out, and so they are persuaded that the common good requires that no one has a duty *not* to cause non-consensual harms of the type suffered by losing competitors. Moreover, if education improves, then the majority's decisions are reasonably expected to become increasingly enlightened. Indeed, this possibility is central to Mill's project in the *Liberty*, since he hopes that deliberative majorities may eventually be persuaded to endorse his maxim of self-regarding liberty.

In principle, Mill's utilitarian liberal democratic political system considers only the higher kind of pleasant feeling associated with the moral sentiment of justice. In other words, it only accepts as inputs for discussion and deliberation a moral kind of individual preference ranking, or judgment, that is defined over alternative possible general rules that distribute and sanction equal perfect duties for all.[15] Such preferences will only be formed by moral agents who have developed their mental faculties. Rules of the sort indicated are the only source of the higher pleasure of justice, and moral individuals will most prefer the rules which they expect will bring them the greatest amount of this higher pleasure, which Mill calls 'security', properly understood as the feeling of enjoyment, including relief from suffering, that the moral individual gets from his assurance that the shared vital interests of all assignable individuals—which ought to be seen as equal rights—as well as the interests of the public, are recognized and protected by society. The rules and duties of justice that are actually recognized at any given time are those chosen by the majority of these moral agents after discussion and debate. Moreover, as long as he acts in accordance with his recognized rights and duties under the rules, the individual is free to pursue other kinds of pleasures without coercive interference by the state.

This distinctive liberal democratic political system works smoothly if most or all members of society are moral agents. Until the level of general education has progressed so far, however, the political system inevitably has shortcomings, and is more or less contaminated by non-moral agents pursuing their narrowly selfish interests. As a result, the recognized rules and duties of justice may not be ones which would be recommended and chosen by moral agents. Mill suggests that the distortions can be minimized, or at least contained, under his distinctive system because it gives the highly educated minority in society more influence in the majority's political deliberations, and this minority may be able to persuade the majority to make better decisions and not meddle with self-regarding actions. And perhaps he is correct about this. There is only one way to find out, and that is for civil societies to actually adopt and experiment with a liberal democratic system of the distinctive sort prescribed by him. Unfortunately, there is no sign that this will happen in the foreseeable future.

Nevertheless, the fact remains that relatively more advanced societies have adopted liberal democratic political systems that are not entirely dissimilar to Mill's distinctive utilitarian system. So, although his self-regarding liberty maxim is not yet properly recognized, there is a good chance that deliberative majorities even at the present low level of education will establish enforceable duties to others with respect to other-regarding conduct that are in the neighbourhood of the duties prescribed by utility in the largest sense: 'On questions of social morality, of duty to others, the opinion of the public, that is, of an overruling majority, though often wrong, is likely to be still oftener right; because on such questions they are only required to judge of their own interests; of the manner in which some mode of [other-regarding] conduct, if allowed to be practised, would affect themselves [and, in particular, harm them without their consent]' (1859c, 284 (IV.12)). Moreover, there may already be sufficient legal recognition of some rights and liberties, especially those involved in the laissez-faire doctrines relating to trade and speech, to hope for continuing social improvement and perhaps eventual widespread acceptance of his distinctive form of liberal democracy. Indeed, if majorities learn to accept the self-regarding liberty principle, the process of social improvement might continue indefinitely.

And yet there is also the danger of social decline if majorities do not learn to accept the self-regarding liberty maxim. If the only outlet left for self-assertion is business, he warns, then society will tend to sink into a quite mindless commercial culture characterized by an endless series of fads which most people pursue in a herd, and accompanied by a restricted range of public expression consisting largely of promotional advertising, consumer entertainment, and political opinions given prominence by commercial groups. Needless to add, the political system in such a banal commercial culture will be driven by money, and the mass of consumers will be apathetic and ignorant about political issues.

I must reiterate that many aspects of Mill's utilitarianism are being left aside in my brief remarks relating to his preferred political system. Some moral rules cannot be expediently enforced as laws, for example, and so it is not the case that duties to others (and thus which forms of non-consensual harm to others are recognized as impermissible) are always determined by political decisions. Rather, some rules evolve as customs that are expediently enforced not by legal sanctions but by coercive public opinion, and so there are customary moral duties not enshrined in law. Indeed, some rules cannot be expediently enforced by external sanctions at all, and so must emerge as shared dictates of conscience protected only by the internal sanctions of guilt. A utilitarian social code of morality is thus akin to a layer cake of rules, including laws, customs and shared dictates of conscience. The laws are expediently enforced by all sanctions, the customs only by stigma and guilt, and the bare dictates only by guilt if obeyed at all.[16]

The customs and dictates of conscience which have actually emerged have been established by actual majorities of the people, however, and not by majorities of moral agents.[17] Actual majorities may only be thoughtlessly imitating the practices of dominant minorities in society, such as aristocratic elites or wealthy classes. Thus, there is a continuing need to assess existing customs and shared dictates of conscience from the perspective of utility in the largest sense. Mill insists that educated individuals who exercise their self-regarding liberty are essential to provide the assessment and to persuade popular majorities to accept better moral customs and rules of conscience. But I cannot further discuss these complicated matters.

WRONGFUL HARM

Wrongful harm is perceptible damage to an individual's interests which deliberative majorities have decided is morally or legally impermissible and thus *ought not* to be consented to by anyone. There is an important complication here, however, which threatens to bring down Mill's whole edifice. The problem is that some competent individuals may nevertheless consent to the harms that have been declared wrongful, and so it seems that these individuals ought to have the self-regarding liberty to do what is wrong.

This problem arises because of interpersonal variation in the identification of harms as consensual or non-consensual. Just as they may disagree over whether to classify a perceptible effect as damaging or beneficial, competent individuals may disagree over whether to consent to some form of perceptible damage to their interests. Whereas some may find it reasonable to consent, others do not wish to consent or participate in the creation of what amounts to the same harm in a descriptive sense. As a result, there is interpersonal variation in the classification of self-regarding and other-regarding actions. Individuals who consent to some form of perceptible damage view interactions with people who cause it as self-regarding, but those who do not consent to it view the same interactions as social, or other-regarding. Thus, the first group of people seem to have a right of self-regarding liberty, and yet the second group can claim that society has authority to consider coercive interference and can legitimately prevent the activity if it decides that the harm produced by it is wrongful. The one group insists on a moral right to experience the harm, while the second group may insist on a moral duty not to cause it.

The problem would disappear, of course, if everybody always agreed on which harms ought to be consensual and which not. Unfortunately, such unanimity cannot reasonably be expected. Even so, society can often find ways to cope. The pattern of actual individual consent and non-consent is observable. Everybody can agree that one individual should not be forced to endure a harm which he does not wish to experience, but that another individual should be free to experience a similar harm if he genuinely consents to it. Thus, crimes are defined such that the harm experienced by the victim is implicitly non-consensual. Nobody wishes to be robbed, raped or physically mutilated by others, given that these terms imply that the harm is non-consensual. And yet similar damage to one's interests may be consensual. The individual may wish to give away his money in the form of gifts to others, for instance, or he may choose to sell his body for sex, or he may decide to ask his companions to cut off his arm if that is the only way he can escape from a glacial crevice in which he will die otherwise. Society can recognize the right of the individual to choose the latter self-regarding actions while at the same time it imposes a duty on all not to engage in those other-regarding actions which it has decided are crimes. Indeed, society properly refuses to allow victims to consent to crimes after the fact: the decision whether to prosecute is given to state officials so as to prevent criminals from intimidating their victims into giving their 'consent' *ex post facto*.[18]

But society cannot make the problem go away by employing this strategy or any others. There are extreme cases where the normative disagreement must be resolved one way or the other because the individual cannot consent to the harm without destroying his self-regarding liberty, that is, without permanently impairing his ability to do as he likes in his self-regarding concerns. Society must decide whether or not to recognize the individual's right to sell himself into slavery, for example. If it recognizes the right, it recognizes the duty of others not to coercively interfere with the individual's self-regarding action of consenting to be a slave and thereby destroying his own self-regarding liberty. If it refuses to recognize the right, it refuses to recognize the duty and thereby permits third parties to coercively interfere with self-regarding conduct. So, society either gives the individual the right to destroy his own liberty as he pleases or it refuses to prevent other individuals from obstructing his destructive self-regarding action. Society cannot avoid this problem: it must decide one way or the other.

Does this problem ruin Mill's doctrine of liberty? Many commentators, including Brink (2013, 190–94) and Feinberg (1984–88, vol. 3), apparently think so. They assume that he is committed to coercive interference in such a case as voluntary slavery and so they convict him of a glaring contradiction, that is, of violating his own 'one very simple principle'. Now, there is no doubt that he disdains selling oneself into slavery as an imprudent and pitiful act. But he never actually advocates coercive interference to prevent voluntary slavery. Indeed, he never prescribes coercion to prevent the individual from negotiating any contracts that involve harm to self. He says only that society should not, and already does not, recognize some self-injurious contracts: 'Not only persons are not held to engagements that violate the rights of third parties, but it is sometimes considered a sufficient reason for releasing them from an engagement, that it is injurious to themselves' (Mill 1859c, 299 (V.11)). In particular, he says that society should be very reluctant to enforce any contracts-in-perpetuity. But society's refusal to enforce a contract is not in itself a coercive measure. Rather, society's enforcement, when called for, is what is coercive.

I don't think that voluntary slavery and similar contracts-in-perpetuity, such as marriage without possibility of divorce, present Mill with an insoluble dilemma. Society can refuse to recognize the *right* to destroy self-regarding liberty, without declaring that coercive interference with a self-regarding action is legitimate. It can express its general disapproval of voluntary slavery without declaring that voluntary slavery is immoral or illegal. It can try to discourage the practice without enforcing a *duty* to refrain from it.

More specifically, the state can refuse to enforce voluntary slavery contracts, without bothering to prevent people from negotiating them. Non-enforcement tends to discourage such contracts since the slave can exit the arrangements at any time. Slave-holders have no way to prevent exit, given that *non-consensual* slavery is a wrongful harm which they have an enforceable duty not to inflict on others. True, society also refuses to recognize the duty not to coercively interfere with voluntary slavery and so refuses to authorize the use of coercion to prevent coercive interference with the practice. Still, society can declare its disapproval not only of voluntary slavery but also of coercive interference with voluntary slavery. There is no reason why it cannot express an opinion that such coercion is illegitimate. The state can declare that officials will not obstruct voluntary slavery, for example, although they may check to make sure that it is genuinely consensual. And the state can also try to persuade others not to meddle with voluntary slavery, instead of enforcing a duty not to meddle.

Far from ruining his doctrine, Mill's claim that the maxim of self-regarding liberty 'cannot require' that the individual 'should be free not to be free' is essential to the doctrine: 'It is not freedom, to be allowed to alienate his freedom' (1859c, 300 (V.11)). The individual cannot have a *right* to destroy his right of self-regarding liberty as he pleases. The right to destroy liberty can be rejected by deliberative majorities without insisting that disapproved self-regarding practices such as voluntary slavery or assisted suicide must be stamped out by force. The rejection does not even imply that such self-regarding activities will disappear of their own accord. But society's rejection of the right to annihilate one's liberty as one pleases, along with its general disapproval of the use of self-regarding liberty for this destructive purpose, is necessary to defend the maxim of self-regarding liberty itself.

At the same time, it should not be thought that deliberative majorities must invariably disapprove of self-regarding activities such as voluntary slavery and assisted suicide in all circumstances. Mill can admit that it is permissible to sell oneself into slavery or to engage in euthanasia once doctors believe that death is imminent from a terminal illness, for example. In such an extraordinary situation, preserving the right of self-regarding liberty becomes pointless because self-improvement is at an end anyway. So majorities can then accept that the right to destroy self-regarding liberty is no longer at odds with maintaining the right of self-regarding liberty. In short, the right to alienate one's freedom is recognized in the extraordinary cases.

THE RIGHT OF SELF-REGARDING LIBERTY IS INALIENABLE

With that caveat about extraordinary situations, we may say that the moral right of self-regarding liberty is *inalienable*, in other words, the individual has no moral power to voluntarily waive it or to appoint an agent to waive it for him, although he may forfeit it along with other rights as a result of his criminal behaviour. His moral disability to alienate his right of self-regarding liberty does not imply that he has an enforceable duty not to waive it. Rather, deliberative majorities will refuse to recognize his attempts at waiver, but without taking any steps to forcibly interfere with them.

The individual's moral disability is properly said to correlate with moral immunities for others. Every person has a disability, whether as principal or agent, to waive rights of self-regarding liberty, and everyone also has an immunity from having the rights waived by others. Although no enforceable duties are involved, these nominal disabilities and immunities can help to create an atmosphere of self-regarding liberty if they are made part of a public programme of moral education. Such a programme may help to persuade people to view their rights of self-regarding liberty as inalienable, except in extraordinary circumstances.

PREVENTION OF WRONGFUL HARM TO OTHERS IS NECESSARY BUT NOT SUFFICIENT FOR COERCIVE INTERFERENCE

For Mill, it is the prevention of *wrongful* harm to others which is necessary for coercive interference. As we have seen, the prevention of just any perceptible damage to their interests is *not* necessary.

It is not necessary to prevent consensual harm, or even to prevent non-consensual harm that deliberative majorities determine is morally and legally permissible. Wrongful harm is still harm in the sense of perceptible damage, however, so there is no inconsistency with the 'one very simple principle'. Wrongful harm is distinctive only because society or its representative body has declared that *this form* of perceptible damage is impermissible.

While necessary, the prevention of wrongful harm is still not sufficient for coercive interference. External sanctions, including legal penalties and public displays of hostility and condemnation such as boycotts and protest marches, cannot always be expediently employed to deter wrongful conduct. They cannot be used to enforce important promises made in secret between intimate friends, for example, even though one party's failure to fulfil his duty without the other's release is a moral crime. Similarly, it would cause more non-consensual harm than it prevents to authorize the police or vigilante groups to forcibly enter private homes and clubs on the mere suspicion, without any clear and convincing evidence to justify a search warrant, that individuals inside the premises are engaging in criminal conduct. In such cases, society can only rely on internal sanctions of guilt to deter people from wrongdoing. As Mill puts it, 'the conscience of the agent himself should step into the vacant judgement-seat, and protect those interests of others which have no external protection' (1859c, 226 (I.11)).

Unfortunately, this means that some utilitarian duties to others will go unfulfilled until all members of society have developed a firm disposition to do right. Moral agents with a powerful conscience will choose to fulfil their duties in the absence of external sanctions or, if they cannot fulfil them for some reason, will express remorse and attempt to compensate the injured parties. But not everyone is a moral agent in the present low level of education, and so some will selfishly ignore their duties to others in these situations.

NECESSARY AND SUFFICIENT CONDITIONS FOR COERCIVE INTERFERENCE

In Mill's doctrine, three conditions are jointly necessary and sufficient to justify coercive interference with an individual's action.

The first is that it is a social, or other-regarding, action that affects others' interests without their consent. The perceptible effect on others' interests is not necessarily viewed as harmful by everyone in society. Moreover, the action is not necessarily even classified as other-regarding by everyone in society. But everyone can see that at least some people do not consent to the perceptible effect on their interests.

The second condition is that a deliberative majority has declared, on behalf of society, that the perceptible effect of the action is *wrongful* perceptible damage that no individual ought to consent to suffer. In short, society decides through its representatives what constitutes wrongful harm, and thus which actions *should* be considered by all as impermissible other-regarding actions, *whether or not they actually are so considered by all*. Society thereby cuts through any observed disagreement over which effects are harmful and which are non-consensual. Moreover, it can do this without authorizing coercive interference with any actions that dissidents insist are self-regarding actions for them, even actions that destroy the agent's self-regarding liberty.

The third and final condition is that it is generally expedient to employ external sanctions to prevent or punish the action.

MULTIPLE HARM PRINCIPLES

In light of the discussion up to this point, we can conclude that Mill's doctrine is comprised of five distinct harm principles, where harm means perceptible damage:

(1) *The 'one very simple principle' of harm*: prevention of harm to others is necessary but not sufficient for coercive interference with an individual's action.
(2) *The principle of consensual harm*: prevention of consensual harm to others is not necessary, and should not even be considered in deliberations as to how and where to employ coercive interference.
(3) *The maxim of social authority, or principle of non-consensual harm*: prevention of non-consensual harm to others is necessary, and always legitimately considered in society's deliberations,

but not sufficient for coercive interference; moreover, society may legitimately decide that some kinds of non-consensual harm (e.g. fair competitive losses) are permissible, so that prevention of these sorts of non-consensual harms to others ceases even to be necessary.

(4) *The principle of wrongful harm*: prevention of non-consensual harm to others which society has decided is of an impermissible kind is necessary but not sufficient for coercive interference.

(5) *The full principle of harm*: prevention of wrongful harm to others which can be expediently prevented by the use of external sanctions is necessary and sufficient to justify coercive interference.

These five harm principles are consistent with one another and may be said to constitute Mill's complex doctrine of social control. As I have already emphasized, he sees it as a utilitarian doctrine but only if utilitarianism is conceived in his *extraordinary* way, as an enlarged doctrine that takes seriously different kinds of pleasant feelings of different qualities in its pursuit of 'utility in the largest sense'.

MULTIPLE LIBERTY PRINCIPLES

There are also five distinct liberty principles corresponding to the five harm principles. The two sets of principles are really the same but expressed in different words. In the liberty principles, liberty means doing as one pleases, always with respect to some given set of actions as indicated in the relevant principle:

(1) *The 'one very simple principle' of liberty*: the individual has a moral right to liberty with respect to actions that are harmless to others.

(2) *The maxim of self-regarding liberty*: the individual has a moral right to liberty with respect to self-regarding actions.

(3) *The principle of laissez-faire, or the principle that the individual has no right to cause non-consensual harm to others and yet he may be permitted by society to do so*: the individual does not have a moral right to liberty with respect to social,

or other-regarding, actions but he may nevertheless enjoy some liberty with respect to some kinds of social actions (e.g. competitive exchanges conducted without force or fraud) if society decides not to coercively interfere with those actions and he is able to successfully get the outcomes he wishes.

(4) *The principle of moral and legal freedom*: the individual does not have a moral right to liberty with respect to wrongful actions and instead has duties to obey the recognized social rules of other-regarding conduct established by deliberative majorities; but he does have a moral right to liberty with respect to permissible actions as determined by his recognized rights and duties under the rules, with the crucial caveat that the rules must distribute and sanction equal rights of self-regarding liberty.

(5) *The full principle of freedom*: the individual does not have a moral right to liberty with respect to wrongful actions and yet he will have some liberty to do wrong in situations where his duties to others cannot be expediently enforced by external sanctions; and he does have a moral right to liberty with respect to permissible actions, as stated above in (4).

These five liberty principles are consistent with one another and may be said to constitute Mill's complex doctrine of individual liberty. Again, he sees it as an *extraordinary* utilitarian doctrine.

It is worth mentioning that these liberty principles can be expressed in different terms, and that Mill himself might prefer to express only the first two of them as liberty principles. More specifically, he may confine the term 'liberty' to contexts in which the individual can get any outcome he wishes by choosing some feasible action. In the self-regarding sphere, for example, the individual can always achieve any outcome he wants in his self-regarding concerns by selecting some self-regarding actions with the desired consequences. This is only possible because the individual does not experience any non-consensual damage, and thus any coercive interference, from others in this context. He may learn that the outcome he gets is not as desirable as he had expected, of course, but that is another matter.

Outside the self-regarding context, liberty in this sense is generally impossible. In a competitive arena, for example, only successful competitors get what they wish for and thus enjoy liberty in the sense of doing as one wishes. The losing competitors have the opportunity to compete – they are free from interference to act – but they do not get the outcome they want, and so do not enjoy liberty in this sense. It is rare that any individual is always a successful competitor, at least if the competitions are fair, that is, conducted without fraud or coercive interference with the competitors.

Even more clearly, in the moral and legal sphere, individuals generally cannot get outcomes that society has decided are impermissible. True, they can generally get outcomes to which their rights entitle them, provided others fulfil their duties. But this is not liberty in the sense of choosing any action one likes to get any outcome one seeks. Unlike the right of self-regarding liberty, other rights do not guarantee such liberty. Instead, other rights, such as property rights or rights to a fair trial, allow the individual to choose only among some limited set of permissible other-regarding actions to get, or try to get, permissible outcomes.

If liberty is interpreted in this more demanding sense, then the statement of the liberty principles in (3)–(5) must be suitably modified. For instance, a distinction might be drawn between liberty in the sense of acting to get what one wishes, and freedom in the sense of being free from coercive interference by others. Freedom thus understood does not imply that one has, or should have, liberty in the more demanding sense. Thus, principles (3)–(5) would be restated accordingly. For example, (3) would be restated as: the individual does not have a moral right to liberty with respect to social, or other-regarding, actions but he may nevertheless enjoy freedom with respect to some kinds of social actions (e.g. competitive exchanges conducted without force or fraud) if society decides not to coercively interfere with those actions. I leave it to the reader to suitably restate principles (4)–(5).

BEYOND MILL'S PRINCIPLES?

Some writers cast doubt on harm principles by arguing that there are wrongs which are legitimately prevented even though the wrongs are harmless to the victims. If they are correct, then coercive interference with conduct that is harmless to others is justified at times, and thus Mill's principles, whether interpreted as harm principles or as liberty principles, must be abandoned. Such arguments are prominent in the literature, and so I will close this chapter by examining an interesting example of one. Similar reasoning, including the argument that mere disgust or offence can be a wrong which coercion is legitimately used to prevent, will be taken up in Part IV.

Ripstein (2006) argues that a focus on preventing perceptible damage to the interests of others cannot account for society's legitimate power to prevent harmless trespasses, wrongs that liberals would typically agree ought to be prevented. He illustrates his argument with the case of an intruder who enters another's home and naps in her bed without detection. She does not perceive his nap, which might be very brief, and, by assumption, he leaves no other traces of his visit. To justify the prevention of this harmless trespass, Ripstein introduces a 'sovereignty principle', according to which 'each person is entitled to use his or her own powers as he or she sees fit, consistent with the ability of others to do the same' (2006, 233). He says that this sovereignty principle is rooted in his understanding of Kant and claims that it, unlike harm principles, can justify prevention of harmless trespasses: 'I wrong you if I nap in your bed even if I do not harm you, because I deprive you of the veto that is essential to your ability to be the one who decides how your means [i.e. external resources or property] will be used' (ibid., 241). The jump from ownership of one's internal powers to ownership of external resources is not made entirely clear but this is not important for my purposes.

Ripstein's argument that harm principles cannot get a grip on this situation is not persuasive. The trespass is *not* harmless to the victim. It harms her by depriving her of the use of the bed, however briefly. It poses a risk of coercively interfering with her choice of getting into her bed if she wishes at a certain time. The fact that she herself does not actually perceive the intruder or detect any traces of his visit is irrelevant. So is the fact that nobody except the intruder perceives his coercive interference with her liberty of using the bed: the non-consensual damage he causes may go undetected by others but he perceives it. What matters is that any suitably situated observer could perceive his coercive interference, and, in this case, he is such an observer.

One person's act of coercively interfering with another person's action always causes non-consensual perceptible damage to that other person's interest in doing as she pleases. As Mill says, 'all restraint *quâ* restraint is an evil' (1859c, 294 (V.4)). Society has legitimate power under the social authority maxim to consider coercively interfering with the individual's coercive actions, although it may sometimes decide that a policy of laissez-faire is more expedient than using its coercive authority to prevent or punish such other-regarding actions. In this case, however, given that the victim can sleep in her bed without causing non-consensual harm to others, the intruder is coercively interfering with her *self-regarding liberty*. And we know from the maxim of self-regarding liberty that the intruder has an enforceable duty correlative with the victim's right of self-regarding liberty. Mill is clear that 'wrongful interference with each other's [self-regarding] freedom' is one of the wrongful harms which society properly recognizes and forbids in its rules of justice (1861b, 255 (V.33)). Society ought to use external sanctions, therefore, to prevent the intruder from ignoring his perfect duty not to invade another person's private sphere by usurping her use of her bed, however briefly.

To elaborate on this case a bit, consider the situation prior to any assignment of rights to own and use the bed. Suppose that the homeowner has made the bed herself, or that she has bought it in a fair exchange, one of a series of such voluntary exchanges leading back to the producer of the bed. She thus has possession of the bed through her self-regarding actions – she has the right, as a consumer, to buy any product with self-regarding uses, even though society may legitimately regulate the sellers to prevent them from causing non-consensual harm to others. Others do not like that she has possession of the bed, however, and wish to use it themselves. So, unless someone is given ownership, a potentially violent competition will arise such that winning competitors alone will get to use the bed, at least while they are awake. Even if she is one of the strongest, she is unlikely to be able to sleep very long in the bed. The assignment of a claim to ownership will preclude this competition, however, since society will enforce the correlative duties. But who should be given the property right?

No doubt, as Mill (1871a, 754–55) insists, the homeowner deserves to own the bed for her exclusive use because she, by assumption, either made the bed herself or bought it in a fair market exchange or series of exchanges stemming from the producer.[19] And, by assigning the property right to her, society also confirms and extends her right of self-regarding liberty: she not only acquired the bed through her self-regarding actions but now she can use her bed as she pleases, as long as she does not cause non-consensual damage to the interests of others. By enforcing the duties correlative with her rights, society guarantees that she will not suffer from wrongful harms such as the wrongful trespass under discussion.

The real difference between Ripstein and Mill is over their respective understandings of both harm and freedom. Ripstein's 'sovereignty principle' works with a conception of freedom that implies that a person is not harmed if she is frustrated from achieving an outcome she wants by another person's use of his powers and external resources for his purposes: the losers in a fair competition are not harmed, despite their wasted exertions and so forth, because the winners do not prevent them from using their own powers and means to achieve their purposes, even though they fail to achieve them (2006, 237–40). In short, the losers have enjoyed equal freedom from coercive interference as well as from domination despite failing to get what they want.

But it hardly seems reasonable to maintain that the winners do not cause the losers to suffer damage, even if we do not blame the winners for doing so. Were it not for the winners, the losers would not be losers. Indeed, on the more demanding notion of liberty, as getting a desired outcome through your own actions, the losers have been deprived of liberty in an other-regarding context. Even if we go so far as to insist that the losers are harmed by 'the invisible hand' and not by any assignable individual winners, the losers still suffer non-consensual perceptible damage to their interests. Society has jurisdiction to consider preventing such damage, even if the harm is not caused by the actions of other identifiable individuals but by market institutions or even by natural forces. The decision as to whether to force others to rescue the losers from such suffering turns on the deliberative majority's opinions as to whether the harm is of a wrongful kind, and whether external sanctions to prevent it are expedient.

SUGGESTIONS FOR FURTHER READING

Many scholars argue that Mill's 'one very simple principle' is really not simple, that his doctrine of liberty is far more complex than he lets on, and that the various concepts and principles of harm, liberty and so on with which he apparently works do not fit together, so that we are left with a mess. Even his admirers are often highly critical. They blame him because they can't make sense of his analysis. And yet they are stirred by his brilliant rhetoric, it seems, and so they turn around and offer doctrines of their own, doctrines that ignore or override important passages in his text, doctrines which seem to them to better capture the spirit of liberalism.

There is no doubt that the structure of Mill's argument is subtle and difficult to uncover. He is extremely concise and probably expects too much of his readers. He does leave clues to help guide us, however, and my interpretation relies on these clues to claim that he has a coherent and appealing doctrine. Still, no one can be absolutely certain that he or she has got him right. *On Liberty* inevitably remains hostage to various interpretations offered by fallible commentators.

It is instructive to study what some of Mill's critics have to say, so as to compare and contrast their various interpretations not only with one another but also with the interpretation offered in this chapter. But there are many alternative critical interpretations, and I cannot list all of those that may be worth considering. The recent publications which I suggest below are no more than a tip of the iceberg. Beyond this limited selection, however, I also make reference in Part IV to a few other prominent critical interpretations.

I suggest looking at the following three works, which offer interpretations that differ widely from one another, as well as from my own reading, of Mill's doctrine of liberty: David O. Brink, *Mill's Progressive Principles* (Oxford: Oxford University Press, 2013), esp. 135–233, 277–89; John Rawls, *Lectures on the History of Political Philosophy*, ed. Samuel Freeman (Cambridge, MA: Harvard University Press, 2007), 249–317; and Arthur Ripstein, 'Beyond the Harm Principle', *Philosophy & Public Affairs* 34 (2006): 215–45. For my critical assessment of Rawls' interpretation, see Jonathan Riley, 'Rawls, Mill and Utilitarianism', in Jon Mandle and David Reidy (eds), *A Companion to Rawls* (New York: Wiley-Blackwell, 2013), 397–412.

For further clarification of Mill's extraordinary version of utilitarianism as I understand it, see the references listed in note 14 to this chapter. I plan to develop this work into a book now tentatively entitled *Genuine Maximizing Utilitarianism*. The title reflects my belief that Mill's liberal utilitarianism, and not crude act utilitarianism, is genuine maximizing utilitarianism. As Mill says, his enlarged utilitarianism promotes both the quantity and the quality of collective happiness in the sense of pleasure including absence of pain (1861b, 214 (II.10)).

NOTES

1 It might be argued that others could judge a self-regarding action as contemptible or degrading without themselves also feeling dislike or displeasure at it. There is some truth in this. For Mill, however, a person who *never* feels dislike for an action must either like it or be indifferent to it. To initially judge an action as contemptible, the person must initially feel displeasure at it, and aversion to it. After repeatedly judging such an action, the judgment can become a habit, and habits of will can become divorced from the desires and aversions, and the pleasures and pains, which first gave rise to them (Mill 1861b, 238–39 (IV.11)). Thus, a person of confirmed habits can judge an action as contemptible and yet no longer be conscious of any feeling of displeasure or aversion at the action himself.

2 While not decisive, his usage shows that the idea of harm as 'perceptible hurt' or 'perceptible damage' has some textual support. In the same sentence, however, Mill suggests that self-regarding conduct does not violate 'any specific duty to the public': it is 'conduct which neither violates any specific duty to the public, nor occasions perceptible hurt to any assignable individual except himself' (1859c, 282 (IV.11)). This might suggest that harm includes something besides perceptible damage but I will argue otherwise in due course.

3 Mill accepts that a perception is an intuitive kind of belief or idea of an object only because he wishes to avoid as much as possible entangling his theory of logic with controversial metaphysical views. He provides a lengthy discussion of his own metaphysical views, including his view that perceptions do not really exist, in Mill 1865a. For him, we know nothing about external objects as things

in themselves; the only information we have is contained in our sensations, which we infer emanate from unknown substances but are modified in unknown ways by our own nervous system; so our idea of an object is not intuitive but rather inferred (usually very rapidly) from our experience of coexistences, successions and resemblances of sensations.

4 The list of objects with which an individual has reason to be concerned may seem similar to Rawls's list of 'primary goods' (1999, 54). Elijah Millgram (2009, 347) and Dale Miller (2010, 120–21), for example, suggest that Rawlsian primary goods correspond to something in Mill's thought. Perceptible damage in the individual's primary goods is certainly a reason for his concern. But he may well be concerned about things besides primary goods. Moreover, in a Millian context, the particular rights, liberties and fair opportunities prescribed by Rawls's theory of justice must be viewed as premoral instruments, not yet endorsed by any utilitarian decision procedure. Mill's utilitarian moral theory may reject some Rawlsian rights or prescribe others, for instance.

5 In the earlier edition, I defined harm as non-consensual perceptible damage, thereby incorporating the *volenti* maxim into the very definition of harm as Mill at times seems to do. Although that approach may be acceptable with some caveats, I now prefer to define harm as perceptible damage, without necessarily tying it to 'against one's wishes'.

6 These public duties might be said to correlate with rights of 'assignable' public officials in whom authority is entrusted by the people or their political representatives to lead the military, collect taxes, organize juries, protect the environment, safeguard public health, and so forth. Yet Mill suggests that the duties are owed to the public at large rather than to any determinate individual. In effect, his view seems to be that the duties are owed to certain 'public offices' created by the people or their representatives and not to the particular inhabitants of those offices. So perhaps we can speak of the rights of the office as correlative with the public duties. Particular office-holders do not possess the claims but they are temporarily delegated the powers to exercise them.

7 See Berlin 1969 and Riley 2015a.

8 An intention to 'do nothing' (that is, not make any physical movements) is always a feasible action, given that actions include inactions. Coercive interference includes forcing a person to act or move when he wishes not to.

9 For further discussion, see Riley 1996, 1998b, 2008a.

10 This does not imply that every individual recognizes the importance of her interest in individuality or that she agrees that the rights of liberty and individuality are necessary for a good life. Mill admits that many people may not care about those rights so he provides various reasons why such people should nevertheless endorse them (1859c, 267–75 (III.10–19)).

11 Despite his repeated dismissal of all talk of essences and of the nature of things in themselves, Mill is continually saddled by commentators with the metaphysical claim that, by spontaneously choosing in accord with his own wishes and judgment, an individual reveals his unique essence or quiddity. He expressly disavows any such claim. See e.g. Mill 1843, 114–15; 1871a, 319.

12 See e.g. Hamburger 1999 and Vogler 2001.
13 Notice that others may include not only 'assignable individuals' but also the public considered as a whole group of 'unassignable' individuals, that is, the individuals are not made determinate as separate members of the group.
14 On Mill's extraordinary utilitarianism as I interpret it, see Riley 2008–9, 2009, 2010a, 2010b, 2010c, 2012, 2013a, 2013b, 2013c, 2014, 2015b, forthcoming-b.
15 Auxiliary special regulations needed to implement the general rules may be considered as well.
16 The bare dictates will be obeyed by moral agents but not by narrowly selfish individuals.
17 Mill does not try to settle the issue as to what extent existing customs and shared dictates of conscience have evolved prior to the formation of the state or only after individuals have become familiar with the workings of an established political and legal system. But he seems inclined to think that the law plays a large role in the creation of customs and shared dictates of conscience (1861b, ch. 3).
18 The state may need to take additional steps to protect victims and witnesses from intimidation and further crimes, of course.
19 For further discussion of what Mill calls 'the principle of private property', see Riley 2008a.

Part IV

GENERAL ISSUES

8

LIBERAL UTILITARIANISM

ISN'T LIBERALISM INCOMPATIBLE WITH UTILITARIANISM?

A traditional complaint against Mill's form of reasoning is that liberalism cannot be consistently combined with utilitarianism. The problem he fails to recognize, according to a long line of complainers, is that utilitarianism may require that individual rights should be given up for the greater good of the other members of society. If a rich man's private property would yield more aggregate happiness when transferred into the hands of some poor people, for example, or if the whole country could be saved from tyranny by sacrificing the life or liberty of a beautiful woman to some evil aggressor, utilitarianism seems to demand, respectively, the property transfer and the sacrifice. Liberalism's concern to protect certain vital personal interests, as moral rights, is putatively overridden by the demands of general utility maximization.

Supposing that liberal utilitarianism (or, equivalently, utilitarian liberalism) is incoherent, many liberal philosophers have turned to some non-utilitarian form of reasoning to give suitable moral importance to individual rights in relation to competing considerations. Rawls (1999, 2005), for example, in his influential theory of justice as fairness, employs an ideal contractarian form of reasoning to argue that a first principle of equal basic rights has absolute priority over a second two-part principle, and that the two principles together constrain any individual's permissible conception of a good life. He imagines that Mill's doctrine is really similar in structure to his own contract theory, to wit, a 'mixed conception' of justice, in which a liberal principle of equal basic rights is given absolute priority over the utility principle itself. Like Hart (1982), he thinks that Mill must import non-utilitarian arguments to justify the liberal principle. Rawls (2007) reaffirms his doubt that Mill offers any adequate utilitarian basis for the priority of liberal rights, although he seems intrigued by Mill's version of utilitarianism and repeats his belief that Mill would favour basic social and political institutions similar to those endorsed by justice as fairness. This Rawls–Hart reading of Mill's liberalism remains highly influential.

Indeed, as Ten (1991) has suggested, the 'revisionist utilitarian' doctrines which Gray (1996), Berger (1984), Skorupski (1989) and others have associated with Millian liberalism seem indistinguishable from what Rawls calls a mixed conception. True, moral considerations internal to utilitarianism itself are said to drive the revisionism. But no good reasons are offered to repel the traditional objection that maximization of collective welfare (or collective autonomy) may demand the sacrifice of individual rights (including rights to self-determination or personal autonomy).[1]

That is not to say that good reasons cannot be offered. In this regard, those who *make* the traditional objection seem to take for granted that they are objecting to an ideal utilitarian conception of the collective good. More needs to be said, however, before anyone should accept their assumption. It does not follow that, because some crude conception of collective welfare admits unjustified trammelling of individual rights, a better conception must do so as well.

Another influential objection to Mill's form of reasoning is that utilitarian liberalism is unworkable because it is impossible that a reasonable and coherent system of rights could ever be grounded in general utility. Such a harmonious rights system is inconceivable altogether, so this objection runs, because our moral world is characterized by tragic conflicts among plural and incommensurable values (including positive and negative aspects of liberty itself). This pluralistic complaint applies equally to Rawlsian forms of reasoning, and receives clear expression in Berlin (1969), C. Taylor (1982) and Gray (1989, 1995, 2000), among others.

Gray, for example, argues that liberal utilitarianism faces 'intractable problems' (1989, 220). We do not know how to compare different persons' utility gains and losses, he says, as required to calculate general utility. Moreover, if (as Mill assumes) there are different kinds or qualities of utility, we remain in the dark even about how to make *intrapersonal* comparisons of the different kinds. Once we recognize these problems of incommensurability, 'Mill's utilitarianism disintegrates ... into a sort of muddled and unwitting value-pluralism. It should be evident enough that, from such a value-pluralism, no "one very simple principle" ... can possibly be derived' (ibid., 224).

He duly traces this perspective to Berlin. Berlin, he says, makes the important 'objection' that 'the idea of happiness has in Mill so mutated that its use in any sort of felicific calculus is not a possibility: it has come to designate precisely that irreducible diversity of human goods which Berlin's pluralism identifies' (1995, 61). Thus, 'contrary to all of his intentions, Mill's liberalism is not, in the end, an application of utilitarian ethics, for liberal utilitarianism is not ultimately a viable position in moral and political thought' (ibid.).

Liberalism must face the pluralistic music, Gray insists, and content itself with conventional sets of conflicting rights, varying across social contexts, any given set a product of a particular cultural history rather than an emanation of universal reason. An ideal liberal conception of the collective good, in which a reasonable system of equal rights is brought into harmony with other social values, is merely another form of rationalistic fiction, as Berlin would have it, and carries the danger that its adherents will embrace some sort of authoritarianism in their deluded 'pursuit of the ideal'. But, again, more needs to be said before anyone should accept the claim that morality is *necessarily* an arena of conflict among plural and incomparable goods. Perhaps further study and Socratic dialogue can generate right answers to what seem on the surface even the most intractable moral dilemmas.

Both the traditional and pluralistic objections to utilitarian liberalism are open to serious doubt. Mill's extraordinary version of liberal utilitarianism seems able to withstand both of them. At one time, and as indicated in the original edition of this book, I thought that a liberal rule utilitarianism might serve as a close approximation to Mill's doctrine (see e.g. Riley 2000). But I no longer hold that view. There are crucial differences between Mill's utilitarianism and rule utilitarianism, which enable the one but not the other to repel the traditional and pluralistic objections.

According to rule utilitarianism, the collective good is best pursued indirectly, by complying with an optimal code of rules, rather than directly, as act utilitarianism assumes, by always trying to calculate and perform the particular act that maximizes general utility. Utilitarians will perhaps find the most happiness by jointly committing themselves to act in accord with a code that assigns liberal rights and duties: the general happiness will be *higher* than it would be otherwise (see e.g. Harsanyi 1992; Riley 2001). Rule utilitarians admit, however, that collective utility may sometimes be increased, at least in the short run, if individuals deviate from the rules. To maximize utility, then, suitable exceptions to the rules must be drawn to cover the situations in which deviations are utility maximizing. In other words, special rules must be framed that override the more general rules in exceptional circumstances. Given that everyone is expected to comply with the code, however, these special rules must proliferate, it seems, until rule utilitarianism becomes extensionally equivalent to act utilitarianism (Lyons 1965, 62–118). But then the traditional objection rears its head again: utilitarians must acknowledge that maximization of collective welfare can require sacrifice of individual rights.

Rule utilitarians try to avoid this disturbing result by arguing that rule utilitarianism is not extensionally equivalent to act utilitarianism for one reason or another: for example, it is too costly for fallible humans to 'internalize' a detailed list of act-utilitarian prescriptions, or it is too psychologically demanding for selfish humans to make the sacrifices required by act-utilitarian duties. Such arguments, while extremely plausible, imply that individuals must follow the rules of an optimal rule-utilitarian code even when deviating from the rules would maximize collective utility in act-utilitarian terms. But, then, rule utilitarians are vulnerable to the fatal objection that they are not genuine utilitarians. They 'worship' rules instead of utility maximization. They attribute some moral value to obeying rules when obedience does not promote collective happiness, and so the value is something other than utility.

Rule utilitarianism also cannot work in the absence of cardinally measurable and interpersonally comparable utilities. Without such rich utility information, we cannot predict which rules among the many possible ones will have the best utility consequences for humans. Thus, rule utilitarians must assert that society can, at least in principle, gather the requisite utility information that enables right answers to be given, and framed in the form of rules, to all moral conflicts, or at least to all that fall within the scope of an optimal rule-utilitarian code. Value pluralists such as Berlin and Gray make the opposing assertion that even if all the pertinent information could in principle be gathered, there would still be conflicts of basic values, or ends, to which no universal rational resolution can be found. No practical compromise acceptable to the warring parties is possible.

I have already given an indication in Part III of how I now understand Mill's extraordinary liberal utilitarianism. It has some resemblance to rule utilitarianism insofar as obedience to recognized social rules of justice is of overwhelming importance for the promotion of collective welfare, with the caveat that the rules must distribute and sanction equal rights of complete self-regarding liberty. But the resemblance is only superficial. For, unlike rule utilitarianism, which does not distinguish different kinds of utilities of intrinsically different qualities, Mill's doctrine gives priority to rules of justice because the higher kind of pleasant feeling that is inseparably associated with the moral sentiment of justice is of a quality that is infinitely superior to all competing kinds of pleasure. This has remarkable implications for the traditional objection.

AGAINST THE TRADITIONAL OBJECTION

Unlike rule and other standard forms of utilitarianism, Mill's doctrine is immune from the traditional objection. The key point is that the higher kind of pleasure experienced by an individual whose vital interests are protected by reciprocal rights and duties assigned to all under a working system of rules of justice cannot be outweighed by any amount of competing kinds of pleasure, including a lower kind associated with the violation of rights: even a bit of the higher pleasure experienced by a single individual is more valuable as pleasure than any finite amount of the lower pleasure, however large, experienced by other people, however many in number. Another way to put this point is to say that the kind of harm and suffering experienced by the individual whose rights are violated can never be outweighed by the subjective pain and dissatisfaction experienced by all those who are forced by society to fulfil their duties, regardless of the total finite amount of their mere dissatisfaction.

True, if situations arise in which conflicts of individual rights occur under the recognized code, then the code must be reformed to remove the conflicts so as to promote utility in the largest sense, as determined by deliberative majorities. But these reform efforts are confined to the system of justice itself, and their goal is to increase the total amount of the higher kind of pleasure associated with justice. It is never the case that competing considerations can justify ignoring, or overriding, recognized rights and duties. Lower pleasures can never offset the higher pleasure of justice. Instead, rights and duties must be rebalanced, or 'adjusted' in the way suggested by Rawls, with a view to increasing the protection, or security, given to the vital personal interests shared by the members of society.

Notice that the higher pleasure of justice, which may be referred to as a feeling of security that can only be experienced by living under a code of rules and rights which protects the vital interests shared by individuals, is a variable and not some fixed quantity either for the individual or for society. Some individuals may experience little if any security, for example, because they are excluded from the system of justice. Even if equal rights are distributed and enforced for all, the total amount of the higher pleasure may vary depending on the content of the recognized rights and correlative duties. But total security is maximized only under some set of universal equal rights which has priority over competing considerations, keeping in mind that, in every civil society, there must be the right of complete self-regarding liberty.

Notice too that, unlike the standard forms of utilitarianism, Mill's unusual version of the doctrine makes room for distinct spheres beyond that of morality and law, namely, those of self-regarding conduct and of competitive behaviour, in both of which the individual is free to pursue other kinds of pleasant feelings than that of security. He has no moral duties to others within his self-regarding sphere since his actions do not cause non-consensual harm to others. He also has no moral duties to others within the competitive sphere because, even though his successful competitive actions cause non-consensual harm to others, the kind of harm is permissible. The competitive sphere is defined such that the individual is within it only if he fulfils his recognized moral and legal duties to others. Within these two spheres, the individual is free to pursue aesthetic pleasures and merely expedient pleasures that are distinct in quality from the moral feeling of security. He has a right to get the aesthetic and material objects of his desire if they have self-regarding uses, whereas he may not actually get the success he seeks within the competitive sphere despite being free from coercive interference.

Even in the present low level of general education, where most are predominantly selfish, there are good reasons for giving priority to, and enforcing widespread compliance with, a social code of liberal justice which deliberative majorities decide is best for regulating other-regarding conduct, with the caveat that any recognized code may have to be reformed over time as new situations arise (e.g. as a result of technological advances), conflicts of recognized rights are discovered, and further knowledge of the utility consequences of rules is gained.

One reason is that most people are just too selfish always to do what liberal utilitarian justice requires in any situation, and it is too costly if not impossible to change biased human characters overnight. In the meantime, and, in fact, to ever undergo the process of self-improvement that might eradicate undue self-interest, people must be forced to obey 'rigid rules of justice for the sake of others'. The rules must always distribute and sanction equal rights of self-regarding liberty so that the individual is able to choose as he likes in his personal concerns and thereby learn what does and does not bring him happiness. Moreover, the social coercion itself facilitates 'the better development of the social part of his nature, rendered possible by the restraint put on the selfish part' (1859c, 266 (III. 9)). As Mill continues: 'To be held to rigid rules of justice for the sake of others, develops the feelings and capacities which have the good of others for their object' (ibid.). Human development, and even self-development or individuality, is not solely a matter of self-regarding liberty. Thus, being made to comply with these rigid rules of justice is essential for individuals to develop the noble Periclean characters required for maximization of utility in the largest sense.

A second reason is that liberal rules and rights generate incentives and assurances that are useful for a society of predominantly self-interested people. To maximize production of consumer goods and services, for example, such a society ought to establish certain rules and rights of private property and market contracting that *assure* self-interested producers of the fruits of their own labour and investment decisions, and provide *incentives* to hard work, saving and entrepreneurship. Similarly, to maximize the physical and financial safety of its people, such a society ought to devise certain rules and rights of criminal and civil due process that assure both accusers and accused of a fair trial, and provide incentives to represent the parties diligently, duly collect evidence, and so on.

Clearly, Mill's idea of collective utility maximization must not be confused with that of crude act utilitarianism or an extensionally equivalent rule utilitarianism. The standard idea of utility maximization does not distinguish among different kinds of utilities of different qualities. Nor does it take account of separate spheres of conduct beyond morality and law. Instead, the standard idea is crude. It makes impossibly stringent demands on individuals to always choose actions that maximize the sum total of a single kind of utility, of the same quality. As a result, the individual is obligated to sacrifice whatever amount of this homogenous utility may be associated with his rights, merely to promote a greater amount of it for others even though they have no claims to it. Indeed, the notion that others have correlative duties to the right-holder is ignored.

The external signs of all liberal rights and duties might conceivably vanish if everybody developed the ideal Periclean character associated with maximization of utility in the largest sense. There would be no need for external sanctions in such an ideal utilitarian liberal society. More importantly, many familiar liberal rules and rights might be recognized as suboptimal in this ideal context, and thus vanish from the code of conscience altogether, given that everybody has educated themselves to become rigidly fair and impartial rather than biased, as they now tend to be, in favour of their own particular interests. If a highly developed person would work hard and invest wisely for the general advantage, with no assurance of anything beyond an equal share of whatever fruits he and his fellows jointly produced, for example, private ownership of productive resources would not need to be recognized by an ideal liberal utilitarian code of justice.

But, whatever the nature of the other rights in an ideal utilitarian society, one right must remain optimal from Mill's perspective, namely, the right to liberty of purely self-regarding conduct. As he makes clear in the *Liberty* (247–48 (II.26–27); 265, 267 (III.6, 11)), highly developed humans, unlike gods or saints, will need at least that core of liberty to *maintain* (as well as to develop) their admirable capacities, including their capacities to remain rigidly impartial when framing and complying with rules of other-regarding conduct. It is wrong to think that the need for complete liberty of discussion and personal lifestyle will disappear as progress unfolds (ibid., 250–52 (II.31–33); 274–75 (III.18–19); see also Chapter 9 below). Thus, an ideal Millian utilitarian code will continue to distribute and sanction such rights to liberty, even if private property and other familiar liberal rights tied to our particularistic inclinations vanish from the code. Those who develop the characters required to act invariably in accord with the code will develop a due balance between the moral disposition to follow reasonable and impartial rules of other-regarding behaviour, and the Pagan drive not only to choose as one pleases among purely self-regarding actions but also to strive for success in fair competitions with others.

AGAINST THE PLURALISTIC OBJECTION

Turning to the pluralistic objection to liberal utilitarianism, it is doubtless true that we cannot conceive of an ideal morality, if by an ideal morality we mean a perfect one in which all bad luck has been eradicated and each and every human virtue flourishes to its fullest extent, never coming into conflict with the others. But it remains an open question whether we can conceive of a best *possible* morality, in which the need to make reasonable compensation for bad luck is recognized and, more generally, a compromise or balance is struck between competing virtues and goods (such as security, subsistence, abundance, equality, liberty and individuality) to maximize the collective happiness. In this regard, given that rights to absolute liberty of self-regarding conduct are *indispensable means to*, as well as constituent elements of, an optimal liberal utilitarian morality, it is palpably absurd to associate Mill's doctrine with the danger of authoritarian repression.

Pluralists also emphasize that we have no idea of how to acquire the rich information about personal welfares required for standard utilitarianism to work. But this criticism is not entirely persuasive because scholars have proposed methods of measuring cardinal utility, such as the von Neumann-Morgenstern method that makes use of a person's attitudes toward risk to ascertain how much utility the person gains or loses between any options, as well as methods of making interpersonal utility comparisons, such as the extended sympathy method in which one person imagines himself in another's shoes, adopts the other's preferences or rankings of pleasures when in the other's position, and then compares them with his own preferences or rankings when back in his own shoes. It remains controversial whether risk-based measures of intensity have moral significance, however, and dubious that society should rely on any individual's interpersonal comparisons if individuals make conflicting comparisons. Why should the majority's comparisons prove decisive over the minority's, for instance? It seems fair to say that there would be no problem if everybody made the same comparisons. In this ideal case of complete identity, any highly educated minority would agree with actual majorities: there would be no conflict between the latter and deliberative majorities guided by the minority pointing out the way to promote utility in the largest sense. And yet in this case, there would be unanimous agreement about which rules should be recognized as rules of justice for the given society: everyone would express identical moral judgments. There would be no need to make interpersonal comparisons to resolve conflicts about what to do, because everybody's moral preferences would already incorporate the same interpersonal comparisons. In short, an aggregation procedure used to decide which rules of justice to recognize could take as inputs the individuals' identical moral utility rankings: there would be no need for interpersonal comparisons of their feelings of security. Thus, rich utility information remains contestable outside the ideal case and is not needed to run the aggregation procedure in the ideal case, where everyone has already become the type of moral agent who makes the same comparisons.

Mill, like Bentham, makes no reference to a mechanical aggregation procedure of the sort assumed by standard utilitarians for generating decisions about which acts or rules will maximize the general happiness. Instead of a standard aggregation procedure that only works with rich cardinal and interpersonally comparable utility information, he seems to rely on a democratic procedure that works with pure ordinalist information (that is, non-comparable individual preference orderings) to generate decisions about which rules to recognize as rules of justice. The democratic procedure, such as majority rule constrained by various checks to promote competent deliberation after discussion and debate of the options, can be shown to satisfy axioms analogous to those satisfied by standard utilitarianism, if allowance is made for the fact that the democratic axioms are defined in the context of pure ordinalist utility information whereas the standard utilitarian axioms are defined in the context of cardinal comparable utility information (Riley 1990). Moreover, the democratic procedure is restricted to considerations of justice: it only accepts as inputs individual preferences or judgments defined over alternative rules or sets of rules that distribute rights and duties, and refuses to consider other kinds of rankings. A similar restriction is placed on the political process by great liberal and republican thinkers such as Locke and Rousseau, when they insist that the people and their representatives should be concerned only to enact general laws as opposed to arbitrary commands and policies.[2]

Given human fallibility, the democratic aggregation process must be viewed as an imperfect process that takes place over time:

it is not a once-and-for-all decision carried out by some fictitious infallible observer. Instead of establishing an optimal code of justice in an instant, the democratic process constructs one in a gradual and piecemeal fashion, inevitably making and correcting mistakes along the way. As a result, this extraordinary liberal utilitarianism, with its assumption of purely ordinalist utility information, can accept the pluralist complaint that society may not know how to resolve some moral conflicts: there may be so much disagreement among individuals, even the most educated individuals with access to the best information currently available, that the political procedure cannot generate a decision that is universally accepted even as a reasonable compromise. Indeed, the political system may cycle over time, settling temporarily on one rule, then replacing it with another, and then coming back to the first rule. Whereas the value pluralist asserts that this sort of cycling must persist indefinitely because some moral conflicts admit of no universal rational resolution, however, the liberal utilitarian makes no such assertion: he allows for the possibility that, with sufficient development of intellectual, moral and practical capacities, in combination with the acquisition of new utility information about the consequences of rules and so forth, society may eventually find reasonable resolutions, acceptable to all competent individuals, of all moral conflicts. But until that far-off day arrives, if it ever does, there need be no discernible difference in practice between liberal value pluralists and liberal utilitarians of a Millian stripe.

HOW CAN UTILITARIANISM PRESCRIBE *ABSOLUTE* LIBERTY OF SELF-REGARDING CONDUCT?

Ten has argued powerfully that *absolute* liberty in self-regarding matters cannot be grounded on utilitarianism as usually defined. As he points out, utilitarians typically must claim that 'the value of liberty ... is wholly dependent on its contribution to utility. But if that is the case', he asks, 'how can the "right" to liberty be absolute and indefeasible when the consequences of exercising the right will surely vary with changing social circumstances?' (1991, 213). His answer is that it cannot be, unless external moral considerations are imported into pure maximizing utilitarianism to guarantee the desired Millian result. In his view, the absolute barrier that Mill erects against all forms of coercion really seems to require a non-utilitarian justification, even if 'utilitarianism' might somehow be redefined or enlarged to subsume the requisite form of reasoning. Thus, 'Mill is a consistent liberal', he says, 'whose view is inconsistent with hedonistic or preference utilitarianism' (ibid., 236).

Against Ten, it must be noted immediately that, given a suitable definition of 'harm', the harmful consequences to others against their wishes of any person's exercise of his right to choose as he likes among self-regarding acts, does *not* vary. As we have already seen, Mill seems to be using the term 'harm' in a fairly straightforward way, as any type of 'perceptible damage' suffered to one's body, material possessions, reputation or freedom of action, with the caveat that the perceptible injury must not be wholly a creation of social authority. With that understanding of harm as excluding mere dislike, self-regarding choices never cause non-consensual harm to others, 'directly, and in the first instance'. The exercise by all of equal rights to absolute liberty of self-regarding choices can never directly cause perceptible damage to anybody against his wishes.

But Ten's objection still has life. He argues that 'Mill's defence of liberty is not utilitarian', because it ignores the mere dislike, disgust and so-called 'moral' disapproval which others feel as a result of self-regarding conduct: 'A utilitarian cannot disregard any of the effects of my conduct since they are all part of its consequences, and help to determine whether the suppression of my conduct or leaving me free will maximize happiness' (1980, 6). Why doesn't the liberal utilitarian count the mere pain and dislike, which the vast majority might well feel at the individual's self-regarding acts? Surely if that is counted, it may outweigh the value of the individual's self-regarding liberty, in which case utilitarianism prescribes coercive interference. What sort of utilitarianism is it that refuses to count mere dislike or displeasure?

But liberal utilitarianism does *not* ignore others' mere dislike of a self-regarding act. Their dislike does count, because it is included in the value of liberty itself. Under Mill's doctrine, society gives others the equal right to complete liberty of self-regarding conduct, including the freedom to select their own friends and to avoid people of whose conduct they disapprove. But your dislike of my self-regarding conduct never justifies suppression of the self-regarding act. That would negate my liberty of self-regarding conduct, and the great good of self-development which depends upon it: 'But to be restrained [by others] in things not affecting their good, by their mere displeasure, developes [*sic*] nothing valuable, except such force of character as may unfold itself in resisting the restraint' (1859c, 266 (III.9)). Rather than count others' dislikes as a potential justification for suppression, liberal utilitarianism counts them by giving everybody an equal right to self-regarding liberty. Any person is free to act on her mere dislike of others' thoughts and personal lifestyles, and, at least to that extent, to develop her own character, or individuality, as she pleases.

Yet why doesn't liberal utilitarianism consider the possibility that aggregate dislike of the individual's self-regarding conduct might outweigh the value of his liberty, and justify suppression of his conduct? True, Mill can reply that the right of self-regarding liberty is an indispensable element of every civil society's code of justice, and that the code is the source of the pleasant feeling of security which is superior in quality to any competing kind of pleasure. But someone might go on to ask: why is that right an indispensable right? And Mill can reply that it protects the individual's vital interest in developing a noble Periclean character. Indeed, he can say that the aesthetic pleasure of imagining this noble individuality, and of striving to cultivate it, is also a higher kind of pleasant feeling, perhaps even the highest kind of all since it does not conflict with the pleasure of security associated with the moral sentiments. The ideal Periclean character is both a moral character and a beautiful one (see Riley 2013b). These answers clarify why a liberal utilitarian moral agent who values self-regarding liberty and self-development will judge that others' mere dislike, however large in total, can never justify coercive interference with self-regarding conduct. Nevertheless, the answers will not satisfy the relatively uncultivated individual who does not think of departing from existing social customs and thus does not place much if any value on self-regarding liberty and individuality.

What can Mill say to convince the undeveloped individual to endorse the right of self-regarding liberty? This is important, of course, because these are the very people calling for suppression of self-regarding conduct which they dislike. And he is aware of its importance: 'it is necessary further to show … those who do not desire liberty, and would not avail themselves of it, that they may be in some intelligible manner rewarded for allowing other people to make use of it without hindrance' (1859c, 267 (III.10)). As we have seen in Part II, he devotes considerable effort to answering this question (ibid., 267–75 (III. 10–19)). Notice that his utilitarian defence of the right of self-regarding liberty thus does not assume that the individual must assign great value to liberty and individuality in his personal conception of a good life.

Mill's doctrine of liberty and individuality maintains that the individual has a moral right to choose as he likes in his self-regarding concerns so that he can promote his permanent interest in self-improvement. Since perceptible damage to others against their wishes is never involved, equal rights of self-regarding liberty can be distributed and enforced. If every individual cultivates his individuality, *social* improvement (that is, the intellectual and moral development of each person in society) is maximized. Promotion of utility in the largest sense thereby implies the free development of a plurality of self-regarding lifestyles, one for each individual. Liberal utilitarianism guarantees, by right, a variety of personal ways of living, without any resort to the metaphysical trappings of value pluralism.

DON'T 'NATURAL PENALTIES' DEFEAT MILL'S SELF–OTHER DISTINCTION?

But the distinction between purely self-regarding and other spheres of life breaks down, some continue to complain, because Mill himself admits that self-regarding conduct can cause harm in the form of 'natural penalties'. Hamburger, for example, claims that the distinction is merely a rhetorical ploy, used by the fake champion of liberty to disguise his true ambition, namely, to destroy prevailing moral ideas and beliefs and replace them with a repressive new utilitarian religion. To that end, the opinions of 'superior' intellectuals like himself would be used as subtle tools of coercion, to force the 'inferior' commercial and Christian majority to refashion even the self-regarding aspects of their lives, including their habits of drinking, gambling, prostitution, idleness and so on. Far from countenancing self-regarding liberty for such people, Hamburger insists, he really aimed to shame and humiliate them to give up their 'selfish' and 'miserable' lifestyles, by means of the natural penalties inflicted by a disapproving 'liberal' vanguard:

> [A]s a consequence, Mill's well-known distinction between conduct harmful to others and self-regarding conduct, which was supposed to demarcate a realm of liberty, is shown not to be viable. It was supposed to distinguish between what was subject to penalties and what was immune from penalties; but, as it turned out, conduct on both sides of the distinction suffered penalties ... He argued eloquently and openly against the pressures and moral coercion of public opinion as it affected self-regarding conduct, giving the overwhelming impression that he was opposed to all such pressure, while, in fact, he regarded the pressure of opinion coming from superior natures with individuality, which was intended to be coercive, as quite legitimate.
>
> (1995, 42, 51–52)

By implication, we miss the point if we take seriously his talk of rights to complete liberty of self-regarding conduct. In fact, he was prepared to employ coercion to stamp out self-regarding conduct and dispositions of which he disapproved.

Hamburger seems far too eager to attribute illiberal ambitions and strategies to Mill, which contradict the text. Moreover, his remarkable thesis is fatally flawed. In the first place, the well-known self–other distinction is not between conduct subject to penalties and conduct immune from them. Mill 'openly' admits that natural penalties may attach to self-regarding conduct. The distinction is a different one, between conduct that is directly harmful to others without their consent and conduct that only harms others with their consent if it harms them at all.

Second, self-regarding conduct does not directly harm *others* without their consent. The natural penalties, which are inseparable from others' mere dislike, fall on the *agent*. True, others' liberty to avoid what displeases them deprives the agent of their company and support, and these are harms to him. If the agent persists with the disliked self-regarding conduct, however, then he consents to these perceptible hurts. All concerned may regret the loss of friendship and other mutual benefits caused by the disagreement over choice of personal lifestyle. But, even though such deprivations are perceptible injuries, nobody suffers them against their wishes. You wish to pursue one personal lifestyle, whereas I wish to pursue another incompatible with the first. Neither of us is harmed without his consent, unless one of us is forced to live as the other wants him to live.

Third, there is not the slightest textual evidence for the claim that Mill was ready to prescribe coercive interference with purely self-regarding conduct that he may have found contemptible. He disdains even the idea of a 'morally superior' self-regarding choice, contrary to what Hamburger suggests. Self-regarding matters are strictly beyond morality, he makes clear, and so are not subject to deliberate social punishment, whether by law or by organized efforts to humiliate in public. Every competent adult (not merely some 'superior' class of intellectuals) ought to enjoy absolute liberty to choose among self-regarding actions. That includes the liberty to avoid others of whose self-regarding conduct we disapprove, as long as we do not cause any non-consensual perceptible damage to their interests.

Fourth, and related, persuasion, advice, counsel, encouragement, attempts to inform and the like are not the same thing as coercion. Such measures are compatible with complete liberty of self-regarding conduct. By contrast, coercion involves non-consensual harm to the victim: it causes perceptible damage to his interest in liberty and individuality against his wishes.

Fifth, Mill is evidently willing to let any 'class struggle' over ideas and personal lifestyles be settled under conditions of complete liberty of discussion and experimentation by all. The intellectual minority should certainly have 'freedom to point out the way' to the majority, in his view. But he explicitly rejects the sort of 'heroic' authoritarianism advocated by Carlyle, whereby some 'strong man of genius' (such as Cromwell or Frederick the Great) forces the masses to 'do his bidding' (1859c, 269 (III.13)). Open discussion, Socratic dialogue, free experiments of living and mass education are held out as the means to a liberal utilitarian society. The coercive machinations of some 'superior' class are not in the picture.

It does not seem to occur to Hamburger that the doctrine of the *Liberty* permits society to evolve in a direction away from that *recommended* by Mill. If people increasingly turn to sex, drugs and rock-and-roll music in their personal lifestyles, for example, sober and straight intellectuals may well tend to face natural penalties for their 'superior' self-regarding choices. Indeed, the possibility of social 'decline' toward 'barbarisms' of this sort usually provokes conservatives and even some liberals to castigate Mill as naive, for proposing a doctrine that is far too permissive.

Jeremy Waldron, while sympathetic to Mill's project in the *Liberty*, makes an argument that bears some similarities to Hamburger's. He seems to think that natural penalties are indistinguishable from coercive public opinion, at least under certain conditions. He presents an example involving Oscar Wilde and the Marquis of Queensberry to illustrate his worry. If Wilde must not be stigmatized for his homosexuality, he says, then this seems to imply that Queensberry has no right to exclude Wilde from his circle of friends. And yet if Queensberry cannot do that, then he is being forced to associate with people whom he despises. 'It seems then that liberty is at risk on both sides of Mill's equation' (2003, 231). But Mill is clear that Queensberry has the right to avoid Wilde if he pleases, and to warn his friends and acquaintances to avoid Wilde too. Waldron's worry is really over the issue of warning others to avoid Wilde since a mass of people avoiding him looks very much like coercive stigma: 'its being permissible for Queensberry to warn others away from Wilde is perilously close to Queensberry's regarding it as permissible to orchestrate boycott and ostracism' (ibid., 235). And so it seems that Mill is faced with a 'conundrum': society must either force Queensberry and others not to ostracize Wilde so as to protect his individuality, or it must permit them to express their individuality by coercively interfering with Wilde's lifestyle. Either way, society must coercively interfere with somebody's individuality: 'Protecting the individuality of people like Wilde seems to mean restricting the individuality of people like Queensberry' (ibid., 233).

But this is a fake dilemma. The fact that many people choose to avoid Wilde does not imply that they are coercing him to change his lifestyle: he is free to continue in his disliked self-regarding conduct, and if he does he signals his willingness to suffer the 'social pressure' associated with their natural penalties. Indeed, he is thereby making clear to them that, for him, his self-regarding liberty is more valuable than their company and support. Moreover, if Queensberry and others do coercively interfere with Wilde's self-regarding liberty by organizing boycotts, public protests and the like against homosexuals, then society legitimately uses coercion to prevent such wrongful non-consensual harm being inflicted on Wilde. For Mill, coercive interference with the individual's self-regarding liberty is always a wrongful harm whereas coercive interference to prevent wrongful harm is legitimate.

Notice that I am not denying Waldron's contention that natural penalties exerted by a mass of people can come 'perilously close' to coercive public opinion. At an extreme, an individual may lose virtually all of his friends and acquaintances if he persists with self-regarding conduct that others strongly dislike in the context of a small-scale homogenous community in which almost everyone thinks alike. Waldron is right to suggest that the person is likely to feel more social pressure to conform in such a context than in, say, a large-scale pluralistic society where diverse personal lifestyles flourish. Even in the extreme case, however, others cannot legitimately *force* the despised person to change his self-regarding behaviour. They have no moral permission to organize a public boycott of his business or that of his employer, for example, or to attack him personally in the media. Instead, they have a moral duty not to do these things. They cannot 'parade their contempt' for his self-regarding conduct in such coercive ways. Nor can they use force to banish him from the community. True, they may be able to exert a lot of pressure by turning to competing businesses and by slandering his reputation in private conversations. But this does not defeat the individual's moral right to do as he pleases, as long as he does not cause harm to others against their wishes. He is free to exit the community if he wants. Or he can continue to own or rent his home if he wishes. Indeed, if he stays, it remains possible that he will eventually persuade others to change their minds and endorse his once-despised opinions and conduct.

Millian liberalism (unlike some modern liberalisms) does not pretend to be neutral between competing personal conceptions of a good life. It is biased in favour of an ideal Periclean character, the development of which by all members of society is associated with the maximization of collective happiness. But the claim that the individual should be *compelled* to develop such a character, through the use of coercion in matters of purely self-regarding concern, is no part of Mill's doctrine. Coercive interference is properly confined to the other-regarding sphere.

ISN'T THERE A DANGER OF ISOLATED AND DISTURBED INDIVIDUALS?

It might seem that liberal utilitarianism carries a grave danger of isolation and anomie among the members of society. Doesn't his right to absolute liberty in self-regarding matters imply that the individual is permitted to live as he pleases within his purely personal sphere, unencumbered by moral duties to other people aside from those which he may voluntarily choose to incur? Isn't it likely, therefore, that Mill's liberal dream is really a nightmare, in which self-obsessed people devote all of their time to their families and businesses but ignore wider social issues of justice and charity? If the individual cannot insulate himself within his self-regarding sphere, on the other hand, how can we say that he has absolute liberty of self-regarding conduct? If he is obligated to perform certain other-regarding acts, does this not imply that his right to liberty is not absolute?

But the doctrine is not plagued by insurmountable difficulties here. Two considerations are relevant. First, a right to choose as one pleases among self-regarding actions does not imply any right to choose as one pleases between self-regarding actions and harmful other-regarding conduct. Absolute liberty within the self-regarding realm is compatible with constraints on one's freedom to move between the realms as one likes. Nobody has a moral right to choose as he pleases among actions, some of which pose a risk of perceptible injury to other people against their wishes.

Second, it is implausible to think that the individual *can* (let alone should) freely choose the choice situations in which he finds himself. Nobody has perfect control over whether, or when, he will have to consider preventing non-consensual harm befalling others. Neptune, a qualified lifeguard, may be innocently reading a book in the privacy of his seaside cottage, for example, when he happens to look through his window to see Venus about to drown. Aware of her distress, he infers immediately that a strong swimmer could rescue her with little risk of harm to himself. Like it or not, he now must choose whether or not to act to prevent non-consensual harm to her, even though the harm does not originate in his actions. Given his qualifications, his failure to do anything might reasonably be thought to constitute a violation of her moral right to be helped in the circumstances. In any case, his purely self-regarding act of reading has been transformed, as a result of events beyond his control, into an *inaction* that may contribute to another's loss of life against her wishes. If he continues to do nothing but read after becoming conscious of her need, he effectively *intends* that she will suffer non-consensual harm, and thereby engages in other-regarding conduct. This sort of inaction might be permissible in some circumstances, e.g. perhaps Nep has recently become paralysed in an auto accident. But it is never a matter of Nep's moral right to choose as he likes. Rather, society properly has jurisdiction, and ought to establish reasonable rules to govern such situations.

There is no necessary conflict between a right to absolute liberty of self-regarding conduct and a duty to assist another in dire need. As the example illustrates, what was once self-regarding conduct has vanished for reasons beyond the control of the agent, to be replaced by other-regarding conduct. It is certainly true that Nep did not *choose* this to happen. But the idea that we can always freely choose the kinds of choices we face, independently of other factors (which we might for convenience subsume under the term 'brute luck'), is not worth taking seriously. The role of luck in this sense raises fascinating questions. How often will the individual be transported outside the self-regarding realm by factors not within his control? When is he obligated to act to prevent non-consensual harm to others?

To take another example, a relatively wealthy person is contemplating his existence behind the walls of his remote castle, when he receives a letter from his impoverished neighbours requesting his financial aid. Even if he ignores the request, factors beyond his control have presented him with a choice whether or not to help others. If he fails to help, he cannot pretend that he is merely choosing as he pleases within his self-regarding realm. He intends to leave unremedied the risk of non-consensual perceptible damage suffered by others.

More generally, other-regarding choices will make their appearance within any person's life, whether or not he chooses them to appear. He may be forced to defend himself from the violent acts of others, for example, if not directly, then indirectly, by participating in the political mechanism for enacting legal rights and duties of other-regarding conduct. Others may also approach him for help, or for advice concerning their projects, which, as a member of their society, he will have reasonable customary obligations to provide. The idea that the individual can or should somehow exist as an isolated being, an atom voluntarily choosing whether, and to what extent, to participate in the society of his fellows, is no part of Mill's liberalism.

Absolute liberty of self-regarding conduct can coexist in harmony with obedience to reasonable rules of other-regarding behaviour. When faced with choices involving non-consensual harm to others, the individual ought to satisfy his moral obligations under the rules, and is properly subject to coercion for that purpose. He ought to satisfy his obligations of justice correlative to others' rights (including their rights to be rescued from grave dangers when little risk is posed to the rescuer), as well as his obligations of charity, which do not correlate to others' rights. These obligations to others may result in a relatively large number of interruptions in the self-regarding activities of some people, as occasions arise more frequently for them to rescue or assist their fellows. But, at least in the present state of education, reasonable rules will not require anything approaching the extreme levels of self-sacrifice associated with crude act utilitarianism.[3] A fortiori, liberal utilitarian rules of justice can exclude, as suboptimal, such measures as Harris' (1975) 'survival lottery', designed to maximize harm-prevention by forcing randomly selected organ donors to sacrifice their equal rights so that a greater number of otherwise doomed patients may live with transplanted organs.[4]

SUGGESTIONS FOR FURTHER READING

For further clarification of Mill's extraordinary liberal utilitarianism as I now understand it, see the list of references to my work cited in Chapter 7, note 14.

Some scholars continue to read Mill as a rule utilitarian. Notably, Dale Miller provides a careful discussion of the debate over whether Mill is a rule utilitarian or an act utilitarian, and comes out in favour of the rule-utilitarian reading. See his *J.S. Mill: Moral, Social and Political Thought* (Cambridge: Polity Press, 2010), 71–110. Miller relies heavily on the insights of David Lyons, although Lyons himself does not defend the rule-utilitarian reading but instead seems drawn to the 'mixed-conception' interpretation. See e.g. David Lyons, *Rights, Welfare, and Mill's Moral Theory* (New York: Oxford University Press, 1994).

The most prominent defenders of rule utilitarianism are Brandt, Harsanyi and Hooker. See e.g. Richard B. Brandt, *Morality, Utilitarianism, and Rights* (Cambridge: Cambridge University Press, 1992); John C. Harsanyi, 'Morality and the Theory of Rational Behavior' (1977), in A.K. Sen and B. Williams (eds), *Utilitarianism and Beyond* (Cambridge: Cambridge University Press, 1982), 39–62, 'Does Reason Tell Us What Moral Code to Follow and, Indeed, to Follow Any Moral Code at All?', *Ethics* 96 (1985): 42–55, 'On Preferences, Promises and the Coordination Problem', *Ethics* 96 (1985): 68–73, and 'Game and Decision Theoretic Models in Ethics', in R.J. Aumann and S. Hart (eds), *Handbook of Game Theory* (Amsterdam: North-Holland, 1992), 1: 669–707; and Brad Hooker, *Ideal Code, Real World* (Oxford: Clarendon Press, 2000).

For interesting discussions pertaining to any attempt to ground moral rights on some system of social rules, see L.W. Sumner, *The Moral Foundation of Rights* (Oxford: Clarendon Press, 1987); and Joel Feinberg, *Freedom and Fulfillment* (Princeton: Princeton University Press, 1993), chs 8–10.

For influential statements of the view that liberal utilitarianism is problematic, see H.L.A. Hart, 'Natural Rights: Bentham and John Stuart Mill,' in his *Essays on Bentham* (Oxford: Oxford University Press, 1982), 79–104; C.L. Ten, *Mill on Liberty* (Oxford: Clarendon Press, 1980), and 'Mill's Defence of Liberty', in J. Gray and G.W. Smith (eds), *J.S. Mill: On Liberty in Focus* (London: Routledge, 1991), 212–38; John Gray, *Liberalisms: Essays in Political Philosophy* (London: Routledge, 1989), ch. 10; and John Gray, *Two Faces of Liberalism* (New York: New Press, 2000).

Hamburger's argument that Mill's self–other distinction is a rhetorical ploy may be found in Joseph Hamburger, 'Individuality and Moral Reform: The Rhetoric of Liberty and the Reality of Restraint in Mill's *On Liberty*', *Political Science Reviewer* 24 (1995): 7–70. See, also, Joseph Hamburger, *John Stuart Mill on Liberty and Control* (Princeton: Princeton University Press, 1999). Waldron's suggestion that natural penalties exerted by many people can come 'perilously close' to coercive public opinion may be found in Jeremy Waldron, 'Mill as a Critic of Culture and Society', in David Bromwich and George Kateb (eds), *On Liberty: John Stuart Mill* (New Haven: Yale University Press, 2003), 224–45.

Further to the discussion of the last section of this chapter, it might be objected against Mill that a self-regarding action is always at the same time an other-regarding action, namely, a failure to prevent non-consensual harm to others. Nep's situation is not rare, so this objection runs. Instead, the individual continually faces obligations to help needy others, whether members of his own society or of other communities. Thus, it is pointless to draw the self–other distinction in the field of individual conduct because society has authority to monitor other-regarding inactions, and can legitimately use coercion to interfere with self-regarding conduct on the grounds that it is preventing inactions that cause wrongful non-consensual harm to others.

But Mill has anticipated this objection. Even if a self-regarding action always did imply a failure to prevent non-consensual harm to others, and even though society has legitimate authority to consider coercive interference with other-regarding inactions, it would not follow that society ought always to declare that the non-consensual damage is wrongful and expediently prevented by external sanctions. A general policy of laissez-faire seems expedient, allowing for exceptions. If the agent has a recognized moral duty to others which he fails to fulfil as a result of his putatively self-regarding action, then, as Mill argues, the action is taken out of the self-regarding class because it is inseparable from duties to others.

The individual who fails to fulfil recognized duties to others causes wrongful non-consensual harm to them, and coercive interference with his conduct is justified if external sanctions are expedient. So Nep is properly punished if he has a recognized enforceable duty to save Venus from drowning. So are individuals who fail to fulfil their duty to pay taxes used to help the needy. Deliberative majorities seeking to promote utility in the largest sense have authority to determine which duties to help others are recognized in the given society.

In any case, it is not the case that everything the individual does is properly described as a failure to prevent non-consensual harm to others. Some actions are self-regarding; they do not involve any intention to harm others without their consent; and the direct consequences of the actions do not alter the circumstances of others against their wishes. Thus, the individual who fulfils his recognized duties to others can be free to engage in self-regarding actions as he pleases.

NOTES

1 Ten is apparently attracted to the non-standard versions of 'utilitarianism' ascribed to Mill by revisionist scholars, but he prefers to treat such interpretations as 'non-utilitarian' (1991, 236–37). His caution is certainly understandable.
2 On Rousseau, see Riley 2005b.
3 For a helpful discussion of various issues surrounding justified coercion against failures to prevent harm to others, see Feinberg 1984–88, 1: 126–86. Feinberg's notion of harm, as setback of an interest which ought to be considered a right, is, however, distinct from Mill's idea.
4 Ten, in contrast, suggests that Mill rejects 'an unrestricted policy of maximizing harm-prevention' because his 'utilitarianism is tempered by the recognition of some *independent* principle of distribution' (1980, 64–65, emphasis added).

9

LIBERTY, INDIVIDUALITY AND CUSTOM

DOESN'T MILL'S IDEA OF INDIVIDUALITY PRESUPPOSE A RADICALLY UNSITUATED INDIVIDUAL?

It is often said that liberalism in general, and Mill's doctrine of liberty in particular, posits an incredible personal character ideal, which is incompatible with every civil society's culture and moral traditions. Gray, for example, claims that 'by individuality Mill means a form of self-realization in which the powers of autonomous thought and choice that mark the human species are exercised [to fulfil] the needs peculiar to each person's nature' (1989, 224). Self-realization in this sense is achieved by means of

> experiments of living ... embodied in plans of life ... conceived and implemented by individuals who have detached themselves critically from the social conventions which surround them and who, once so detached, are able to discover the unique needs of their natures.
>
> (Ibid.)

The growth of knowledge fuelled by those experiments of living is apparently central to Mill's account of human progress or development. 'For Mill', says Gray, 'progress is an inherent tendency of the human mind, with historical development being controlled ultimately by innovation in the realm of ideas. What is most noteworthy is that the growth of knowledge is theorized as an autonomous tendency of the mind' (ibid., 227), manifested in the conception and implementation of experiments of living by critically detached individuals.

Gray rightly claims that there are fatal objections to this way of thinking about individuality and progress. The conception of individuality is incredible because it requires the individual to be 'radically unsituated', that is, 'unencumbered' by any social conventions when engaging in discussion or conducting experiments of living. Self-development in that sense is simply not feasible, given that the individual cannot transcend altogether the social context in which he finds himself. Moreover, the approach misleads us into condemning as devoid of individuality all traditional forms of living: 'The man who accepts the way of life in which he was born ... and who has no interest in trying out alternatives to it, cannot for Mill exhibit individuality, however stylish his personality may be' (ibid., 224–25).

Similarly, the 'idea of an experiment of living is a rationalistic fiction' because it assumes that each individual has 'a quiddity, or unique nature, that is his to realize', independently of cultural circumstances (ibid., 225–26). Custom is then falsely seen as hostile to self-realization when in fact 'personal individuality and human flourishing [depend] on a cultural tradition' (ibid., 226). Tradition is not the *enemy* of liberty and progress, Gray emphasizes. Instead, 'social conventions [are] a precondition not only of peace, but also of liberty', because they play an 'indispensable role ... in enabling diverse individuals and ways of living to coexist without constant recourse to legal coercion. A society without strong conventions would unavoidably be chaotic, resembling ... a Hobbesian state of nature' (ibid.). Thus, 'convention and tradition are to be regarded as conditions of progress and not (as Mill ignorantly supposes) obstacles to it' (ibid.). Indeed,

> if there is such a thing as an experiment of living, it is collective and not individual, it is conducted by social groups held together by common traditions and practices and it is tried, not over a single lifetime, but across the generations.
>
> (Ibid.)

But Mill surely does not think of individuality and progress in the way attributed to him by Gray. By individuality, he apparently means a character that has been developed by the individual through liberty in the positive sense of making choices in accordance with his own judgment and inclinations. Strictly speaking, a person who never chooses as he pleases has no character or individuality: 'One whose desires and impulses are not his own, has no character' (1859c, 264 (III.5)). Consistent with this, individuals can be described as having strong, active characters or weak, passive ones: 'If, in addition to being his own, his impulses are strong, and are under the government of a strong will, he has an energetic character' (ibid.). Unlike a person whose individuality is energetic, a person with a weak individuality has only a weak desire for liberty, and thus rarely chooses as he wishes. Instead of choosing as he pleases, this person of weak character usually lets others (including long-dead ancestors) make his choices for him.

Mill suggests that the individual who has a vigorous character is more likely than not to develop an ideal Periclean character. He seems to believe, in other words, that a person with a strong disposition to do as he wishes will tend to develop a noble and moral individuality. By contrast, the individual with a weak desire for liberty will tend to display a miserable individuality. In short, his character will not show much development beyond a blind acceptance of the prevailing customary norms and choices.

As we have seen, Mill recommends that the individual should develop a noble Periclean character, and, to that end, insists on a moral right to complete liberty of purely self-regarding conduct. Outside the purely self-regarding sphere, however, individual liberty is not necessarily permissible. Rather, society legitimately has the authority to employ coercion to prevent non-consensual harm to others. External sanctions should be expediently used to prevent harm deemed wrongful by deliberative majorities, even though the individual thereby loses the means of self-improvement which 'gratifying his inclinations to the injury of others' would make possible (ibid., 266 (III.9)). A person with noble individuality understands this, and voluntarily conforms to the moral and legal rules of other-regarding conduct recognized by majorities in the given context.

The Millian idea of individuality (noble or otherwise) does *not* presuppose a radically unsituated self. Since his judgments and inclinations are themselves situated in some institutional setting, any person's *liberty* (the choices he freely makes, without interference by others, in accord with his own judgment and inclinations) as well as his *individuality* (his character formed by his repeated choices) are both inseparable from his cultural beliefs and practices. But the fact of situatedness does not imply that personal character and desires are mechanically determined by existing social conventions. Otherwise, custom would inevitably establish a homogeneous society of distressingly similar individuals, who imitated each other's way of life in all particulars.

Given that we observe the contrary, we are entitled to infer that a person encumbered by popular norms and beliefs is nevertheless capable of deciding to choose differently than the majority of his fellows. No great ingenuity is required to see that the situated individual can do this, provided he can remember and/or imagine beliefs and practices other than those which currently happen to prevail among the majority. He need not be critically detached in the absurd sense that his self-image transcends his society entirely, including its traditions and conceivable futures. How could any reasonable person altogether ignore his society's accepted rules of correct inference, for example, let alone simply abandon its rules of language?

If memory and imagination are not arbitrarily banished from human nature, the idea of an experiment of living is straightforward, independently of all metaphysical talk about quiddities or unique personal natures. Such an experiment is in effect any uncommon choice or practice, that is, any way of living rejected by most people as peculiar or eccentric. By definition, such experiments must be carried out by the individual or by a voluntary group of persons comprising a minority of society.

AGAINST QUIDDITIES

It is worth emphasis that quiddities – unique *noumena* whose properties are not contingent on social circumstances – are precisely the sort of merely intuitive entities which Mill seeks to eradicate from his lean *phenomenalist* epistemology (see Riley 1988, 133–63). So far as I am aware, he never makes the assertion often attributed to him that each of us has some such unique essence awaiting discovery. Rather, he repeatedly asserts the contrary. In his *Political Economy*, for instance, he says: 'Of all vulgar modes of escaping from the consideration of the effect of social and moral influences on the human mind, the most vulgar is that of attributing the diversities of conduct and character to *inherent* natural differences' (Mill 1871a, 319, emphasis added). Indeed, the idea that plural and incommensurable quiddities inhere in different persons or groups seems to rest more easily within a value-pluralistic moral universe, of the sort posited by Gray and Berlin, than within liberal utilitarianism.

As opposed to being possessed of quiddities, Mill suggests that individuals are sufficiently similar by nature that they might ideally come to display unity in their moral and political judgments and opinions. Even if such rational unity were attained, however, their personal desires, dispositions and characters may continue to differ in important respects, provided their personal circumstances (including their endowed capacities) remain heterogeneous. In general, he emphasizes that 'the circumstances which surround different classes and individuals ... shape their characters' (1859c, 274 (III.18)). Diverse characters are apparently caused by diverse environments, not by unique individual essences. Thus, he dismisses the Romantic notion that a 'superior excellence' inheres in some individuals, classes or nations. When any such distinction exists, it 'exists as the effect, not the cause' of individuality (ibid.).[1]

His claim that individuals are unequal with respect to their endowed capacities (including their given powers of will) should not be conflated with the claim that each person has a unique essence awaiting discovery. All adults to whom the liberty doctrine applies apparently possess intellectual and moral capacities *to some degree*, although generally to unequal degrees. Individuals do not differ in kind on this score (see e.g. Mill 1833). All are fallible and subject to weakness of will.

An unequal distribution of choice-making capacities across individuals does not imply that different persons have distinct essences, or that they must have plural and incommensurable basic values. Despite their unequal powers of judgment, reasoning and willing, for example, all individuals may share a similar nature, insofar as each is motivated in decipherable ways by some basic notion of happiness.

Gray has reiterated that Mill wanted to combine two distinct empirical claims, namely, that what makes man happiest is the exercise of his capacities of autonomous thought and action, and that his exercise of those powers will lead each person to the discovery of his unique and peculiar quiddity: 'Mill's theory of individuality, then, combines the claim that man is his own maker with the claim that, for each man, a nature exists which awaits discovery' (1991, 207). The first claim may be empirical, although we must be careful about what Mill is claiming. He does not claim that all persons now actually *do* take pleasure in making their own choices. Most are observed to imitate others blindly, he thinks. Nor does he claim that people *ought* to assign priority to autonomous choice-making if it conflicts with reasonable rule-abidingness and security in other-regarding matters. His claim is that people will be most happy if they develop a certain ideal liberal character, in which autonomy or individuality has come to mean choosing as one pleases in self-regarding matters, and also choosing to obey reasonable moral and legal rules in other-regarding matters.

As for the second claim attributed to Mill by Gray, I have already suggested that Mill never makes it. Moreover, it is difficult to see how quiddities could ever be inferred from empirical observation. What empirical evidence could support such a hypothesis? If two persons had identical choice-making capacities and always occupied the same circumstances, then perhaps we could test it. But such stringent conditions are never met, even in the case of identical twins reared in the same family. Even Kant admits that knowledge of noumena is inaccessible to human beings, in which case we can never really know whether each of us is comprised of some unique substance that distinguishes us from everyone else. The question is irrelevant for practical purposes.

NO RELIANCE ON IDEAL OBSERVERS

Whether or not they are blessed with quiddities, fallible individuals arguably *need* rights to discuss ideas and experiment with distinctive personal environments freely, to improve their imperfect intellectual and emotional capacities. Prior to such discussion and experimentation, we may be expected to hold various more or less ignorant opinions of happiness, and to come into conflict accordingly.

Intellectual and moral development is not, for Mill, some autonomous tendency of the human mind (whether individual or collective). He does not rely on unsituated ideal observers to produce warranted opinions, personal lifestyle choices or reasonable rules of permissible other-regarding conduct in any social context. Rather, he says that:

> [T]he source of everything respectable in man either as an intellectual or as a moral being [is] that his errors are corrigible. He is capable of rectifying his mistakes by discussion and experience ... Wrong opinions and practices gradually yield to fact and argument: but facts and arguments, to produce any effect on the mind, must be brought before it. Very few facts are able to tell their own story.
>
> (1859c, 231 (II.7))

Complete liberty of thought and discussion among situated and fallible people replaces the fictitious observer who is 'sufficiently capacious and impartial' to distil truth from conflicting opinions. Similarly, complete liberty of self-regarding experimentation replaces the fiction of an ideal mechanism that automatically recognizes the best social rules of other-regarding conduct when confronted with conflicting possibilities. More must be said to clarify how liberty of *self-regarding* conduct is linked to the choice of a liberal democratic political procedure for selecting laws of *other-regarding* conduct. It remains true, however, that self-regarding liberty underlies and accounts for the moral obligation which is felt by individuals who have developed their individuality, their character, to construct and participate in a liberal democratic political process of the sort prescribed by Mill for this purpose.

The motor that drives the halting and imperfect process of social improvement is the individual's strong desire to choose in accord with his own judgment and wants. Of course, this desire for liberty, together with the self-improvement, that is, cultivation of character or individuality, which flows from choosing as one wishes and learning from the consequences, is situated within and constrained to some extent by a given society's existing customs and beliefs, including its rules of correct inference. But human fallibility implies that existing customs and beliefs can never be assumed the best possible. There is inevitably room for the individual to discover novel and surprising causal regularities among phenomena (including mental phenomena). In that sense, the idea of 'truth' is open-ended. The individual can always discover better alternatives to existing rules and practices. As Mill emphasizes, 'no routine or rule of thumb can possibly make provision' for the 'ever-varying circumstances' in which our mental capacities have occasion to be exercised (1832, 338). Liberty and individuality remain indispensable for bringing about generally expedient reforms in response to ever-varying circumstances. Thus, every civil society seeking progress should protect, by right, the individual's liberty to form his own opinions, discuss them, and act upon them without causing non-consensual harm to other people. And, once some threshold of material and moral advance has been achieved, society should also permit individuals the freedom to engage in fair competitions, even though the winners will cause non-consensual harm to the losers.

HOW CAN DOING AS ONE PLEASES LEAD THE INDIVIDUAL TO DEVELOP A NOBLE PERICLEAN CHARACTER?

As mentioned in the preceding section, there is a need to clarify how liberty of *self-regarding* conduct is linked to the choice of a liberal democratic political procedure for selecting laws of *other-regarding* conduct. More generally, it may seem puzzling that choosing as one pleases can promote the development of a noble character that includes not only dispositions to assert oneself in self-regarding and competitive matters but also dispositions to comply with reasonable moral and legal rules of other-regarding conduct.

But this puzzle dissolves when we appreciate that liberty in the sense of doing as one pleases enables a competent individual to discover the higher kinds of pleasant feelings which human nature is capable of experiencing. In particular, competent adults will tend to learn that the kind of pleasure inseparably associated with the moral sentiments, and especially with the sentiment of justice, has a superior quality to any competing kinds of pleasures. True, individuals who do not develop their characters, who display a miserable individuality, will not learn this. Even if most people more or less thoughtlessly follow existing laws and customs, including rules that wrongly invade the self-regarding sphere, however, there will be some who insist on their liberty, and who develop their individuality, even in the absence of a recognized right to self-regarding liberty. This cultivated minority will discover the qualitative superiority of the pleasure of justice, and, as moral agents, seek to persuade the majority to establish social rules that distribute and sanction equal rights, including rights of self-regarding liberty. To the degree that this minority of people with more developed characters can influence political deliberations, the political authorities will establish such laws of justice. This remains so in a representative democracy, where the political authorities are elected by the people.

Popular majorities and their elected representatives will establish laws that distribute and sanction equal rights, including rights of self-regarding liberty, if they are persuaded to do so by educated minorities. Mill's preferred form of liberal democratic political system, with its distinctive system of counter-majoritarian checks and balances, is designed to promote the influence of the educated minority in the majority's political deliberations (Riley 2007). Indeed, that is why individuals who have developed their individuality, and who thus appreciate the qualitative superiority of the pleasant feeling of security which would be experienced by any conscientious person who lives under a working social code of equal rights and duties, will feel a duty to others to help construct and maintain some such liberal democratic political process. Such a political process, responsive to majorities and yet also designed to discourage them from abusing individual rights, is more likely than any other form of political process to construct a social code of justice. Other political systems are more prone to degenerate into corrupt processes, in which unjust laws are enacted that promote the 'sinister interests' of narrowly selfish factions instead of the collective good. The construction of a social code that distributes and sanctions equal rights and duties for all, including equal rights of self-regarding liberty and their correlative duties, has absolute priority for maximizing what Mill calls 'utility in the largest sense'.

Of course, in the ideal case where all are moral agents with a noble Periclean character, counter-majoritarian checks would no longer be needed in the democratic political process. Actual majorities would also be ideal deliberative majorities: they would voluntarily seek out expert opinions on any special topic of legislation, and they would not think of abusing individual rights. Nor would the social code of justice need to include external sanctions: everyone would voluntarily comply with the rules, after they had been made public and everyone knew which equal rights and duties had been recognized as best for their community.

Some critics complain that Mill is prevented from saying anything like this because he relies on a defective moral psychology and lacks an adequate model of practical reason. Candace Vogler (2001) and Elijah Millgram (2009), for example, argue along these lines. They seem to have somewhat different notions of what higher pleasures are, and I will return to this point in due course, but otherwise their complaints are similar. Roughly, the gist of their objection seems to be as follows, although they do not express it quite in these terms. First, Mill supposedly works with an outdated associationist psychology in which cognitions, including ideas, beliefs and judgments, are sharply separated from feelings, including sensations of pleasure and pain. As Vogler puts it, 'the moral psychology with which Mill is working does not allow for reasoned feelings' (2001, 82). Since pleasure is only a subjective non-cognitive feeling that might be associated with any external objects, it is difficult to understand how Mill can say that a higher kind of pleasure, more valuable as pleasure than the usual sensations regardless of quantity, is associated with one object rather than another, unless he implicitly smuggles in something besides pleasure to assess the different objects. He might argue that reason judges that certain personalities or characters are intrinsically better than others for human beings, for example, and then rely on that rational assessment to assert that a better character is a source of pleasure of a higher quality. True, that would require him to abandon his explicit commitment to hedonism since the rational assessment of characters is made independently of feelings of pleasure per se. But he can't make such an argument even if he wanted to, so the complaint as I'm expressing it runs. That's because he adopts a purely 'instrumentalist' model of practical reason, according to which reason is confined to ascertaining the best means to given ends and has nothing to say about the choice of ends per se. Thus, Mill is stuck. He really has no way to defend his grand claim that liberty in the sense of self-assertion is justified by the ultimate end of utility in the largest sense. He lacks the tools to say that liberty can lead the individual to develop a noble character which all individuals must develop for themselves if the collective happiness is to be maximized.

But Millgram and Vogler are attributing to Mill views that he rejects, and thus are attacking a straw man of their own making. First, he doesn't hold a purely instrumentalist model of practical reason. As he makes clear in *Utilitarianism*, he thinks that reason can show us that pleasure is the sole 'ultimate end' of human action, even though this conclusion evidently cannot be proved in the usual way, by deducing it from premises that are yet more ultimate: 'The subject is within the cognizance of the rational faculty; and neither does that faculty deal with it in the way of intuition' (1861b, 207 (I.5)). The challenge is to figure out his justification for saying that reason can determine ultimate ends, and not pretend that he does not say it. This large topic is beyond the scope of this study, of course, but one may reasonably expect to find in his *System of Logic* the bulk of whatever justification he has.

Second, Mill does not hold a psychological theory in which cognitions are sharply separated from feelings. In *Utilitarianism* again, for example, he insists that the desire for an object, the belief or expectation that the object is a source of pleasure, and the judgment that the object is desirable are in fact 'the same phenomenon' or mental state (ibid., 237–38 (IV.10)). We give the mental state different *names* in our ordinary language, and draw logical distinctions between the names for our purposes. But the names refer to the same thing, in his view, and it is simply a metaphysical delusion to insist that the different names must correspond to different things. Moreover, given that humans are fallible, we can have mistaken desires, mistaken beliefs about which objects are pleasant and which painful, and mistaken judgments about what is desirable—all amounting to the same mistake.

Even more important for present purposes, higher pleasures as Mill depicts them are complex feelings that are generated in a quasi-chemical fashion from myriad ingredients, including cognitive elements. The pleasant feeling of security inseparably associated with the moral sentiment of justice, for example, is a complex feeling involving a chemical combination of: animal instincts, including the instinct to sympathize with one's kin and the instinct to retaliate against anything perceived as threatening harm to oneself or one's kin; sensations of pleasure, including relief from pain, or their copies in memory or imagination; and moral concepts and principles constructed by reason, including ideas of rights and principles that guide the infliction of retaliation by limiting it to individuals who violate the recognized rights of others (ibid., 248–51 (V.16–25)). Strictly speaking, this higher pleasure is a property of the sentiment of justice, which grows up around the idea of a social code of justice that distributes and sanctions reciprocal rights and duties. When attention is focused on this pleasant feeling of security per se, it is felt by most if not all of those individuals who have developed the capacities required to feel it to be superior in quality to any competing kinds of pleasant feelings. Given that reason has gone into the construction of the idea of justice around which the sentiment of justice grows up, reason supports the qualitative superiority of the pleasant feeling of security which is a property of the moral sentiment (see also Riley 2012, 2014).

Vogler and Millgram fail to appreciate the higher pleasures thus understood. Vogler sees that higher pleasures are a chemical blend of myriad ingredients but she seems to think that they are invariably aesthetic feelings associated with objects of art, including personalities or characters fashioned by individuals for themselves. She acknowledges that higher pleasures are superior in quality to lower ones, at least insofar as a small amount of the higher can outweigh some (but perhaps not all) larger amounts of the lower, but she offers no explanation for this. And it does seem impossible to explain in terms of pleasure why blended pleasures are qualitatively superior to simple ones, given her understanding of pleasures as non-cognitive feelings. Moreover, why should higher pleasure attach to one character rather than another on her understanding? The only way a noble character can be picked over a miserable one, it seems, is by bringing in some standard other than pleasure to do the work. By saddling Mill with her interpretation of what a higher pleasure is, it is hardly surprising that she finds fault with his utilitarian argument for the rights of liberty and individuality.

Millgram offers another interpretation of higher pleasures, which he thinks makes Mill's argument somewhat more plausible in terms of the supposedly 'outdated' hedonistic psychology. I should mention that, although he does not acknowledge this, the interpretation which Millgram calls 'standard and almost correct' is my own, namely, that higher pleasures have lexical priority over lower ones and, in particular, that the higher pleasure of justice has lexical priority over all competing pleasures.[2] In any case, Millgram's alternative interpretation relies on Mill's claim that certain means to pleasure—such as money, virtue, power, fame and rules of justice— become valued for themselves, independently of pleasure (e.g. 1861b, 234–37 (IV.4–7)). These things are such fecund sources of pleasure that an individual may lose sight of the goal of pleasure and instead treat the objects as concrete components of his notion of happiness. How does this happen? As Mill makes clear, part of the explanation is that these objects are means to such a wide scope of pleasant feelings that they become closely associated with pleasure itself. But the main point is that they become valued for themselves through habit: repeated use of them as means makes for habitual use so that we wish to have them purely out of habit and think of them as basic ends, forgetting that they were once only means to pleasure (ibid., 238–39 (IV.11)).

But the fact that some objects are considered intrinsically desirable out of habit has nothing to do with higher pleasures. Objects such as money, virtue and codes of rights are not themselves feelings of pleasure, and can't be seen as either higher or lower kinds of pleasant feelings. Millgram has confused pleasant feelings with objects or sources of pleasure, a common confusion insofar as objects are often called 'pleasures' in the vernacular. Moreover, the force of habit cuts across different kinds of pleasant feelings. The miser who values his wealth for itself and refuses to spend his money out of habit no longer cares about the merely expedient kind of pleasant feelings which he could get from consuming scarce material goods, for example, whereas the person of confirmed virtue who habitually displays honesty, charity, courage and so forth can be counted on to act this way even though he no longer cares about the higher kind of moral pleasure, including relief from moral suffering or guilt, which once motivated his virtuous activities.

Mill is careful to emphasize that there is nothing intrinsically good about habit. Habit is only good insofar as it imparts certainty to actions that promote some kind of pleasant feeling, including the higher kinds: 'Both in feeling and in conduct, habit is the only thing which imparts certainty; and it is because of the importance to others of being able to rely absolutely on one's feelings and conduct, and to oneself of being able to rely on one's own, that the will to do right ought to be cultivated into this habitual independence' (ibid., 240 (IV.11)). In other words, habit itself is only valuable as a means to happiness: 'this state of the will is a means to good, not intrinsically a good; and does not contradict the doctrine that nothing is a good to human beings but in so far as it is either itself pleasurable, or a means of attaining pleasure or averting pain' (ibid.). Imprudent, vicious and ugly habits ought to be broken because they are means to pain and harm.

Clearly, the force of habit, and the fact that some objects are valued as basic ends out of habit, cannot account for the distinction between higher and lower pleasant feelings. Nor can habit explain why a noble Periclean character is so valuable as compared with a miserable character for achieving utility in the largest sense. The miser's habits have given him a miserable character and imparted certainty to his miserable conception of happiness. But the person of confirmed virtue has a virtuous character and a moral conception of happiness. And a person who values the recognized social code of justice for itself and habitually follows its rules has a just character and a just conception of happiness.

Millgram's mistaken understanding of higher pleasures leads him into other severe interpretive difficulties. For example, noticing that the objects like wealth, power and virtue which he calls higher pleasures might come into conflict, he attributes to Mill the absurd view that these objects cannot vary in amount but instead constitute a class of fixed and apparently mutually compatible objects. Yet it is obvious that these 'higher pleasures' can vary in amount and conflict with one another. Should some amount of virtue be traded off for some amount of wealth?[3] Should deviations from recognized rules of justice be permitted in return for some degree of the virtues of charity and mercy? Millgram implies that Mill has no way of answering such questions. But it is really Millgram who has no way of answering them, given his mistaken reading of higher pleasures.

Millgram also joins the chorus that chants of Mill's defective hedonistic theory of psychology. And the chanting might well prove to be correct, although a careful investigation of the issue has yet to be carried out. Millgram is wrong, however, to suggest that Mill's associationist version of hedonism is a forerunner of behaviourism, or of neuroscience, or of that ambiguous discipline known as 'cognitive science' which seems to have more to do with the internal processes of computing machines than with those of conscious human beings. Such disciplines are, for Mill, not even 'psychology', which he understands as the science of regularities— successions and coexistences—among mental states, that is, states of consciousness. Introspection is essential to psychology thus understood. It is also worth pointing out that there is something of a revival of hedonism going on within psychology and economics, led by Daniel Kahneman and his colleagues (see e.g. Kahneman *et al.* 1999). I don't mean to endorse any particular form of the new 'hedonic' psychology. But perhaps hedonism is not dead yet.

ISN'T THE NEED FOR LIBERTY INVERSELY RELATED TO SOCIAL PROGRESS?

Gray claims that Mill's argument from human fallibility is ultimately self-defeating:

> If human nature is progressively knowable, and moral knowledge cumulative, the sphere of liberty will wane as human knowledge waxes ... That progressive enlightenment about the conditions and content of the good life may weaken toleration of forms of life which enlightenment has discredited, is an irony that haunts all those liberalisms which ground the worth of liberty in the fact of human fallibility.
>
> (1986, 245)

But is that claim valid?

Assume for the sake of argument that all members of society have progressed as far as human capacities can allow. Does it follow that liberty is no longer desirable? It may seem so because any person of noble character could serve as an infallible dictator, whose enlightened judgments and commands could be recorded and passed down to everybody else (including subsequent generations) as the only beliefs and actions which are tolerable in the best possible human society. Liberty to deviate would carry a chance of social regress. Thus, blind obedience by all to certain utilitarian laws and customs would seem to be called for.[4]

But appearances are deceiving. For the need to *maintain* one's advanced understanding and highly developed moral and aesthetic dispositions remains. Mill implies that even the most developed human faculties would atrophy if left idle (1859c, 263 (III.4), 265 (III.6)). Even the best people may lose their *acquired* wisdom and noble dispositions through lack of mental exercise. Blind obedience gives the mind no exercise, and thus maintains nothing valuable. In short:

> There shall be as much room and as much necessity for genius when mankind shall have found out everything attainable by their faculties,

as there is now; it will still remain to distinguish the man who knows from the man who takes upon trust.

(1832, 334)

It follows that in an ideal liberal utilitarian society, individuality and its two requisites – liberty and social pluralism – would remain essential to prevent decline.

THE PERMANENT VALUE OF LIBERTY

Liberty in the positive sense of forming, discussing and to some extent even acting upon any ideas one pleases remains essential because humans ultimately have no other criterion of truth, including truth about their own natures (1859c, 231–32 (II.6–8), 247 (II.26), 250–52 (II.31–33), 260–63 (III.1, 3–4)). By implication, humans can never be absolutely certain that they have attained the best possible society. Infallibility is not really feasible for human beings. Any person's claim of infallibility is merely an attempt to deny liberty to others (ibid., 234 (II.11)). In the absence of liberty of discussion and of personal experimentation, no human can properly claim that his beliefs are warranted by the best available evidence. Thus, even in the best possible society, each person must retain a moral right to make whatever self-regarding choices he likes.

It is true that mere 'automatons in human form' could blindly adhere to the best social beliefs and practices, once established. But human beings are not 'pleasure-machines'. Automatons could never by themselves acquire the wisdom of which human nature is capable. Nor can humans automatically preserve their acquired knowledge by virtue of some innate personal excellence that persists independently of their own mental exercise. Even a person of noble Periclean character, to retain it, needs to exercise, and thereby preserve, his acquired ability to judge wisely the grounds of his opinions, as well as his acquired strength of will to make not only the self-regarding but also the competitive and moral choices he prefers on the basis of those judgments. Without such mental exercise, he will gradually lose his capacities to enjoy the 'higher' intellectual and moral activities and pleasures, which mark the noble character: 'it really is of importance, not only what men do, but also what manner of men they are that do it' (ibid., 263 (III.4)).

THE PERMANENT VALUE OF SOCIAL PLURALISM

Social pluralism, as the other requisite of individuality, must also remain a feature of liberal utilitarian society. Critics sometimes suggest that if any ideal utilitarian society were ever realized, then the participants in that ideal social way of life would necessarily be choosing to live every detail of their personal lives in the same way. But that implication simply does not follow. Mill is committed only to the much weaker claim that every participant would choose to conform to reasonable social rules of justice that distribute and protect the same basic rights for all, including equal rights to liberty with respect to purely self-regarding concerns; that every member would also choose to conform to rules of charity and goodwill that enjoin each person to give help to others when he can reasonably afford to do so; and that, within these limits of justice and charity, every member would also choose to accept fair competitive processes, conducted without force or fraud, to allocate economic goods and services, broadly defined. Even if all are possessed of the same noble character, many personal choices, both self-regarding and other-regarding, may differ. Different personal circumstances may continue to generate different personal judgments and inclinations. Social pluralism need not vanish unless two additional assumptions are introduced arbitrarily, namely, that such highly developed individuals must unanimously want an entirely homogeneous society; and that, having agreed thus, these individuals are omnipotent, having the power to eradicate all genetic and acquired differences among individuals. The second assumption may be safely ignored. Moreover, the first is clearly rejected by Mill. Thus, there is nothing incoherent about the idea of an optimal collective way of life that itself admits complete liberty for the individual and voluntary group to experiment with a plurality of self-regarding lifestyles.

WHY DOESN'T THE INDIVIDUAL HAVE A RIGHT TO PARADE HIS BAD MANNERS AND INDECENT BEHAVIOUR IN PUBLIC?

If the individual has a right to complete liberty of self-regarding conduct, it may be asked, doesn't that imply a right to behave indecently and cause offence in public? Granted that he may be situated in a particular social context, doesn't he still have the right to defy the polite conventions of the majority, since these rules seem to have nothing to do with the prevention of harm to others? And, assuming he has such a right, isn't it reasonable to fear that these social conventions would tend to erode under Millian liberalism? Indeed, by ushering in this social decline, wouldn't the liberty doctrine indirectly cause a form of severe harm to the public at large?

If three adults engage in consensual sex in a public place to the astonishment of onlookers, for example, or if one person publishes the intimate details of his love affair without the consent of his friend, why is the shock of the onlookers, or the offence taken by the friend, anything other than mere dislike or emotional distress? What is the *perceptible damage* suffered by any of these people? Given that none can be identified, shouldn't the great good of individuality be safeguarded, despite the fact that its pursuit in these ways causes shock and outrage to others?

Similar questions arise when an individual desecrates the flag in front of a group of army veterans, or rudely tells his wife in front of the neighbours to go fuck a donkey, or parades as a member of the Ku Klux Klan down the main street of a city where blacks are residents, or hands his dying Jewish mother a local newspaper ad in which he expresses his joy at her impending death and announces his plan to bury her ashes in an urn engraved with Hitler's image. All of these acts, and countless more like them, may cause intense dislike to other people. But why are they not self-regarding actions on the Millian notion of harm?

Many who consider themselves liberal have decided to jump off the Millian ship at this point. Perhaps the most influential strategy is to admit that these cases cannot be adequately covered by a harm-prevention principle (however 'harm' to others is conceived), and to add a supplementary principle, according to which society has legitimate authority to employ coercion to prevent the individual from causing offence or shock to others in public. Hart, for example, argues that an admittedly fine distinction can and should be drawn between 'shock or offence to feelings caused by some public display', and distress caused by 'the bare knowledge that others are acting in ways you think wrong' or by 'the belief that others are doing what you do not want them to do' (1963, 46–47). The consequences of an act done in public are thereby distinguished from the consequences of the same act done in private. In particular, person A's mere dislike of B's action in public has a different quality, it appears, than A's mere dislike of B's act in the privacy of, say, B's own home. The first sort of dislike may justify coercive interference, whereas the second sort does not.

But Hart does not clarify why the source or the locale of a person's mere dislike should have this significance. Rather, he jumps quickly to the conclusion that utilitarianism can justify a right to not suffer distress from witnessing an action in public, even if a right to not suffer distress from thinking about the same action done in private must be denied for the value of individual liberty to receive any social recognition. As it stands, this seems to give society unlimited jurisdiction over all individual behaviour in public. Remarkably, Hart appears undisturbed by this alarming extension of the legitimate field of coercion by law or stigma. He says only that the individual who is prohibited from engaging in offensive conduct in public is left 'at liberty to do the same thing in private, if he can' (ibid., 48). Why being left free to do the thing in private, 'if he can', provides a reason for prohibiting the thing in public merely because others dislike it remains mysterious.[5]

The various ways in which Hart's approach has been elaborated in the literature are worth further study (see e.g. Feinberg 1984–88, vols 1–2). But it is more important for our purposes to consider whether the argument of the *Liberty* really requires such modification. Recall that Mill says 'it is unnecessary to dwell' on public violations of good manners, 'as they are only connected indirectly with our subject' (1859c, 296 (V.7)). These cases fall outside the ambit of the principle of self-regarding liberty, he seems to be saying, because non-consensual harm really is suffered by the victims of others' bad manners or shocking behaviour in public. There is something about public performance that can transform what is otherwise a purely self-regarding act into an action that causes perceptible damage to the interests of others against their wishes. What requires clarification from a Millian perspective is how bad manners and indecent conduct in public can be seen to involve non-consensual harm thus understood, 'directly, and in the first instance'.

Mill clearly views as wrongful the individual's failure to satisfy obligations distributed and enforced by recognized social rules of justice and goodwill (including 'good manners') that regulate interactions in 'public' among the members of society to their mutual benefit. Disappointment of legitimate expectations emanating from these laws and customs is a type of wrongful perceptible injury, even if the expectations are not protected by recognized rights. As he insists, 'inasmuch as every one, who avails himself of the advantages of society, leads others to expect from him all such positive good offices and disinterested services as the moral improvement attained by mankind has rendered customary, he deserves moral blame if, without just cause, he disappoints that expectation' (1865b, 338).

According to the liberty doctrine, however, social rules must not create obligations to refrain from causing other people to feel mere dislike or distress. Rather, obligations must be designed solely to prohibit actions which cause or fail to prevent perceptible injury to others against their wishes. Consistently with this, he complains that existing customs of politeness do inhibit the individual from expressing his mere dislike of others' behaviour. One person ought to be far more free than is customary to tell others that he thinks them foolish or despicable in their self-regarding affairs, for example, and to warn them that their company will no longer be welcome unless they smarten up:

> It would be well, indeed, if this good office were much more freely rendered than the common notions of politeness at present permit, and if one person could honestly point out to another that he thinks him in fault, without being considered unmannerly or presuming.
>
> (1859c, 278 (IV.5))

So, he is not defending the existing social rules of politeness and decency. But he evidently believes that reasonable rules of polite behaviour and courtesy in public are justified to protect people from suffering impermissible forms of perceptible damage to their interests. The argument of the *Liberty* goes through, therefore, provided we can identify the relevant forms of non-consensual harm.

There are various types of non-consensual harm to others which may be caused by rude and indecent conduct in public, and which deliberative majorities may reasonably declare wrongful.

PREVENTION OF DISEASE

Some reasonable rules of decent or polite behaviour in public can perhaps be seen as social precautions against the spread of disease. Public displays of urination, defecation, vomiting and even coughing and sneezing may be prohibited and punished to prevent perceptible damage to the health of others. 'Public display' seems here to mean 'acting so as to endanger others' health', as determined by social authority (including the sewerage and health authorities). Recall that even if the damage to any assignable individual's health is indeterminate and seems imperceptible, Mill has the resources to say that repeated displays of urination, defecation and the like by many people will cause grievous perceptible damage to the interests of the public at large.

It should also be kept in mind that reasonable rules of polite public behaviour need not rely on any conventional distinction between private and public. It may be permissible to defecate in remote woods but not in a city street, for example, or in the toilet of another person's private home but not on the floor. The key issue in this context is whether others are forced to experience a significant health danger.

PREVENTION OF NUISANCE

Other reasonable rules of decent behaviour in public seem to be time and place restrictions to prevent nuisances, as argued by Feinberg and Ten. Sexual intercourse between consenting adults may be prohibited in busy public parks or office buildings, for example, because it can be freely practised in less crowded settings, such as homes, hotels and country fields, where it does not inconvenience others by interfering with their activities. The deliberative majority has legitimate authority to allocate scarce public space between *competing* uses (each of which necessarily interferes with the others), and ought to enforce effectively such restrictions as it thinks are reasonable and fair. Given that most think sexual intercourse is not a high priority use of the public space, people who ignore such a restriction *do* pose a threat of perceptible damage to others against their wishes. By ignoring the restriction, a couple engaging in sexual activity sets a bad example and tends to attract imitators to similarly engage in this low-priority use of the public space. Crowds of imitators and onlookers may block the free flow of traffic, for example, costing others time and money as they are forced to wait. Given that the flow of traffic is a high-priority use under the rules, those forced to wait are suffering non-consensual harm which they had legitimate expectations of avoiding.

It is not that any of the alternative uses of the scarce public space would cause no inconvenience to others. Giving high priority to the flow of traffic, for example, inconveniences those who want to engage in public sex. *Any* permitted use will render some competing uses impermissible, and thus cause non-consensual perceptible damage to people who wish to pursue those competing uses freely. But the uses permitted are reasonably judged to be less generally inconvenient than public shows of sexual intercourse.

This argument that rules are justified to prevent public nuisances is of wide application. People who chatter away on their mobile phones in hospitals, airports, trains and so forth are disturbing others and preventing them from getting needed rest or from concentrating on their own work. It is legitimate to post signs or make announcements to remind people to be reasonably quiet in these contexts so as not to harm others by unduly disturbing them. Of course, drivers who distract themselves by texting on their phones are more likely to cause accidents and injure others. So prohibiting the use of mobile phones in cars is not paternalistic interference with self-regarding conduct.

Many activities which are liable to draw crowds of imitators and onlookers, including parades, demonstrations, marches and other forms of public expression, are also properly subject to suitable time and place restrictions. And the liberty principle does not imply that society has to adopt a laissez-faire policy toward those who make it their business to solicit demonstrations or protests which are designed to insult other individuals or groups, or those who sell 'hate literature' and the like for a profit. Analogous things may be said about the producers and sellers of 'pornographic literature', designed to degrade women or other groups. As Mill suggests repeatedly, generally expedient regulation of the producers and sellers of these forms of public expression is compatible with perfect liberty of the consumer to view them, in times and places deliberately established by society to shield other adults from undue inconvenience and to protect children, and others unable to manage their own affairs, from undesirable influences.

'Special' restrictions, analogous to the special prohibitions against consumption of alcohol which he recommends for individuals with a history of violent drunken behaviour toward others (ibid., 295 (V.6)) may also legitimately be established for individuals or groups (including Nazis and the Klan) with a history of violence toward others of a particular religion, ethnic background, gender or race. Nazis and the Klan have wantonly killed and tortured minorities in the past. Anyone who affiliates himself with such odious organizations, by wearing their uniforms and brandishing their symbols, reveals (intentionally or otherwise) a sympathy for that history. As such, special bans against Nazi marches in communities with Jewish residents may be entirely appropriate, for example, to remove a credible threat that the marchers and their sympathizers will inflict physical injury, property damage and the like on the residents.[6]

Indeed, special restrictions against the public display and dissemination for profit of hate literature, pornography and the like by such groups might also be justified on similar grounds.

PROTECTION OF REPUTATION

Still other rules of decent public behaviour are designed to prevent wrongful perceptible damage to the *reputations* of others. Someone's reputation may be grievously damaged by another's misrepresentation to third parties of his personal character or his intimate affairs. By spreading malicious gossip about his personal affairs, for example, the other can harm his standing in the community against his wishes. Idle rumours may be worked to provoke broad, though unwarranted, resentment against him, and all that that implies. To prevent this sort of non-consensual harm to reputation, customs against malicious gossiping and the like are legitimate rules of other-regarding conduct.

Mill himself provides an illustration, in which someone publishes personal correspondence not intended by the author for publication. In a letter to Elizabeth Cleghorn Gaskell, probably written during July 1859, he says that the discretion of an editor properly does not extend to such publication:

> The case being simply that in the exercise of the discretion of an Editor you neglected the usual and indispensable duties which custom (founded on reason) has imposed of omiting [sic] all that might be offensive to the feelings of individuals ... Miss [Charlotte] Bronte [sic] was entitled to express any foolish expression that might occur to her [about Mill's wife Harriet] in a private letter – It is the Editor who publishes what may give just offence who is alone to blame.
>
> (1859b, 629–30)

Gaskell herself, in her comments on Mill's letter, refers to the customary obligation 'of omitting what would be offensive to the feelings and perhaps injurious to the moral reputation of individuals' (Haldane 1930, 269–71). Legitimate offence is linked here to perceptible damage to moral reputation, where the latter is inseparable from existing social conventions ('founded on reason') of decent public behaviour.

Harm to another's reputation can also occur in other ways, perhaps more subtle. Thus, when a husband rudely tells his wife in front of the neighbours to go fuck a donkey, he forces her to endure a public misrepresentation of her character to others, which tends to damage her reputation in the community. By showing her so little courtesy and respect in comparison to what a wife may legitimately expect under existing customs, he raises doubts in the minds of others about her character (not to mention his own) if she continues to live openly with him, unless he makes a similarly public apology. Repeated instances of this sort of thing may force her to consider a separation, in order to preserve her reputation and self-respect. Otherwise, she may be ostracized along with him against her wishes, by neighbours who wish to preserve common standards of public decency.

Rules to prevent loss of reputation may extend far inside what is conventionally considered private space. When a son threatens to bury his Jewish mother's ashes in an urn engraved with Hitler's image, for example, it does not matter whether he advertises the plan in the local newspaper or whispers it confidentially in her ear. In either case, he threatens perceptible damage to her reputation against her wishes. Even if it is unheard by anyone else, his whispered threat may properly be prohibited by rules of decent public behaviour. Perhaps the rules cannot be expediently enforced by law or opinion in cases of whispered as opposed to open threats, so that enforcement is left to the relevant person's conscience, admittedly non-operative in the case at hand. But that does not alter the fact a Millian liberal can legitimately assess the son's action as immoral, by arguing that his mother (and anyone else in her circumstances) ought to have a right to be protected from impermissible harm to her reputation. A liberal utilitarian code can then legally prohibit the son's burial plan, unless he can provide witnessed documentation attesting to her consent. Such precautions arguably help to promote general security of legitimate expectations.

PROTECTION OF SPECIAL RELATIONSHIPS

But perhaps it will be objected that harm to reputation is not really at issue in some of these cases. In the Jewish mother case, for example, it is not wrongful damage to any assignable person's reputation which is the worry but wrongful damage to the notion of a special relationship between parents and children which the deliberative majority values and aims to protect for all members of society. In short, society has advanced to the point where the 'disinterested services' involved in this special relationship are considered customary. The social rules that govern the special parent–child relationship are not illegitimate conventions that invade the son's self-regarding sphere by prohibiting him from causing his mother mere dislike or disgust. Instead, they recognize reciprocal rights and duties tied to the idea that children owe their parents due care and respect in return for their parents' efforts to raise them. These special rights and duties may be set aside in unusual circumstances, for instance, perhaps the son was abused by his mother. In general, however, a son's failure to fulfil his special duties to his elderly mother constitutes wrongful harm. Society can thus legitimately prevent the son from carrying out his burial plan on the grounds that such an action inflicts wrongful damage to the public interest, more specifically, the public's interest in fostering special parent–child relationships of the sort it values.

Of course, there are other social rules that define and regulate other special relationships, for example, the relationships between close friends, between siblings, between parties to a promise, and so on. Deliberative majorities legitimately decide that these special relationships are valuable too. Who thinks that the individual should have a right to breach these social conventions as he pleases? Instead, if he fails to fulfil his recognized special duties to others, he disappoints their legitimate expectations and causes impermissible harm to them under the rules.

HARMLESS INDECENCY?

Despite what has been said, it may still seem that Mill has a problem. Critics may concede that social rules of decent public behaviour can be properly enforced by law or stigma to prevent at least some of the various aforementioned forms of non-consensual harm deemed impermissible by majorities. They may still insist, however, that the individual's indecent public conduct is sometimes harmless to others and yet virtually everyone agrees that such self-regarding conduct ought to be prohibited and at least stigmatized (even if not punished by law) because it is so disgusting and offensive. For example, a few people, or even a crowd, walking around in skimpy clothing or buck naked in the city may look ridiculous but are they really causing a public nuisance? Someone who swears at his wife in front of the neighbours, or friends who swear at each other in a public restaurant, may be offensive but is there really any damage to reputation or any perceptible hurt to special relationships of the sort which society values? Again, a couple of jackasses who have a farting contest on Feinberg's bus may be disgusting but do they really cause any perceptible damage to the interests of other passengers? There really doesn't seem to be any harm involved and so these tasteless actions and many more like them are self-regarding actions which, according to Mill, the individual should be free to perform as he pleases. And yet even most liberals would agree, so the objection runs, that these actions are legitimately prohibited as disgusting and offensive.

I agree that these actions in public, however contemptible to some people, are really self-regarding actions. Others have rights to complain, to warn the agents that they are behaving like fools, to try to persuade them to change their conduct, and so forth. But society does not have authority to employ external sanctions. Admittedly, it is unclear whether Mill himself would accept that these public actions are self-regarding. As pointed out earlier, however, he does not defend existing rules of polite or decent public behaviour. Moreover, he clearly views public indecency as something wrongful, and thus legitimately prohibited and punished. The assumption that he would recommend coercive interference with these particular actions in public is unwarranted. It remains an open question just how far he would extend rules of decent or polite public behaviour.

Alexander Brown, following Daniel Jacobson (2000), argues that 'the real point' of Mill's doctrine is to defend 'a substantial realm of liberty for all' but 'not rule out the prohibition of violations of good manners' (Brown 2009, 15). This argument is just another way of saying that the 'very simple' harm principle should be supplemented with another principle that authorizes society to prevent mere disgust or shock to the feelings of others in public. Presumably, Brown would not rule out prohibition of the tasteless self-regarding actions listed above. But that just takes for granted that Mill endorses the existing rules of polite public behaviour, which is not the case. His defence of individual liberty is arguably more robust than Brown allows.

THE DANGER OF SOCIAL DECLINE

This discussion of bad manners and indecency in public raises the issue of whether Mill is sufficiently alert to the danger of social decline. If society refuses to coercively interfere with even the most tasteless and disgusting self-regarding actions, isn't there a risk that majorities will emerge that walk around the streets naked (at least on warm days and nights) and fart as they please in public? Moreover, although public discussion or expression is not truly self-regarding conduct, recall that he thinks it should 'almost' always be treated as such because the non-consensual harm it causes is 'almost' always outweighed by various benefits, including benefits of self-development, associated with it (1859c, 225–26 (I.12)). Again, if society virtually never interferes with the content and manner (as opposed to the time and place) of public expression, isn't there a danger that most people will eventually hurl insults and 'hate speech' at one another instead of maintaining a decent level of respect for others in public?[7]

It is doubtless true that public rudeness and incivility may become more common in a society that implements Mill's doctrine of liberty. Reconsider the example of the rude husband telling his wife to fuck off in front of the neighbours. If she relishes this form of public 'expression' and returns the same in kind to him, then their ugly 'conversation' is mutually consensual. Given that children are not present, any non-consensual harm to others (to others' reputations, for example, or to their understanding of issues related to the 'discussion', including their ideas about the nature of marriage) seems minimal, so that censorship cannot, under liberal utilitarianism, be generally expedient. Such a rude and tasteless couple might suffer 'natural penalties', as neighbours freely choose to avoid the company of both. Yet, if sufficient numbers engage in this crude sort of public behaviour, such that existing rules and expectations begin to erode, general civility and politeness are in decline. Society is regressing toward a state of barbarism, in other words, where individuals are as frank and intimidating to one another in public as they please.

Of course, some may protest that this is not regression but instead progress in the direction of a more free and open society, even if it looks rowdy, turbulent and impolite in terms of our customs and expectations. But that protest is unconvincing. Accepting that the danger of social decline is real, has Mill been overly optimistic in his judgment that every civilized society ought to implement his doctrine of liberty? It might be claimed with considerable plausibility that his judgment ought to be reconsidered in the context of societies like ours, involving public media, such as television and the Internet, which he could not have anticipated. Perhaps laws and other measures are needed to regulate the posting of insults and misleading information on the Net, for example, and to discourage the lightning speed with which 'flash mobs' and protests can be organized to occupy city streets and parks. But I suspect that he would stick to his guns, and reassert that the danger of social decline is unavoidable even if external sanctions are used to try to prevent it. Certainly, on his view, social decline cannot be prevented by *suppressing* self-regarding liberty or cognate liberties such as freedom of expression. We can only hope that competent individuals will tend to use their freedom to develop the kind of moral character that includes firm dispositions to treat others with decency and respect in public.

NO NEED FOR MODIFICATION

Social rules of decent other-regarding conduct in public are justified under Mill's doctrine, to prevent various forms of perceptible injury to others against their wishes. The deliberative majority properly has authority to employ such forms of coercion as are considered generally expedient to prevent the spread of disease, the undue waste of time or money associated with nuisance, the loss of reputation, and so on, which would otherwise be suffered unwillingly by others. Society may sometimes decide to leave enforcement of the rules to the internal sanctions of conscience, or to rely on stigma rather than legal penalties. But it has legitimate jurisdiction, and the maxim of self-regarding liberty does not apply.

At the same time, rules of decent public conduct cannot legitimately invade the individual's self-regarding sphere. Self-regarding conduct, however tasteless and disgusting, doesn't cause non-consensual harm to others and cannot legitimately be called wrongful or impermissible. Moreover, it is rarely generally expedient to regulate by law or stigma the content and manner (as opposed to time and place) of public discussion and expression. Even violent and pornographic materials should rarely be prohibited, for example, since, with suitable caveats relating to those with a history of violence toward other people, consumers of these materials can and do use them without causing non-consensual harm to others. Virtually perfect freedom to engage in a public debate over some dirty book or to watch a live sex show at a public theatre is, however, quite compatible with expedient time and place restrictions, as well as expedient regulation of the for-profit producers and sellers of the relevant goods and services.

In short, there is no need to modify Millian liberalism in the directions proposed by Hart and others. Indeed, from Mill's perspective, Hart's approach essentially begs the question. For that approach does not bother to identify the forms of perceptible damage which are suffered unwillingly by the victims of offensive or indecent behaviour in public. The prevention of wrongful harm to others is a *necessary* Millian condition of legitimate social coercion. It is that condition which sets a *limit* to social regulation of individual actions, in public as much as in private.

SUGGESTIONS FOR FURTHER READING

For arguments that liberalism fails to appreciate adequately the normative significance of the fact that the individual is situated in a particular community, see Michael Sandel (ed.), *Liberalism and Its Critics*, 2nd edn (Cambridge: Cambridge University Press, 1995).

For Gray's attack on what he takes to be Mill's view of individuality, see John Gray, *Liberalisms: Essays in Political Philosophy* (London: Routledge, 1989), ch. 10, and 'Mill's Conception of Happiness and the Theory of Individuality', in J. Gray and G.W. Smith (eds), *J.S. Mill: On Liberty in Focus* (London: Routledge, 1991), 190–211. Gray's claim that any defence of liberty from human fallibility is self-defeating may also be found there.

For a liberal view that rational self-determination or autonomy is compatible with the affirmation of reasonable moral rules and obligations, see Gerald Dworkin, *The Theory and Practice of Autonomy* (Cambridge: Cambridge University Press, 1988).

For the arguments of Vogler and Millgram that Mill's defence of the importance of liberty and individuality is problematic given their understanding of his theory of moral psychology and model of practical reason, see Candace A. Vogler, *John Stuart Mill's Deliberative Landscape* (New York: Garland, 2001); and Elijah Millgram, 'Liberty, the Higher Pleasures, and Mill's Missing Science of Ethnic Jokes', *Social Philosophy and Policy* 26 (2009): 326–53.

Hart's suggestion that Millian liberalism requires a separate principle recognizing society's legitimate authority to employ coercion to prohibit public offence, was offered in the context of his well-known debate with Lord Devlin over the 1957 Wolfenden report. The debate revolved around the issue of whether homosexual behaviour between consenting adults in private should be outlawed. More generally, Hart argued that society ought not to use the law to enforce ideas of morality in private settings, whereas Devlin argued the reverse, suggesting that society could properly prohibit any conduct which aroused the intense disgust of the average man in the street. In 1967, the report's recommendation to drop legal restrictions on homosexual conduct in private was implemented, in the Sexual Offences Act. Meanwhile, in the US, the Supreme Court, in a 2003 decision (*Lawrence et al. v. Kansas*, 539 U.S. 558), finally recognized the fundamental right of homosexuals to enter into relationships and have sex in the privacy of their homes. The Lawrence decision overruled the 1986 decision (*Bowers v. Hardwick*, 478 U.S. 186), in which the Court declined to nullify essentially moribund state laws against sodomy and other sexual practices as unconstitutional, preferring to leave it up to the state legislatures to repeal them. For further insights into the Hart–Devlin debate, see H.L.A. Hart, *Law, Liberty, and Morality* (Oxford: Oxford University Press, 1963); Patrick Devlin, *The Enforcement of Morals* (Oxford: Oxford University Press, 1965); C.L. Ten, *Mill on Liberty* (Oxford: Clarendon Press, 1980), 86–108; Joel Feinberg, *The Moral Limits to the Criminal Law*, 4 vols (Oxford: Oxford University Press, 1984–88), vol. 4, esp. ch. 30; and Michael Martin, *The Legal Philosophy of H.L.A. Hart* (Philadelphia: Temple University Press, 1987), 239–71.

For Feinberg's elaboration of Hart's suggestion that a liberal principle of public offence is needed, see Feinberg, *The Moral Limits to the Criminal Law*, vol. 2. Despite its interest, Feinberg's approach is a far cry from the liberalism of Mill's 'text-book', a point taken up more generally in Chapter 10 of this book. Indeed, Mill's original argument is in danger of being obliterated by Feinberg's type of liberal revisionism. For example, some have claimed, apparently under Feinberg's influence, that a Millian liberal can consistently support an outright ban on all violent pornography for one reason or another. No careful reader of the *Liberty* can agree with such a remarkable claim, unless the pornographic materials themselves involve children, mentally ill or challenged people, unwilling adults or animals. For the claims in question and discussion surrounding them, see David Dyzenhaus, 'John Stuart Mill and the Harm of Pornography', *Ethics* 102 (1992): 534–51; Robert Skipper, 'Mill and Pornography', *Ethics* 103 (1993): 726–30; Richard Vernon, 'John Stuart Mill and Pornography: Beyond the Harm Principle', *Ethics* 106 (1996): 621–32; and Danny Scoccia, 'Can Liberals Support a Ban on Violent Pornography?', *Ethics* 106 (1996): 776–99. I plan to publish a separate monograph on *Mill's Liberal Feminism*, which will include a critique of this debate. For further discussion of Mill's feminism, see Maria Morales (ed.), *Mill's 'The Subjection of Women': Critical Essays* (Lanham, MD: Rowman & Littlefield, 2005); and Wendy Donner, 'Mill's Moral and Political Philosophy', in W. Donner and R. Fumerton, *Mill* (Malden, MA: Wiley-Blackwell, 2009), ch. 7.

Many scholars insist that Mill's brief remarks on good manners and decency in public are inconsistent with his 'very simple principle' (whether interpreted as a harm principle or a liberty principle). Alexander Brown makes such an argument, for example, in 'J.S. Mill and Violations of Good Manners', *Philosophy Now* 76 (2009): 12–15. See also Jonathan Wolff, 'Mill, Indecency and the Liberty Principle', *Utilitas* 10 (1998): 1–16; and Daniel Jacobson, 'Mill on Liberty, Speech, and the Free Society', *Philosophy & Public Affairs* 29 (2000): 276–309.

NOTES

1 Given his defence of 'moral causationism' (determinism) as opposed to the free will doctrine, Mill's view that circumstances (including our given power of will) determine individual character is hardly surprising. He argues that the doctrine of universal causation is compatible with our practical feeling of moral freedom,

i.e. our feeling that we do have some power to alter our circumstances, if we wish. We do not choose our innate power of will but we have it and can strengthen it by exercising it. See Mill 1843, 836–43; and 1865a, 437–69.
2 As far as I'm aware, the so-called standard interpretation was not published by anyone prior to Riley 1988. Even Rawls, who noted in his 1971 *Theory of Justice* that higher pleasures have lexical priority over lower ones, did not conceive of a higher kind of pleasant feeling that is a property or quality of the moral sentiment of justice.
3 Millgram tries to exclude money from the class of his 'higher pleasures' but has no grounds for doing so. Great wealth is a permanent source of many pleasant feelings, just as virtue is, and both can be desired for themselves out of habit.
4 In a similar vein, Plato surmised that in an ideal city, where all were highly developed philosophers, nobody would wish to be bothered with political administration, preferring instead to rely on the wise judgments and commands of others.
5 Wolff (1998) defends Hart's approach on grounds that coercive interference with the conduct in public does not have a significant impact on liberty and individuality because the individual can often do the same thing in private. Even if it were true that the 'same thing' could be done in private, however, Wolff doesn't explain why mere disgust or offence can trigger coercive interference with the public conduct. He seems to assume that Mill is just inconsistent because there is no justification for coercion here in terms of preventing harm to others.
6 Feinberg arrives at a similar conclusion. Yet he argues that harm to others is not involved, in his revisionist sense of harm, thereby suggesting that this type of case cannot be handled by Mill's doctrine. See Feinberg 1984–88, 2: 86–96, 162–64.
7 Indeed, Mill suggests that society should rarely use coercion even against the *manner* of a public debate (1859c, 258–59 (II.44)). But his remarks may not have been intended to apply to potentially more boisterous forms of public expression, such as parades, demonstrations and the like. At the same time, there seems little doubt that he would support restrictions on the manner in which, say, sexually explicit materials are sold to the public, e.g. suitable packaging of 'dirty magazines' to prevent exposure to children.

10

THE DOCTRINE OF *LIBERTY* IN PRACTICE

HOW CAN ANYONE SERIOUSLY THINK THAT MILL'S DOCTRINE IS WORKABLE?

A familiar complaint, pressed initially by religious and moral idealists such as Green and Bosanquet, and resonant in the literature ever since, is that Mill's doctrine of liberty—and, in particular, his maxim of self-regarding liberty—provides little, if any, practical guidance. Various related reasons have been offered in support of the charge. The self-regarding liberty principle is misleading in practice, some have said, because it relies on an arbitrary distinction between self and other, which even Mill himself abandons in his 'specimens of application'. Or it is vacuous because there are no purely self-regarding actions. Or it is inapplicable because it is inseparable from complex utilitarian mechanics that no one can really carry out. Or it is simplistic because, on any sensible idea of harm, it must be supplemented by other principles (such as a principle of public offence) to explain adequately our moral intuitions about justified coercion. These and other reasons have been put forward to create the impression that any attempt to actually implement the doctrine of *Liberty* would result in chaos.

But, as even Plamenatz (hardly a defender of liberal utilitarianism) suspected, any such sweeping objection to the practicality of Mill's doctrine is unpersuasive. There may not be any actions in the abstract which are always and everywhere properly described as self-regarding, he seems to suggest, because the classification of an action as self-regarding or social depends on its concrete consequences, which can vary with circumstances. Getting drunk at home with the cat can be purely self-regarding, for example, whereas getting drunk on duty as a police officer poses a risk of perceptible injury to others against their wishes, since the officer may fail to perform his duties. So we cannot hope to apply the self-regarding liberty maxim if we insist on abstracting actions from their consequences in given concrete circumstances: the term 'getting drunk' is too loose by itself to specify a particular action. 'But this in no way invalidates Mill's criterion', Plamenatz points out, anticipating a central argument of Ten's, 'nor does it make it less easy to apply than any other' (Plamenatz 1965, 130). To apply the self–other distinction, we need to specify the relevant circumstances to have a workable definition of a particular concrete action: the action can then be classified as self-regarding or other-regarding on the basis of its consequences for other people.

The fact that an action's entry into the self-regarding realm is contingent on the consequences of the action may make the realm seem ambiguous, yet 'Mill has as much right to be vague as any other moralist in a matter in which greater precision is not possible' (ibid.). Moreover, 'the objection that Mill's criterion leaves almost no liberty to the individual ... is not well founded' (ibid.). There are many actions which harm other people 'not at all, or so little as to be not worth regarding', he insists:

> [W]e all know they are many, and that people love to interfere with what does not concern them. We may argue, then, that Mill's criterion is not strictly consistent with his utilitarian principles, but we cannot say that it is impossible to apply it or unimportant to do so.
>
> (Ibid.)

Plamenatz seems quite right about this, even if his strictures against the possibility of liberal utilitarianism are unfounded, and even if he exaggerates the imprecision that attaches to any definition of the self-regarding sphere.

On the latter point, the fact that the class of purely self-regarding actions can only be defined *after* we infer the likely consequences of particular actions, does not make its definition ambiguous. True, we must abandon the notion that we can simply pick out broad categories of actions (such as 'getting drunk') that will enable us to see the boundaries of the self-regarding realm in some sort of pristine clarity, *prior* to our experience of their consequences in concrete situations. But who, other than perhaps a mad idealist seeking after Plato's timeless concepts, would think to complain about this? Those who seek such precision as is possible to fallible humans must discover the particular consequences of particular actions through experience and discussion, and properly build those consequences into more qualified (and thereby more precise) definitions of actions (getting drunk while home alone with the cat, getting drunk while serving as a police officer, and so on).

Mill treats as a warranted induction from 'ordinary experience' the proposition that there are actions which are self-regarding or private in the descriptive sense that they do not directly cause non-consensual perceptible damage to the interests of others; and he also argues that individual rights to choose among those actions as one pleases are justified by a liberal version of utilitarianism, in which the immense value of individuality or self-development is recognized. His main concern in *On Liberty* is to defend this maxim that the individual has a moral right to complete liberty of self-regarding conduct. For him, liberty is the only permanent and unfailing source of self-development, of cultivating an improved and perhaps noble character. This maxim of self-regarding liberty is not, however, the sole element of his utilitarian liberalism.

Given that society has legitimate authority to consider using coercion to prevent other-regarding actions that cause non-consensual harm to others, questions remain about which forms of non-consensual harm are properly considered wrongful and thus deserving of prevention and punishment. Moreover, even after impermissible harms have been identified, further questions remain about whether external sanctions can be expediently employed in the case at hand, and, if so, in what form (i.e. law or stigma). The answers to those questions, he makes clear, depend on further utilitarian calculations, which he seems content to leave to informed majority opinion in any given social context. In the *Liberty*, however, he does not spell out his extraordinary version of utilitarianism. Nor does he supply what he considers reasonable utilitarian answers to such questions in a wide range of cases. Rather, he focuses exclusively on the practical implications of his argument that every civil society must recognize the right of self-regarding liberty. His argument implies that every civil society must also recognize the correlative duty not to coercively interfere with the individual's self-regarding conduct: such interference must be identified as a wrongful harm.

I've provided an outline of Mill's extraordinary utilitarian doctrine of liberty as I understand it in Part III of this study. To the extent that I've made reference to the workings of his utilitarianism itself, however, I've relied on his other writings, especially *Utilitarianism*, as opposed to the *Liberty*. When considering applications of the argument of the *Liberty*, the reader should keep in mind that Mill is talking for the most part about applications of the maxim of self-regarding liberty and its corollary, the maxim of social authority, both of which are easily seen to be compatible with the 'one very simple principle'. He is not trying to explain how his extraordinary utilitarianism is applied to identify moral rights other than the right of self-regarding liberty, for example, or to identify wrongful harms, that is, violations of duties to others, other than the wrongful harm of obstructing another person's self-regarding liberty.[1] True, he takes for granted that we will recognize that there are utilitarian arguments for social policies of laissez-faire with respect to trade and speech. Even so, he does not really bother to explain in the *Liberty* what those arguments are. Moreover, he doesn't clarify why the non-consensual harm suffered by the losers in a fair competition is different in kind from the non-consensual harm which is properly deemed impermissible by those seeking to promote utility in the largest sense. For all we are told in the *Liberty*, it is mysterious why a policy of leaving the winners alone to get what they want in an *unfair* competition is not recommended but forbidden by his unusual utilitarianism.

In addition to outlining in Part III the structure of his doctrine of freedom, including the central role of the maxim of self-regarding liberty, I have argued in Chapter 6 that Mill does not abandon his self–other distinction in his 'specimens of application' designed to illustrate his two maxims in practice. Now I propose to make some further remarks relating to the influential charge, levelled by a great many commentators—including prominent philosophers such as Hart (1963), Ten (1980), Feinberg (1984–88), Gray (1989, 1996, 2000) and Brink (2013)—that Mill's doctrine is simplistic. This charge misfires because it is based on the mistaken assumption that his entire doctrine can be *reduced* to 'one very simple principle', usually called *the* harm principle and variously interpreted. As we have seen in Part III, however, Mill's doctrine consists of multiple harm principles and corresponding liberty principles, all of which are compatible with the 'one very simple principle'. Considerations in addition to the prevention of harm to others implicitly enter into the utilitarian use of coercion because society must decide which forms of harm are wrongful and which of these wrongful forms can be expediently prevented through external sanctions.

Of course, if reduced to a single harm principle, Mill's doctrine could properly be attacked as simplistic. But his doctrine is far more interesting than that. Moreover, as we have seen, the entire doctrine does accept the 'one very simple principle' as a necessary but not sufficient condition for coercive interference. Even what I have called the 'full harm principle', which states necessary and sufficient conditions for coercion, is compatible with the very simple principle. But many leading philosophers reject the very simple principle as even a necessary, let alone sufficient, condition for coercion. The prevention of harm to others may be a reason for coercive interference, they say, but it needs to be supplemented with other reasons. By calling for principles to replace the simple harm principle in situations where harm to others does not exist in their view, they destroy Mill's doctrine at its root and replace it with some other one that ignores the distinctive right of self-regarding liberty.

NOT SIMPLISTIC BUT RADICAL

Mill's doctrine of liberty is certainly not simplistic. Those who object that it is naive or crude fail to appreciate its sophisticated structure as outlined in Part III. Their call for principles of public offence and the like to supplement 'the' harm principle is really an objection to the maxim of self-regarding liberty. In short, they are really saying that the maxim gives the individual too much liberty. But it is incumbent on them to explain why others' mere disgust or offence at self-regarding conduct ever ought to outweigh the agent's liberty and individuality. Given that self-regarding conduct doesn't cause any non-consensual perceptible damage to the interests of others, others are never obstructed by such conduct from pursuing their own lives as they please: they can ignore or avoid the agent of any self-regarding action that annoys and upsets them, if they can't persuade him to change his conduct. So why shouldn't they be told to mind their own business instead of calling for society to use coercion to suppress the agent's liberty and individuality in his own concerns?

For his part, the agent will learn from the consequences of his self-regarding conduct. He will come to understand when others are made upset and, if the conduct really is injurious to his own interests, he will come to appreciate that as well. But the decision what to do remains his to make in his own concerns. Moreover, everyone is fallible. Perhaps others will discover that their disgust is misplaced or at least not a reason for them to feel endangered. They may learn that the despised conduct yields more pleasure than pain to the agent and is not injurious for *him* whereas it might be for *others* who engaged in it. Indeed, many might learn that his despised opinions and actions are actually improvements on their own and are fit to be incorporated into their own way of life.

Put in other words, Mill's critics need to make a convincing case against his argument that there is no wrong if others are not forced to suffer perceptible damage to their interests. Unlike the critics, he implicitly distinguishes between harm in the descriptive sense of perceptible damage and harm in the moral sense of *wrongful* perceptible damage that ought to be prevented or punished. The definition of self-regarding conduct does not depend on any moral determination (utilitarian or otherwise) of wrongful harm. Instead of accusing him of equivocation or worse in his conception of harm, critics ought to be asking themselves why they are apparently willing to settle for a less robust sphere of liberty than he demands for competent individuals. Again, instead of being so anxious to protect others from feeling mere dislike or disgust, why not focus attention on the individual's vital interest in self-development? Protection of this 'principal ingredient of human happiness' demands recognition of the right of self-regarding liberty, where liberty means choosing the outcome one desires for oneself and not only having an opportunity to compete on fair terms with others to get that outcome. A fair competition is conducted without force or fraud: no competitor is thwarted by coercive interference or undue concentration of political power. Nevertheless, only the winners get their desired outcomes. Thus, a fair competition cannot provide security for *each individual's* vital interest in individuality. The equal right of self-regarding liberty alone can provide it.

Even liberal commentators often ignore the descriptive idea of harm as perceptible damage and so they miss the main point of *On Liberty*, namely, Mill's defence of the right of self-regarding liberty. A society that recognizes this right necessarily also recognizes that duties not to cause others to feel mere dislike or disgust must be rejected. By ignoring the descriptive idea of harm and focusing attention instead on some notion of wrongful harm such as the setback of an interest that ought to be considered a right, these liberal revisionists mislead readers into thinking that he is trying to present a more or less complete moral and legal account of situations in which coercive interference is justified. But he has no such ambition in the essay. True, by making reference to his other writings, it is possible to infer necessary and sufficient conditions for coercion as summarized in the 'full harm principle' stated in Part III. As already indicated, however, the *Liberty* contains no general utilitarian account of wrongful harms, or of cases in which external sanctions are justified to prevent wrongful harms to others, or of situations in which public stigma but not legal punishment is justified, and so forth. Rather, the focus is on where the individual should have a right to do as he pleases and on what measures society can adopt consistently with that right.

Mill is not attempting in the *Liberty* to paint anything like a complete picture of where the individual should be free from coercive interference or, equivalently, of where society ought to employ coercion. Roughly, and ignoring certain caveats, he indicates that the individual should be free from coercive interference not only within the self-regarding sphere but also to some extent within the social, or other-regarding, sphere; and that society should restrict its use of coercion to the sphere of morality and law within the social sphere (see Figure 1 of Part III). Consistently with this, the individual ought to be free from coercive interference within the sphere of fair competition as well as within that of morality and law itself provided he acts in accordance with his recognized rights and duties to others. Although he gives intimations of this picture in the *Liberty*, Mill doesn't give it prominence there. Indeed, he makes no effort to discuss any basic rights except the right of self-regarding liberty and correlative duties. Readers must turn to his *Political Economy* to find his arguments in favour of capitalistic property rights, for example, as well his defence of the principle of free trade or economic laissez-faire and its limitations. They must also turn to *Considerations on Representative Government* to discover that he rejects in principle a moral right to an equal vote. And, as I have repeatedly emphasized, they must study *Utilitarianism* to gain any insight into his extraordinary utilitarian theory of morality and justice.

Mill's aim in his essay is to focus our attention on the self-regarding realm where the individual ought to have a right to absolute liberty. That an action is self-regarding, in the sense that it directly causes no perceptible damage to other people against their wishes, is said to be sufficient – but not necessary – to render coercive interference illegitimate. The individual has a moral right to choose among self-regarding acts as he pleases. Thus, an irreducible core of liberty ought to be recognized and protected by every civil society, Mill insists, to promote the cultivation of individuality, that is, the development of a noble character.

The charge of oversimplification generally seems to be conflated with a different charge, namely, Mill's doctrine of liberty is radical and 'extreme'.[2] It is one thing to say that harm-prevention cannot be the only good reason for interfering with liberty of action, quite another to say that the failure to take seriously other reasons is an extreme (as opposed to mild) departure from our moral convictions about the issue. The latter assertion immediately invites the question: which theory of morality and law is (at least implicitly) being offered as an alternative to Mill's liberal utilitarianism?[3]

But critics are quite right to insist that the principle of self-regarding liberty is a radical departure from conventional social rules of morality and justice in modern industrial societies like our own. Purely self-regarding actions include sexual activities among consenting adults, for example, provided the consent is genuine – no force and no lying about diseases or about obligations of marriage – and there is no significant risk of non-consensual perceptible damage to the interests of others not involved in the activities (including absent marriage partners as well as any potential children who might be called into being by the activities). The sex is self-regarding only under suitable conditions, therefore, including adoption of birth control measures, fulfilment of any promises made to others, and finding a place and time not likely to inconvenience, and thereby offend, others in the pursuit of their projects. It does not matter, however, whether the consenting adults are homosexuals, or partners in a polygamous marriage, or single people participating in a group orgy in a private club. Nor does it matter if one person is a stranger buying sex from another: society has no legitimate power to prohibit prostitution.[4] At the same time, the state does have authority to regulate brothels and other sellers of sex to promote safe working conditions for sex workers, for example, or to curtail biased promotional public advertising of prostitution.

Despite the state's authority to regulate the marketing of sex, Mill (1871b) opposed the Contagious Diseases Acts, which forced women suspected of being prostitutes to undergo painful and humiliating medical examinations to prevent the spread of venereal diseases. He argues that by assuring male clients of disease-free sex, the state creates the impression that prostitution is acceptable or a necessary evil and thereby encourages it to flourish. In his view, there is an important distinction between society's refusal to approve self-regarding conduct and coercive interference with such conduct. Society should not give the impression in its laws that it approves of self-regarding prostitution when deliberative majorities disapprove of prostitution, for example, but that is not the same thing as coercive interference with prostitution.

Moreover, if the goal is to prevent the spread of disease to innocents, there is a strong case that the clients should be required to undergo medical checks. In general, he sees no reason to single out sexually transmitted diseases for special treatment: society ought to deal with them in the same way that it tries to prevent the spread of other contagious diseases. Thus, people who catch the illness ought to be given remedial treatment; those with symptoms of a dangerous infection ought to be put into quarantine so that they can receive treatment; those who knowingly or negligently infect unsuspecting partners ought to be duly punished; wives who get the diseases from cheating husbands ought to be granted divorce and compensation from the husband—and so on.[5]

Many other widely despised actions are self-regarding under suitable conditions. These include: a person's expression of his atheistic beliefs; his consumption of opium, heroin, cocaine and any other drug of choice; his gambling activities; his reading obscene books and viewing pornographic photos and films as long as the pictures themselves do not involve children or animals or unwilling adults; his engaging in strenuous physical activity that is potentially injurious to himself—and so on. According to the self-regarding liberty principle, the individual has a moral right to do these things as he pleases, short of perceptible damage to others against their wishes. Moreover, he has a right to do such things with other consenting adults. Consenting adults have a right to fight each other (perhaps even to the death) in gladiatorial contests cheered on by paying fans, for example, and they also have a right to have orgies in private clubs or arenas rented for the purpose. This does not mean that society must approve of the self-regarding activities. It need not enforce contracts; it may refuse to permit promotional public advertising—and the like. But it cannot legitimately prevent the activities if people genuinely wish to do them. Needless to add, such a right of self-regarding liberty is far from being recognized in modern societies, where it is likely to be seen by most as a serious danger to established religion and morality, if not to the very survival of the community.

Moreover, Mill is surely not guilty of oversimplification in his defence of absolute liberty of self-regarding conduct. He is careful to set out the 'obvious limitations' to his principle in practice. His masterful discussion of the matter in the fifth chapter of his essay is concise and to the point, giving rise to auxiliary insights or precepts relating to application of 'the two maxims which together form the entire doctrine *of this Essay*' (1859c, 292 (V.1), emphasis added).

AUXILIARY PRECEPTS

Based on our earlier discussions, the main precepts might be stated as follows:

- The absolute liberty of the individual to consume products and services without causing non-consensual harm to others must be carefully distinguished from a policy of laissez-faire in production and marketing.
- An individual's liberty can be legitimately circumscribed to facilitate the prevention of crimes, or accidents, not only in cases where uncertainty inherent in the situation itself makes it impossible to know beforehand that he intends to engage in self-regarding conduct—as opposed to conduct harmful to others against their wishes or unintentionally injurious to self—but also in cases where special personal circumstances transform into harmful other-regarding action what in most people is self-regarding.
- The liberty of the individual can properly be limited if his otherwise self-regarding action is performed in public, in violation of reasonable social rules of decent and polite public behaviour which assign duties not to cause certain forms of non-consensual harm to others.
- Although general expediency dictates a presumption in favour of treating solicitation of self-regarding actions as if it too were self-regarding, that presumption can be defeated when special classes of producers and sellers make it their occupation to publicly advertise and encourage self-regarding actions (gambling, for example, or fornication) of which the deliberative majority disapproves.

- Taxation of self-regarding conduct can be legitimate for the purpose of raising essential state revenues, though never merely to prohibit or discourage the conduct in question.
- Although, as a general rule, utility in the largest sense dictates that society ought to enforce contracts negotiated by people in their jointly self-regarding affairs, there are exceptions, for example, voluntary slavery contracts, where non-enforcement is justified to preserve liberty and individuality.
- Beyond the moral right of the parties to release each other by unanimous consent, general utility sometimes dictates that society should permit one party to be released from his legal obligations to another, against the wishes of the other, under a contract negotiated by them in their jointly self-regarding concerns—with the caveat that complete liberty is improper in these situations since breaking a contract is not a self-regarding action.
- The self-regarding liberty principle does not give any individual or group a moral right to exercise power as one pleases over other people, including husbands over wives, political officials over citizens or parents over children.
- The self-regarding liberty maxim does not require society to recognize or approve of self-regarding actions so long as it does not coercively interfere with them.
- Independently of the self-regarding liberty maxim, though for similar reasons, utility in the largest sense dictates that society ought to encourage individuals and groups to perform voluntarily many actions beneficial to other people, rather than rely on government provision of the benefits.

These practical precepts clarify how the maxim of self-regarding liberty ought to be applied to promote utility in the largest sense. Expedient application of the liberty maxim is essential to expedient application of its logical complement, the social authority maxim, and vice versa. There is no inconsistency in any of this with the 'one very simple principle'.

In the remainder of this chapter, some further remarks are offered, to combat the view that Mill's doctrine is simplistic, or otherwise fatally flawed, for practical purposes.

ISN'T IT UNREASONABLE TO DEMAND A COMPLETE BAN ON PATERNALISM?

An obvious implication of the self-regarding liberty principle is that paternalism is unjustified, where paternalism refers to any coercive interference with the individual's self-regarding conduct for his own good. Such interference is designed to prevent the agent from directly causing himself perceptible injury, or to make him, for his own good, do something that he does not want to do. His self-regarding action doesn't cause any non-consensual harm to others, keeping in mind that harm excludes mere dislike or offence. Paternalism in this Millian sense is always wrongful. It involves violating the individual's moral right to choose among his self-regarding actions as he pleases. Paternalists insist that they know better than the competent individual does what is best for him in his personal affairs.[6]

Mill's absolute ban on paternalism in this sense is often presented in a confusing way, because different meanings are placed on the term in the literature.[7] Hart suggests that any departure from economic laissez-faire is paternalistic, for example:

> [P]aternalism – the protection of people against themselves – is a perfectly coherent policy. Indeed, it seems very strange in mid-twentieth century to insist upon this, for the wane of laissez-faire since Mill's day is one of the commonplaces of social history, and instances of paternalism now abound in our law, criminal and civil.
>
> (1963, 31–32)

But government intervention in the market for the purpose of preventing grievous non-consensual harm to others, including loss of public goods which some people wish to have, is thereby conflated with obstruction of a self-regarding action solely for the agent's own good. There is a crucial difference between prohibiting a competent adult from consuming a narcotic in the privacy of his own home without causing any perceptible damage to others against their wishes, for example, and preventing him from producing pollutants that pose a risk to others' health, or preventing him from misleading others into buying dangerous products or bogus 'medicines'. Similarly, there is a crucial difference between meddling with his self-regarding consumption, and forcing him to obey regulations and pay taxes so that government can provide public goods, even if government only provides them as a last resort because people refuse to co-operate to produce them through voluntary associations.

Mill, of course, favoured a general doctrine of laissez-faire (though with important exceptions) with respect to markets, and he favoured a general doctrine of limited government power. But his principle of self-regarding liberty must not be conflated with those doctrines. Moreover, Hart compounds the problem by suggesting that so-called paternalistic government regulations are often clearly desirable (ibid., 32–34). Indeed, 'Mill carried his protests against paternalism to lengths that may now appear to us fantastic' (ibid., 32).

Feinberg's treatment of paternalism is also perplexing from a Millian perspective. He recognizes that talk of paternalism is pointless if there is no purely self-regarding realm of conduct: 'all "paternalistic" restrictions, in that case, could be defended as necessary to protect persons other than those restricted, and hence would not be (wholly) paternalistic' (1984–88, 3: 22). From his revisionist perspective, however, the self-regarding realm is apparently comprised of actions that do not wrongfully set back others' interests or cause them offence, in other words, violate their moral rights. He also maintains that consensual harm is not wrongful harm under the *volenti* maxim so that the harm principle as he reads it is not concerned to prevent consensual harm. Yet he changes his notion of harm in the context of his principle of legal paternalism. Paternalism involves coercive interference to prevent the individual from harming himself in the descriptive sense of damaging his own interests even if he wishes to do so. Harm is no longer wrongful harm and may also be consensual: 'Whereas the harm principle is understood to employ the word "harm" in the sense of "wrongful injury" (so that "to harm" means in part "to wrong"), legal paternalism ... employs the word "harm" in the sense of simple setback to interest whether "wrongful" or not' (ibid., 11). While this conception of paternalism is acceptable, needless confusion is created because of the two different ideas of harm involved in Feinberg's principles.

More specifically, a self-regarding action as Feinberg conceives it does not cause *wrongful* harm to others but it may cause *permissible non-consensual* perceptible damage as well as consensual damage to their interests. In short, self-regarding conduct in his sense can be other-regarding conduct in Mill's sense. But coercive interference with other-regarding conduct is within society's jurisdiction and does not constitute paternalism in the Millian sense. Society can legitimately point to the prevention of non-consensual harm to others and not solely to the individual's own good as a reason for coercive interference, even though the social decision (after due deliberation) may be not to use coercion, because the non-consensual harm is held to be permissible.

Obstruction of self-regarding conduct as conceived by Feinberg is no longer necessarily wrongful, as it is for Mill. Coercive interference with self-regarding conduct as conceived by Mill is always wrongful because it violates the individual's moral right to choose as he pleases among self-regarding actions that, by definition, do not cause non-consensual harm to others. What Feinberg views as 'paternalistic' legislation is not necessarily paternalistic in Mill's sense because there are reasons in addition to the individual's own good for enforcing the law. Feinberg himself is sensitive to the general point that what is often called 'justified paternalism' is not really paternalism, but he fails to see that his own approach is open to this objection if we restrict the meaning of paternalism to coercive interference with self-regarding conduct, as conceived by Mill, for the agent's own good.

But even in cases where his notion of self-regarding conduct coincides with Mill's (i.e. because the conduct doesn't cause any non-consensual harm, wrongful or otherwise, to others), Feinberg appears more receptive than Mill to paternalistic interference. Like Hart, he seems to find Mill's brand of anti-paternalism too adamant and absolutist. There are various reasons why one gets this impression. One is that Feinberg ties paternalism to benevolent motivations (ibid., 5–7, 17–18). Non-benevolent meddling with someone's self-regarding conduct is apparently seen as non-paternalistic, having an 'alternative rationale' in pure moralism – the view that the conduct is inherently immoral, regardless of its consequences. As a result, paternalists are seen as well-intentioned rather than mean-spirited or indifferent meddlers in others' personal concerns. A second reason for Feinberg's seemingly more receptive attitude towards paternalism is that he interprets the harm principle narrowly such that it covers wrongful harm caused by one person to others but does not cover cases in which one person ought to act benevolently to prevent harm to others that arises independently of his own actions. The latter cases are thereby made to seem as if they fall under a distinct principle of paternalism.

A third reason is that Feinberg seems to think that coercive interference with conduct that directly causes no perceptible damage to others against their wishes can at times be justified in terms of prevention of indirect harm to the public interest. He leaves the impression, for example, that laws prohibiting the consumption of drugs like opium, heroin and marijuana may be justified, if too many people engage in such self-regarding conduct (ibid., 17–23). And yet another reason is that he also suggests that coercive interference might be justified to prevent others from suffering shock or offence to their feelings, as when they witness horrific car accidents and the like, despite suffering no perceptible injury to their own interests (ibid., 139–41).

Admittedly, Feinberg is reluctant to let these various considerations decisively tip the balance in favour of paternalism. Taken together, however, they imply that he, unlike Mill, is open to coercive interference with self-regarding conduct as Mill conceives it. For Feinberg, the paternalist has powerful arguments that coercive interference with self-regarding conduct is sometimes justified, even though the competent agent does not agree that his interests, as perceived by himself rather than by other people, are likely to suffer any setback. Thus, Feinberg raises doubts that self-regarding liberty and individuality are as valuable as Mill insists they are. This opens the door to the illiberal conclusion that they can be rightly overridden by competing considerations.

SOFT (ANTI-)PATERNALISM

Mill's absolute ban on paternalism *can be* compatible with what is often called 'soft' or 'weak' paternalism. That milder sort of paternalism, which, as Feinberg (ibid., 14–15) remarks, is better viewed as anti-paternalism, is meant to assure others that the individual has common knowledge of the likely consequences of his proposed action, sufficient to permit the action to be classified as a choice that could be made by a minimally rational agent. Feinberg makes a strong case that soft (anti-)paternalism along these lines is compatible with any plausible version of liberalism.

Evidently, alternative criteria of rational choice will give rise to alternative versions of the soft approach. Indeed, if suitably thick criteria are imposed, the approach might merely serve as a guise for true ('hard' or 'strong') paternalism. But thin criteria are apparently what Mill has in mind, whereby the individual is made aware of common beliefs about the consequences of actions, which any competent person is expected to want to know before acting. Such knowledge might be highly speculative, however, and will surely not obviate myriad mistakes on the part of the decision-maker.

In any case, once assured that he possesses such information, others must not coercively interfere with the individual's self-regarding choices. Does the person intend to incur the risk of self-injury which most believe is associated with crossing a particular dangerous bridge, for example, or with consuming a particular poisonous substance? By temporarily seizing him to warn him of the danger, or by posting warning signs or labels without his consent, others may assure themselves of his intentions, without really interfering with his liberty. Again, liberty means doing as one wishes. But one does not wish to fall into the river, perhaps, or to be made ill by the poison. If not, there is no interference with his *liberty* in these cases. Moreover, by preventing unintentional self-injury, the so-called interference does prevent *non-consensual harm* to self. Indeed, far from violating his right to choose as he pleases, those who intercede on his behalf prevent perceptible damage to another against his wishes.[8]

At the same time, of course, if a person is not minimally rational, true paternalism is justified because the self-regarding liberty principle does not apply. We can never be confident that a child, or an insane adult or a savage barbarian, understands the likely consequences of his behaviour. Thus, others must take responsibility for that individual's good, with a view to developing his intellectual and emotional capacities, if possible. Paternalistic coercion is justified in these cases, because the agent is not informed by minimal standards of rationality in what he wishes to do.

MUST REASONABLE LIBERALS BE FOR HARD PATERNALISM?

Despite these caveats, Mill's anti-paternalism remains dubious to some. Most of the arguments offered in defence of paternalistic coercion of minimally rational adults are of little interest from a Millian perspective. The attempt to justify paternalism by distinguishing between earlier and later selves of the individual, for example, such that coercion of the former prevents harm to the latter, is problematic.[9]

Nevertheless, it is commonly agreed even by those who consider themselves liberals that hard paternalism is justified in some cases such as compulsory seat-belt or motorcycle helmet legislation. But driving a motor vehicle on a public street or highway is not a self-regarding activity in Mill's sense. Rather, it is an other-regarding action that poses a significant risk of grievous non-consensual damage to others through accidents. To prevent such harm, the state legitimately has power to enforce rules of the road and to ban people from driving if they don't have a licence attesting to their ability to drive competently and safely. So there are reasons in addition to the individual's own good for regulating the operation of cars, trucks and motorcycles. It is fair to ask whether legal requirements to wear seat belts or motorcycle helmets are essential elements of an expedient regulatory programme. The individual's own good is not the sole consideration, however. It must also be considered whether these elements are likely to reduce non-consensual harm to others. A case can be made, for example, that mandatory seat-belt legislation is expedient to prevent drivers from losing control of their vehicles in minor scrapes on crowded roads so that the vehicles fly into others or injure pedestrians on the side of the road. Feinberg mentions that motorcycle helmets with suitable windshields might prevent drivers from being hit by rocks, insects and other objects that cause loss of control. Similarly, these elements may significantly reduce the medical and health costs of accident victims, which must ultimately be borne by the taxpayer and/or consumers of insurance. True, self-financing private-sector insurance schemes could in principle be designed so that different classes of consumers would pay different premiums according to the risks which they, respectively, choose to bear. But it may be very costly to implement and enforce such schemes, in which case it is just not feasible to give individuals the option of not wearing seat belts or helmets.

The point is that such calculations of non-consensual harm to others are properly considered by society when deliberating over whether to use coercion to enforce wearing seat belts and motorcycle helmets. It is conceivable that deliberative majorities may decide against enforcement and instead adopt a policy of laissez-faire on grounds that seat belts and helmets would not in fact reduce non-consensual harm, including loss of life and medical costs to others. The freedom of individuals not to wear these things would not be the sole consideration. If there is evidence of a significant reduction of non-consensual harm outweighing any benefits of doing as one pleases in other-regarding matters that are legitimately of society's concern, however, then society properly enforces seat-belt and helmet legislation and makes it wrongful not to comply with the law.

Feinberg seems to think that appeals to prevention of non-consensual harm to others in these cases are 'strained' and unconvincing. He assigns far more importance to the prevention of others' shock and distress ('psychic costs') consequent on causing or witnessing the accidents of those not wearing belts or helmets (1984–88, 3: 139–41). It is not clear that there would be a reduction in such costs: why would people feel less distress at causing or witnessing accidents in which the severely injured if not dead victims are wearing belts or helmets? Even if they would feel far less disgust, however, the agents and witnesses do not thereby suffer any non-consensual perceptible damage to their own interests: the victims are harmed, not them. In any case, Feinberg himself indicates that if psychic costs don't tip the balance in favour of coercion, he is prepared to accept a laissez-faire policy instead of mandatory helmet or seat-belt legislation.

It should be re-emphasized that the question of whether to adopt a laissez-faire policy or to enact mandatory seat-belt and helmet legislation is the sort of question that is beyond the scope of Mill's argument in *On Liberty*. For him, since self-regarding conduct is not involved, the answer to such a question depends on further utilitarian calculations as to which forms of non-consensual harm are wrongful and which are not. The maxim of self-regarding liberty does not apply.

Of course, the relevant utilitarian calculations required to decide such a question are complex. What should society do about uninsured or underinsured accident victims, for example, who refuse to wear seat belts or helmets? In a wealthy modern industrial society, utility in the largest sense may well recommend a universal public health care programme, financed by taxpayers, with legal rights to adequate care for all. Society may try to recoup some costs from those who choose to not wear seat belts or helmets. Just because the majority enacts generous public health care measures, however, it does not necessarily follow that coercion (as opposed to education, advice and the like) is justified to keep down the costs of care.

Even so, critics continue to argue that Mill implicitly accepted hard paternalism in some situations such as voluntary slavery. Specifically, given that minimally rational persons can choose to become slaves, it seems to follow that his call for non-enforcement of voluntary slavery contracts constitutes an exception to his anti-paternalism. Feinberg echoes received opinion when he asserts that 'his solution' to the problem of voluntary slavery 'is paternalistic in spirit' (ibid., 72). According to the received view, liberals who claim to value individual autonomy must respect the competent individual's choice to become a slave. Although Mill speaks metaphorically of the individual being 'sovereign' in his personal concerns, he does not accept the liberal outcome in this context because he apparently believes that utility or individuality is more valuable than freedom. Interference with voluntary slavery can only be justified, it seems, by casting doubt on the voluntariness of the agreement, or by what amounts to paternalistic interference with self-regarding conduct (ibid., 71–81).

But, as Ten (1980, 118–19) and others suggest, Mill's approach to slavery does not seem to contradict his anti-paternalism. I have already presented in Part III my own interpretation of his approach.

For Mill, promotion of utility in the largest sense requires society to recognize that the individual has an inalienable moral right to choose as he wishes in his self-regarding concerns. So a liberal utilitarian society cannot recognize that slavery has any moral or legal status. Mill's extraordinary utilitarianism provides a solid ground for the sovereignty of the individual in his personal concerns. The right of self-regarding liberty is an essential component of a social code of justice because it secures the vital interest in individuality: the feeling of security associated with the moral sentiments is a higher kind of pleasure that overrides all competing kinds of pleasure, regardless of quantity; and individuality is a principal ingredient of human happiness because it is principally through self-assertion that the individual is able to cultivate the noble 'Periclean' character which most must develop for society to maximize utility in the largest sense. And society's refusal to enforce voluntary slavery agreements does not prevent the individual from choosing to be a slave as he pleases. He may not find many masters willing to offer him much compensation, however, since he retains a right to cease to be a slave whenever he likes. His moral and legal disability to conclude a binding contract-in-perpetuity will make it difficult to negotiate a slavery contract that serves his interests. Instead, he will tend to find it more attractive to conclude binding temporary contracts for limited purposes.[10]

Another complication for Mill's anti-paternalism arises in the case of suicide and assisted suicide. Despite von Humboldt's suggestion that liberty must extend to these extremes, Mill seems inclined to interfere with a person's freedom to commit suicide by venturing onto a condemned bridge (1859c, 294 (V.5)), for example, even if, elsewhere, in 'Utility of Religion', he suggests that those who have found happiness during a long life 'would have had enough of existence, and would gladly lie down and take their eternal rest' (1874, 427). Moreover, by analogy with voluntary slavery contracts, he might well argue against enforcement of voluntary euthanasia contracts, where one party resigns his life and liberty to another. Those contracts too are permanently irrevocable, and destroy all possibility of liberty and self-development in the future.

To try to justify coercive interference with suicide and euthanasia agreements, Mill might argue that a minimally rational adult would never voluntarily conduct himself thus: to behave in such a way, the person must either be coerced by others, or be too young, deluded or depressed to understand the consequences of his behaviour. As Feinberg suggests, however, the premises of that argument are too strong (1984–88, 3: 344–74). Again, Mill can adopt an approach similar to that which I have attributed to him in the case of voluntary slavery. Without resorting to coercion, society can express disapproval of suicide, establish various agencies to discourage it through advice and counselling, and refuse to enforce voluntary euthanasia contracts. Such an approach is consistent with the maxim of self-regarding liberty and also seems to capture Mill's apparent reluctance to endorse suicide.

Indeed, a Millian can go further and endorse suicide in special circumstances. For instance, society could agree to enforce assisted suicide agreements in tragic situations where the individual faces an imminent and horrible death with no hope of recovery. By contrast with the case of voluntary slavery, there is no worry that the person might change his mind in the future. So there is no worry that a doctor helping a patient to die might be harming another person who subsequently withdraws his consent. There is no uncertainty, in other words, about whether this arrangement will always remain a self-regarding activity. Moreover, by enforcing this particular contract-in-perpetuity, society would encourage voluntary euthanasia in such tragic circumstances since doctors and other assistants would have enforceable rights to fair compensation from the patient for their services. It is not like the slavery case where society properly discourages slavery. The point of the self-regarding liberty principle is defeated for terminally ill individuals whose only reasonable option is a quick and peaceful death with dignity: such persons are, tragically, incapable of self-improvement.

MILL AND PATERNALISM

Mill doesn't actually use the term 'paternalism' in *On Liberty*. But he probably wouldn't object to its use provided the term is defined appropriately in accordance with his argument. Paternalism must be understood in this context to mean coercive interference with a competent person's conduct solely for his own good. In other words, it means coercive interference with the individual's self-regarding conduct merely because other people dislike his conception of his personal good and are confident that their conception of it is better than his. For Mill, paternalism in this strong sense is always wrongful and ought never to be considered. An absolute ban against it is just and right.

Mill does refer to paternalism in some of his other works (see e.g. 1871a, 758–65). He appears to mean by this supervision of one group by another which claims to rule disinterestedly or for the good of the supervised group, even though in truth the powerful always govern in their own interests. The rich owners of land and capital claim to organize production and markets for the good of the working classes, for example, while denying the workers a vote. Or a political elite insists that it governs in the collective interest while denying the popular majority any voice in the process of determining the rules that supposedly promote the collective good. Or a political majority claims to rule disinterestedly while excluding minorities from having any say in the political process. Paternalistic government thus understood involves treating some excluded group as children who can't appreciate or assess the consequences of alternative rules and actions for the collective good. It is analogous to strong paternalism at the level of the individual. They are both forms of oppression. To avoid oppression at the level of the polity, popular majorities have a moral right to pursue the collective good as they see fit, provided they make rules that distribute and sanction equal rights and duties for all. To avoid it at the level of the individual, the competent individual has a moral right to pursue his personal good in his own way, provided he does not cause non-consensual harm to others.

These two notions of paternalism operate at different levels and must not be conflated. Moreover, unless paternalism at the level of the individual is defined as coercive interference with self-regarding conduct for the agent's own good, Mill's doctrine is lost in a cloud of confusion. It is false, for example, that he rejects paternalism if it is defined loosely to include coercive interference with the individual's *other-regarding* conduct for his own good. Other-regarding conduct causes non-consensual harm to others and so the agent's own good is never the sole reason for interference with such conduct.

In this regard, Mill says that a competent person's own good is not *sufficient* to justify coercive interference with his conduct: 'His own good, either physical or moral, is not a sufficient warrant' (1859c, 223 (I.9)). Nor is it necessary. The only essential condition is the prevention of harm to others. But prevention of harm is not always sufficient either: 'it must by no means be supposed, because damage, or probability of damage, to the interests of others, can alone justify the interference of society, that therefore it always does justify such interference' (ibid., 292 (V.3)). For example, if the harm is genuinely consensual, then coercive interference should not be considered. This leaves open the possibility that a person's own good can help, in conjunction with the prevention of non-consensual harm to others, to constitute 'a sufficient warrant' for interference.

And, in *On Liberty*, Mill makes clear that the individual's own good *is* a reason that, together with the prevention of non-consensual harm to others, does justify compelling him to comply with social rules of justice:

> And even to himself there is a full equivalent in the better development of the social part of his nature, rendered possible by the restraint put upon the selfish part. To be held to rigid rules of justice for the sake of others, developes [sic] the feelings and capacities which have the good of others for their object.
>
> (Ibid., 266 (III.9))

This reading is confirmed by his argument in the *Examination of Sir William Hamilton's Philosophy* that the good of the criminal himself is one of the reasons that justifies the punishment of criminals for breaking rules of justice. Referring explicitly to his argument in *On Liberty*, he asks rhetorically: 'did I say, or did any one ever say, that when, for the protection of society, we punish those who have done injury to society, the reformation of the offenders is not one of the ends to be aimed at, in the kind and mode, at least, of the punishment?' (1865a, 459 n.).

Mill's position appears to be this. A person's own good is not a sufficiently weighty reason by itself for coercive interference. That much is needed to defend individual rights of self-regarding liberty and individuality. There is an absolute ban on interference with self-regarding conduct because such conduct does not harm others without their consent. Harm to others must be non-consensual for society to even legitimately *consider* interference, where harm excludes mere displeasure or distress. So the person's good cannot be a sufficient warrant because, if it were, it could justify interference with self-regarding conduct, contradicting the claim that coercion can only be justified to prevent or punish non-consensual harm to others. Self-regarding conduct can never be properly viewed as immoral or criminal conduct since it does not cause any non-consensual harm to others.[11]

By contrast, society legitimately considers whether to coercively interfere with other-regarding conduct that inflicts non-consensual harm on others or poses a significant risk of doing so. The individual does not have a moral right of *other-regarding* liberty. The person's own good may enter into society's deliberations about interference with some positive weight in this context. Its weight may help us to decide when non-consensual harm to others ought to be prevented or not. Society may decide to compel individuals for their own good to develop strong aversions to certain non-consensual harms considered blameworthy by competent majorities, for example, and yet also encourage individuals to tolerate other non-consensual harms such as the losses suffered by losers in a competitive market.

If paternalism is taken loosely to mean forcing an individual to do something for his own good, Mill allows paternalism in this weak sense as a reason for compelling obedience to rules of justice that protect people from suffering certain grievous harms to interests that ought to be considered as rights. I have argued, however, that Mill would not call this paternalism because the individual's own good is not the sole reason for coercion. Some might make the distinct argument that paternalism in the weak sense should not be called 'paternalism' if everyone has a voice in the making of the rules. That argument relies on the claim that liberal democratic government and paternalistic government are opposites. But democracy must not be conflated with individual autonomy.

Mill endorses individual self-assertion with respect to self-regarding conduct, and liberal democratic government for the regulation of other-regarding conduct. This does not preclude the idea that the individual is justifiably forced for his own good to obey democratic rules of justice designed to prevent grievous non-consensual harms to others. What Mill rejects is the idea that the individual's good alone is *sufficient* to justify coercion. Paternalism in that strong sense would justify obstructing self-regarding actions, whereas he defends rights of self-regarding liberty and individuality.

DOESN'T THE MAXIM OF SELF-REGARDING LIBERTY GIVE CRUDE ANSWERS TO SOME HARD PROBLEMS?

MORMON POLYGAMY

Mill's remarks on Mormon polygamy have been widely criticized. For example, Richard Posner, despite praising *On Liberty* as the 'bible' of 'libertarianism', charges that 'Mill's discussion of polygamy is particularly unsatisfactory' (2003, 207, 205). As I pointed out in Chapter 5, Mill defends the moral right of consenting adults to choose polygamy as they like and yet he also says that he disapproves of polygamous marriage contracts as 'a mere riveting of the chains of one-half of the community' (1859c, 290 (IV.21)). Sensing confusion, Posner wonders why Mill believes that it would be 'improper' for government to employ coercion to 'extirpate' polygamy given that polygamy is tantamount to the enslavement of women (2003, 205).

But Mill makes clear in *The Subjection of Women* that he also disapproves of monogamous marriage contracts under the patriarchal laws and customs of contemporary civil societies like England and America. Under those rules, the husband owned all property, including any assets which the wife brought to the marriage, and divorce was virtually impossible so that, by consenting to marriage, a woman effectively resigned forever her liberty to manage her self-regarding concerns. Such marriage contracts-in-perpetuity strike him as patently unreasonable and he argues that a civil society should refuse to recognize them. Instead, society should only enforce marriage contracts (monogamous or polygamous) that contain sunset clauses and thus come up for periodic renegotiation, with provision for unconditional freedom of divorce if the relevant parties unanimously consent and provision for freedom of divorce under certain conditions even if the relevant parties do not unanimously consent. Mill does not recommend that society should abolish all types of monogamous marriage contracts, so there is no reason for him to recommend that the government should 'extirpate' all polygamous ones.

Posner goes on to suggest that Mill, if he is consistent, must defend the liberty of racist whites in the old South to practice public school segregation, because segregation is analogous to polygamy as long as blacks are free to leave the community. But black residents evidently did not consent to segregation whereas Mill assumes that Mormon women widely endorsed polygamy as part of their culture. Segregation was merely a guise for unjust treatment of blacks by whites. By forcing black children to attend separate public schools with far fewer resources per student than the schools attended by whites, southern state governments sanctioned other-regarding conduct that directly injured black children against the wishes of their parents. Evidently, Mill's doctrine says that any civil society may rightfully consider regulating such conduct, and ought to legally prohibit it if (as seems obvious) doing so advances utility in the largest sense.

Posner apparently forgets the central distinction between self-regarding conduct and social conduct because he ignores the difference between consensual polygamy and non-consensual racial discrimination. A voluntary scheme of segregated public schools is, however, also conceivable. Suppose that blacks and whites in a given state never intermarry and they mutually consent to segregated schools. But they adopt measures to ensure that each and every school in the state receives equal resources on a per student basis. Parents have a right to send their children to any local school they like but they always choose to send their kids to a school whose students are of the same racial identity as their own. Suppose too that anyone who tires of this voluntary segregation scheme can freely leave. Moreover, members of other communities have equal rights to avoid the state as they wish if the segregationists cannot be persuaded to abandon the practice. Others can also destabilize the practice to some degree by freely moving into the state and sending their children to 'incorrect' schools, that is, local schools whose students have a different racial identity from their own. Any attempt to prohibit this by state authorities would constitute non-consensual damage to the interests of the newcomers, which the federal government legitimately decides is wrongful and ought to be prevented. Even if large numbers of newcomers move into the state and gain control of the state government, though, coercive interference with those who engage in voluntary segregation remains illegitimate. Moreover, it may turn out that few if any people choose to move into the state because most are disgusted by the existing voluntary segregation. In that case, a separate community of voluntary segregationists may persist for quite a while.

In this hypothetical case, Mill's doctrine implies that the consenting adults have a moral right to freely practice segregation. But so what? As Posner admits, this does not mean that a Millian must view racial segregation as admirable. Mill emphasizes that self-regarding conduct may well be tasteless and disgusting. But self-regarding liberty is absolute. It cannot be reduced to some limited liberty to choose *only* that self-regarding conduct of which some majority approves.

Posner badly distorts Mill's doctrine of liberty in various ways. He implies that Mill's toleration of polygamy is incompatible with a belief that in a marriage of equals 'the terms of the marriage would be the free choice of the [equal partners]' (ibid.). But Posner just can't accept that women who choose polygamy can do so as equals. Polygamy is compatible with equal rights of self-regarding liberty: all of the participants may wish to engage in an unusual marriage of this sort, despite any mere disgust felt by onlookers. Posner is also off-track when he claims that 'Mill thought people extraordinarily submissive ... to the point where ... just being accused of immorality was likely to have the same coercive force as the law' (ibid., 206; see also 203). On the contrary, Mill did not believe that 'just being accused of immorality' was coercive in the absence of legal penalties or public humiliation by pressure groups (see e.g. 1859c, 279–80 (IV.7)). Rather, he thought that most people, even meddlesome people, consider their own private concerns not properly of concern to others. In other words, most think that society ought not to coercively interfere with their private concerns, although they may blindly accept mistaken customary notions of private or self-regarding conduct. Thus, they have a rough understanding, which they can learn to improve upon, that being *falsely* accused of immorality does not, and should not, deter self-assertion in self-regarding matters.

Posner also has some disturbing libertarian ideas of his own which a Millian properly rejects. For instance, he finds 'obnoxious' Mill's claim that society can legitimately prohibit couples from producing children which they have no means of feeding, housing, providing a basic education and, in general, giving a fair chance of success in life: 'it is difficult to imagine a more obnoxious interference with private conduct than requiring prospective spouses to prove their solvency to the state's satisfaction' (2003, 205). But if the parents cannot afford to support their child, they inflict a significant risk of non-consensual harm on the child – indeed, Mill says that the harm is immoral and ought to be prevented or punished. Given parental failure, the state must often step in to do what the parents ought to have done. Private philanthropy cannot reasonably be expected to always fulfil the moral duties of supporting the child. And the state must have revenues to rescue these children, which in turn requires the general taxpayer to supply the funds. But Posner believes that coercive taxation to finance the education of the children 'is not justified by the harm principle, for the inability of a person to finance his children's education will not ordinarily be the result of culpable conduct by the well-to-do' (ibid., 206). Taxation for that purpose certainly is justified in Mill's view to prevent wrongful harm to the children, however, even though the harm is not the direct result of any wealthy individual's own actions. Since Posner regards the harm principle, as he (but not Mill) understands it, to be at the core of his libertarianism, we can only conclude that Posner would permit irresponsible couples to produce as many children as they please and yet he would also deny that the general taxpayer has any duty to prevent the children from suffering grievous harm: 'If failure to assist strangers is a form of doing harm to them (a very strained sense of harm)', he claims, 'the liberty principle disintegrates' (ibid.). Such a view is not only far from Mill's but also obnoxious in itself.

Libertarians like Posner are not the only critics of Mill's remarks on Mormon polygamy. Many others are also critical, including those who think of themselves as liberal feminists. Wendy Donner, for instance, says that his remarks 'come as something of a surprise' after his 'strong defense of individuality and autonomy' (2009, 69). According to her, 'he does not sufficiently question the strange and disquieting supposedly "voluntary" acceptance of polygamy by the women and girls of the community' (ibid., 70). She sees the contemporary Mormon community as a fundamentalist religious group that forced women into polygamous marriages in order to preserve its traditional way of life. So, for her, 'Mill displays a lack of empathy and sympathy for the vulnerable and powerless women and girls who are coerced into polygamous unions' (ibid.). Even so, his 'reflections on polygamy ... do not expose a problem with his theory' (ibid., 72). Rather, the problem is that he doesn't know how to apply his own theory in this case: 'what this particular example exposes', she argues, 'is weakness in Mill's application of his theory, rather than a weakness in the theory itself' (ibid.). More specifically, he supposedly loses sight of the rights of individual women to choose as they like in their personal concerns and instead defends the community's right to preserve its traditional practice of polygamy by oppressing the women. Indeed, Donner accuses Mill of working with a 'stereotype' of the Mormon community: he sees the community as a 'homogenous mass' of people who 'all have the same "voluntary" choices in marriage' (ibid., 70). Remarkably, the great defender of diversity is said to be blind to the diversity of attitudes towards polygamy within the group.

Perhaps Mill was incorrect about the facts of Mormon polygamy in the remote Utah Territory. Contrary to his assumption that polygamy was widely accepted in the community, the women may well have been unwilling participants.[12] In the absence of a careful empirical investigation, it is difficult to decide whether the men coerced the women into polygamous unions. Although women were legally free to remain single or to practise monogamy, public stigma may have pressured all but a few eccentric rebels into polygamy. Certainly the freedom to leave the remote Utah Territory was essentially vacuous, given that women lacked property and were extremely vulnerable to physical attack. So Donner might be right that Mill made a mistake by using the example of contemporary Mormon polygamy to illustrate his maxim of self-regarding liberty. Even if he got the facts wrong and this led him to misapply his theory, however, I agree with Donner that this does not tell against his theory of liberty. Where I disagree with her is over the possibility of consensual polygamy. Mill is correct that consensual polygamy is conceivable, whether or not polygamy was really consensual in the old Utah Territory. Under certain conditions, polygamy is a self-regarding activity: consenting adults have a moral right to practice it as they please. I will return to this point in a moment.

Donner refuses to take seriously the possibility of consensual polygamy. Her comments reveal her prejudice that competent women cannot genuinely consent to be one of plural wives to the same man under any conditions. She depicts plural marriage as necessarily involving wrongful harm to women: 'polygamy relies upon sanctions ranging from control and oppression to abuse and violence against young women and girls of the community' (2009, 74). She seems to think that polygamy can only be practised by a criminal group such as the Fundamentalist Latter Day Saints, in which male perverts conspire to kidnap young women and sexually abuse them. Just as a scheme of voluntary segregation is conceivable, however, so is a scheme of voluntary polygamy.

Suppose that men and women in a given community all agree that polygamous unions are the best way to manage their personal concerns. The plural participants in any union treat each other as equals and set the terms of the marriage as they jointly please. They are firmly committed to fulfilling their duties to their children and they never cause any non-consensual damage to people outside their family. Suppose too that anyone who comes to disapprove of voluntary polygamy can freely leave the community. Moreover, members of other communities have equal rights to avoid the community as they wish if the polygamists cannot be persuaded to abandon the practice. Others can also freely move into the community and practice monogamy or polyandry or whatever, short of injury to others. Any attempt to prohibit this by community leaders would constitute non-consensual damage to the interests of the newcomers, which the larger society legitimately decides is wrongful and ought to be prevented. Even if large numbers of newcomers move into the community and gain control of the communal government, however, coercive interference with the existing voluntary polygamy remains illegitimate. Or it may turn out that few if any people choose to move into the community because most are offended by voluntary polygamy. In that case, a separate community of voluntary polygamists may be far from a temporary phenomenon.

Again, in this hypothetical example, Mill's doctrine implies that the consenting adults have a moral right to practise polygamy as they please. Others may find the polygamy disgusting but they are not harmed by it or entitled to coercively interfere with it. It is not intrinsically immoral. Nor do the children of the polygamists need to be rescued and taught the virtues of, say, monogamous marriage. Donner is confident that polygamy is incompatible with liberalism: 'When the proper liberal educational and social conditions are secure, it is doubtful that many women would choose polygamy ... Polygamy is not likely to survive as a popular option when children are educated for freedom' (ibid., 74). But her confidence should be seen for what is, namely, an assumption of infallibility of the sort to which Mill is opposed. Against such dogmatism, he defends the right to engage in experiments in living, short of non-consensual damage to others. Voluntary polygamy is such an experiment and, although he is inclined to think that a monogamous marriage of equals is the ideal arrangement, he does not pretend to know for certain that monogamy is the best arrangement for everyone to adopt in their personal concerns.

People have rights to establish customs of monogamy or polygamy as they like, based on experience of alternative arrangements. And deliberative majorities have authority to express their approval of one custom or another, by withholding legal recognition of practices of which they disapprove. Majorities in the future may also disagree with majorities in the past. In the meantime, majorities need not recognize polygamous marriage contracts of which they disapprove, as long as they do not use coercion to prevent voluntary polygamy. Just as he opposes the Contagious Diseases Acts on grounds that society should not give the impression that it approves of prostitution when it doesn't approve, Mill can oppose legal recognition of polygamous marriage contracts, and not only contracts-in-perpetuity, in countries such as Britain or the USA where deliberative majorities disapprove of polygamy. But non-enforcement of polygamous marriage contracts is not coercive interference with voluntary polygamy: people can still choose to engage in polygamy if they wish and society can't legitimately prevent them from taking steps to assure that they receive the same insurance benefits and so on that partners in legally recognized unions receive. A fortiori, one society's decision not to recognize polygamy contracts certainly doesn't justify a missionary expedition to stamp out voluntary polygamy in a separate society where the majority approves of voluntary polygamy and enforces polygamous marriage contracts.

ABORTION

Abortion is a difficult social issue.[13] Feinberg suggests that freedom of abortion (the pro-choice view) may be justified, at least in the early stages of pregnancy, because nobody is harmed by the death of a foetus prior to its becoming a *person*, with interests and rights of its own. 'A prepersonal fetus ... presumably has no actual interests', he says, 'from which it follows that no actual harm can be done to it while it is in that state' (1984–88, 1: 96). True, the foetus will have interests and rights once it evolves into a person. But the act of abortion defeats that process of evolution, so that no setback of any actual person's interests ever takes place:

> Death to a fetus before it has any actual interests ... is no harm to it. The aborted fetal preperson has no actual interests that can be harmed, and since it dies before any 'potential interests' can become actual, no harm can be done to these either.
>
> (Ibid.)

Feinberg recognizes that his argument will hardly impress anyone who claims that personhood begins with conception, although he finds the latter view 'extremely implausible' (ibid.). Yet what makes abortion such a difficult issue for many, it seems, is the obvious bias underlying any such boundary between persons and prepersons. After all, the line is drawn by people who are judges in their own cause, with no voice accorded to prepersons.

In the end, Feinberg is not prepared to defend the pro-choice view because he takes 'no stand ... on the complicated question

THE *LIBERTY* DOCTRINE IN PRACTICE 321

of the point of onset of personhood' (ibid.). If personhood begins at conception, then abortion even in the first semester of pregnancy is *pro tanto* immoral (the pro-life view) because it wrongfully harms the unborn person by violating his basic right to a minimally decent life. This conclusion might be defeated in special circumstances where the mother's right to life is at stake and negates that of the unborn child, for example, or where the foetus is so defective that a minimally decent life would be impossible for the newborn. Even so, there is no question that the act of abortion would directly harm the foetus in a descriptive sense.

Mill does not provide a statement of his own views on abortion, although he certainly favoured birth control measures. As I understand his extraordinary utilitarianism, he must say that it is up to deliberative majorities to decide whether abortion causes wrongful harm to the foetus without consent (because consent is impossible in this case), and the decision may vary across different societies. But we don't know which abortion policy he might have recommended to promote utility in the largest sense in any social context.

Even so, the difficulties of abortion have nothing to do with Mill's maxim of self-regarding liberty. Abortion might be classed as a self-regarding action by those who argue that it causes no perceptible damage to other actual persons. But the argument is a red herring for at least two reasons. First, even if it is not yet a person with interests and rights, a prepersonal foetus is likely to become such if its natural development is not prevented by others. Thus, the destruction of a foetus is validly inferred, from 'ordinary experience', to involve a significant risk of perceptible damage to another person without his consent, where the risk refers to the probability that the foetus would develop into a person in the absence of coercive interference. As Feinberg admits, a prepersonal foetus has 'future interests' as a person even if it is not yet a person. So, even if we accept his assertion that it is implausible to assume that personhood begins with conception, his argument that abortion is harmless because it renders these future interests 'non-existent' and not 'real' is unconvincing (ibid., 97). The act of abortion, by interrupting the natural course of development, is the very action that destroys the future interest in a minimally decent life. On those grounds alone, it is an other-regarding action that poses a risk of damage to another person's interests without his consent by killing him before his likely natural development into a person is complete. Even if the harm is not seen as a wrongful harm for one reason or another, it is certainly not a consensual harm. As such, abortion is beyond the ambit of the self-regarding liberty principle.

The argument that abortion is a self-regarding action is also mistaken for a second reason. A foetus may not be a person but it is a sentient creature at some point. The descriptive idea of harm is not necessarily restricted to perceptible damage suffered by *persons*. It can, and probably should, be extended to include perceptible injury suffered by sentient creatures, including not only prepersonal foetuses but also many non-human animals. That extension would narrow somewhat the self-regarding realm of absolute liberty. But a general policy of laissez-faire with exceptions remains an option for those who favour pro-choice.

Society clearly has legitimate authority to regulate abortion. Even if utility in the largest sense recommends in favour of a general policy of laissez-faire (pro-choice), that policy must be distinguished sharply from any moral right to absolute liberty of abortion. Leaving a pregnant woman alone to make up her mind free from coercion does not imply that she ought to choose as she pleases in the matter. It may be that external sanctions are inexpedient and yet she still faces a moral choice properly guided by internal sanctions. So she ought to follow the dictates of conscience, in other words, make a choice which she could in good faith recommend as best for anyone else (including the hypothetical person whom the foetus could become) to make in circumstances like hers. In a context where many qualified people are willing to adopt children, the implication may be that she should decide to abort only in quite unusual circumstances, including rape, incest and a risk of serious damage to her own health posed by bringing her pregnancy to term.

Unlike the self-regarding liberty principle, a general policy of laissez-faire allows for exceptions. Legal prohibition of abortion may well be generally expedient in some situations, including where pregnant children seek abortions without the knowledge or consent of their parents, for example, or where women seek procedures during the third trimester, none of the excuses mentioned earlier being applicable. Or, as Wayne Sumner (1981, 143–54) suggests, if the foetus first becomes sentient at some time in the second trimester, prohibition may be justified to prevent the killing of sentient creatures earlier than the third semester.

At the same time, sellers of abortion services may properly be required by law to post suitable warnings of the risk of surgery, provide advice and educational materials relating to the feasible options, and ensure that any decision to abort is made without force or fraud, after due deliberation.

PARFIT'S BABY PROBLEM

Just as the issue of a morally defensible abortion policy is beyond the scope of the maxim of self-regarding liberty, the so-called 'Parfit baby problem' creates no difficulties for the maxim.[14] The problem arises in situations like the following. A woman deliberately gets pregnant, despite her doctor's warning that her child will certainly suffer from a permanent handicap sufficiently severe to render his life miserable, for example, his arms and legs will be withered as a result of some diseased condition of her own. The damage to the child is not so severe, however, as to render non-existence preferable to his wretched life: his right to a minimally decent life has not been violated.

Such a case is 'puzzling', Feinberg insists, because the mother's culpable act of giving birth does not harm her child by putting any interest of his 'in a worse condition than it would have been' had she not acted (1984–88, 4: 26). Despite the reprehensible behaviour of his parents, the defective baby is not wrongfully *harmed* because he would be even worse off if he had never been conceived. Still, the parents do engage in harmless wrongdoing: 'There is no doubt that the mother did act wrongly … She must be blamed for wantonly introducing a certain [non-grievance] evil into the world, not for harming, or for violating the rights of, a person' (ibid., 28). Feinberg is willing to abandon his otherwise 'bold liberal' convictions to prevent or punish such a victimless crime. Thus, in his view, 'cautious' liberals should make room, though rarely, for criminal laws that are justified only on the grounds of pure moralism (ibid., 324, 326–28).

But this type of case is not problematic for Mill's doctrine. Feinberg's argument that the irresponsible mother has not harmed her child is unpersuasive. By assumption, the child has suffered a damaged body as a result of his parents' sexual intercourse, and such damage constitutes harm in the descriptive sense without his consent. There is no need for any reference to a baseline of non-existence to perceive this damage to his interests. Indeed, the act of causing the existence of another person is *never* a purely self-regarding act, even if the sexual intercourse is between consenting adults, and even if the parents are assumed to know beforehand that their child will *not* be born with a severe and permanent handicap. Any person (however normal or healthy) faces myriad risks of perceptible damage against his wishes during his lifetime. The act of causing his existence is thus of a kind that poses risks of non-consensual harm to others, and is properly within society's jurisdiction. Deliberative majorities can properly decide that the negligent parents in the Parfit baby case have caused wrongful harm to their child and so deserve punishment. It is not a case of harmless immorality.

Nobody has a moral right to produce children as he or she pleases. Rather, society has legitimate authority to regulate such social acts of production. It can properly use coercion against those who intentionally or negligently bring others into the world with terrible deformities or incurable diseases Moreover, Mill makes clear that couples ought to be prevented from giving birth to children who will not have 'at least the ordinary chances of a desirable existence' (1859c, 304 (V.15)). Indeed, he argues that in countries 'either overpeopled, or threatened with being so', coercive interference with even the most caring and well-off couples seeking to produce children 'beyond a very small number', may also be justified, to prevent harm to labourers, whose competitive wages tend to be driven below a customary subsistence level by overpopulation (ibid.).

To force people to satisfy their moral obligations in this matter, marriage may be prohibited between parties who cannot 'show that they have the means of supporting a family' (ibid.).

Compulsory birth control legislation might also be expedient in some contexts. Even harsh legal measures might be appropriate to protect unlucky children and punish their irresponsible parents, including placement of the children in foster homes, fines and compulsory work programmes for the parents in aid of child support, and so on.

Many people seem to assume even today that society has no business meddling with the freedom of couples to expand their families as they see fit. But the assumption is 'misplaced' from the perspective of Mill's liberty principle:

> It still remains unrecognized, that to bring a child into existence without a fair prospect of being able, not only to provide food for its body, but instruction and training for its mind, is a *moral crime*, both against the unfortunate offspring and against society; and that if the parent does not fulfil this obligation, the State ought to see it fulfilled, at the charge, as far as possible, of the parent.
>
> (Ibid., 302 (V.12), emphasis added)

WOULD IMPLEMENTATION OF THE DOCTRINE RESULT IN A SOCIAL REVOLUTION?

It seems that J.T. Mackenzie may have been on to something back in 1880, when he insisted that Mill's doctrine of liberty reaches into all corners of life as we know it in modern commercial societies, and contains the seeds of 'a social revolution' (as reprinted in Pyle 1994, 397–98). Among many other things, its implementation would put a stop to the employment of any form of coercion against harmless wrongdoing and all that.

From a Millian perspective, so-called 'harmless wrongdoing' is an incoherent phrase. There is no such thing, notwithstanding Feinberg's impressive classification of putative acts of this sort (1984–88, 4: 19, diagram 28-1). Purely self-regarding actions are properly beyond morality. If there is no perceptible damage to others against their wishes, there can be no wrongdoing. Rather, there is a moral right to absolute liberty of self-regarding conduct. Any form of coercion against self-regarding actions is itself wrongdoing and constitutes unjustified paternalism. Such paternalism can be hidden by redescribing others' mere dislike of self-regarding conduct as some type of 'impersonal' evil that lurks in the social atmosphere, independently of any perceptible damage to them. But, underneath the patina of murky terminology, it remains unjustified paternalism.[15]

Mill's simple and radical liberal defence of a moral right of complete self-regarding liberty vanishes under a cloud of redefinitions and distinctions in Feinberg's revisionist approach, where it is replaced by a complex defence of a cautious form of 'liberalism' that ignores the right of self-regarding liberty and does not depart very far from the prevailing norms of American legal culture. Like other revisionists, Feinberg makes it seem as if Mill's theory of individual liberty is crude and simplistic in its exclusive focus on harm-prevention. In addition to preventing harm in the revisionist sense of a wrongful setback of interests that ought to be considered as rights, an adequate liberalism supposedly must accommodate other reasons for coercive interference. For Feinberg, coercion may be justified to prevent mere offence in public as well as harmless wrongdoing. Moreover, he suggests that Mill strays from liberalism by calling for non-enforcement of certain contracts such as consensual slavery contracts.

With respect to harmless wrongdoing, Feinberg argues that liberals must consider coercion to prevent what he calls 'non-grievance evils', that is, allegedly regrettable consequences of acts and omissions which are not 'grounds for personal grievances' because nobody's rights are violated. Non-grievance evils are said to be of two types: 'welfare-connected', which are indirectly related to personal interests and yet either do not involve any setback of such interests (as in the Parfit baby example), or do not involve any wrongful setback because it was willingly courted; and 'impersonal' or 'free floating' evils, which are unrelated to anybody's interests.

In terms of Mill's doctrine as I have interpreted it, the first type of evil may involve direct non-consensual perceptible damage to others, although coercive interference should never even be considered when the damage is consensual. The second type never involves direct non-consensual damage to others, and includes at least four subspecies: an inherently 'sinful' or 'immoral' quality that attaches to some acts; cultural change or erosion; consented-to exploitation, as in some forms of blackmail, where ill-gotten gains for some are consented to by their victims; and degradation of character and taste.[16]

Feinberg assigns little if any weight to these various non-grievance evils within his liberalism, with the notable exception of the sort exemplified by the Parfit baby case, discussed earlier. Millian liberalism is not bothered by the baby case, which is properly within society's jurisdiction. Moreover, it also assigns an infinitesimal weight to the remaining non-grievance evils in comparison with the value of liberty to do as one pleases. Actions said to generate free-floating evils or consensual welfare-connected evils are really self-regarding actions from a Millian perspective. Indeed, the terms 'free-floating evil' and 'welfare-connected' setbacks of interests willingly accepted are guises for the mere dislike or distress felt by others at such actions.

People who want to preserve traditional cultural norms, for example, redescribe their mere dislike of the individual's critical opinions, or of his uncommon self-regarding lifestyle, as a justified concern on their part to prevent evil social change or to prohibit inherently immoral acts. Similarly, people who do not like to see the individual played for a sucker, or to see him consent to self-injury, redescribe their dislike as a legitimate concern to promote his own good or to prevent unjust exploitation of him by third parties. And those who want to elevate the character and tone of social life also regard their mere disgust at the person's beliefs or private lifestyle as a legitimate basis for prohibiting that of which they disapprove. But, in all these cases, nobody can identify any perceptible damage directly caused to others against their wishes by the self-regarding conduct.

The situation is very different, of course, if these non-grievance evils are in effect the icing on the cake of non-consensual harm to others. If a perfectionist argues for coercion to elevate the characters of minimally rational adults if and only if such coercion is already justified in order to prevent perceptible damage to other people against their wishes, for example, then, as Feinberg admits, perfectionism 'becomes a mere redundancy, or epiphenomenon' (1984–88,4: 287). Harm-prevention is, for Mill, the essential reason for coercion in this situation, even if the promotion of a virtuous character is superadded to it.

Thus, Mill might argue that rigid rules of justice ought to be enforced not only to prevent grievous perceptible injuries to others against their wishes, but also to encourage people to develop the dispositions comprising an ideal Periclean character. That argument does not presume that coercion itself can produce the requisite moral and aesthetic dispositions, nor that coercion would be justified if non-consensual harm to others was not involved. Rather, by preventing the individual from wrongfully harming others, or punishing him when he does so, legal and social sanctions may encourage him to develop the dispositions required to refrain voluntarily from violating the recognized rights of others, or otherwise ignoring their reasonable requests for help. Needless to add, coercive interference with any person's purely self-regarding conduct remains illegitimate. Each individual ought to learn for himself which opinions and self-regarding actions bring him the most personal happiness, and which cause him the most pain.

SUGGESTIONS FOR FURTHER READING

Refer also to the suggestions for further reading in Chapters 6–9 above.

For Waldron's discussion of Mill's objections to the Contagious Diseases Acts passed during the 1860s, see Jeremy Waldron, 'Mill on Liberty and on the Contagious Diseases Acts', in Nadia Urbinati and Alex Zakaras (eds), *J.S. Mill's Political Thought: A Bicentennial Reassessment* (Cambridge: Cambridge University Press, 2007), 11–42. More detailed discussions of Victorian attitudes towards prostitution and the Acts are provided by Judith R. Walkowitz, *Prostitution and Victorian Society: Women, Class and the State* (Cambridge: Cambridge University Press, 1980); and Paul McHugh, *Prostitution and Victorian Social Reform* (New York: St Martin's Press, 1980; reprinted 2013 by Routledge).

On paternalism, see C.L. Ten, *Mill on Liberty* (Oxford: Clarendon Press, 1980), 109–23; Richard J. Arneson, 'Mill versus Paternalism', *Ethics* 90 (1980): 470–89; Joel Feinberg, *The Moral Limits to the Criminal Law*, 4 vols (Oxford: Oxford University Press, 1984–88), vol. 3; and Rolf Sartorius (ed.), *Individual Conduct and Social Norms* (Belmont: Wadsworth, 1975).

For the critiques of Mill's remarks on Mormon polygamy by Posner and Donner, see Richard A. Posner, '*On Liberty*: A Revaluation', in David Bromwich and George Kateb (eds), *On Liberty: John Stuart Mill* (New Haven: Yale University Press, 2003), 197–207; and Wendy Donner, 'Mill's Moral and Political Philosophy', in W. Donner and R. Fumerton, *Mill* (Malden, MA: Wiley-Blackwell, 2009), 68–74.

On such life and death issues as wrongful conception, abortion and euthanasia, see Feinberg, *The Moral Limits to the Criminal Law*, vol. 1: 95–104, vol. 3, ch. 27, and vol. 4: 27–33, 325–28, and his *Freedom and Fulfillment* (Princeton: Princeton University Press, 1993), chs 1–2, 8–12; Ronald Dworkin, *Life's Dominion: An Argument about Abortion, Euthanasia, and Individual Freedom* (New York: Vintage Books, 1994); and L. Wayne Sumner, *Abortion and Moral Theory* (Princeton: Princeton University Press, 1981). For Parfit's original discussion of the baby problem, see Derek Parfit, 'On Doing the Best for Our Children', in M.D. Bayles (ed.), *Ethics and Population* (Cambridge, MA: Schenkman, 1976).

Feinberg's discussion of 'harmless wrongdoing' may be found in his *The Moral Limits to the Criminal Law*, vol. 4.

NOTES

1 This point should be kept in mind with respect to the discussion in Chapter 9 of bad manners and indecency in public. Mill is not concerned in *On Liberty* to explain in concrete detail what he considers the moral duties of polite and decent behaviour towards others in public.

2 Feinberg (1984–88) defines as 'extreme liberalism', for example, the doctrine that prevention of harm to others is the sole reason for legal coercion. Mill's liberalism is thereby classed as extreme, unless his definition of harm is carefully distinguished from Feinberg's.

3 Feinberg is deliberately obscure about his own theory of morality (1984–88, 1: 6–7, 14–19, 25–26).

4 Mill's maxim of self-regarding liberty is violated by Sweden's Sex Purchase Act of 1999, for example, which prohibits the purchase of sex. This illiberal 'Swedish model' seems to be increasingly popular among some conservatives and feminists in Europe and Canada. For Mill, self-regarding activities cannot be immoral. By contrast, kidnapping and trafficking of young people (male or female) for sex is criminal behaviour that ought to be prevented at all costs.

5 For a discussion of Mill's views in this context, see Waldron 2007. Unfortunately, Waldron rejects Mill's self–other distinction. For Mill, however, the buyer

of sex (male or female) rightfully has liberty to do so because sex can be enjoyed without causing non-consensual perceptible damage to others. Moreover, the Contagious Diseases Acts did not expediently employ external sanctions to prevent non-consensual harm to others: the Acts authorized the police to bring any woman suspected of prostitution before a magistrate who could force her to undergo a genital examination, and yet male clients were left free to spread the diseases to wives, mistresses and other males.

6 From a Millian perspective, it is impossible to disentangle paternalistic interference with self-regarding conduct from interference to prevent others from experiencing mere dislike or disgust. Others dislike the individual's conception of his own good and are prepared to force him to behave in accordance with their conception of his good.

7 For some of the diverse meanings, see Feinberg 1984–88, 3: 3–26.

8 For further discussion of soft or weak (anti-)paternalism, see Ten 1980, 109–17; and Feinberg 1984–88, 3: 12–16, 98–343. In defending such an approach as part of his liberal doctrine, Feinberg refers to criteria of voluntary choice as opposed to minimally rational choice. I avoid that terminology, so as to allow for the possibility that voluntary choice may fall short of standards of minimal rationality. Otherwise, if we say that some individuals (children, for example, or the insane) engage in non-voluntary behaviour, then we literally cannot even speak of coercing them, because they have no wishes with which to interfere. But coercion is essential to the meaning of paternalism in Mill's sense.

9 For a devastating critique, see Ten 1980, 119–23.

10 Ten argues that 'if there is a "slavery" contract, renewable at frequent intervals, and imposing limits to what may be required of a slave without his existing consent, this should be enforceable' (1980, 119). Perhaps so. But such a personal services contract is surely not a slavery contract, whose essential feature is that it is revocable only at the discretion of the slave master (who does not have to sell the slave to anyone else – including the slave himself – unless he wishes).

11 Mill's doctrine also allows the government to compel sellers to 'nudge' consumers for their own good, provided the consumers are not *prohibited* from buying products and services with self-regarding uses. Nudging is not coercive interference. See e.g. Thaler and Sunstein 2009.

12 Mill apparently doesn't mean to say that little girls genuinely consent to polygamous unions. He argued in his testimony before the Royal Commission examining the Contagious Diseases Acts, for example, that the age of consent in Victorian Britain ought to be raised to at least seventeen or eighteen years (1871b, 369). Girls as young as twelve could marry at the time and this occasionally happened in the lower classes. The Mormons were not alone in exploiting children.

13 For a liberal defence of the existing state of American constitutional law on abortion, rooted in the Supreme Court's decision in *Roe v. Wade*, 410 U.S. 113 (1973), see Dworkin 1994.

14 The baby problem is discussed by Feinberg (1984–88, 1: 95–104; 4: 26–33, 325–28). He attributes it to Parfit (1976).
15 For a revisionist liberal rejection of this Millian equation of pure moralism with paternalism, see Feinberg 1984–88, 4: 7–8.
16 For detailed discussion of these various 'non-grievance evils', see Feinberg 1984–88, 4: 39–317.

BIBLIOGRAPHY

MILL'S WORKS

All references are to J.M. Robson (gen. ed.), *The Collected Works of John Stuart Mill* (henceforth *CW*), 33 vols (Toronto and London: University of Toronto Press and Routledge, 1963–91).

Mill, J.S. (1832) 'On Genius', *CW* 1:327–39.
——(1833) 'Thoughts on Poetry and Its Varieties', *CW* 1:356–64.
——(1840a) 'Coleridge', *CW* 10:117–63.
——(1840b) 'De Tocqueville on Democracy in America, Part II', *CW* 18:153–204.
——(1842) 'Puseyism', *CW* 24:811–22.
——(1843) *A System of Logic*, *CW* 7–8.
——(1846) 'Grote's History of Greece, Vols. I, II', *CW* 11:271–305.
——(1849) 'Grote's Greece, Vols. V and VI', *CW* 25:1128–34.
——(1853) 'Grote's History of Greece, Vols. IX, X, XI', *CW* 11:307–37.
——(1859a) 'A Few Words on Non-intervention', *CW* 21:109–24.
——(1859b) Letter of (perhaps) July to E.C. Gaskell, *CW* 15:629–30.
——(1859c) *On Liberty*, *CW* 18:213–310.
——(1861a) *Considerations on Representative Government*, *CW* 19:371–577.
——(1861b) *Utilitarianism*, *CW* 10:203–59.
——(1862) Letter of 10 January to G. Grote, *CW* 15:761–64.
——(1865a) *An Examination of Sir William Hamilton's Philosophy*, *CW* 9.
——(1865b) *Auguste Comte and Positivism*, *CW* 10:261–367.
——(1867) 'Inaugural Address at St Andrews', *CW* 21:215–57.
——(1869a) 'Endowments', *CW* 5:613–29.
——(1869b) *The Subjection of Women*, *CW* 21:259–340.

——(1870) 'Treaty Obligations', *CW* 21:341–48.
——(1871a) *Principles of Political Economy* (1848), 7th edn, *CW* 2–3.
——(1871b) 'The Contagious Diseases Acts', *CW* 22:349–71.
——(1873) *Autobiography*, *CW* 1:1–290.
——(1874) *Three Essays on Religion*, ed. H. Taylor, *CW* 10:369–489.
——(1879) 'Chapters on Socialism', *CW* 5:703–53.
Books 4 and 5 and some passages from Book 2 of the 7th edition of the *Political Economy*, together with the 'Chapters on Socialism', are also reprinted in J. Riley (ed.), *John Stuart Mill: Principles of Political Economy and Chapters on Socialism* (Oxford: Oxford University Press, 2008).

OTHER WORKS

Adair, D. (ed.) (1945) 'James Madison's Autobiography', *William and Mary Quarterly*, 3rd series, 2: 191–209.
Alexander, E. (1965) *Matthew Arnold and John Stuart Mill* (New York: Columbia University Press).
Arneson, R.J. (1980) 'Mill versus Paternalism', *Ethics* 90: 470–89.
Arnold, M. (1968) 'Marcus Aurelius' (1863), in his *Essays in Criticism: First Series* (1865), ed. Sister T.M. Hoctor (Chicago and London: University of Chicago Press), 204–24.
——(1993) 'Doing as One Likes', chapter 2 of *Culture and Anarchy* (1869), in *Arnold: Culture and Anarchy and Other Writings*, ed. S. Collini (Cambridge: Cambridge University Press), 53–210.
Arrington, L.J. and Bitton, D. (1992) *The Mormon Experience: A History of the Latter-Day Saints*, 2nd edn (Champaign: University of Illinois Press).
Azoulay, V. (2014) *Pericles of Athens*, trans. J. Lloyd (Princeton: Princeton University Press).
Bain, A. (1882a) *James Mill: A Biography* (London: Longmans, Green).
——(1882b) *John Stuart Mill: A Criticism, with Personal Recollections* (London: Longmans, Green).
Baker, C.E. (1989) *Human Liberty and Freedom of Speech* (Oxford: Oxford University Press).
——(2002) *Media, Markets and Democracy* (Cambridge: Cambridge University Press).
——(2006) *Media Concentration and Democracy: Why Ownership Matters* (Cambridge: Cambridge University Press).
Beiser, F.C. (2006) *The Romantic Imperative: The Concept of Early German Romanticism* (Cambridge, MA: Harvard University Press).
——(2008) *Schiller as Philosopher: A Re-examination* (New York: Oxford University Press).
Bentham, J. (1983) *Constitutional Code*, vol. 1 (1830), ed. F. Rosen and J.H. Burns, in *Collected Works of Jeremy Bentham*, gen. ed. J.R. Dinwiddy (Oxford: Oxford University Press).
Berger, F. (1984) *Happiness, Justice and Freedom: The Moral and Political Philosophy of John Stuart Mill* (Berkeley: University of California Press).
Berlin, I. (1969) *Four Essays on Liberty* (Oxford: Oxford University Press).

——(1981) 'The Originality of Machiavelli' (1972), in his *Against the Current*, ed. H. Hardy (Oxford: Oxford University Press), 25–79.

——(1991) 'The Pursuit of the Ideal' (1988), in his *The Crooked Timber of Humanity*, ed. H. Hardy (New York: Knopf), 1–19.

——(2013) *The Roots of Romanticism*, ed. H. Hardy, 2nd edn (Princeton: Princeton University Press).

Bhattacharya, S. (2011) *Secrets and Wives: The Hidden World of Mormon Polygamy* (Berkeley: Soft Skull Press).

Blocker, J.S. (1989) *American Temperance Movements: Cycles of Reform* (Boston: Twayne).

Bosanquet, B. (1923) *The Philosophical Theory of the State* (1899), 4th edn (London: Macmillan).

Bouwsma, W.J. (1968) *Venice and the Defense of Republican Liberty* (Berkeley: University of California Press).

Brandt, R.B. (1992) *Morality, Utilitarianism, and Rights* (Cambridge: Cambridge University Press).

Brink, D.O. (1992) 'Mill's Deliberative Utilitarianism', *Philosophy & Public Affairs* 21: 67–103.

——(2013) *Mill's Progressive Principles* (Oxford: Clarendon Press).

Bromwich, D. and Kateb, G. (eds) (2003) *On Liberty: John Stuart Mill* (New Haven: Yale University Press).

Brown, A. (2009) 'J.S. Mill and Violations of Good Manners', *Philosophy Now* 76: 12–15.

Buckley, T.E. (1977) *Church and State in Revolutionary Virginia, 1776–1787* (Charlottesville: University Press of Virginia).

Burrow, J.W. (1988) *Whigs and Liberals: Continuity and Change in English Political Thought* (Oxford: Clarendon).

——(2000) *The Crisis of Reason: European Thought, 1848–1918* (New Haven: Yale University Press).

Capaldi, N. (2004) *John Stuart Mill: A Biography* (Cambridge: Cambridge University Press).

Carlyle, T. (1841) *On Heroes, Hero-Worship, and the Heroic in History* (London: Fraser).

Cassirer, E. (1945) 'Goethe and the Kantian Philosophy', in his *Rousseau-Kant-Goethe: Two Essays*, trans. J. Gutmann, P.O. Kristeller and J.H. Randall Jr (Princeton: Princeton University Press), 61–98.

Chapman, J.K. (1954) 'The Mid-nineteenth-Century Temperance Movement in New Brunswick and Maine', *Canadian Historical Review* 35: 43–60.

Citron, D.K. (2014) *Hate Crimes in Cyberspace* (Cambridge, MA: Harvard University Press).

Clarke, M.L. (1962) *George Grote: A Biography* (London: Athlone Press).

Clarkson, F. (1996) *Eternal Hostility: The Struggle Between Theocracy and Democracy* (New York: Common Courage Press).

Clor, H.M. (1996) *Public Morality and Liberal Society: Essays on Decency, Law, and Pornography* (Notre Dame: University of Notre Dame Press).

Coleridge, S.T. (1818) *The Friend*, 3 vols (London: Rest Fenner).
——(1839) *On the Constitution of Church and State, and Lay Sermons*, ed. H.N. Coleridge (London: Pickering).
Cowling, M. (1990) *Mill and Liberalism* (1963), 2nd edn (Cambridge: Cambridge University Press).
DeLaura, D.J. (1969) *Hebrew and Hellene in Victorian England: Newman, Arnold, Pater* (Austin: University of Texas Press).
Devigne, R. (2006) *Reforming Liberalism: J.S. Mill's Use of Ancient, Religious, Liberal, and Romantic Moralities* (New Haven: Yale University Press).
Devlin, P. (1965) *The Enforcement of Morals* (Oxford: Oxford University Press).
Dingle, A.E. (1980) *The Campaign for Prohibition in Victorian England: The United Kingdom Alliance, 1872–95* (New Brunswick, NJ: Rutgers University Press).
Donner, W. (1991) *The Liberal Self: John Stuart Mill's Moral and Political Philosophy* (Ithaca: Cornell University Press).
——(2009) 'Mill's Moral and Political Philosophy', in W. Donner and R. Fumerton, *Mill* (Malden, MA: Wiley-Blackwell), 13–143.
Dow, N. (1898) *The Reminiscences of Neal Dow, Recollections of Eighty Years* (Portland, ME: Evening Express Publishing Co.).
Dworkin, G. (1988) *The Theory and Practice of Autonomy* (Cambridge: Cambridge University Press).
Dworkin, R. (1977) *Taking Rights Seriously* (London: Duckworth).
——(1985) 'Do We Have a Right to Pornography?', in his *A Matter of Principle* (Cambridge, MA: Harvard University Press), 335–72.
——(1994) *Life's Dominion: An Argument about Abortion, Euthanasia, and Individual Freedom* (New York: Vintage Books).
——(2000) *Sovereign Virtue: The Theory and Practice of Equality* (Cambridge, MA: Harvard University Press).
——(2011) *Justice for Hedgehogs* (Cambridge, MA: Belknap Press of Harvard University Press).
Dyzenhaus, D. (1992) 'John Stuart Mill and the Harm of Pornography', *Ethics* 102: 534–51.
Eisenach, E. (1995) 'Mill's Reform Liberalism as Tradition and Culture', *Political Science Reviewer* 24: 71–146.
Feinberg, J. (1984–88) *The Moral Limits to the Criminal Law*, 4 vols (Oxford: Oxford University Press).
——(1993) *Freedom and Fulfillment* (Princeton: Princeton University Press).
Freeden, M. (1978) *The New Liberalism: An Ideology of Social Reform* (Oxford: Oxford University Press).
Goethe, J.W. von (1987) *Faust, Part One* (1808), ed. and trans. D. Luke (Oxford: Oxford University Press).
——(1994a) *Faust, Part Two* (1832), ed. and trans. D. Luke (Oxford: Oxford University Press).
——(1994b) 'Winckelmann and His Age' (1805), in J. Geary (ed.), with E. von Nardoff and E.H. von Nardoff, trans., *Goethe: The Collected Works* (Princeton: Princeton University Press), 3: 99–121.

Goldhill, S. (2011) *Victorian Culture and Classical Antiquity: Art, Opera, Fiction, and the Proclamation of Modernity* (Princeton: Princeton University Press).

Gordon, S.B. (2002) *The Mormon Question: Polygamy and Constitutional Conflict in Nineteenth-Century America* (Chapel Hill: University of North Carolina Press).

Gray, J. (1984) *Hayek on Liberty* (London: Routledge).

——(1986) *Liberalism* (Minneapolis: University of Minnesota Press).

——(1989) *Liberalisms: Essays in Political Philosophy* (London: Routledge).

——(1991) 'Mill's Conception of Happiness and the Theory of Individuality', in J. Gray and G.W. Smith (eds), *J.S. Mill: On Liberty in Focus* (London: Routledge), 190–211.

——(1993) *Post-Liberalism: Studies in Political Thought* (London: Routledge).

——(1995) *Berlin* (London: Fontana).

——(1996) *Mill on Liberty: A Defence* (1983), 2nd edn (London: Routledge).

——(2000) *Two Faces of Liberalism* (New York: New Press).

Gray, J. and Smith, G.W. (eds) (1991) *J.S. Mill: On Liberty in Focus* (London: Routledge).

Green, P. (1972) *The Shadow of the Parthenon: Studies in Ancient History and Literature* (Berkeley: University of California Press), 11–93.

Green, T.H. (1986a) 'Lecture on "Liberal Legislation and Freedom of Contract"' (1881), in P. Harris and J. Morrow (eds), *T.H. Green: Lectures on the Principles of Political Obligation and Other Writings* (Cambridge: Cambridge University Press), 194–212.

——(1986b) 'On the Different Senses of "Freedom" as Applied to Will and to the Moral Progress of Man' (1885), in P. Harris and J. Morrow (eds), *T.H. Green: Lectures on the Principles of Political Obligation and Other Writings* (Cambridge: Cambridge University Press), 228–49.

Grote, G. (1846–56) *A History of Greece: From the Earliest Period to the Close of the Generation Contemporary with Alexander the Great*, 12 vols (London: John Murray).

Haldane, E. (1930) *Mrs. Gaskell and Her Friends* (London: Macmillan).

Hamburger, J. (1965) *Intellectuals in Politics: John Stuart Mill and the Philosophic Radicals* (New Haven: Yale University Press).

——(1991a) *How Liberal Was John Stuart Mill?* (Austin: University of Texas Press).

——(1991b) 'Religion and *On Liberty*', in M. Laine (ed.), *A Cultivated Mind: Essays on J.S. Mill Presented to John M. Robson* (Toronto: University of Toronto Press), 139–81.

——(1995) 'Individuality and Moral Reform: The Rhetoric of Liberty and the Reality of Restraint in Mill's *On Liberty*', *Political Science Reviewer* 24: 7–70.

——(1999). *John Stuart Mill on Liberty and Control* (Princeton: Princeton University Press).

Hamburger, J. and Hamburger, L. (1985) *Troubled Lives: John and Sarah Austin* (Toronto: University of Toronto Press).

Harris, J. (1975) 'The Survival Lottery', *Philosophy* 50: 81–87.

Harrison, B. (1971) *Drink and the Victorians: The Temperance Question in England 1815–72* (Pittsburgh: University of Pittsburgh Press).

Harrison, R. (1985) *Bentham* (London: Routledge).

Harsanyi, J.C. (1982) 'Morality and the Theory of Rational Behavior', in A. Sen and B. Williams (eds), *Utilitarianism and Beyond* (Cambridge: Cambridge University Press), 39–62.

——(1985a) 'Does Reason Tell Us What Moral Code to Follow and, Indeed, to Follow Any Moral Code at All?' *Ethics* 96: 42–55.

——(1985b) 'On Preferences, Promises and the Coordination Problem', *Ethics* 96: 68–73.

——(1992) 'Game and Decision Theoretic Models in Ethics', in R.J. Aumann and S. Hart (eds), *Handbook of Game Theory* (Amsterdam: North-Holland), 1: 669–707.

Hart, H.L.A. (1963) *Law, Liberty, and Morality* (Oxford: Oxford University Press).

——(1982) 'Natural Rights: Bentham and John Stuart Mill', in his *Essays on Bentham* (Oxford: Oxford University Press), 79–104.

Hayek, F. (1951) *John Stuart Mill and Harriet Taylor* (London: Routledge & Kegan Paul).

Henry, M.M. (1995) *Prisoner of History: Aspasia of Miletus and Her Biographical Tradition* (Oxford: Oxford University Press).

Himmelfarb, G. (1974) *On Liberty and Liberalism: The Case of J.S. Mill* (New York: Knopf).

——(1994) 'Liberty: "One Very Simple Principle?"', in her *On Looking into the Abyss: Untimely Thoughts on Culture and Society* (New York: Knopf), 74–106.

——(1995) *The De-moralization of Society: From Victorian Virtues to Modern Values* (New York: Knopf).

Hinchliff, P. (1987) *Benjamin Jowett and the Christian Religion* (Oxford: Clarendon Press).

Honderich, T. (1982) '"On Liberty" and Morality Dependent Harms', *Political Studies* 30: 504–14.

Hooker, B. (2000) *Ideal Code, Real World* (Oxford: Clarendon Press).

Hume, D. (1975) *Enquiries Concerning Human Understanding and Concerning the Principles of Morals* (1777), ed. L.A. Selby-Bigge with revisions by P.H. Nidditch, 3rd edn (Oxford: Clarendon Press).

——(1978) *A Treatise of Human Nature* (1739), ed. L.A. Selby-Bigge with revisions by P.H. Nidditch, 2nd edn (Oxford: Clarendon Press).

Jacobson, D. (2000) 'Mill on Liberty, Speech, and the Free Society', *Philosophy & Public Affairs* 29: 276–309.

——(2003) 'J.S. Mill and the Diversity of Utilitarianism', *Philosophers' Imprint* 3: 1–35.

——(2008) 'Utilitarianism without Consequentialism: The Case of John Stuart Mill', *Philosophical Review* 117: 159–91.

Jefferson, T. (1982) *Notes on the State of Virginia* (1785), ed. W. Peden (New York: Norton).

Jensen, R.L. and Thorp, M.R. (eds) (1990) *Mormons in Early Victorian Britain* (Salt Lake City: University of Utah Press).

Justman, S. (1990) *The Hidden Text of Mill's Liberty* (Lanham, MD: Rowman & Littlefield).

Jessop, C. (2007) *Escape* (New York: Broadway Books).

Kagan, D. (1991) *Pericles of Athens and the Birth of Democracy* (New York: Free Press).

Kahneman, D., Diener, E. and Schwarz, N. (eds) (1999) *Well-Being: Foundations of Hedonic Psychology* (New York: Russell Sage Foundation).

Kaplan, F. (1983) *Thomas Carlyle: A Biography* (Ithaca: Cornell University Press).

Kateb, G. (2003) 'A Reading of *On Liberty*', in Bromwich and Kateb 2003, 28–66.

Kelly, P.J. (1990) *Utilitarianism and Distributive Justice* (Oxford: Clarendon Press).

Kinzer, B.L. (2007) *J.S. Mill Revisited: Biographical and Political Explorations* (New York: Palgrave Macmillan).

Kinzer, B.L., Robson, A.P. and Robson, J.M. (1992) *A Moralist in and out of Parliament: J.S. Mill at Westminster 1865–68* (Toronto: University of Toronto Press).

Kymlicka, W. (2002) *Contemporary Political Philosophy: An Introduction*, 2nd edn (Oxford: Oxford University Press).

Laband, D.N. and Heinbuch, D.H. (1987) *Blue Laws: The History, Economics, and Politics of Sunday Closing Laws* (Amherst: Lexington Books).

Livingston, J.C. (1986) *Matthew Arnold and Christianity* (Columbia: University of South Carolina Press).

Lyman, E.L. (1986) *Political Deliverance: The Mormon Quest for Utah Statehood* (Champaign: University of Illinois Press).

Lyons, D. (1965) *Forms and Limits of Utilitarianism* (Oxford: Oxford University Press).

——(1994) *Rights, Welfare, and Mill's Moral Theory* (New York: Oxford University Press).

MacCall, W. (1843) *The Doctrine of Individuality* (London: Green).

——(1844) *The Individuality of the Individual* (London: Chapman).

——(1847) *The Elements of Individualism: A Series of Lectures* (London: Chapman).

McHugh, P. (1980) *Prostitution and Victorian Social Reform* (New York: St Martin's Press).

Madison, J. (1973) 'Memorial and Remonstrance against Religious Assessments' (1785), in Robert A. Rutland and William M. E. Rachal (eds), *The Papers of James Madison* (Chicago and London: University of Chicago Press), 8: 295–306.

Martin, M. (1987) *The Legal Philosophy of H.L.A. Hart* (Philadelphia: Temple University Press).

Mill, James (1979) 'Education' (1818?), in F.A. Cavenagh (ed.), *James and John Stuart Mill on Education* (Westport, CT: Greenwood Press), 1–73.

Miller, D. E. (2010) *J.S. Mill* (Cambridge: Polity Press).

Millgram, E. (2004) 'On Being Bored Out of Your Mind', *Proceedings of the Aristotelian Society*, n.s., 104: 165–86.

——(2009) 'Liberty, the Higher Pleasures, and Mill's Missing Science of Ethnic Jokes', *Social Philosophy and Policy* 26: 326–53.

Mineka, F.M. (1944) *The Dissidence of Dissent: The Monthly Repository 1806–1838* (Chapel Hill: University of North Carolina Press).

Morales, M. (ed.) (2005) *Mill's 'The Subjection of Women': Critical Essays* (Lanham, MD: Rowman & Littlefield).

Morley, J. (1873) 'Mr. Mill's Doctrine of Liberty', *Fortnightly Review* 20: 234–56. Repr. in A. Pyle (ed.), *Liberty: Contemporary Responses to John Stuart Mill* (Bristol: Thoemmes Press), 271–97.

Musser, R. (2013) *The Witness Wore Red: The 19th Wife Who Brought Polygamous Cult Leaders to Justice* (New York: Grand Central Publishing).

Neff, E. (1964) *Carlyle and Mill*, 2nd edn, rev. (New York: Octagon Books).
Niblett, B. (2011) *Dare to Stand Alone: The Story of Charles Bradlaugh, Atheist and Republican* (Oxford: Kramedart Press).
Nockles, P.H. (1994) *The Oxford Movement in Context: Anglican High Churchmanship, 1760–1857* (Cambridge: Cambridge University Press).
Noel, J.N. (1995) *Canada Dry: Temperance Crusades before Confederation* (Toronto: University of Toronto Press).
O'Rourke, K.C. (2001) *John Stuart Mill and Freedom of Expression: The Genesis of a Theory* (London: Routledge).
Packe, M. St John (1954) *The Life of John Stuart Mill* (London: Secker & Warburg).
Parfit, D. (1976) 'On Doing the Best for Our Children', in M.D. Bayles (ed.), *Ethics and Population* (Cambridge, MA: Schenkman).
Pater, W. (1985) *Marius the Epicurean* (1885), ed. M. Levey (Harmondsworth: Penguin).
Pestalozzi, J.H. (1886) *Enquiries concerning the Course of Nature in the Moral Development of Human Race* (1787, in German) (Zurich: Hunziker).
Peterson, M.D. and Vaughan, R.C. (eds) (1988) *The Virginia Statute for Religious Freedom: Its Evolution and Consequences in American History* (Cambridge: Cambridge University Press).
Plamenatz, J. (1965) *The English Utilitarians*, 2nd edn (Oxford: Blackwell).
Posner, R.A. (2003) '*On Liberty*: A Revaluation', in Bromwich and Kateb 2003, 197–207.
Postema, G.J. (2006) 'Bentham's Utilitarianism', in H.R. West (ed.), *The Blackwell Guide to Mill's Utilitarianism* (Oxford: Blackwell), 26–44.
Prochaska, F. (2012) 'John Stuart Mill: The Tyranny of Conformity', chapter 2 of his *Eminent Victorians on American Democracy: The View from Albion* (Oxford: Oxford University Press), 23–46.
Pyle, A. (ed.) (1994) *Liberty: Contemporary Responses to John Stuart Mill* (Bristol: Thoemmes Press).
Quinn, D.M. (1998) *Early Mormonism and the Magic World View*, 2nd edn (Salt Lake City: Signature Books).
Radcliff, P. (ed.) (1969) *Limits of Liberty: Studies of Mill's On Liberty* (Belmont: Wadsworth).
Raeder, L.C. (2002) *John Stuart Mill and the Religion of Humanity* (Columbia: University of Missouri Press).
Rawls, J. (1999) *A Theory of Justice* (1971), rev. edn (Cambridge, MA: Harvard University Press).
——(2005) *Political Liberalism* (1993), exp. edn (New York: Columbia University Press).
——(2007) *Lectures on the History of Political Philosophy*, ed. S. Freeman (Cambridge, MA: Harvard University Press), 249–317. (Lectures on Mill.)
Raz, J. (1986) *The Morality of Freedom* (Oxford: Clarendon Press).
Rees, J.C. (1956) *Mill and His Early Critics* (Leicester: University of Leicester Press). Repr. in part in his *John Stuart Mill's On Liberty*, ed. G.L. Williams (Oxford: Clarendon Press, 1985), 78–105.
——(1985) *John Stuart Mill's On Liberty*, ed. G.L. Williams (Oxford: Clarendon Press).
Reeves, R. (2007) *John Stuart Mill: Victorian Firebrand* (London: Atlantic).

Riley, J. (1988) *Liberal Utilitarianism* (Cambridge: Cambridge University Press).
——(1989) 'Justice under Capitalism', in J. Chapman and J.R. Pennock (eds), *Markets and Justice: Nomos XXXI* (New York: New York University Press), 122–62.
——(1989–90) 'Rights to Liberty in Purely Private Matters', pts 1 and 2, *Economics and Philosophy* 5: 121–66, and 6: 27–64.
——(1990) 'Utilitarian Ethics and Democratic Government', *Ethics* 100: 335–48.
——(1991a) 'One Very Simple Principle', *Utilitas* 3: 1–35.
——(1991b) 'Individuality, Custom and Progress', *Utilitas* 3: 217–44.
——(1991c) 'Philanthropy under Capitalism', in D. Burlingame (ed.), *The Responsibilities of Wealth* (Indianapolis: Indiana University Press), 69–96.
——(1996) 'J.S. Mill's Liberal Utilitarian Assessment of Capitalism versus Socialism', *Utilitas* 8: 39–71.
——(1998a) 'Mill on Justice', in D. Boucher and P. Kelly (eds), *Social Justice* (London: Routledge), 45–66.
——(1998b) 'Mill's Political Economy: Ricardian Science and Liberal Utilitarian Art', in J. Skorupski (ed.), *Cambridge Companion to John Stuart Mill* (Cambridge: Cambridge University Press), 293–337.
——(1999) 'Is Qualitative Hedonism Incoherent?' *Utilitas* 11: 347–58.
——(2000) 'Defending Rule Utilitarianism', in B. Hooker, E. Mason and D. Miller (eds), *Morality, Rules and Consequences* (Edinburgh: University of Edinburgh Press), 40–70.
——(2001) 'Constitutional Democracy as a Two-Stage Game', in J. Ferejohn, J. Rakove and J. Riley (eds), *Constitutional Culture and Democratic Rule* (Cambridge: Cambridge University Press), 147–69.
——(2003) 'Interpreting Mill's Qualitative Hedonism', *Philosophical Quarterly* 53: 410–18.
——(2005a) 'J.S. Mill's Doctrine of Freedom of Expression', *Utilitas* 17: 147–79.
——(2005b) 'Rousseau, *The Social Contract*', in J. Shand (ed.), *Central Works of Philosophy*, 5 vols (London: Acumen), 2: 193–222 (chapter 9).
——(2006a) 'Liberal Rights in a Pareto-Optimal Code', *Utilitas* 18: 61–79.
——(2006b) 'Utilitarian Liberalism: Between Gray and Mill', *Critical Review of International Social and Political Philosophy* 9: 117–35.
——(2006c) 'Mill, *On Liberty*', in J. Shand (ed.), *Central Works of Philosophy*, 5 vols (London: Acumen), 3: 127–57 (chapter 5).
——(2007) 'Mill's Neo-Athenian Model of Liberal Democracy', in Urbinati and Zakaras 2007, 221–49.
——(2008a) Introduction to J. Riley (ed.), *John Stuart Mill: Principles of Political Economy and Chapters on Socialism* (Oxford: Oxford University Press), vii–xlvii.
——(2008b) 'Racism, Blasphemy and Free Speech', in Ten 2008, 62–82.
——(2008c) 'What are Millian Qualitative Superiorities?' *Prolegomena* 7: 61–79.
——(2008d) 'Rule Utilitarianism and Liberal Priorities', in M. Salles and J. Weymark (eds), *Justice, Political Liberalism, and Utilitarianism* (Cambridge: Cambridge University Press), 411–33.
——(2008–9) 'Millian Qualitative Superiorities and Utilitarianism', pts 1 and 2, *Utilitas* 20: 257–78, and 21: 127–43.

——(2009) 'The Interpretation of Maximizing Utilitarianism', *Social Philosophy and Policy* 26: 286–325.
——(2010a) 'Mill's Extraordinary Utilitarian Moral Theory', *Politics, Philosophy & Economics* 9: 67–116.
——(2010b) 'Justice as Higher Pleasure', in P.J. Kelly and G. Varouxakis (eds), *J.S. Mill – Thought and Influence: The Saint of Rationalism* (London: Routledge), 99–129.
——(2010c) 'Optimal Moral Rules and Supererogatory Acts', in B. Eggleston, D. Miller and D. Weinstein (eds), *John Stuart Mill and the Art of Life: A Critical Reader* (Oxford: Oxford University Press), 185–229.
——(2012) 'Happiness and the Moral Sentiment of Justice', in L. Katz (ed.), *Mill on Justice* (London: Palgrave Macmillan), 158–83.
——(2013a) 'Rawls, Mill and Utilitarianism', in J. Mandle and D. Reidy (eds), *A Companion to Rawls* (New York: Wiley-Blackwell), 397–412.
——(2013b) 'Mill's Greek Ideal of Individuality', in K.N. Demetriou and A. Loizides (eds), *John Stuart Mill: A British Socrates* (London: Palgrave Macmillan), 97–125.
——(2013c) 'The Greatest Happiness Principle', in H. LaFollette (ed.), *The International Encyclopedia of Ethics* (Oxford: Blackwell).
——(2013d) 'John Stuart Mill', in J.E. Crimmins (ed.), *The Bloomsbury Encyclopedia of Utilitarianism* (New York: Bloomsbury Academic), 346–56.
——(2014) 'Different Kinds of Pleasures', in A. Loizides (ed.), *Mill's System of Logic: A Critical Guide* (London: Routledge), 170–91
——(2015a) 'Liberty', in C. McKinnon (ed.), *Issues in Political Theory*, 3rd edn (Oxford: Oxford University Press), pp. 30–53.
——(2015b) 'Is Mill an Illiberal Utilitarian?', *Ethics* 125: 781–96.
——(forthcoming-a) *Mill's Radical Liberalism* (London, Routledge).
——(forthcoming-b) 'Is Utilitarianism Dead?' *Critical Review of International Social and Political Philosophy.*
Ripstein, A. (2006) 'Beyond the Harm Principle', *Philosophy & Public Affairs* 34: 215–45.
——(2009) *Force and Freedom: Kant's Legal and Political Philosophy* (Cambridge, MA: Harvard University Press).
Robbins, W. (1959) *The Ethical Idealism of Matthew Arnold: A Study of the Nature and Sources of his Moral Ideas* (London: Heinemann).
——(1966) *The Newman Brothers: An Essay in Comparative Intellectual Biography* (Cambridge, MA: Harvard University Press).
Robson, J.M. (1966) 'Harriet Taylor and John Stuart Mill: Artist and Scientist', *Queen's Quarterly* 73 (Summer): 167–86.
Rosen, F. (1983) *Jeremy Bentham and Representative Democracy* (Oxford: Clarendon Press).
——(1992) *Bentham, Byron and Greece: Constitutionalism, Nationalism, and Early Liberal Political Thought* (Oxford: Oxford University Press).
——(1996) Introduction to J. Bentham, *The Principles of Morals and Legislation*, ed. J.H. Burns and H.L.A. Hart (Oxford: Clarendon Press).
——(2003) *Classical Utilitarianism from Hume to Mill* (London: Routledge).
——(2013) *Mill* (Oxford: Oxford University Press).

Rossi, A.S. (ed.) (1970) *Essays on Sex Equality: J.S. Mill and Harriet Taylor Mill* (Chicago: University of Chicago Press).

Ryan, A. (1987) *John Stuart Mill*, 2nd edn (London: Macmillan).

Sandel, M. (ed.) (1995) *Liberalism and Its Critics*, 2nd edn (Cambridge: Cambridge University Press).

Sartorius, R. (ed.) (1975) *Individual Conduct and Social Norms* (Belmont: Wadsworth).

Scanlon, T. (1972) 'A Theory of Freedom of Expression', *Philosophy & Public Affairs* 1: 204–26.

——(1979) 'Freedom of Expression and Categories of Expression', *University of Pittsburgh Law Review* 40: 519–50.

Schauer, F. (1982) *Free Speech: A Philosophical Enquiry* (Cambridge: Cambridge University Press).

Schiller, J.C.F. von (1983) *On the Aesthetic Education of Man in a Series of Letters*, ed. E.M. Wilkinson and L.A. Willoughby (Oxford: Oxford University Press).

Schofield, P. (2006) *Utility and Democracy: The Political Thought of Jeremy Bentham* (Oxford: Oxford University Press).

Scoccia, D. (1996) 'Can Liberals Support a Ban on Violent Pornography?', *Ethics* 106: 776–99.

Semmel, B. (1984) *John Stuart Mill and the Pursuit of Virtue* (New Haven: Yale University Press).

Sen, A.K. (1970) *Collective Choice and Social Welfare* (San Francisco: Holden-Day), 78–88.

——(1985) *Commodities and Capabilities* (Amsterdam: North-Holland).

——(2010) *The Idea of Justice* (Cambridge, MA: Harvard University Press).

Sen, A.K. and Williams, B. (eds) (1982) *Utilitarianism and Beyond* (Cambridge: Cambridge University Press).

Shiman, L.L. (1988) *Crusade against Drink in Victorian England* (New York: St Martin's Press).

Sidgwick, H. (1988) *Outlines of the History of Ethics*, 5th edn [1902], (repr., Indianapolis: Hackett).

Silber, K. (1973) *Pestalozzi: The Man and His Work* (New York: Schocken Books).

Skipper, R. (1993) 'Mill and Pornography', *Ethics* 103: 726–30.

Skorupski, J. (1989) *John Stuart Mill* (London: Routledge).

——(2006) *Why Read Mill Today?* (London: Routledge).

Spitz, D. (1962) 'Freedom and Individuality: Mill's Liberty in Retrospect', in C.J. Friedrich (ed.), *Liberty: Nomos IV* (New York: Atherton Press), 176–226.

——(1965) *The Liberal Idea of Freedom* (Chicago: University of Chicago Press).

——(1982) *The Real World of Liberalism* (Chicago: University of Chicago Press).

Stadter, P. (1989) *A Commentary on Plutarch's Pericles* (Chapel Hill: University of North Carolina Press).

Stephen, J.F. (1967) *Liberty, Equality, Fraternity* (1873), ed. R.J. White (Cambridge: Cambridge University Press).

Sterling, J. (1848) 'Simonides', in *Essays and Tales*, ed. J.C. Hare, 2 vols (London: Parker).

Sumner, L.W. (1981) *Abortion and Moral Theory* (Princeton: Princeton University Press).

——(1987) *The Moral Foundation of Rights* (Oxford: Clarendon Press).
——(1996) *Welfare, Happiness and Ethics* (Oxford: Clarendon Press).
——(2004) *The Hateful and the Obscene: Studies in the Limits of Free Expression* (Toronto: University of Toronto Press).
Sunstein, C. R. (1993) *Democracy and the Problem of Free Speech* (New York: Free Press).
——(2009) *Republic.com 2.0* (Princeton: Princeton University Press).
Taylor, C. (1982) 'The Diversity of Goods', in Sen and Williams 1982, 129–44.
Taylor, M. (1982) *Community, Anarchy and Liberty* (Cambridge: Cambridge University Press).
——(1987) *The Possibility of Cooperation* (Cambridge: Cambridge University Press).
Ten, C.L. (1980) *Mill on Liberty* (Oxford: Clarendon Press).
——(1991) 'Mill's Defence of Liberty', in J. Gray and G.W. Smith (eds), *J.S. Mill: On Liberty in Focus* (London: Routledge), 212–38.
——(1995) 'Mill's Place in Liberalism', *Political Science Reviewer* 24: 179–204.
——(2002) 'Was Mill a Liberal?', *Politics, Philosophy & Economics* 1: 355–70.
——(ed.) (2008) *Mill's On Liberty: A Critical Guide* (Cambridge: Cambridge University Press).
Thaler, R.H. and Sunstein, C.R. (2009) *Nudge: Improving Decisions about Health, Wealth and Happiness*, rev. exp. edn (Harmondsworth: Penguin).
Thompson, D.F. (1979) *John Stuart Mill and Representative Government* (Princeton: Princeton University Press).
Turner, F.M. (1981) *The Greek Heritage in Victorian Britain* (New Haven: Yale University Press).
——(1993) 'The Triumph of Idealism in Victorian Classical Studies', in his *Contesting Cultural Authority: Essays in Victorian Intellectual Life* (Cambridge: Cambridge University Press), 322–61.
Turner, P.N. (2014) '"Harm" and Mill's Harm Principle', *Ethics* 124: 299–326.
Tyrrell, I.R. (1979) *Sobering Up: From Temperance to Prohibition in Ante-bellum America, 1800–1860* (Westport, CT: Greenwood Press), 252–89.
Urbinati, N. (2002) *Mill on Democracy: From the Athenian Polis to Representative Government* (Chicago: University of Chicago Press).
Urbinati, N. and Zakaras, A. (eds) (2007) *J.S. Mill's Political Thought: A Bicentennial Reassessment* (Cambridge: Cambridge University Press).
Van Wagoner, R.S. (1989) *Mormon Polygamy: A History*, 2nd edn (Salt Lake City: Signature Books).
Vanberg, V. (1986) 'Spontaneous Market Order and Social Rules: A Critical Examination of F.A. Hayek's Theory of Cultural Evolution', *Economics and Philosophy* 2: 75–100.
Varouxakis, G.E. (2002) *Mill on Nationality* (London: Routledge).
——(2013) *Liberty Abroad: J.S. Mill on International Relations* (Cambridge: Cambridge University Press).
Vernon, R. (1996) 'John Stuart Mill and Pornography: Beyond the Harm Principle', *Ethics* 106: 621–32.
Vogler, C.A. (2001) *John Stuart Mill's Deliberative Landscape* (New York: Garland).

von Humboldt, K.W. (1969) *The Limits of State Action* (1851, in German), ed. J.W. Burrow (London: Cambridge University Press).

Waldron, J. (2003) 'Mill as a Critic of Culture and Society', in Bromwich and Kateb 2003, 224–45.

——(2007) 'Mill on Liberty and on the Contagious Diseases Acts', in Urbinati and Zakaras 2007, 11–42.

Walker, R.W., Turley, R.E., Jr, and Leonard, G.M. (2008) *Massacre at Mountain Meadows* (New York: Oxford University Press).

Walkowitz, J.R. (1980) *Prostitution and Victorian Society: Women, Class and the State* (Cambridge: Cambridge University Press).

Wallas, G. (1951) *The Life of Francis Place, 1771–1854*, 4th edn (London: George Allen & Unwin).

Warren, J. (1852) *Equitable Commerce: A New Development of Principles, as Substitutes for Laws and Governments, for the Harmonious Adjustment and Regulation of the Pecuniary, Intellectual, and Moral Intercourse of Mankind: Proposed as Elements of a New Society* (1846), ed. S.P. Andrews (New York: Fowlers & Wells).

Whitman, W. (1871) *Democratic Vistas*, in J. Kaplan (ed.), *Walter Whitman: Complete Poetry and Collected Prose* (New York: Library of America), 929–94.

Wilkinson, E.M. and Willoughby, L.A. (2002) *Models of Wholeness: Some Attitudes to Language, Art and Life in the Age of Goethe*, ed. J. Adler, M. Swales and A. Weaver (Oxford: Peter Lang).

Wolff, J. (1998) 'Mill, Indecency and the Liberty Principle', *Utilitas* 10: 1–16.

Wollheim, R. (1973) 'John Stuart Mill and the Limits of State Action', *Social Research* 40: 1–30.

INDEX

Note: the index covers the main text but not the bibliography or each chapter's suggestions for further reading. The notes at the end of each chapter are also covered, although no attempt is made to mark the names of authors whose works are merely cited in the notes. The page references to entries from Chapter 7 are given in bold type. That chapter summarizes my interpretation of Mill's liberal utilitarian doctrine of individual liberty and social coercion.

abortion 320–23, 330 n13
accidents, prevention of 153–56
act utilitarianism 232, 236, 250; *see also* utilitarianism
action 73 n5, **225 n8**
anomie 248
Aristotle 106
Arnold, M. 42, 94 n2,
art of life, spheres of **202, 206–10**; *see also* Mill's extraordinary utilitarianism
Aspasia 27, 49 n13, 107
assisted suicide *see* suicide
atheism 297
Aurelius, M. 79, 94 n2
Austin, C. 17

Austin, J. 16, 25
autonomy 48 n5, 254–57, 259, 307, 312; *see also* moral autonomy

Bain, A. 8, 31, 40, 41, 47 n2, 50 n20
Beauchamp, P. 17
Bentham, J. 4, 11, 17, 18–21, 25, 29–33, 48 n8&9, 156, 239; *see also* utilitarianism
Bentham, S. 11, 54
Benthamite radicalism *see* utilitarianism, Bentham's form of
Berger, F. 42, 230
Berlin, I. 39, 42, **196, 197, 225 n7**, 231, 233, 258
Bingham, P. 17

birth control 21, 30, 33, 174–75, 296, 320–25
blackmail 326–27
Blanc, L. 25
Bosanquet, B. 38, 50 n20, 288
Bowring, J. 17
Bradlaugh, C. 8–9
Bradley, F. 50 n20
Brink, D. 42, **212**, 292
Brontë, C. 278
Brown, A. 281
Browning, R 6, 49 n11
bureaucracy 180–83

Cabet, E. 25
Cairnes, J. 41
Calvin, J. 106
Cambridge University 49 n17
capitalism 151
Carlyle. T. 6, 9, 17, 39, 109, 245
character 99–100, 105–7, 235–36, 242–43, 254–61, 277–83, 327–28; *see also* Greek ideal of character; quiddity
children, as properly subject to paternalism 13, 61–62, 172–75, 282, 314, 316, 318–19, 320–25; and their special relationship with their parents 279–80
China, as example of despotism of custom 112
Christ 40, 41, 79, 89, 94 n3&5, 95 n8
Christianity 4, 21, 39–41, 43, 44, 45, 71, 75, 79, 83–85, 88–90, 94 n3, 4&6, 95 n7&8, 100, 105–6, 111, 243; corruption of 83–85, 94 n3&4; as incomplete morality 88–90, 105–6; and paganism 89–90, 95 n8, 100, 105–6; persecution of 78–79; and Platonism 100, 106
clerisy 109, 116 n3
coercion, where legitimate 101–4, 117–20, 148, 151, **215–16**, 246–48, 272–84, 290–91, 300–325; as opposed to advice and criticism 119, 245, 307; *see also* natural penalties
Coleridge, S. 6, 17, 25, 109
Comte, A. 3, 28, 71
Condillac, E.B. de 17
Condorcet, M.J., Marquis de 18
conscience, as desire to do right 63, 102–3, **210**, **215**; and legitimate coercion 102–3, **215–16**, **226 n17**, 236–37, 279, 283, 322
consensus, as enemy of truth 85, 269–71
Contagious Diseases Acts 296–97, 319, 330 n5&12
Contarini, G. 54
contracts 135–36, 165–71, **212–14**, 299, 305–9, 313–14
cooperation 175–83
Cowling, M. 44, 50 n22
crimes, prevention of 153–57
critical period 3–4, 34–35, 36, 41, 71, 80
Cromwell, O. 245
custom, influence of 13–16, 58, 100, 103–4, 108–9, 177–78, 181, 254–57, 272–84, 327

decency 157–58, 272–84, 329 n1
Deism 17
Demosthenes 11
Devine, R. 42
dialectical method *see* Socratic method
Dickens, C. 9
Diderot, E. 18
discussion *see* public expression
divorce 170–71; *see also* marriage
dogma 80–83
Donner, W. 42, 317–20
drugs 158–63, 297, 300, 303
Dumont, E. 17
Durant, S. 49 n11
Dworkin, R. 70

East India Company 5, 7, 12, 17, 35
Edgeworth, F.Y. 19
education policy 73 n7, 173–74

Eisenach, E. 50 n20
euthanasia *see* suicide
experiments of living 254–57, 319
Eyre, Governor E.J. 9

fallibility 76–88, 260–61, 269–71, 293
Fawcett, H. 41
Feinberg, J. 37, 41, 42, 49 n17, **212**, 253 n3, 275, 281, 287 n6, 292, 301–9, 320–27, 329 n2&3, 331 n14
Fichte, J.G. 6, 38
Findlater, A. 8
Flower, E. 6, 49 n11
Flower, S. 6
Fourier, F.M.C. 25
Fox, W.J. 6, 48–49 n11
Frederick the Great 245
free markets 144–52, 294–95; *see also* laissez-faire
free trade *see* free markets
free will doctrine 286–87 n1
freedom *see* liberty; autonomy
full harm principle *see* harm principle, full version of

gambling 158–63, 244, 297
Gandhi, M. 95 n7
Gaskell, E. 278
Goethe, J.W. von 5, 25, 34, 116 n1
gossip 49n12, 277–79
Gray, J. 42, 230, 231, 233, 254–60, 269–71, 292
Greek ideal of character 12, 105–7, 112–13, 180, **200**, 236, 242, 248, 261–68, 270–71, 328; as Periclean rather than Platonic 106–7; *see also* individuality
Green, T.H. 38, 39, 50 n20, 288
Grote, G. 12, 17, 47 n2, 47–48 n3, 49 n12&17, 50 n20,
Grote, H. 12, 49 n12&13
Guicciardini, F. 94 n4

habit 266–68
Hamburger, J. 44, 50 n22, 73 n3, **226 n12**, 243–46

Hamilton, A. 73 n1
Hamilton, Sir W. 28
Hare, T. 8, 32
harm, meaning of 40, 60–61, 98–99, 113, 121, 125–27, 142, **189–92**, **222–23, 225 n5**, 293–94, 301–2, 320–25; of silencing another person 76–88; *see also* wrongful harm
harm principle *see* 'one very simple principle'
harm principle, full version of 217, 292, 294
harmless wrongdoing **219–23**, 280–84, 323–28
Harris, J. 250
Harsanyi, J. 70, 232
Hart, H.L.A. 37, 42, 49 n15, 230, 273, 284, 287 n5, 292, 301–2
Hartley, D. 17, 20
hate literature 277, 282
hedonism 261–68
Hegel, G.W. 6, 38
Helen of Troy 106
Helvetius, C.A. 17, 18
Hickson, W. 25
higher pleasures 261–68
Himmelfarb, G. 43, 50 n22
history, as cyclical process 86
Hitler, A. 272, 279
Hobbes, T. 255
Humboldt, W. von 27, 34, 99, 116 n1, 170–71, 308
Hume, D. 17, 140 n2

ideal observer 86–88, 260–61
idealism 38–39, 50 n20, **197**, 288
immorality *see* morality
inalienable right of self-regarding liberty **214**
indecency *see* decency
individual liberty 38, 48 n5, 100, 170, **189**, 257, 304; meaning of **196–99**; as negative freedom from coercion 40, 146, 151, **196–97, 218–19, 222**; as positive freedom to do whatever

one wishes 38, 147, 151, **196–97, 218–19, 222**; as essential to individuality 100, **198**, 269–71; Mill's doctrine of **201–19**; misapplied notions of 172–75, 325; as properly absolute in self-regarding matters 68–69, 240–43; as spontaneity 99–101; utilitarian basis of a right to absolute liberty in self-regarding matters 62–63, 107–13, 229–50; where expedient 146–53; *see also* political liberty

individuality, meaning of **199–200**, 254–60; as ideal character 99–100, 105–7, 110–13, 180, **200**, 242–43, 269–71; as miserable character 44, **199**, 235–36, 244, 256, 262, 267–68; and liberty 96–97, 100, **198**; and obedience to social rules 101–4, 272–84; as permanent interest 63, **225 n10**, 243, 269–71, 294–95, 308; and progress 97–104, 111–12, 255, 269–71; *see also* Greek ideal of character

infallibility, assumption of 76–78, 319
interpersonal comparisons of utility 231, 238–40

Jacobson, D. 42, 281
Jamaica Committee 9
Jay, J. 73 n1
Jefferson, T. 59, 68, 73 n4
Jevons, S. 19
Jews 272, 277, 279
Johnson, S. 79
Justman, S. 42, 50 n22

Kahneman, D. 268
Kant, I. 6, 25, 38, **220**, 259
Kateb, G. 42
Kelly, P. 33
King, M.L. 95 n7
Klu Klux Klan 272, 277

laissez-faire, doctrines of 62–63, 73 n6, 119–20, 133–35, 144–52, 158–63, 165, 170, 175–83, **209**, **217–18**, 276–77, 291–92, 294, 295, 298, 300–301, 306–7, 322–23

liberalism 69–72, 229–50, 254–84, 326
liberty *see* individual liberty; political liberty

liberty, Mill's doctrine of **201–19**; *see also* social control, Mill's doctrine of

liberty, Mill's maxim or principle of self-regarding 35, 65–66, 69–70, 126, 142–53, 175–78, 182–83, **190**, **203–5**, **213**, **214**, **217**, **221**, 236–37, 240–43, 248–50, 290–91, 293, 313–25; and animals 322; applications of 142–83, 288–328; auxiliary precepts of 298–99; as opposed to a right to dominate others 172, 299; *see also* social authority, Mill's maxim or principle of

liberty of expression 74–91, 98–99, 127, 260–61, 270; as exceptional case 67–68, 75–76, 93, 98–99, 119, 152–53; limits of 93 n1, 157–63; as test of warranted belief 77–78, 80–81, 86–88, 260–61, 270; as utilitarian 86–88; *see also* Socratic method

liberty of self-regarding action 44, 96–97, 290; as test of warranted belief about one's own nature and character 97, 100–101, 107, 112, 260–61, 270; as essential to individuality 100, **198**, 237; as utilitarian 107–13, 240–43; *see also* experiments of living; individuality

liberty of thought and discussion *see* liberty of expression

Locke, J. 17, 54, 239
London Debating Society 17
London and Westminster Review 24
luck 238, 249, 325
Lyons, D. 232

Macaulay, T.B. 32
Maccall, W. 34
Machiavelli, N. 54, 94 n4
Mackenzie, J.T. 37, 40, 325
Madison, J. 59, 69, 73 n1&4
Maine laws 132–33
majority tyranny 71, 83, **201–3**, **205–16**, 238; *see also* custom, influence of
manners 157–58, 272–84, 329 n1
Marmontel, J.F. 22
Marquis of Queensberry 246–47
marriage 6–7, 135–36, 170–71, 174–75, 313–20, 324–25; *see also* divorce; polygamy
Marshall, A. 19
Marx, K. 94 n3
Maurice, F. 17, 20
mental exercise 101, 254–61, 269–71
Mill, H. 4, 12
Mill, James 4–5, 11–16, 20, 21, 31–32, 47 n2, 47–48, n3, 50 n20, 54
Mill, J.S. biography 3–9; on birth control 174–75; his early education 5, 11–16; on education policy 173–74; his fear of rising religious intolerance 59–60, 70–72, 75, 78–80, 83–84, 88–90, 105, 111, 132–36, 174; on foreign intervention 136–37; his love for Harriet Taylor 26–28; on marriage and divorce 135–36, 165, 170–71; his mental crisis 21–25; his doctrine of liberty and social control, summary of **201–19**; his 'one very simple principle' 60–62, **201–3**, **216**, 291, 292; his maxim of self-regarding liberty 35, 65–66, 69–70, 126, 142–53, 175–78, 182–83, **190**, **203–5**, **213**, **214**, **217**, **221**, 240–43, 248–50, 290–91, 293, 313–25; his maxim of social authority 142–53, **205–7**, **216–17**, **221**, 299; his process of self-development 10, 16–33; his relations with his father 12–16; *see also* Mill's extraordinary utilitarianism

Mill's extraordinary utilitarianism 24–33, 42, 62–63, 86–88, 107–13, **201–19**, 229–50, 261–68; and its multiple harm principles **216–17**; and its multiple principles of liberty **217–19**; applications of 142–83, 288–328
Miller, D.E. 42, **225 n4**
Millgram, E. **225 n4**, 263–68, 287 n3
Millian radicalism *see* Mill's extraordinary utilitarianism
Molesworth, W. 24, 49 n12
Monthly Repository 6, 48 n11,
moral autonomy *see* principle of moral and legal freedom
moralism 302, 324, 326, 331 n15
morality 123–25; improperly attached to opinion or self-regarding action 76, 78–79, 124–25, 132–37, 141 n3, 312
Morley, J. 40, 41, 50 n19
Mormons 133, 135–36, 170, 313–20, 330 n12
motorcycle helmets, compulsory 305–6
Muller, M. 37

Napoleon 9
National Reformer 8
natural penalties 121–24, 130, 142, 243–48, 282; as opposed to social punishment 123–24, 140 n1, 243–48
Nazis 272, 277
negative liberty, as freedom from coercive interference by others 40, 146, 151, **196–97**, **218–19**, **222**, 231
Neptune 249
neutrality 247–48
New Testament 83, 84, 88
Newman, J. 50 n20, 94 n4
Nietzsche, F. 39, 45
Novalis (alias of F. von Hardenberg) 5, 25
nuisances 275–77; *see also* public offence

obedience, worth of 101–4, 269–71; as Christian ideal 105; as component of ideal character 105–6; *see also* social rules

Old Testament 88

'one very simple principle' 41, 60–62, **201–3**, **216**, 231, 291, 292; as simple harm principle 60–62, **201–3**; as simple principle of liberty 60–62, **201–3**; *see also* Mill's extraordinary utilitarianism

opinion, as beyond morality 76, 80; *see also* self-regarding conduct

organic period 3–4, 34–35, 41, 71, 83

other-regarding conduct, meaning of **195–96**; and paternalism 310–13; and public decency 272–84; *see also* morality; social rules; self-regarding conduct

Owen, R. 17, 25

Oxford Movement 50 n20, 94 n4

Oxford University 49 n17

paganism 88–90, 95 n8, 237

Parfit, D. 323, 324

Parfit baby problem 323–25, 326, 327, 331 n14

Parliamentary History and Review 17

Paruta, P. 94 n4

Pater, W. 41, 94 n2

paternalism 14, 60, 61–62, 131–32, 164, 172, **212–14**, 303–13, 325–26, 330 n6

Pattison, M. 50 n20

Peloponnesian War 106

perception **190**, **224–25 n3**

perceptible damage **190–91**, **215–16**

perfectionism 327

Pericles 9, 27, 49 n13, 95 n8, 106–7, 180, **200**, 236, 242, 248, 256, 261, 263, 267, 270, 308, 328

permanent interests 19–20, 30, 33; *see also* individuality; security

Pestalozzi, J.H. 34

philosophical radicalism: 'official' or Benthamite kind 18–21; Millian kind *see* Mill's extraordinary utilitarianism; *see also* radicalism

Plamenatz, J. 289–90

Plato 11, 81, 100, 106, 111, 287 n4, 290; *see also* Socratic method

pluralism of basic values 231–33, 237–40, 258; as distinct from social pluralism 243, 271

Plutarch 107

police authority 153–57

political liberty, doctrines of 53–56; *see also* individual liberty

political radicalism *see* radicalism

polygamy 133, 296, 313–20, 330 n12

pornography 277, 283–84, 297; *see also* prostitution

positive liberty, as freedom to do as one likes 38, 147, 151, **196–97**, **218–19**, **222**, 231, 270

Posner, R.A. 42, 50 n2, 313–16

Postema, G. 48 n9

practical reason 263–65

principle of consensual harm **216**; *see also* principle of self-regarding liberty

principle of laissez-faire **217–18**; *see also* principle of social authority

principle of moral and legal freedom **218**; *see also* principle of wrongful harm

principle of self-regarding liberty 35, 65–66, 69–70, 126, 142–53, 175–78, 182–83, **190**, **203–5**, **213**, **214**, **217**, **221**, 236–37, 240–43, 248–50, 290–91, 293, 313–25; *see also* principle of consensual harm

principle of social authority 142–53, **205–7**, **216–17**, **221**, 291, 299; *see also* principle of laissez-faire

principle of wrongful harm **217**; *see also* principle of moral and legal freedom

private conduct, as self-regarding conduct 59, 64, 66–68, 147–48

private property, justification of **198**; and self-regarding liberty **198**, **219**, **221–22**
private versus public, different ideas of 147–48, 157–58, 272–84, 313–25
progress *see* social progress
prostitution 158–63, 244, 296–97; *see also* pornography
public, as a group of unassignable individuals **226 n13**
public expression, morality of 90–91, 276–84; case of advertising 158–63; *see also* liberty of expression
public goods 176–78, 300–301
public harm **193–95**, 272; *see also* public, as a group of unassignable individuals
public offence 157–58, 272–84, 303, 306–7
public offence principle 273–74, 281, 284, 287 n5, 288, 293
public solicitation 158–63
punishment, forms of 118–25; for the wrongdoer's own good 311
Pusey, E.B. 50 n20, 94 n4
Pyle, A. 37, 40, 325

quiddity 39, **225 n11**, 257, 258–60

radicalism, in politics 44, 48 n10; *see also* philosophical radicalism
Raeder, L. 44
Rawls, J. 42, 69–70, **225 n4**, 230, 231, 234, 287 n2
Raz, J. 42
Rees, J. 36, 40, 42
Religion of Humanity 4, 41, 43, 44, 89–90, 94 n5, 243–44; *see also* Mill's extraordinary utilitarianism
religious liberty, as absolute by right 58–60, 68–69, 70, 174
reputation 277–79, 282–83
Ricardo, D. 11, 21
rights, meaning of **197–99**, **225 n6**; illiberal kinds 126, 172; and liberalism 69–70, 229–43, 261–63, 265, 279–80, 288–99; as opposed to moral permissions to compete 151–52, **199**; as opposed to moral trusts 172, 185–86 n4
Ripstein, A. **220**, **222**
Roebuck, J. 48 n6; 49 n12
Rosen, F. 42
Rousseau, J.J. 38, 54, 86, 239, 253 n2
rules *see* social rules
rule utilitarianism 232–37; *see also* utilitarianism
Ruskin, J. 9

Sabbatarian legislation 133
Saint Paul 40, 88
Saint-Simon, C.H. Comte de 3, 25
Sarpi, P., Fra 94 n4
Schiller, J.C.F. 15, 25
Schlegel, A. 5
Schlegel, F. 5
seat belts, compulsory 305–6
security, as permanent interest 63, **208**, 233–34, 259, 262–63, 265, 308
self-assertion, as pagan ideal 99–106
self-denial, as Christian ideal 103–6
self-protection *see* security
self-regarding conduct 35, 38–39, 42, 43, 44, 64–65, 66–68, 98–99, 120–32, 142–51, **204–5**, **224 n1**, 240–48, 272–84, 289–90, 293–98, 302, 314–16, 321–22, 324; meaning of **192–95**; as beyond morality 124–25, 132–33, 141 n3, 312; *see also* perceptible damage
Sex Purchase Act (Sweden) 329 n4
Sidgwick, H. 19, 20, 48 n8
Skorupski, J. 37, 40, 42, 49 n15, 230
slavery 88, 166–70, **212–14**, 307–9, 330 n10
Smith, A. 11
Smith, W.H. 9
social authority, meaning of **200–201**; Mill's maxim or principle of 142–53, **205–7**, **216–17**, **221**, 291, 299; and birth control 174–75; and education

policy 173–74; and enforcement of contracts 166–71; and limits to authority of police 153–57; and manners of politeness 157–58, 272–84; and regulation of the number of sellers of intoxicants 164–65; and regulation of public solicitation 158–63; and special taxation of self-regarding consumption 163–64; *see also* liberty, Mill's maxim or principle of self-regarding; paternalism
social control, Mill's doctrine of **201–19**
social conduct *see* other-regarding conduct
social decline 281–83; *see also* social stagnation
social pluralism, as essential to individuality 271; as distinct from pluralism of basic values 243, 271
social progress, as not inevitable 70–72, 86, 108–9, 111–12, 181–82, **209**; and individuality 97, 102–3, 183, 255–71
social rules 101–4, 116 n2; of other-regarding conduct, legitimacy of 101–4, 272–84; of self-regarding conduct, illegitimacy of 110, 237, 240–50, 274–75, 281, 283–84
social stagnation, possibility of 70–72, 86, 111–12, 181–82, **209**, 246, 281–83; *see also* social progress
socialism 28, 32–33, 151
Society of Students of Mental Philosophy 17
Socrates 79, 106–7; *see also* Socratic method
Socratic method 11, 13, 48 n3, 81, 85, 231, 245, 260–61
sovereignty principle **220**, **222**
spheres of conduct **202**, **206–10**, 235–36, 295; *see also* art of life; Mill's extraordinary utilitarianism
spontaneity, worth of 99–101; required compression of 101–4; as component of ideal character 105–6, 256, 270–71; *see also* self-assertion
Stephen, J.F. 40, 50 n19
Sterling, J. 6, 17
stigma 79, 118–19, 120, 158, 171, 175, 283; as opposed to natural penalties 123–24, 140 n1, 243–48
suicide **213**, 308–9
Sumner, L.W. 323

taxation, on sales of stimulants 163–64
Taylor, C. 231
Taylor, Harriet 6–7, 15, 26–28, 35–36, 41, 43, 49 n11, 107, 278
Taylor, Helen 6–7, 26, 28
Taylor, J. 6–7
temperance crusades 133
Ten, C.L. 37, 42, 49 n15, 230, 240–41, 253 n1&4, 275, 289, 292, 307, 330 n10
Tocqueville, A. 32, 56
totalitarianism 44, 45, 71, 180–83
treaties 135–37
trespass **219–23**
truth, as warranted belief 77–78; liberty as test of 78–81, 86–88; *see also* fallibility

Ulpian 65
United Kingdom Alliance 133
United States Constitution 41, 68, 70, 73 n1, 2&4, 330 n13
University College London 49 n17
Utilitarian Society 17
utilitarianism: and elitism 82–83, 110, 180–82, 243–48, 310; and ideal observers 86–88, 260–61; and liberal democracy **207–10**, 262–63; as anti-liberal 229–50; as foundation for doctrine of individual liberty 62–70, 86–88, 107–13, **201–19**; Bentham's form of 18–21, 24; Mill's form of *see* Mill's extraordinary utilitarianism; *see also* act utilitarianism, rule utilitarianism

utility in the largest sense 26, 62–63; and high importance of individuality 97, 105–7; *see also* Mill's extraordinary utilitarianism

value pluralism *see* pluralism, of basic values
Venus 249
vices 120; moral kinds 123–25; self-regarding kinds 123; *see also* virtues
virtues 120; moral kinds 123–25; self-regarding kinds 123; *see also* vices
Vogler, C. **226 n12**, 261–66
volenti maxim 65, 66, 166, **204**, **205**, **225 n5**, 301

volenti non fit injuria, maxim of *see volenti* maxim
Voltaire, F.M.A. 18
voluntary association, liberty of 67, 165–71

Waldron, J. 246–47, 329–30 n5
Warren, J. 34, 42
Weber, M. 94 n3
Westminster Review 17
Whitman, W. 40
Wilde, O. 37, 246–47
Wolff, J. 287 n5
Wordsworth, W. 6, 23, 25
wrongful harm **210–16**, 301–2

eBooks
from Taylor & Francis

Helping you to choose the right eBooks for your Library

Add to your library's digital collection today with Taylor & Francis eBooks. We have over 50,000 eBooks in the Humanities, Social Sciences, Behavioural Sciences, Built Environment and Law, from leading imprints, including Routledge, Focal Press and Psychology Press.

Free Trials Available

ORDER YOUR FREE INSTITUTIONAL TRIAL TODAY

We offer free trials to qualifying academic, corporate and government customers.

Choose from a range of subject packages or create your own!

Benefits for you
- Free MARC records
- COUNTER-compliant usage statistics
- Flexible purchase and pricing options
- 70% approx of our eBooks are now DRM-free.

Benefits for your user
- Off-site, anytime access via Athens or referring URL
- Print or copy pages or chapters
- Full content search
- Bookmark, highlight and annotate text
- Access to thousands of pages of quality research at the click of a button.

eCollections

Choose from 20 different subject eCollections, including:

- Asian Studies
- Economics
- Health Studies
- Law
- Middle East Studies

eFocus

We have 16 cutting-edge interdisciplinary collections, including:

- Development Studies
- The Environment
- Islam
- Korea
- Urban Studies

For more information, pricing enquiries or to order a free trial, please contact your local sales team:

UK/Rest of World: **online.sales@tandf.co.uk**
USA/Canada/Latin America: **e-reference@taylorandfrancis.com**
East/Southeast Asia: **martin.jack@tandf.com.sg**
India: **journalsales@tandfindia.com**

www.tandfebooks.com